THE SCOTTISH MEDIEVAL TOWN

Edited by
MICHAEL LYNCH
MICHAEL SPEARMAN
GEOFFREY STELL

JOHN DONALD PUBLISHERS LTD
EDINBURGH

© The Editors and Contributors severally 1988.

All rights reserved. No part of this publication
may be reproduced in any form or by any means
without the prior permission of the publishers,
John Donald Publishers Ltd., 138 St Stephen Street,
Edinburgh, EH3 5AA.

ISBN 0 85976 170 3

Distributed in the United States of America
and Canada by Humanities Press Inc., Atlantic
Highlands, NJ 07716, U.S.A.

Phototypeset by Quorn Selective Repro Ltd., Loughborough.
Printed in Great Britain by Bell & Bain Ltd., Glasgow.

Preface

In recent decades the medieval town has been discussed in general works relating to medieval Scotland and to Scottish urban history, and it has been the object of much intensive archaeological investigation. It now seems appropriate to bring together into a single volume many of the different strands of current research, and to explore and re-examine those aspects of the organisation and life within and around the medieval Scottish town that remain obscure or misunderstood.

The essays in this volume have been brought together under the auspices of the Urban History Group of the Conference of Scottish Medieval Historical Research. They represent some of the first fruits of a burgeoning of research into various aspects of the medieval urban history and archaeology of Scotland, a large, complex and relatively uncharted area of study. For clarity and convenience, an analytical arrangement has been adopted, the essays being grouped into sections relating to broad but interrelated ecclesiastical, economic, social and administrative themes; the first section is devoted to an assessment of the available evidence. The emphasis throughout is on the social and economic realities of the 'town', as opposed to the theoretical legal privileges of the 'burgh', but the coverage within each section is, of necessity, selective. Similarly, some of the essays summarise detailed work in progress, which is destined for publication elsewhere. They all show the direction and exciting potential of current research.

The editors wish to record their grateful appreciation of the work of the contributors, and hope that they will all feel rewarded by the results of this collective enterprise. Our thanks go to John Torrie and the Anderson Dunlop Fund trustees for financial assistance, as well as to Ray Harris of the Geography Department, University of Edinburgh, for his cartographic work. We also wish to acknowledge the encouragement given to this project in its early stages by Professor G. W. S. Barrow, Professor A. A. M. Duncan, Dr Walter Makey, Dr Atholl Murray, Dr Grant G. Simpson and Mrs Anne T. Simpson. To all are accorded our grateful thanks.

Contributors

Dr Harold W. Booton, whose postgraduate research was undertaken in the Department of History, University of Aberdeen

Professor Ian B. Cowan, Department of Scottish History, University of Glasgow

Judith Cripps, City of Aberdeen District Council

David Ditchburn, currently postgraduate student, Department of Scottish History, University of Edinburgh

Dr Elizabeth L. Ewan, Department of History, University of Guelph, Canada

Iain Flett, City of Dundee District Council

Dr Michael Lynch, Department of Scottish History, University of Edinburgh

Dr Hector L. MacQueen, Department of Scots Law, University of Edinburgh

Norman F. Shead, Hutchesons' Grammar School, Glasgow

R. Michael Spearman, Department of Archaeology, Royal Museum of Scotland, Queen Street, Edinburgh

Geoffrey P. Stell, Royal Commission on the Ancient and Historical Monuments of Scotland, Edinburgh

Dr Alexander Stevenson, London, whose postgraduate research was undertaken in the Department of History, University of Aberdeen

Dr Wendy B. Stevenson, Aberdeen, formerly of the Department of History, University of Aberdeen

Dr Elizabeth P. D. Torrie, North Queensferry, whose postgraduate research was undertaken in the Department of Scottish History, University of Edinburgh

William Windram, currently postgraduate student, Department of Scots Law, University of Edinburgh

Contents

Maps

Illustrations

1

Introduction

A reasonably acceptable working definition of a Scottish, as well as an English medieval town, is that 'a significant proportion (but not necessarily a majority) of its population lives off trade, industry, administration, and [a variety of] other non-agricultural occupations', but the extent to which any Scottish town also 'forms a social unit more or less distinct from the surrounding countryside'[1] is less certain. In Scotland, town and country were bound closely together in an intimate and many-sided relationship. Also, compared with the early origins of a number of English or Irish towns, the term 'medieval' as applied to a Scottish town is of more restricted chronological definition; it usually refers to the period from the early twelfth century when the first surviving documents relating to Scottish 'burghs' coincided with a phase of urban revival and growth throughout Europe. Thereafter, from at least the middle and possibly from the early fourteenth century until after 1500, Scottish towns shared in a general experience of commercial decay which profoundly affected the nature of their institutions and economies in the later middle ages.[2]

The much-debated question of continuity of urban settlement through Roman into later times does not apply to Scotland, where successive Roman occupations were little more than temporary military extensions of their more protracted and successful conquest of southern Britain. For Scotland and the greater part of 'barbarian' Europe questions of urban origins and continuity revolve instead around assessments of native settlement and economic patterns. For although Rome's considerable political and economic influence and stimulus extended well beyond the official limits of its empire, the seeds and eventual fruit of urbanisation in Scotland, and northern Europe as a whole, appear to have germinated in quite a different soil.

The first tentative roots of urbanisation may have been formed in the late iron age hillforts of central and southern Scotland. Although not as vast as some of the great southern English *oppida*, each of the two largest, Eildon Hill North and Traprain Law, enclosed at various times areas of up to sixteen hectares. At Eildon Hill field survey has identified over 300 house-platforms with space for a further 200 houses in areas of the fort that have since been disturbed.[3] Even if only a small proportion of these houses

1

were occupied simultaneously, these settlements would have represented works of considerable economic and social organisation and would have achieved comparable densities of settlement to those which eventually re-emerged in medieval burghs. Although many may have been abandoned before or during the Roman occupation, some, including Traprain Law, survived and prospered.[4] For, whatever the political effects of the Roman presence, it seems clear that trade was stimulated by the provisioning of Roman garrisons, by the establishment of *vici* (extra-mural civilian settlements) and ports, together with the construction and improvement of a road system.

The factors which contributed to and followed from the removal of Rome's interest in the British Isles also appear to have been responsible for sweeping away any remaining large-scale centres of population such as Traprain Law. The smaller, more defensible forts which rose to prominence in the fifth, sixth and seventh centuries may not, however, have been the products of an entirely new political and economic framework. At Edinburgh, Perth/Scone, Haddington/Dunbar/Traprain, and elsewhere, the focus of settlement appears simply to have been transferred to adjacent sites which may have been better suited to the military requirements of these tumultuous centuries, but the general geographical, agricultural and social attractions of these established *loci* otherwise remained unchanged.

From scant documentary and archaeological sources it seems that the inhabitants of these fortresses, like those of the late iron age hillforts, practised mixed, and especially pastoral farming, channelling agricultural produce from surrounding areas to meet their needs. The slaughter of numerous animals for each settlement of this kind has implications for more than just diet; hide, horn, gut, sinew, tallow and all the other carcass produce would have been processed for use in the fortress and perhaps among the surrounding communities as well. Likewise, grain gathered into the fortress would have been stored and processed into bread, malt and ale. Purely through the concentration of foodstuffs and these processing operations there would have developed a basis for local industry and trade. The success of these settlements in converting agricultural wealth into fine jewellery, wine, clothes, weapons and other trappings of power is amply attested by archaeological excavations at sites such as Dundurn, Dunadd, Dumbarton and Mote of Mark.[5] Despite their smallness of area these fortresses possessed many of the attributes of later urban settlement, and indeed several were described as *civitas* or *urbs* by Bede and Eddius.[6]

This developing economy attracted the Norse, first as traders, then raiders, and finally as settlers. The known geography of Norse settlement must partly reflect the substantial trade between Ireland and Scandinavia which flowed around Scotland via the Western and Northern Isles, hence the main Norse trading stations in Scotland, such as Brough of Birsay in Orkney and Freswick Links in Caithness, and an apparent avoidance of established centres of power in the fertile lands of eastern and central Scotland. However, whilst acknowledging that survival of archaeological evidence in the more intensively farmed and developed lands is inevitably less complete than that for the Highlands and Islands, it is fair to say that the Norse presence has been less thoroughly investigated in other parts of Scotland.

Although not producing a steady, ordered progression of settlement types, there were early political and economic systems capable of organising and sustaining substantial centres of population, and it would be unrealistic to suppose that urban economies and settlements were suddenly created by the title, 'burgh', conferred by King David I (1124–53) and his successors. It is against a background of emerging states and increasing trade in Europe that David's introduction of the term and its subsequent legal identity should be viewed. As kingdoms and settlements increased in size, it became more difficult to exercise direct royal control over residences, settlements and associated agricultural hinterlands. Authority was delegated and legislation enacted in order to define and formalise these new relationships throughout twelfth-century Europe, the *Burgh Laws* of David I and the burgh charters of William I (1165–1214) being parts of this international movement.[7] And just as the histories of the emergent nation states are surrounded with the remnants of ancient kingdoms, so the history of urbanisation has its lists of abandoned settlements, both before and after the twelfth century. A charter of privileges carried no automatic guarantee of their successful application, and not all early burghs remained, or even became towns.

The hilltop and hillside settings of a number of successful burgh foundations are clearly reminiscent of their suggested ancestors, for, although the general locational advantages of places like Edinburgh and Stirling can be readily appreciated, the fact remains that their medieval communities were perched upon the tails of natural rock citadels in time-honoured fashion. Less obvious and in some ways more enigmatic are those urban settlements that have grown up on the slopes or brows of gentle rounded hills of a non-defensible character, as appears to have been the case at, for example, Lanark, Selkirk and Dunfermline.

Unfortunately, the evidence for the actual scale of settlement in Scottish medieval towns is very slight. It is easier to trace the physical extent of settlement by a combination of archaeological evidence and town-plan analysis than it is to come to even the most general conclusions about sizes of urban populations. Few towns appear to have overspilled their original layouts before the sixteenth century. Although there was modest suburban expansion in Perth in the fifteenth century, a more significant growth of its suburbs seems to belong to the very end of the sixteenth century when the kirk session agreed to the representation of three suburbs on that body.[8] Composite town-plan analysis suggests that fourteenth-century Perth, one of the 'four great towns of Scotland' (as viewed from Bruges) and paying 9% of all customs in the 1370s, had some 370 burgage plots. By that date Edinburgh paid 24% of customs, more than any other town, yet, according to one foreign visitor, had only 400 houses in 1400. Stirling, an increasingly important royal centre from the reign of James III, was ranked eighth of the royal burghs in terms of royal taxation in 1550 but had only 385 householders.[9]

The clearest pattern in the history of Scottish towns after the Wars of Independence is that of the continual rise of Edinburgh, which can be measured by its progressively larger share of the export trade: it had 21% of the wool trade in the 1320s, 32% by the 1370s, 57% by the 1440s, and over 90% by the 1590s. Its domination of other sectors, such as hides and cloth, was not so overwhelming in these centuries but was still marked by the later fifteenth century.[10] Yet it is difficult to find evidence of anything more than modest population growth before 1500. By 1560 Edinburgh had a population of some 12,500; by 1635 it had 4,000 households and over 20,000 inhabitants[11]. The example of Edinburgh is a cautionary one, illustrating that there may be no direct correlation between population increase and economic growth, whether measured by trade or investment in municipal and private building projects. A medieval town such as Edinburgh may have increased the range of its activities, diversified its economy, built and vastly extended its parish church, without significantly enlarging its resident population.

So far as the special character of urban life is concerned, it is customary for historians to emphasise the distinctiveness of the medieval town within the community of the realm and in its place in the landscape and economy of medieval Scotland: that a king's burgh was given a distinct constitutional position within the feudal polity, with its own laws, privileges and institutions; that in its range and concentration of specialist occupations it formed a natural contrast to the surrounding countryside; and that it controlled the country's commerce through a monopoly of overseas trade.[12] There are elements of truth in these orthodoxies but each, as various essays in this collection make plain, needs qualification.

When viewed closely, the *Burgh Laws* prove not to have been peculiar to Scotland, nor was the system of burgh courts inherently different from, or at variance with, other feudal courts within the realm.[13] In Scotland, as in

England, the medieval burgh can best be understood as one expression of feudal society and economy rather than as a contradictory element within it,[14] particularly as military feudalism and royal burghs arrived in Scotland almost simultaneously and each spread under the patronage of successive twelfth- and thirteenth-century kings. Nor should the pace or the extent to which burghs were granted common privileges or jurisdictions be exaggerated: Berwick, by far the largest of the thirteenth-century burghs, had been granted, in the form of burgess tenure of the office of coroner, virtual shrieval jurisdiction some time before 1286 but only Perth, nearest in size to Berwick, was explicitly granted this – in 1394; Edinburgh, the largest of the late medieval burghs, had to wait until 1482 and Aberdeen was refused it as late as 1445.[15]

Urban parishes emerged within a parochial system that was essentially rural in character, and they remained closely associated with their landward areas.[16] The medieval town also depended for its livelihood on the exploitation of the resources of the surrounding countryside. In a largely pastoral farming economy, it drew especially on wool, hides and skins, which formed the basis of much of its occupational structure.[17] That structure was itself significantly affected by the highly distinctive patterns taken by Scottish overseas trade in the medieval period, in which most exports took the form of raw materials – hides, skin, fish and, pre-eminently, raw wool – and imports were largely made up of a wide variety of manufactured goods.[18] The core of the Scottish economy before 1300 lay in the wool trade, yet towns were less involved as finishing centres for wool than they were for other raw materials. The clothing industry was important in thirteenth-century Berwick and Perth but far less so in any of the principal towns in the following two centuries.

The increasing dependence of the Scottish economy on the export of raw wool to Flanders had its price: after Bruges, as the staple port, came to monopolise much of Scotland's overseas trade in the fourteenth and fifteenth centuries, cheap and coarse quality Scottish cloth, much of it perhaps the work of rural weavers, was still allowed into Flanders, but cloth of a better quality was not. One result was that the dyers who were prominent in the Perth guild merchant in 1209 disappeared into obscurity in that town until the seventeenth century.[19] The clothing and textile trades, often taken to be the touchstones of urban wealth and industry, usually became a minor element in most Scottish towns unless they were able to find new markets, as Dundee was able to find in the Baltic. The occupational structure of the leading towns altered appreciably after 1300 as they strove to accommodate themselves to the changed economic climate which set in after the beginning of the Wars of Independence. There also emerged major differences in the specialisms of each of the new 'four great towns of Scotland' – Edinburgh, Perth, Aberdeen and Dundee – as recognised by Bruges by 1350.[20] A series of short-term crises, trade wars, eight outbreaks of plague between 1349 and 1455, coupled with an increasingly adverse balance of trade and falling exchange rate after the 1370s,[21] combined to provoke a long-term decline in wool exports and a scramble to diversify urban economies to counter the worsening conditions.

The burghs became the prisoners of their own monopoly of overseas trade. That monopoly had brought with it an unusual dependence on a narrow range of staple exports and a vulnerability to factors outside their control. In the absence of sources akin to the English poll taxes or lay subsidy returns of the fourteenth century,[22] urban decay in late medieval Scotland is unquantifiable, but it is difficult to believe, given the evidence of falling customs returns, shortage of coin and worsening exchange rates,[23] exaggerated by the growing stranglehold of Edinburgh over key sectors of overseas trade, that there was not a serious commercial decline in many, if not most, Scottish towns until 1500 or later. Some towns found it possible to diversify reasonably quickly, and by 1378 Stirling, for example, was paying more in custom for hides than wool.

But the decline in exports affected more than the wool towns. The prolific fisheries of the thirteenth century must have provided the foundation of the prosperity of east coast ports like Crail, with its elaborate town plan, as well as underpinning the predominance of major burghs like Berwick and Aberdeen. The collapse of the overseas market for cod and herring, if not for salmon, until the late fifteenth century must have had a proportionately greater effect on small ports, some languishing until well into the sixteenth century. Yet recovery, when it came, could be swift. Only five burghs paid less tax than Crail in 1535, but by 1579 its assessment had risen fourfold.[24]

The 'urban revival' of the eleventh and twelfth centuries[25] gave way to urban crisis and retrenchment for much of the fourteenth and fifteenth centuries. Admittedly, there were short-lived minor booms in wool and leather in the 1370s and 1420s, and some increases in both the cloth and timber trades;[26] there was even some physical extension of settlement in Perth,[27] and prestigious church-building operations were promoted in most of the major towns of eastern and central Scotland.[28] But the period was indelibly marked by a long-term decline in trade. This was followed by a certain expansion, still uneven, fluctuating and confined to parts of the urban economy, in the last quarter of the fifteenth century when there was some increase in trade with France and the Baltic.[29] Yet smaller inland towns like Elgin and Forres continued to lose ground to major provincial centres such as Aberdeen;[30] and the burgh tax returns, which become available from 1535, reveal a recurrent pattern of short-term crisis in many middle-ranking and smaller towns which began to evaporate only in the 1570s.[31] There was no general revival of overseas trade until the 1560s, and real improvement did not come until the 1590s.[32] It seems an inescapable conclusion that, outside the larger towns, and especially Edinburgh, there was no general urban recovery before the last quarter of the sixteenth century.

With only a few notable exceptions, much Scottish urban history has tended to dwell on form rather than function, that is, on the burgh rather than the town. Both the thirteenth-century *Statutes of the Guild*, which were copied out by the Dunfermline guildry two centuries later, and the twelfth-century *Burgh Laws*, transcribed by an Inverness burgess a century later still,[33] in a real sense linked burghs and burgesses in 1200 and 1600 and gave a greater uniformity to Scottish burghs than was possessed by English boroughs.[34] Yet the homogeneity of burgh institutions and law needs to be set against the diversity of Scottish towns, whether as market places, occupational or finishing centres, ports, or centres of land communication. The *Burgh Laws*, which have been described as 'a jumble'[35] even when first drawn up, provided at best a common core of customs and regulations which would be embellished, qualified or ignored by each burgh as it saw fit in much altered economic circumstances of later centuries.

The other key document describing early burgh institutions, the *Statutes of the Guild*, makes clear that already by the thirteenth century the Berwick guild merchant was evolving into a guild of burgesses.[36] Historians have held that by the fifteenth century, if not earlier, in most towns this institution had narrowed to a guild of merchants, excluding craftsmen from both the guild and burgh government. But the way in which relations between merchants and craftsmen have been viewed seldom takes into account the wider circumstances of slumps in trade and reduced economic activity, nor of manufacturing processes and retailing habits. Berwick was the focus and sole exit-point for a huge natural hinterland; its guild merchant was filled with provision merchants and entrepreneurs who controlled the key stages in cloth manufacture.[37]

About nineteen burghs are known to have had a guild merchant by the fourteenth century[38] but they operated in a very different Scottish economy from that of a century earlier and tended to concentrate in the wool and leather trades rather than in the cloth industry. Much of the history of the Scottish town from the 1370s onwards thus needs to be told in terms of the markets for wool and leather and the boundaries between middlemen and manufacturers, rather than the conventional story of administrative conflict between merchants and craftsmen.[39] As in

Berwick, middlemen could still control the relatively small cloth industry, much of which may have been rural or suburban, but the bulk of wool was still exported untreated. The leather trade was more evenly balanced between the export of skins and the manufacture of leather products. In the fifteenth century control of the wool trade was restricted by various means (including the connivance of the crown from the 1420s onwards) to a small elite of established merchants.[40] Similarly within the leather trade entrepreneurs, usually skinners, gained increasing control of the long manufacturing processes by being granted the right (by town councils or parliaments) to fix prices and wages and to prescribe standards. The formal incorporation of craft guilds completed the trend, and it is no coincidence that the skinners became – in 1474 – the first Edinburgh craft to be granted a 'seal of cause'. The metal workers, another amalgamated craft, followed shortly after. Power and control over the economic monopolies which had long been the mainspring of urban life were passing to the 'best and worthiest' in the burghs and this was true of both the retailing and the manufacturing sectors. The larger merchants tended to deal in a variety of commodities; the more prosperous craftsmen tended to supervise a number of stages in long manufacturing processes. A new urban aristocracy, comprising merchants *and* craftsmen, was thus emerging, but as yet only in the larger towns.

When the records of various merchant guilds become available in the fifteenth century, it is clear that the composition of the guilds varied from one town to another: in Dunfermline the guildry, on average about fifty strong, encompassed a third of the male inhabitants of the town; in Perth, a much larger town, numbers were not much greater than the Dunfermline average but they included craftsmen as well as merchants; in Aberdeen the numbers were much higher because, unlike other burghs, no distinction was made between inland and overseas traders, both categories being admitted as burgesses of guild, but craftsmen usually not; in Edinburgh some 15% of the merchant guildry was composed of craftsmen by the middle of the sixteenth century.[41] The shape of the merchant guild thus varied significantly from one town to another, reflecting the different shapes of their economies and the fluctuating boundaries between retailing and manufacture, merchant and craftsman.

Over the course of the centuries the sources of burgh customs and law shifted: in the twelfth century they were based largely on those of Newcastle; by the fourteenth and fifteenth centuries many constitutional and religious changes, including the adoption of the cult of the Holy Blood by merchant guilds, stemmed from the staple port of Bruges;[42] from the 1470s onwards the main influence was 'the example of Edinburgh'. The re-drawn Edinburgh constitution of 1583, giving increased representation to some of the crafts and itself the result of a royal commission, was used as a model solution to the ills of a number of burghs, which helps to explain the apparent similarity of so many burgh constitutions.[43] Yet much of this is misleading; the Aberdeen constitution of 1587 was largely ineffectual, just as the legislation stemming from the parliaments of the reign of James III, but prompted by other burghs, had been ignored for a century and more. There may have been such a thing as a typical burgh in the twelfth century, when most royal charters had an avowed common purpose of granting legal status and privileges to wool towns; but by the fifteenth century there was not.

The nature of royal patronage and political circumstances altered almost as much as the economic. The tight grip which the crown had maintained on the king's burghs before 1300 slackened thereafter. The interference, albeit inconsistent, of James I in the details of burgh life and government during the 1420s[44] must therefore have come as a surprise to urban rulers who had grown accustomed to being allowed a loose rein by the crown. The most important royal interventions were in the realm of foreign trade, and took two forms: the encouragement of certain sectors of the export trade, especially cloth, both by fiscal and diplomatic means; and the repeated attempts to restrict access to the export trade to a smaller circle of established merchants.[45] Equally significant was what the crown did not do: there was no concerted attempt to increase royal taxation on the burghs until the personal reign of James V.[46]

A reading of the legislation of fifteenth-century parliaments may produce too sharp a picture of increasing interference by the crown or other agencies of the king's government in burgh matters. It has been suggested, for instance, that the legislation of 1458 prohibiting bonds of manrent between landed men and towns resulted from the lobbying of the burgh of Aberdeen. The much-quoted act of 1487 ordering burgh elections to select only 'the best and worthiest indwellaris' also almost certainly stemmed from an attempt to resolve an Aberdeen dispute, the burgh election of 1486 having resulted in a controversy which had forced the king and his council to intervene.[47] If this act was intended to provide a model election procedure, the irony is that it was ignored in Aberdeen itself for over a century.

Just as important as changing attitudes of the crown was the transformation of the higher nobility, which was nearly complete by the 1450s.[48] There are signs that it often had the effect of re-casting in a more clear-cut way local or regional spheres of magnate interest, and had a lasting effect on the perception of many burghs, large and small, about their standing in the community of the realm. Burghs and burgesses alike made bonds with landed men, most notably Aberdeen with the earl of

Huntly in 1463. The fifth earl of Crawford was paid a pension by no less than six burghs, as far apart as Banff and Crail and ranging in size from Aberdeen to Forfar.[49] The subject remains largely unexplored but there is as much evidence of the need for noble protectors felt by the burghs, as of a 'problem' of magnate interference.

Certainly by the sixteenth century the relationship between burghs and landed men had become one of the most important issues in urban politics, perhaps *the* key relationship which affected all the others, including the uneasy mutual dependence of the crown and royal burghs.[50] In Aberdeen, for example, the long dynasty of the Menzies family was begun in 1487 and ended in 1593 on much the same grounds, for, having claimed power as an antidote to an excess of landed influence, they were ironically displaced for acting too much like 'landward barons'.[51] The issue was particularly difficult in Aberdeen where the great market place in the Castlegate, fronted by the town houses of many rural landowners, symbolised the vast countryside on which so much of the town's economy depended and the close mutual interests of burgesses and landed men.

As in other towns, Aberdeen's chartered status as a burgh gave it clearly defined privileges in its rural hinterland, and bound the town closely to the surrounding countryside rather than setting it apart. A string of nobles and lairds either owned property within the town of Aberdeen or had interests on the urban periphery in the form of leases of burgh lands, mills and fishings.[52] Conversely, from at least the fourteenth century Aberdeen burgesses are known to have invested in rural estates and married into the families of rural lairds. Similarly, the Dunfermline guild owned substantial grazing lands outside their town.[53] Although the occupational structure of a town was more concentrated and specialised than in its landward areas, it was tied to the cycle of rural farming for the supply of materials and casual labour; the Perth authorities were still worried by the annual influx of male and female shearers at harvest time in the 1590s.[54]

Town and country fed on each other for materials, labour and capital, but the nature and extent of a town's zone of influence varied. Aberdeen had a huge hinterland, virtually contiguous with the sheriffdom, and remained unchallenged in its domination of it; Dunfermline's was hewn out of a patchwork of jurisdictions in south-west Fife and contained a number of anomalies and 'grey' areas disputed by its neighbours;[55] but the majority probably lay somewhere between these two extremes in terms of size and character. Edinburgh, as in so many other respects, was a significant exception: by the fifteenth century its harbour at Leith had become the entrepôt for much of Scotland's overseas trade; its fourteen markets, spread throughout the town, also became a mecca for finished products from as far away as Perth and Dumfries, as well as being the hub of a vast hinterland stretching far into the Borders, an area which it had inherited after the final loss of Berwick to the English in 1482. Since no early market charter had been granted to any seaport on the south side of the River Forth, the loss of Berwick also gave an impetus to the overseas trade of towns like Linlithgow and Haddington as well as Edinburgh,[56] and was thus a turning point in the general relationship between town and country over much of Scotland south of the Forth.

In the later medieval period there was also a shift in the nature of the landed influence itself. Early burghs, most notably Berwick, contained large grants of property that had been made to religious houses, but such grants became much less common after 1300.[57] Nonetheless, most towns, whether diocesan centres like St Andrews and Glasgow[58] or not, maintained a larger proportion of ecclesiastically owned property than holdings of the nobility.[59] Noble interest in towns certainly existed but it, like the nobles themselves, tended to be peripatetic; a number of fifteenth-century major nobles seem to have been regularly on the move, visiting and issuing writs in various towns,[60] but the extent of their influence remains incalculable because it was rarely pushed to the issue. The long relationship between Aberdeen and the earls of Huntly is unlikely to have been typical, but even Aberdeen's position was more subtle than that of noble fief.[61]

Indeed, one of the most striking differences between Scottish and English urban history in the medieval period lies in the respective proportions of royal and seigneurial foundations: two-thirds of all English medieval boroughs were seigneurial; in 1400 nearly half of all Scottish burghs were royal.[62] There was no headlong rush of Scottish lords to gain charters for village markets in the thirteenth century. That rush came in the century after 1450 when over ninety private burghs were erected or confirmed, and even then almost a quarter of the new erections had ecclesiastical superiors.[63] In terms of landholding, the church had a relatively greater presence in the Scottish medieval town than in its English counterpart. The noble presence was correspondingly slighter, and for this reason Scotland escaped the jumble of overlords and jurisdictions which so characterised and blighted relations between English towns and magnates in the middle ages.

Other major differences distinguish the history of the Scottish medieval town from that in England. Every Scottish town, great or small, was a single-parish burgh, a *corpus christianum* as well as a community of burgesses, until the 1590s when population growth in some of the larger towns forced a subdivision of parishes.[64] The Scottish burghs were, relatively speaking, more uniform in burgh law and custom, and from perhaps as early as 1405 had a much more unified voice in national politics than was the case in England.[65] They were also far more lightly taxed than English boroughs, both in terms of the frequency and weight of royal taxation and the proportion of the community subjected to taxation. The only Scottish tax rolls extant before the sixteenth century belong to Aberdeen, the second or third largest town in fifteenth-century Scotland which had 445 taxpayers in 1448. This figure would have placed Aberdeen well below such English towns as Wells, Bridgnorth, Cirencester and Barking which had taxpaying populations of about 900 and ranked fortieth and below in the league table of towns paying the lay subsidy of 1377.[66] Even Edinburgh had only 1,245 taxpayers in 1583, but this amounted to no more than 10% of the total population which is measurable by other means.[67] The fact is that Scottish towns were as lightly taxed as the rest of the country, and although the crown sharply increased burgh taxation in the sixteenth century, it still strove to ensure that the urban poor escaped the tax net.[68] Comparisons of taxpaying populations in English and Scottish towns are therefore meaningless, as are calculations of Scottish urban populations using English multipliers on numbers of taxpayers. There were contrasts too in the overall forms and varieties of towns: in Scotland there were no single-industry towns, perhaps because of the slightness of the cloth industry; a much greater proportion of towns were directly engaged in overseas trade; and, conversely, there were fewer inland regional centres of any size.

Within the towns themselves the occupational structure and the composition of craft guilds showed marked differences from those common in English towns. Because of the unusual pattern of the Scottish export trade, which was highly concentrated in raw materials or only partly finished commodities, and because Bruges craftsmen were allowed to flood the domestic market with a wide range of quality manufactured goods, urban craft skills remained severely restricted, at least until the late fifteenth century. Even later, English observers commented on the smallness of the range of handicrafts in Scottish towns.[69] There were, in consequence, far fewer craft guilds in Scotland: fourteen in Edinburgh, and nine each in Dundee and Perth by 1540; most of these were conglomerate organisations, embracing a series of different trades and giving the opportunity for a craft aristocracy to emerge quickly within each guild.

A final contrast lies in the fact that the history of the Scottish medieval town was closely interwoven with the distinctive habits of Scottish medieval kingship. The twelfth and early thirteenth centuries saw important changes, stemming from the crown, in the legal status of urban settlements, and royal patronage almost certainly resulted in significant increases in urban populations, a demographic trend which was not repeated until the sixteenth century. The history of the Scottish medieval town is becoming better known in the relatively prosperous years up to the 1280s; its history in the very different environment of a prolonged slump in the export trade and the revised expectations of the crown after 1300 is still generally unfamiliar. The fourteenth, it has been argued, was the key century, which saw both the consolidation of the community of the burgh and its full absorption into the community of the realm.[70] From another perspective, the century and a half after 1350 was a transitional phase where, although precise points of change cannot be pinpointed, nothing less than a transformation of the medieval town took place. By 1500 the relationships between town and country, burgh and feudal realm, as well as the underlying occupational structure of towns were all vastly different from what they had been in 1300. The change was real and fundamental, but it was partly camouflaged by apparent continuity in burgh custom, law and institutions. The course of the sixteenth century would reveal how much had already changed. It saw a rise in overseas trade and marked growth of populations, at least in most of the major towns, as well as the more persistent demands, political as well as fiscal, of the crown. It was little wonder that towns then looked to their medieval charters in order to confirm their position in a changing world.[71]

NOTES

1. These characteristics are further discussed in Reynolds, *English Towns*, pp. ix–x.

2. See Stevenson, Ch. 11 and Lynch, Ch. 15, below.

3. R. Feachem, 'The hillforts of northern Britain', in *The Iron Age in Northern Britain*, ed. A. L. F. Rivet (Edin., 1966), 59–88.

4. See the various reports on the Traprain Law excavations and finds which appear in *PSAS* from vol. xlix (1914–15) onwards.

5. L. Alcock & S. T. Driscoll, *Excavations at Dundurn, St Fillans, Perthshire, 1976–77. Revised Interim Report* (Glas. Univ. Archaeology Dept., 1985); L. Alcock, *Arthur's Britain* (Penguin Bks., 1971); L. Lang, *The Archaeology of Late Celtic Britain & Ireland* (London, 1975).

6. C. Plummer (ed.), *Bede's Ecclesiastical History* (1986); B. Colgrave, *Eddius Stephanus, Life of Wilfred* (1927).

7. See MacQueen & Windram, Ch. 12 below.

8. Spearman, Ch. 3, below; MS Perth Kirk Session Recs., 1597.

9. Spearman, Ch. 3, below; Stevenson, 'Thesis', 228n; Hume Brown, *Early Travellers*, 10; 'List of inhabitants of Stirling', *Scottish Antiquary*, vi (1892), 175–8.

10. These calculations, based on *ER*, vols. i–vi, were kindly made available by Dr A. Grant; those after 1460 depend on Guy, 'Thesis'.

11. Lynch, *Edinburgh*, 10; Makey, 'Edinburgh in mid-seventeenth century', in Lynch (ed.), *Early Modern Town*, 205–6.

12. Grant, *Scotland*, 69.

13. See MacQueen & Windram, Ch. 12, below.

14. Cf. R. Hilton, 'Towns and societies in medieval England', *Urban History Yearbook* (1982), 7.

15. Duncan, *Scotland*, 496; Nicholson, *Scotland*, 263, 389, 452.

16. Cowan, Ch. 5, below.

17. Spearman, Ch. 8, below.

18. Ditchburn, Ch. 10, below; Stevenson, Ch. 11, below.

19. Stevenson, Ch. 11, below; Duncan, *Scotland*, 490, 500.

20. Lynch, Ch. 15, below.

21. See Grant, *Scotland*, 72-3, 80-1.

22. Cf. S. H. Rigby, 'Urban decline in the later Middle Ages: the reliability of the non-statistical evidence', *Urban History Yearbook* (1984), 48-9.

23. See the convenient table in Grant, *Scotland*, 240.

24. Stevenson, 'Thesis', 254, 262-3; Guy, 'Thesis', 116, 125-8, 134; Lynch, *Early Modern Town*, 12.

25. Duncan, *Scotland*, 464.

26. Grant, *Scotland*, 70, 79-80.

27. Spearman, Ch. 3, below.

28. Stell, Ch. 4; also Ewan, Ch. 13, below.

29. See Ditchburn, Ch. 10, below; Stevenson, 'Thesis', 283-4.

30. As evidenced by the contrast in tax assessments on burghs in an isolated roll of 1485 and that of 1535; *Burghs Conv. Recs.*, i, 514, 543; Lynch, 'Towns', 188n.

31. Lynch, *Early Modern Town*, 5.

32. Guy, 'Thesis', 166-7.

33. Torrie, Ch. 14, below; the Inverness collection forms the basis of SCA, Fort Augustus MS A1.

34. Barrow, *Kingship*, 84.

35. Duncan, *Scotland*, 482.

36. *Ibid.*, 497.

37. *Ibid.*, 490, 499.

38. Ewan, Ch. 13; Torrie, Ch. 14, n. 6, below.

39. For the details of this argument, see Lynch, Ch. 15, below; also Spearman, Ch. 8, below.

40. Stevenson, Ch. 11, below.

41. Torrie, Ch. 14; Lynch, Ch. 15, below. The information on Perth was kindly supplied by Marion Stavert, who is preparing an edition of the Perth Guild Book, which begins in 1452, for SRS.

42. D. McRoberts, *The Fetternear Banner* (Glasgow, n.d.), 16-17.

43. Lynch, *Early Modern Town*, 14, 61.

44. Duncan, *James I*, 9-10.

45. Ditchburn, Ch. 10; Stevenson, Ch. 11, below.

46. Lynch, *Early Modern Town*, 72-3.

47. Wormald, *Lords and Men*, 138, 141; see ACA, CR, vii, 27, which was followed by the passing of *APS*, ii, 178, c. 14.

48. Grant, *Scotland*, 178-9.

49. C. A. Kelham, 'Bases of magnatial power in later fifteenth-century Scotland' (Edin. Univ. Ph.D., 1986), 337.

50. Lynch, *Early Modern Town*, 19-26.

51. White, 'Thesis', 309, 319, 321–4, 329–32; *Burghs Conv. Recs.*, i, 313–15.

52. Booton, Ch. 9, below.

53. Ewan, 'Thesis', Ch. 3; Torrie, Ch. 14, below.

54. MS Perth Kirk Session Recs., 27 Aug. 1593.

55. Cf. Booton, Ch. 9, and Torrie, Ch. 14, below.

56. The editors are grateful to Dr Walter Makey, who is engaged on a general history of Edinburgh, for this point.

57. Stevenson, Ch. 6, below.

58. See Shead, Ch. 7, below, for the example of Glasgow.

59. See Ewan, 'Thesis', 148.

60. Kelham, 'Thesis', 52.

61. Cf. Wormald, *Lords and Men*, 143; White, 'Thesis', *passim*, an extended discussion of the ambivalent relationship of noble patron and urban client. Booton, 'Economic and social change', 51–2, discusses the relationship in the fifteenth century.

62. Hilton, 'Towns and societies', 11; Pryde, *Burghs*, nos. 1–45, 82–132.

63. *Ibid.*, 51–9.

64. Cowan, Ch. 5; Lynch, Ch. 15, below.

65. Nicholson, *Scotland*, 265; Duncan, *James I*, 10–11, 21.

66. ACA, CR, iv, 512–18; W. G. Hoskins, *Local History in England* (2nd ed., 1972), 176.

67. Lynch, Edinburgh, 378. An ecclesiastical census of 1592 revealed 8,000 adult communicants; Lynch, 'Whatever happened to the medieval burgh?', 7.

68. Lynch, *Early Modern Town*, 72.

69. Stevenson, Ch. 11; Lynch, Ch. 15, n. 9, below.

70. Ewan, 'Thesis', Ch. 6.

71. Flett & Cripps, Ch. 2, below.

Part One

Sources and Evidence

2

Documentary Sources

Iain Flett and Judith Cripps[1]

The sources for the study of the Scottish medieval town are scattered and fragmentary, but underexploited.[2] The major difficulty confronting the historian is the fact that no continuous urban archive survives which predates the very end of the fourteenth century and most begin or expand to a useful degree only a century later. There are also for Scotland no sources akin to the detailed English fourteenth-century poll tax records or lay subsidy returns, which makes it difficult to quantify the extent of urban decay in late medieval Scotland. There are fewer extant bishops' registers and no evidence, other than in the form of incidental references in monastic cartularies or similar sources, as to the rents of urban properties before the sixteenth century. No petitions for financial relief, common for many English medieval boroughs, exist before the 1530s.[3] Information about the individual wealth of urban dwellers is unobtainable in the virtually complete absence of testamentary records until the 1560s or later.

It is hardly surprising that historians of the Scottish medieval town have relied heavily on the few sources which do exist as a corpus of readily available material: burgh charters, where they survive; the two detailed sets of municipal regulations drawn up at an early stage in burgh history, the *Burgh Laws* and the *Statutes of the Guild* of Berwick; a few descriptions made by foreign visitors of Scottish towns, although most are vague or unreliable;[4] and the stream of legislation relating to burgh life, government and trade emanating from parliaments from the fifteenth century onwards. Yet other sources do exist, if in forms which are less manageable or convenient. There is a legacy of ecclesiastical records, mostly in the shape of cartularies of religious houses, which gives some indication of the strikingly large presence of the church in Scottish towns.[5] Records relating to both trade and exchange rates, whether in the various records of the Exchequer or lying in foreign archives, were often examined and partly printed in the nineteenth century but have until recently lain largely neglected;[6] taken together, they provide a reasonably firm context for an analysis of the economic history of towns in the medieval period. The evidence, such as it is, has yet to be taken to its cultivation limits.

With documentary sources so varied in quality and coverage, it is all the more important to remember that historic buildings, drawings, maps, objects, and the towns themselves all contribute to the study of medieval towns. Three chapters of this book deal at some length with the main available, unwritten evidence: buildings, maps and archaeological excavation.[7] They make use of a variety of major plan and photographic archives, museum collections, and excavation reports which are regrettably not normally considered by urban historians. The National Monuments Record of Scotland, which holds information on both buildings and excavations, is attached to the Royal Commission on the Ancient and Historical Monuments of Scotland, Edinburgh. The main museum collections which hold medieval urban material are the Royal Museum of Scotland (formerly the National Museum of Antiquities of Scotland) in Edinburgh, Perth Museum & Art Gallery, Glasgow Art Gallery & Museum, and Inverness Museum. The majority of excavation reports appear in *PSAS* or the Monograph Series of SAS. Many await publication and in most instances interim information is available through SUAT.

The most basic, early source in documented form for the study of the medieval town is the charter;[8] it is testimony to the granting or confirmation of property or other legal rights. Although valuable documentary evidence for the burghs may be found in later private charters, for the early period almost the only source for the burghs are charters granted by the king to his burgesses and other vassals. Royal charters would normally have been engrossed on rolls, but unfortunately, as a result of the intervention of Edward I in Scottish government, the earliest public records of this type date only from the reign of Robert I. There are other gaps in the series, especially before 1424, but these records are printed in the *Register of the Great Seal* down to 1668 with full texts in the first volume and abridgements in the others. However, prior to Robert I, and for certain years until 1424, Scottish historians have to rely on the original charters and cartularies compiled from them. Fortunately, as charters provided evidence of title to specific rights, they were normally retained by the owners or inheritors of the lands and rights to which they related, and it has been possible for historians to reconstruct a large proportion of the missing registers.[9] Because of their better maintenance of written records, it has inevitably been the religious houses and municipal corporations, rather than individuals and families, which have preserved the majority of royal and other charters. However, the movement of title deeds in association with land or families, especially following the Reformation, has meant that many relevant charters have been dispersed to sometimes unexpected and apparently obscure manuscript collections.

A great many of the important charter collections and monastic cartularies have been published by the various Scottish historical clubs of the nineteenth century.[10] Amongst this great wealth of evidence, transcribed and printed to variable standards, are a number of important collections of charters from the urban religious houses, churches and cathedrals.[11] The Burgh Records Society was primarily concerned with the great mass of later urban records but they remain an important source for early charters generated by or relating to the burghs. Some burghs have retained their accumulations of charters from medieval times; others have deposited them, along with the rest of their burgh archives, in the Scottish Record Office.[12] Family muniments are far more difficult to sift for urban information; although Sir William Fraser's family histories provide much basic information on the more important private collections, it is necessary for urban historians to examine the original charters, many of which are to be found in the Scottish Record Office.[13]

Closely related to royal charters granted to individual burghs are the 'Laws of the Four Burghs', which are usually held to have initially been drawn up almost verbatim from the customs of Newcastle-upon-Tyne during the reign of David I. They are, however, a compilation from various sources made over an uncertain period of time.[14] Both their provenance and their use by historians as a prescriptive custumal of Scottish urban life are called into question in this volume.[15] Yet the *Burgh Laws*, when taken in conjunction with apparent borrowings from them in burgh charters, do at least imply the emergence of a common burgh and mercantile law by the late twelfth century.

Most of the records of early Scottish parliaments are lost but the second volume of the *Acts of the Parliaments of Scotland*, beginning in 1424, has in it a stream of legislation about towns, covering a range of topics such as the nature of burgh government and elections, the fixing of prices of basic foodstuffs and the regulation of overseas trade, and even the siting of brothels on the periphery. It is a much-used source,[16] but it, like the *Burgh Laws*, may, if taken in isolation, give a misleadingly uniform picture of Scottish urban life.[17] Some legislation, such as that on trade and prices, was clearly intended to be general; other acts, such as those of 1458 and 1487, dealing respectively with landed influence in towns and the conduct of burgh elections, were devised to solve specific, local disputes; others again, such as the act of 1427 banning craft deacons, may have reflected an *ideé fixe* of a particular parliament.[18] It is important in dealing with such a convenient source to bear in mind these distinctions, even if they cannot always be firmly established. It is too easy to construct a general problem, which may in fact not have existed, out of such a source.

The other major government record in print relating to the burghs, the *Exchequer Rolls*, is more voluminous than the *Acts of Parliament* and more difficult to use. Although Exchequer records are known to have been kept from at least 1180, they survive as a regular series only from 1326. They thus reveal in particular the new revenues which the crown drew from the royal burghs – in particular the 'new' or 'great' customs on wool exports, which were first introduced sometime between 1275 and 1282. They reveal little of older forms of income, the petty customs and the 'cain' or 'custom of ships'.[19] The *Rolls* essentially consist of the accounts of the various collectors of crown revenues; of most interest to urban historians are the accounts of the custumars, the lessees of burgh customs and dues. Yet entries can include narratives of burgh charters, a wealth of incidental information on the range of raw materials required, marketed and manufactured in Scottish towns, and, though usually from a comparatively late date, reasons for delay in submitting accounts. Although there were imposts levied on specific categories such as English goods, Scotland had otherwise no import duties, as distinct from anchorage dues, until 1597. Some indication of imported commodities can be gleaned, however, from the custumars' expenses, which also occasionally reveal the names of foreign merchants.[20]

The most valuable part of the *Rolls* are the customs accounts, which record the volume and duty payable on staple commodities exported from Scottish ports. They do not take the form of English particular customs accounts of the same period, and even Berwick during its English occupation yields few particular accounts. The Scottish records, while both fragmentary and laconic in the fourteenth century, do include references to numbers of ships, and often distinguish between ships and boats, although they do not usually provide the names or nationality of merchants or skippers. Some impression of these can be gleaned, however, from other incidental records stemming from instances of piracy or shipwreck.[21] The customs accounts do, however, provide material for a continuous analysis of the staple goods passing through each of the exporting burghs from the 1360s onwards as well as for giving a detailed picture of the patterns of Scotland's overseas trade as a whole.[22] The first surviving port books date from the very late fifteenth century, although they are fairly common by 1600, so detailed analysis both of shipping and of skippers and individual exporters is not possible before the sixteenth century.[23] Yet a comprehensive view of Scotland's main trade, with the Low Countries, Germany and the Baltic, is now available. What remains to be done, in the light of this newly provided context, is systematic analysis of the fluctuations in customs returns in order to chart the decay or diversification of the economies of individual towns.[24] They comprise the best, indeed the only, index of the urban economy in the medieval period.[25]

Two other kinds of official record, both of which survive only from the late fifteenth century, are worth noting. The Treasurer emerged during the reign of James I, and the first Treasurer's account to survive is for 1473/4. It is not until the 1490s, however, that the accounts survive in any quantity. The Treasurer was responsible for the collection of various dues. He also made casual payments on behalf of the crown, and it is from this activity that information on international diplomacy and trade can be gained. James IV's close ties with Denmark are clearly illustrated by payments to ambassadors and merchants trading there.[26] There are also references to the commodities of trade with other parts of Europe and occasionally merchants, skippers and their ships are named. The crown's foreign correspondence also probably contained considerable information relating to trade. Much of this has been lost,[27] but attempts have been made to add to the patchy Scottish survivals from the reigns of James IV and V with foreign records. Both of these printed collections reveal a good deal of the problems which merchants faced, such as seizure of goods, as well as the extent to which kings intervened in foreign trade.[28]

The bulk of Scotland's overseas trade for most of the medieval period was with Flanders and Artois but it is not reflected in a convenient or readily accessible body of material. The Walcheren toll records, which recorded the anchorage dues paid by foreign ships, show little Scottish activity;[29] but other records, especially Halyburton's ledger,[30] make clear that there was widespread evasion of tolls. The archives of each of the three staples in the Low Countries which in their turn held a monopoly of trade with Scotland have suffered serious damage: the loss of early Bruges records in a fire in 1280 casts a veil over the earlier history of the Scottish expatriate community there, which was large enough to have its own district by the 1290s;[31] the virtually complete destruction of Middleburg's records and much of Veere's during the Second World War forces a reliance on earlier printed histories.[32] The burgess lists for Veere have survived from the late fifteenth century,[33] as have those for the more easterly port of Bergen-op-Zoom, where there are also land registers of the same date;[34] all record Scottish names in numbers.[35] There is a scattering of records elsewhere in the Netherlands, particularly in The Hague;[36] yet for other parts of the Low Countries, including Antwerp, there seem to be few records of Scottish traffic, except at St Omer.[37] Much material does, however, lie in the Burgundian state records housed in Lille, and there is a large file of records (which are virtually all sixteenth century or later) in the Archives Générales du Royaume in Brussels.[38] The single most important archive, is that of Bruges,[39] which has a large and valuable inventory detailing the town records.[40] There are burgess records (*poorterboeken*) for

Bruges but, since they do not include entrants to the merchant guild, they lack details of Scottish merchants.[41] The file of Scottish papers compiled by Anselm Adornes, containing important correspondence relating to the reign of James III, is not listed in any of the standard works but has re-emerged in the Bruges Stadsarchief, uncatalogued and unnumbered.[42]

The material in print for the study of Scotland's relations with Germany and the Baltic, the other main component of its medieval trade, are less well known to Scottish historians. Archives there are *terra incognita*. Although some archives, such as Münster and Szczecin, suffered early losses to their collections, most amassed a considerable corpus of records. Much of this has been calendared or printed in the *Diplomatarium Norvegicum, Hanse Recesse, Hansisches Urkundenbuch* and other regional source books.[43] The publication of these before 1939 was fortunate since during and after the Second World War many of the relevant archives wandered. Some came west. Part of the records from Reval (Tallinn) are now at the Bundesarchiv in Koblenz; those of the Staatarchiv Schwerin in the Bundesarchiv Aussenstelle in Frankfurt-am-Main; and (of most interest to Scottish medievalists) the Teutonic Order's records, formerly at Kaliningrad (Königsberg), have eventually found a home in the Geheimes Staatarchiv, Preussischer Kulturbesitz, in West Berlin. Other records moved east. Material from Lübeck journeyed via a salt mine to Potsdam, Lübben and Leningrad. Some Hamburg records are also now in East Germany. Evacuations and bombings also caused the loss of documents. Bremen's holdings are thus sparse, while certain early fifteenth-century Teutonic Order records, which certainly included Scottish references, are now missing. Nevertheless, some archives continue to hold extensive records, most notably those of Gdańsk and Cologne (which also holds material from the Hansa's Bruges and London *Kontors*). The current holdings of Hanseatic archives have been detailed elsewhere.[44]

The types of record to survive vary enormously. Because the Hansa was such an amorphous body, central records are limited. Much of what survives (diet proceedings and their correspondence) is printed.[45] At the local level, correspondence, especially for Cologne (from 1350), Gdańsk and the Teutonic Order (from the fifteenth century), is relatively voluminous and revealing. Council and judicial records are more patchy, but useful on the activities of individual merchants and settlers. Customs records are sparse, though those of Gdańsk, dating from 1460, include one book devoted solely to Scottish trade in 1477. The first extant Sound Toll Register is for 1497 and others, though not in an unbroken run, date from the early sixteenth century.[46] Some German merchants' handbooks also survive. Those of Reval are particularly numerous, but include little on Scotland.

B

Of all the foreign archives those of England are probably the fullest for the medieval period and they reveal a good deal about various aspects of Scotland's international trade. During periods of Anglo-Scottish hostility, the English government attempted to disrupt Scottish trade with the continent, while foreign merchants in England were dissuaded from trading with Scotland. Suspicion that such rules were being ignored during the Wars of Independence resulted in numerous seizure orders on foreign merchants' goods. Scots merchants too came into contact with the English authorities when their ships were shipwrecked on the English coast or when their vessels were captured at sea. Much of the material relating to such matters has been published. The *Rotuli Scotiae* include some information and Bain's *Calendar of Documents* is an indispensable guide to references in other parts of the English archives. Nevertheless the various collections of state papers, especially the calendars of Close Rolls and Patent Rolls, collections of correspondence and Rymer's *Foedera* have often to be turned to for the details.[47] These collections are also of use for the sadly neglected topic of Anglo-Scottish trade, recording safe-conducts granted to merchants and the problems which beset Scottish merchants in England. One of the most valuable sources for the study of bilateral trade, the English particular customs accounts, has not, however, been published and it is to them that one must turn for detailed figures on the size and nature of the trade.[48] The English records are also of great use in unravelling Berwick's history. Evidence on the burgh's decline as a trading centre after it was cut off from its Scottish hinterland has been published. In addition a few of the town's customs accounts dating from the fourteenth century survive, as do some guild minute books from 1505.[49]

Urban records proper survive only from the fifteenth century, taking one or other of two basic forms: a record of the guild merchant or of the burgh court. Records of guilds merchant have survived only sparsely; three folios dating from 1428 to 1432 outline very briefly proceedings of the guild court of Ayr, but the Dunfermline guild court book, commencing in 1433, is the oldest extant record.[50] There is a reference to the *curia gilde* of Aberdeen in 1437, and for thirty years from 1441 guild court records exist as a separate section of the register; after 1470 guild court business was, however, reduced to the election of councillors and admission of burgesses of guild.[51] A reference to a meeting of the Edinburgh guild court in 1403 should correctly be dated 1453, and thereafter there are isolated entries relating to the guild, but no guild court book as such survives before 1550.[52] The 'Guildrie Book' of Perth dates from 1452[53] and a manuscript parchment roll for 1460–1475 outlines dealings of the guild merchant in Stirling.[54]

In several towns burgh court records survive from an earlier date than those of the guildry. Aberdeen possesses three membranes from a parchment roll recording proceedings before the baillies from August to October 1317.[55] On the authority of the first inventory of court records compiled in 1591,[56] similar scrolls were produced until the 1390s. The earliest paper register, or book of proceedings of the burgh court for Aberdeen begins in 1398.[57] Edinburgh[58] and Dundee[59] possess only extracts from court books for the fifteenth century. Among smaller royal burghs, Ayr's court book begins in the 1420s,[60] those for Montrose[61] and Peebles[62] in the 1450s, and the Dunfermline burgh court book series begins in 1488.[63] Newburgh (Fife), a burgh of regality, has a court book beginning in 1459,[64] and a fragment of a similar book just survives for Prestwick.[65] From the 1450s, Scots is increasingly the language of record, but the Aberdeen scribes continued to write some entries in Latin well into the sixteenth century.

Within this select group, Aberdeen stands out by virtue of the bulk of its fifteenth-century records, 4,000 pages in seven volumes before 1501, despite the loss of the registers for 1413–33.[66] Alongside the elections of provosts, councillors and office bearers, registrations of property transfer, admissions of burgesses, amercements of forestallers, promulgations of statutes to regulate the conduct of the inhabitants and the prices of staple foodstuffs, and the proceedings of the chamberlain's ayre, the clerks of Aberdeen recorded numerous cases of mercantile and property-based debt, and law and order offences. On half-used pages they jotted down the cargoes of foreign vessels. Some of the non-judicial business was registered in the head courts, but much spilt over into regular sittings of the burgh court. Administrative records entered in the early court books include accounts of the alderman's expenses, rentals and assedations of town lands and fishings, royal missives and tax rolls arranged by the quarters. The last account to be entered is for 1433–6; once kept separately, accounts have not survived before the 1540s.[67] Assessment lists for royal taxation, ambassadorial and military expenses and the charges of the chamberlain's ayre are entered in the registers between 1408 and 1470. Once kept apart from the register, they were easily lost or destroyed, and the earliest in this format dates from 1576.[68]

Property transfers continue to be recorded in the Aberdeen registers on behalf of the inhabitants throughout the fifteenth century, but the existence of a bulky minute book of sasines 1484–1502[69] is indicative of the need to create new record series to cope with the growing demand for registration. Peebles appears to have reacted to the same problem by ceasing to record court business in the main register book. The Peebles protocol books begin in 1484 and contain admissions of burgesses, common good accounts and decreets of lining in addition to sasines. The

court books after 1484 have largely disappeared.[70] In a similar manner
Edinburgh chose in 1487 to record the admissions of burgesses in a
separate register which is now the earliest volume in the burgh archive.[71]
The earliest series of protocol books of private notaries deposited in a
burgh archive is that compiled by James Young of the Canongate and
begins in 1485.[72] An embryonic burgh protocol book survives from much
earlier in the century. The court book of Haddington 1423–1514 is in fact
an intermittent record of actions in the burgh court for property and
inheritance, together with sasines and charters registered between 1423
and 1471, the remainder of the volume blank except for one charter dated
1514.[73]

Records of proceedings in burgh courts, however catalogued, are the
predominant survivors of the archives created by burghs in the fifteenth
century. None can be deemed typical. Aberdeen demonstrates the record-
keeping capabilities of a major burgh, and it must be assumed that
Edinburgh, Dundee and Perth once had archives to match. The contrast
with the sheer bulk of material surviving from the next century is too great
to think otherwise. Despite the damage to local records caused by the
'rough wooing' of the 1540s and the destruction during the Cromwellian
invasion of both local and national records, the substance and extent of
surviving Scottish archives of the sixteenth century is so overwhelming
that only recently has any concerted attempt been made to depart from
studies of individual towns and to commence on a programme of broad
comparative work.[74]

The important national records have been systematically published, and
through the consistency of disciplined editorships they present a
formidable, if accessible, repository of factual, statistical, political and
sociological information.[75] Local records, on the other hand, have been
published by a bewildering assortment of individuals, publishing clubs,
local history societies and institutions,[76] with a resulting lack of consistency
in accuracy, selection of extracts, or choice of record series.[77] However,
although it is always preferable to consult an original record to really
appreciate its form and provenance, it is unfortunate that the uneven
development of provision of local record offices[78] means that access to
original documents is still difficult or inconvenient, and that printed
sources must still be used extensively.

While there are new series such as port books in the late sixteenth
century directly being created as the result of legislation,[79] what is
remarkable about the principal vehicle of information, the court, guildry,
or council minute book, is not its creation but its expansion. It is clear that
council minute books were kept in major burghs in the fifteenth century,
but their haphazard survival,[80] in contrast to the contents of town charter

chests which survived pillage and pestilence,[81] point to a change in emphasis on record keeping rather than a creation of a burgh record. The sixteenth century, with its emphasis on the growing stability and juridical power of the crown,[82] brought realisation to community, guildry, craft, and later, kirk session, that their power lay as much in the faithful and witnessed recordings of their decisions, as in the production of writs, charters, and 'evidentis', although the testing of burgh privileges by the crown in the 1580s led to a temporary reversal in this trend.[83]

Minute books were kept in various forms in both royal burghs and in burghs of barony and regality. The policy and community decisions were entered in volumes described as 'registers' in Aberdeen and in Edinburgh,[84] or as 'council minute books' elsewhere.[85] There could also exist contemporary or later abstracts of important policy decisions, as in Dundee[86] and Edinburgh.[87] The loose description of 'sederunt books', meaning minute books with complete attendance lists, is used widely by some later inventories to cover council, guildry and trade incorporation decisions.

Judgments of the provost and magistrates acting in the burgh or head court were entered in court books, and sometimes these were the same volume as the minutes of town council. The unfortunate habit of some published editions to omit the full headings of record entries has meant that it is not possible to distinguish the function of a council meeting without referring to the original.[88] The other unfortunate habit of omitting sederunts or attendance lists in published editions is now creating obstacles in the development of psephological studies.[89] Now that interest is being shown in the decision makers, as well as their decisions, it has been shown that sederunts have proved invaluable in identifying economic and political figureheads through comparison with other sources such as stent rolls, and have in turn brought new light on the social and economic background of the Reformation.[90]

Burghs also possessed the judicatory of the Dean of Guild Court, which dealt with mercantile cases and, later, building consent. The early sixteenth century saw seals of cause consolidating the guildry in Edinburgh and Dundee.[91] The dean of guild had an automatic seat on the town council, and in some burghs the guild court records form part of the burgh archive,[92] although in Dundee the guildry was to divorce itself from the town council in 1817, together with its records.[93]

The matters dealt with in these minute books include civil and criminal jurisdiction, weights and measures and price regulation, administration of common works, public health, the burgh church and the burgh schools, collection of customs, issue of birth brieves,[94] negotiations on rights or disputes with the Convention of Royal Burghs, with parliament, or with the privy council. The sheer volume of these series presents a managerial as well as an analytical problem to the researcher. For those burghs with lacunae it is necessary to consult central government records and miscellaneous documents to establish what their areas of activity were,[95] but for those series in existence the lack of comprehensive indices makes research a laborious process. Judgments on civil cases relate to payment of debt or settlement of contract,[96] and on criminal cases to a description of the crime and of the punishment.[97] Much effort was spent on actually encouraging townsfolk to obey and revere their magistrates.[98] Price regulation, particularly of bread, is recorded in the earliest Aberdeen records, but not on a regular basis. By the mid-sixteenth century it occurs with such frequency that P. H. Brown thought that burgesses were more concerned with prices than religion,[99] but although fixed prices led to baker craft riots,[100] the price of oats, the diet of the poor people, was seldom included.[101]

Public works included walls, tolbooths, burgh churches, town mills, piers, harbours and bridges. Undue activities on any of these are good indicators of unrest, reforming zeal, and economy respectively. Public health in such confined and unhealthy areas as burghs was a constant source of despondency and alarm, and a stream of burghal legislation about middens, cesspools, burying grounds,[102] offal trades, hygiene at wells, lepers and plague victims[103] paints a corroborative picture of ordure. Concern about burgh churches widened in the sixteenth century as town councils found themselves with not only the kirk fabric to administer, but also, after 1567, the lands of the former dispossessed monastic and mendicant orders with their former responsibilities of poor hospital and general alms,[104] and the upkeep of ministers and their eventual families. Education was inseparable from religious provision,[105] and dispute about the nature of education, and those who were nominated to dispense it, was a reliable barometer of the progress of the Reformation.[106]

However, the burgh was a centre of economic activity, whether craft or merchant orientated,[107] and the minute books reflect this. Acts regulating the quality of goods, the sale of goods, the markets for goods and the producers of goods fill successive head court meetings.[108] Traditional mercantile rivalries between towns such as Perth/Dundee,[109] Edinburgh/ Leith,[110] and Glasgow/Dumbarton[111] were a centre for constant irritation, as were the attempts by surrounding landowners to secure influence in burgh government so that they could participate in this economic activity.[112] The minute books of the guildry, where they exist separately, can still in the sixteenth century consist of a register or roll of burgesses or guild brethren with interspersed proceedings,[113] or alternatively as separate rolls and sederunt volumes.[114] The dean of guild as a spending magistrate covered the responsibility of kirk fabric in some burghs,[115] thus fulfilling the role carried out by kirk masters in the others.[116]

The next major class of burgh records, the accounts, supplement the minute books by detailing expenditure, usually in pedantic detail, and they can provide administrative detail where there are gaps in the minute books, or where scant reference is made to a subject like witch burning in the minute books.[117] Because treasurers kept their accounts simply under charge (income) and discharge (expenditure), it is a straightforward exercise to recreate the proportion of fiscal responsibilities undertaken in the burghs. Difficulties arose, however, when the duties of spending magistrates started to overlap. The kirkmaster's and hospitalmaster's duties tended to overlap in Dundee in the sixteenth century, and by the nineteenth century had become hopelessly interwoven.[118] Other burghs had similar problems as they assumed administration of pre-Reformation ecclesiastical and monastical rents and incomes after 1560.[119] Edinburgh collectors had the additional heavy burden of occasionally taking in levies for national purposes, with the result that their accounts then became national ones.[120]

A remarkable amount has survived of miscellaneous charters, bonds, papers, correspondence and title deeds for the sixteenth century, and like accounts they can supplement or in some cases provide an alternative source of information.[121] Even legal inventories of papers, when the items listed have been dispersed, can be illuminating.[122] Crown charters or grants under the great or privy seal are usually to be found in the respective royal registers if the burgh originals are not extant and relate to the confirmation of old rights. They can also relate to the acquisition of new ones like shore dues,[123] or to the creation of a burgh or burgh of barony[124] or the conversion into a royal burgh of a burgh of barony. Stent or tax rolls in Edinburgh have provided a corroborative guide to mercantile influence and may also, with caution, be used to give some indication of occupational structure;[125] shipping lists in Aberdeen and Dundee have shown both trade statistics and trading patterns.[126] In the case of Paisley, Dundee, Glasgow, Edinburgh and Montrose miscellaneous papers and title deeds provide some information on burgh activity in the first half of the sixteenth century before the bulk of their minute books start to survive.[127]

An act of parliament of 1567[128] ordained that the protocol books (records of transactions) of deceased notaries within burghs should be sent to the provost and baillies for safe keeping. Later acts ordained that they should be sent to the Clerk Register,[129] with the result that burgh protocol books can be found both in local record offices and in Register House.[130] The variety and richness of the social, economic and genealogical information which they hold has been mirrored by the sustained and serious programme of publication which legal history and other societies have carried out over the last century.[131]

Although guildry records have been associated with burgh records and mostly survive with them, the records and minute books of the trade incorporations, which mostly date from their incorporation in the sixteenth century,[132] have usually been regarded as the private property of these trades, with the result that many are still in private custody or have been dispersed. Some published histories have been commissioned privately by trade incorporations with various degrees of precision.

Kirk session records are now the property of the Church of Scotland, but they could be regarded in the sixteenth century as a burgh record in the sense that the kirk session often consisted of the same people as the town council, and the renaissance of moral laws in burgh legislation in the second half of the sixteenth century upheld the concept of the civil magistrate as a godly magistrate. Like contemporary Imperial cities, the Scottish burgh after the Reformation could still be considered a *civitas christiana*,[133] and therefore much can be found in magisterial edicts that would otherwise have existed in kirk session records. Similarly the registers of baptism and marriage, which formed part of the kirk session records, were split from those series in the Registration Act of 1855,[134] and taken into the custody of the Registrar General. They contain registrations for some burghs before any extant kirk session records, and the selection of those burgesses who chose to register is a useful indicator of reformed families. Of the central church records, the Edinburgh Commissary Court gradually established a general jurisdiction throughout the realm, and accordingly local matrimonial causes can be found in their registers of deeds and records of testaments, which give detailed genealogical and social information. The records of the commissary courts, the courts of the reformed church which inherited the jurisdiction of the medieval bishops, are a rich and largely untapped source for burgh history in the last thirty years of the sixteenth century. Commissary court records include decreets, processes and deeds but are most often used for the records of testaments. The testmanets in every case include and inventory of the 'goods, gear, debts and sums of money' of the deceased. There are printed indexes of persons published by the Scottish Record Society.[135]

A substantial number of diet books and act books survive for this period for sheriff courts, and these give names of parties in law suits in the rural surrounds of the burghs. Influential burgesses often had landed as well as town interests, and sheriff court entries will reflect this.[136] The papers of important landed families will also contain valuable material for this period. The larger collections are held either in the Scottish national repositories or by the owners themselves, but some smaller collections are available at local record offices.[137] Two remarkable and unusual private account books survive for this period – one for David Wedderburne for his transactions as a merchant trading in and around Dundee 1587–1603, and one for Andrew Halyburton for his transactions as Conservator of the Privileges of the Scotch Nation in the Netherlands 1492–1503.[138]

Scottish society in the sixteenth century was still sufficiently de-centralised for a full interrelationship to exist at a local and national level. Local records, especially in Edinburgh, contain much of national importance, and conversely central government records contain a wealth of information about local and burghal matters. The halfway house between the burghs and central government lay in the Convention of Royal Burghs and in the estate of the burgesses in parliament. The records of the former have been comprehensively published[139] and the influence of the latter[140] can by the sixteenth century be traced in the legislation of a number of burghs, where parliamentary acts about diverse subjects such as lodging houses, weights and measures, beggars, wappinshaws, the selling of bread in Edinburgh, and Flemish craftsmen were invariably echoed.[141]

An extremely useful state series, beginning in 1545, is the *Register of the Privy Council*, which contains acts, decreets, subsidiary papers and warrants, and as the record of the day-to-day government of the country 'probably constitute the most important single source for the long period they cover'.[142] For the period 1592–9 alone the *Register* covers a riot by Edinburgh High School boys, the forced detention at Wigtown of two inhabitants of Dumfries, the dispute among Perth burgesses about the location of the fishmarket, the complaint by burgesses of St Andrews about the misappropriation of the common good by the magistrates, and the liberation by a Dundee shipmaster of a cargo in a Danzig ship, belonging to the duke of Florence, which was wrecked in Shetland.[143]

The miscellaneous papers of central government in Scotland can be found in the private papers of the various families who were involved at various times in the government. These include the Hamilton Papers, now in the SRO, the Warrender Papers[144] and the Balcarres Papers.[145] The Scottish state paper archives have been widely dispersed and it is necessary to reconstitute some of the series by copying records of the cor-respondents.[146] This can be done by examining the holdings of foreign governments, and especially those of England. As Professor Donaldson noted, 'It is pleasant to record that our southern neighbour, which was responsible for the heaviest losses suffered by the Scottish records, has in this respect served Scotland well'.[147] English state papers relating to Scotland are extensive, although as in Scotland influential families still retain the secretarial papers of their ancestors.[148] It has already been seen how useful the printed selection of the *Calendar of State Papers relating to*

Scotland[149] has been in documenting burgh life in the English strongpoints during the 'rough wooing'.

Other foreign state papers important to understanding trading, religious and family links with the continent are the French,[150] Norwegian,[151] Swedish,[152] Danish,[153] German,[154] Swiss,[155] and the Vatican.[156] Scotland's relationship with the Vatican, however, was quite unique because of its religious association before 1560 and particularly since the church of Glasgow had been declared to be the 'special daughter' of the Roman Church.[157] As a result the registers of the Vatican are disproportionately rich in Scottish material right up to the Scottish Reformation, and the Scottish History Department of Glasgow University, active in retrieving microfilm copies of Scottish entries in the Vatican registers, has just completed extracting material from the archives of the Sacred Penitentiary for 1436–1560, which give information on burgh church pluralities, monastic rent increases and land descriptions, and case descriptions of manslaughter committed by burgh clergy.

The overwhelming volume of material in existence, if not readily available, on the administrative, political, economic and religious history of the burgh in Scotland still makes Anderson's comment on Aberdeen records in 1890 a current one: '. . . the amount of material that still remains for the future burgh historian to explore, is truly astonishing . . .'.[158]

NOTES

1. We are grateful to many of the other contributors to this volume for their general help as well as advice on many specific points. Particular thanks go to David Ditchburn.

2. There are two useful, modern commentaries: B. Webster, *Scotland from the Eleventh Century to 1603* (Cambridge, 1975); G. Donaldson, *The Sources of Scottish History* (Edinburgh, 1978).

3. See *Convention Burgh Recs.*, i, 545, for an early example (Kinghorn).

4. Conveniently available in P. Hume Brown, *Early Travellers in Scotland* (Edinburgh, 1891).

5. See Stevenson Ch. 6, and Shead, Ch. 7, below, which both make heavy use of such evidence.

6. See esp. the pioneering work in foreign archives in Stevenson, 'Thesis'; it and Guy, 'Thesis', which deals with the later period 1460–1599, make systematic use of customs accounts. See Ch. 11, below, for a review of some of Stevenson's conclusions.

7. Stell, Ch. 4, and Spearman, Chs. 3 and 8, below.

8. The use of charter evidence has been described and discussed in various general works on Scottish historical sources, as well as in the introductions to the various volumes of the *Regesta* (Donaldson, *Sources*, 10–14; Webster, *Scotland*, 59–92; *RRS* i, ii, vi).

9. *ESC* and *RRS* i & ii, vi. The *Regesta* will eventually continue until 1424; for the moment, however, there are also useful handlists by J. Scoular, *Alexander II* (1956) and G. G. Simpson, *Alexander III, Guardians & John* (1960).

10. Whose work is catalogued in C. S. Terry, *A Catalogue of the Publications of Scottish Historical Clubs* (Glasgow, 1909), continued by C. Matheson, *A Catalogue of the Publications of Scottish Historical and Kindred Clubs 1908-1927* (Aberdeen, 1928).

11. The list of works is extensive and many appear in the bibliography to this volume. Of special importance are: *Ayr Friars*; 'Edinburgh Blackfriars' in *Edin. Accts.; Abdn. Friars.*, which includes a calendar of the important collection, AUL, Marischal College Charters, MS M.390, Mass. 1-19; *Perth Blackfriars; Glasgow Friars Muniments; Dunf. Reg.; Lind. Cart.; Lind. Lib.; Scone Lib.; Newb. Reg.; Kelso Lib.; Cold. Cart.* Urban parish records with charter material include *St Nich. Cart.; St Mary Lib.* and *St Giles Reg.* Of the urban cathedrals *Abdn. Reg.; Glas. Reg.; Moray Reg.; Brechin Reg.*; and *St And. Lib.* are of note.

12. The SRO inventory of burgh records, held both there and retransmitted elsewhere, is an essential tool. For burgh charters in general see A. Ballard, *British Borough Chrs., 1066-1216* (1913) and A. Ballard and J. Tait, *British Borough Chrs., 1216-1307* (1923). Early Scottish burgh charters appear in the following collections: prior to 1214 *RRS* i & ii; 1214-1286 in *Lanark Recs.; Ayr Burgh Chrs.; Abdn. Chrs.; Glas. Chrs.*; the important Dumbarton charters survive in a seventeenth-century confirmation to be found in *RMS*, vii, no. 190.

13. Among Fraser's numerous works there are of specific interest to urban historians: *Fraser, Douglas, Eglinton, Grandtully, Grant, Melville, Southesk, Sutherland* and *Wemyss*. Many smaller collections of family papers which include charters have been listed by HMC and NRA, while within SRO there are major collections of charters in the Gifts and Deposits series (SRO GD/) as well as among the Register House Charters (SRO RH/); see e.g. Ewan, 'Thesis', 348, for a useful fourteenth-century list.

14. Available in *APS*, i, and *Ancient Burgh Laws*, but neither can be taken as a properly critical text. Cf. the description of them in Barrow, *Kingship*, 97-8, and Duncan, *Scotland*, 481-5.

15. In MacQueen and Windram, Ch. 12, and Lynch, Ch. 15, below. They do, nonetheless, remain useful when corroborated by other evidence; see Ewan, Ch. 13, below.

16. See e.g. Donaldson, *Scottish Historical Documents*, 84-5.

17. Similar care needs to be exercised in dealing with apparently similar burgh constitutions, dating from the late sixteenth century onwards, conveniently printed in *SBRS Misc.* (1881); most resulted from the crown's attempts to impose a uniform solution on troublesome towns. See Lynch, *Early Modern Town*, 13-14.

18. See Introduction, Ch. 1, above for details; also Duncan, *James I*, 10. The 1427 act quickly fell into disuse.

19. Duncan, *Scotland*, 156-7; see *ER*, i, 50. There is a list of burgh fermes in 1327 in *ER*, i, p. lxxxviii, and a useful comparison of fermes and customs income from the burghs in Stevenson, 'Thesis', 228n.

20. The most useful discussion of the contents of *ER* is in the introductions to the volumes themselves; see esp. i, pp. lxxix-cii, and i, pp. cxxxv, 314-22, for English dues.

21. As in *CDS*, iv, nos. 162, 462.

22. Totals of customs returns 1327-1469 are given in Grant, *Scotland*, 236-7, and for 1327-1520 in Stevenson, 'Thesis', 290, both on the basis of five-year averages. The individual returns of the leading burghs are tabulated, on ten-year averages, for the sixteenth century in M. Lynch, 'Continuity and change in urban society, 1500-1700', in R. A. Houston and I. D. Whyte (eds.), *Scottish Society, 1500-1800* (Cambridge, 1988), 98; and

the returns for burghs exporting hides for 1445–99, on five-year averages, in Lynch, 'Towns', table 1; see also Stevenson, Ch. 11, below, tables 1–5.

23. SRO, E71/1/1 (Aberdeen Cocket Bk., 1499–1500); E71/29/2–3 (Leith, 1510–11, 1512–13); they are analysed in Stevenson, 'Thesis', 317–25. For an analysis of Edinburgh exporters of skins and hides, based on E71/30/12, a port book of 1561–3, see Lynch, Ch. 15 below.

24. This is attempted for the four largest towns in Lynch, Ch. 15, below. See also Introduction, Ch. 1. A more complete analysis would be time-consuming but viable.

25. Note should also be taken of the falling exchange rate of the £ Scots; see J. Gilbert, 'The usual money of Scotland and exchange rates against foreign coin', in *Coinage in Medieval Scotland*, ed. D. Metcalf (BAR Reports, xlv, 1977); W. W. Scott, 'Sterling and the usual money of Scotland', *Scottish Economic and Social History*, v (1985), 4–22. A convenient table of the worsening exchange rate of Scots and English currency is given in Grant, *Scotland*, 240.

26. *TA*, i, pp. cviii, cxii; iii, pp. lxxii–lxxvi.

27. James III's interest in trade can be illustrated by the MS letterbook of Anselm Adornes; see n. 42, below.

28. *James IV Letters; James V Letters.*

29. *De Tol van Ierskeroord, 1321–1572*, ed. W. S. Unger (The Hague, 1939); see table of incoming ships in *Bronnen tot de geschiednis van Middelburg in den Landsherrlijken Tijt*, ed. W. S. Unger (The Hague, 1923–31), iii, 818–22.

30. See n. 138, below.

31. Stevenson, 'Thesis', 16–18.

32. J. Davidson and A. Gray, *The Scottish Staple at Veere* (London, 1909); M. P. Rooseboom, *The Scottish Staple in the Netherlands* (The Hague, 1910); J. Yair, *Account of Scotch Trade in the Netherlands* (London, 1776); Rijksarchief, Middelburg still has Accounts of the Water Bailiff; see also *Inventaris van het oud archief der stad Middelburg, 1217–1581*, ed. J. H. Stoppelaar (Middelburg, 1873); *Geschiednis Middelburg*.

33. Gemeentearchief, Veere, Poorterboeken, no. 920.

34. Gemeentearchief, Bergen-op-Zoom, Poorterboeken, no. 955; ibid., Obdrachten, R. 215–16.

35. They are listed in Stevenson, 'Thesis', table viii, pp. 326–9.

36. *Bronnen tot de geschiednis van den handel met Engeland, Schotland en Ierland*, ed. H. J. Smit, 4 vols. (The Hague, 1928–51).

37. G. Espinas, *La draperie dans la Flandre française*, 2 vols. (Paris, 1923), at ii, 50–53.

38. Lille, Archives départmentales du Nord, Chambre de Comptes, sèrie B; further details are given in Stevenson, 'Thesis', 331–2. Brussels, Arch. Gén. du Royaume, Papiers d'état et de l'audience, no. 405.

39. Bruges, Stadsarchief; there is also some material in Bruges, Rijksarchief, Registre du Franc de Bruges.

40. *Inventaire des archives de Bruges*, ed. L. Gilliodts van Severen, 9 vols. (Bruges, 1871–85).

41. They are printed in *Inventaire*; see also W. H. Finlayson, 'The Scottish Nation of Merchants in Bruges' (Glasgow Ph.D., 1951).

42. Bruges, Stadsarchief, Letterbook of Anselm Adornes.

43. References to many of the regional source books appear in Ch. 10, below. Other useful ones are mentioned in T. A. Fischer, *The Scots in Germany* (Edinburgh, 1902) and *The Scots in Eastern and Western Prussia* (Edinburgh, 1903). Fischer, however, seems to have drawn more on material from the more easterly archives rather than that in the

westerly archives such as Bremen and Cologne. For an overall guide see E. Keyser, *Bibliographie zur Städtegeschichte Deutschlands* (Köln-Wien, 1969).

44. R. Sprandel (ed.), *Quellen zur Hanse-Geschichte* (Darmstadt, 1982), 519–24, gives a brief survey of the holdings of Hanseatic archives in East and West Germany. For the Teutonic Order's correspondence (OBA), see E. Joachim and W. Hubatsch (eds.), *Regesta Historico Diplomatica Ordinis S. Mariae Theutonicorum 1198–1525* (3 parts, Göttingen, 1948–73), though since this was published the archive references have been changed. There is no printed guide to the Order's folio volumes (OF). For Gdańsk, the sixteenth-century holdings were recorded in *Inventare Hansischer Archive* (3 vols., Leipzig, 1896–1913). There is no easily accessible guide to Polish archives before this, other than in Polish, for which see *Archiwum Miasta Gdańska* (Warsaw, 1970).

45. The proceedings of Hanseatic diets are recorded in the four series of the *Hanse Recesse* to 1537. For the regional affairs of the Prussian towns, important for the activities of small-time Scottish traders, see M. Toeppen (ed.), *Acten der Ständetage Preussens unter der Herrschaft des Deutschen Ordens* (5 vols., Leipzig, 1878–86), and M. Biskup *et al, Akta Stanów Prus Królewskich* (6 vols., Toruń, 1955–75).

46. The printed edition of the tolls (N. Bang (ed.), *Tabeller over skibsfart og varetransport gennem Øresund 1497–1660*, 2 vols., Copenhagen, 1906–33) does not include the names of merchants who are recorded in the originals. These are preserved in the Rigsarkivet, Copenhagen. For a survey of other Danish archival material relating to Scotland, see *The 45th Annual Report of the Deputy Keeper of the Public Records* (London, 1885), app. ii, no. 1, 1–56; *The 46th Annual Report* .... (London, 1886), app. ii, no. 1, 1–75; *The 47th Annual Report* .... (London, 1887), app. no. 5, 9–77; T. Jexlev, 'Scottish history in the light of records in the Danish National Archives', *SHR* xlviii (1969), 98–106. TKUA Skotland are available on microfilm in Scottish History Dept., Glasgow University, and in Orkney Library, Kirkwall. Dr. T. Riis used Scottish east coast burgh sources extensively, both for *Should Auld Acquaintance be Forgot: Scottish-Danish Connections, 1406–1707* (forthcoming, Edinburgh and Odense), and his 'Scottish-Danish relations in the sixteenth century', in T. C. Smout (ed.), *Scotland and Europe, 1200–1850* (Edinburgh, 1986), 82–96.

47. D. Macpherson *et al* (eds.), *Rotuli Scotiae* (2 vols., London, 1814–19); J. Bain (ed.), *CDS* (5 vols., 1881–1986); *Calendar of Close Rolls* (London, 1900–); *Calendar of Patent Rolls* (London, 1901–); *Foedera* ... (Record Comm. ed., London, 1816–69; original ed., London, 1704–35; also The Hague, 1739–45); Henry IV's correspondence has been collected in F. C. Hingeston (ed.), *Royal and Historical Letters during the reign of Henry IV* (2 vols., London, 1860–1965). See also J. Gairdiner (ed.), *Letters and Papers of the Reigns of Richard III and Henry VII* (2 vols., London, 1861–3). There are many other printed collections of state and other papers also useful, especially those cited by J. Dilley, 'German merchants in Scotland, 1297–1327', *SHR* xxvii (1948), 142–55. Stevenson, *Documents*, *James IV Letters* and *James V Letters* include material from English as well as continental archives. Many foreign source books also include English material: see e.g. H. Smit, *Bronnen; HUB*; and K. Kunze (ed.), *Hanseakten aus England, 1275 bis 1412* (Halle, 1891). Most of the original documents included in the above works and others are in the PRO, but some are to be found elsewhere. BL, Cotton MSS e.g. include references to Scottish trade with Bremen and Danzig in the early fifteenth century, while a collection of Scottish ambassadors' reports relating to marriage treaties in Harleian MSS, 4367, iii, contains also material on international trade. BL, Add. MSS. 33245, Registrum de Aberbrothock, has assorted material on Perth.

48. PRO, E122/(various classifications). PRO, Ancient Correspondence, SC1/(various classifications), also contains much material relating to English and Scots trade, especially in Flanders.

49. C. Fraser (ed.), *Northern Petitions* (Surtees Soc., 1981); PRO, E122/3/ ..., E122/193/ ..., E122/219; Berwick, Borough Council Archive, B1/1; B2/1.

50. SRO, 'The Ayr Manuscript', PA5/2, fos. 8v–10, 85v, which has been published in *Archaeological and Historical Collections relating to the Counties of Ayr and Wigton*, i (1878), 223–30; *Dunfermline Gild Court Book*, ed. E. P. D. Torrie (SRS, 1986).

51. ACA, CR, v(2).

52. *Edin. Recs.*, i, 1–2.

53. Perth Archive 1/1; an edited version by Marion Stavert will shortly be published by SRS.

54. CRA, PD61/1.

55. *Abdn. Recs*, 3–17.

56. ACA, Press 18/64, extract printed in Archivists's Report to Council, 29 June 1981. An earlier draft is printed in Louise B. Taylor (ed.), *Aberdeen Council Letters*, i (Oxford, 1941), 47–50.

57. ACA, CR, i (1398–1407), partly transcribed in *Abdn. Recs.*

58. ECA, MS Council Register, compiled c. 1580; NLS, Adv. MS 31.4.9.

59. DA, 'Book of the Church', c. 1480–1524, Burgh Court Book, ii.

60. Ayr, Carnegie Library, B6/12/1 (1428–78).

61. SRO, B51/10/1 (1455–67).

62. SRO, B58/8/1 (1456–84); extracts in *Peebles Chrs.* (SBRS, 1872).

63. SRO, B20/10/1 (1488–1584).

64. St Andrews Univ. Lib., B54/7/1 (1459–79).

65. Ayr, Carnegie Library; condition fragmentary.

66. ACA, CR, i–vii. Only very limited extracts are printed in *Abdn. Counc.*, i.

67. ACA, Guildry Accounts, i, includes one from 1452–3; an account for 1470–71 has recently been located by Dr R. J. Lyall in Yale Univ. Lib., Gordon of Gordonstoun MSS.

68. ACA, 1851 Inventory L, Parcel F.

69. ACA, SR i.

70. SRO, B58/1/1.

71. ECA, Guild Register, i (1487–1579).

72. SRO, B22/22/1–12; calendared in G. Donaldson (ed.), *Protocol Book of James Young, 1485–1515* (SRS, 1952).

73. SRO, B30/9/1.

74. Lynch, *Early Modern Town*, 1–4.

75. A good practical modern commentary is available in Donaldson, *Sources*, 9–24; M. Livingstone, *Guide to the Public Records of Scotland* (1905) [replacement guide is in preparation and typescript draft of vol. i can be consulted at the Historical Search Room]; copies of *Short Guide to the Records* (SRO, Leaflet No. 7) are available from the SRO; J. A. Inglis, 'Financial and administrative records, 1264–1724', in *Sources of Scots Law*; W. K. Dickson, 'Privy council records, 1545–1707', *ibid.*; *British National Archives* (HMSO Sectional List no. 24) lists volumes out of print as well as those available for purchase.

76. Coverage by Terry and Matheson (see n. 10, above) varies from the startlingly sparse for Dundee (one compendium volume of charters, documents and minutes, one volume of burgess roll extracts and one volume of shipping lists), to the virtually complete for Glasgow (extracts from council books, accounts, charters, documents and protocol books).

77. The only printed edition of the Dundee Guildry minutes is to be found in A. J. Warden, *Burgh Laws* (Dundee, 1872). Sederunt lists are not included, and the text slips from transcript to summary without clear definition. Both the *Ayr Burgh Accounts 1534–1624*, ed. G. S. Pryde (SHS, 1937) and the *Kirkintilloch Court Book* offer wide comparative

studies about the type of record considered, while M. Wood and R. K. Hannay in *Records of the Burgh of Edinburgh 1589–1603* (Edinburgh, 1927) not only clearly stated their view that publication should strive to avoid arbitrary selection (p. ix), but pointed out the drawbacks of the particular Edinburgh series in that the Council Register extracts already in print contained arbitrary omissions, while the Accounts had been covered 'with a perhaps lavish completeness' (p. vii).

78. Collecting record offices are listed in *HMC Record Repositories in Great Britain* (HMSO, 1982). Individual collection notes are useful on record offices and libraries in J. Foster and J. Sheppard, *British Archives* (London, 1982), although the geographical index is misleading – the Leighton Library at Dunblane has been placed under Lothian Region and the former County of Angus has been indexed on its own without references to its location within Tayside Region. The SRA has published Datasheet No. 5, giving basic contact information about archival repositories, and No. 6, containing summaries of holdings of official and private records. Although the SRO has retransmitted many burgh records to local repositories, many burgh (class B) charters, documents, and court and council records relating mainly to the Borders and to the North East are still located in Register House, which maintains an internal office catalogue of the present known location of all burgh records.

79. The concession of shore dues by James VI to the burgh of Dundee in 1580 (MS Dundee Town Charter Chest 1, no. 71) led to the creation of the Dundee Shipping Lists in that year (see 'Shipping Lists of Dundee' in *Compt Bk.*), as did his similar grant to the burgh of Aberdeen in 1596 (*Aberdeen Shore Work Accounts 1596–1670*, ed. L. B. Taylor (Aberdeen, 1972), 3).

80. A fragment of a Dundee head court minute of 1461 survives in a composite collection of an inventory of 1454 and burgh court minutes of 1520s in 'The Book of the Church'. The inventory appears to have been in the possession of a Spanish Jesuit in the 1570s and this raises questions about the itinerary of the other portions (see Maxwell, *Old Dundee*, 556); the Montrose Head Court Book 1458–1476 was returned to the town clerk this century after appearing in a private English collection; it was the interest of an antiquarian in 1579 in Edinburgh that preserved material from the court books from 1442 through transcription. See *Edin. Recs.*, i (1403–1528), p. xxxii; NLS, Adv. MS. 31.4.9.

81. The confirmation charter by Robert I to the burgh of Dundee in 1327, together with the preceding commission to the abbot of Arbroath and his subsequent return, form the only known surviving process of confirmation known to survive in Scotland (DA, MS Dundee Town Charter Chest 1, nos. 14, 14A, 16). Only one compilation volume of court minutes survived the destruction of the English occupation of 1547/8. Similarly, Edinburgh's earliest surviving charter of 1329 and associated documents contrast with the main source of burgh court books extant from 1507 (see Pryde, *Burghs*, 4, and *Sources of Scots Law*, 106). However, charters were small, light and portable in crises.

82. Accounts of the Lord High Treasurer from 1473, Acts of the Lords of Council and Session from 1532, Register of the Privy Council from 1545, and the Register of the Privy Seal from 1497 (see Webster, *Scotland*, 204ff.).

83. For an explanation of the haste by Aberdeen, Edinburgh and Dundee to consolidate their registers, cartularies and writings after 1575, see Lynch, *Early Modern Town*, 67–8.

84. Aberdeen Report (see n. 56, above); *Edin. Recs.*, 1589–1603, p. viii.

85. SRA Datasheet No. 6.

86. DA, MS Dundee Burgh Laws drawn furth of the Acts of this Burgh 1550–1646.

87. *Brevis et Compendiosa Collectio veterum et maxime utilium statutorum ex antiquis libris curiae Edinburgh*, c. 1579, *Edin. Recs.*, i, p. xxxii.

88. *Sources of Scots Law*, 100.

89. Lynch, *Early Modern Town*, 2.

90. Lynch, *Edinburgh*, 29, 277.

91. Edinburgh in 1518 (Mackenzie, *Scottish Burghs*, 105); Dundee in 1515 (MS Dundee Town Charter Chest 2, no. 265).

92. *Sources of Scots Law*, 104ff.

93. Warden, *Burgh Laws*, 106ff. After dissatisfaction with the harbour bill promoted by Dundee Town Council in 1813, the Guildry commenced proceedings which culminated in their withdrawing their records from Dundee Town Council in 1817. They have now placed their records on loan with the Dundee District Archive Centre.

94. Attestations of parentage for merchants travelling abroad; for examples, see Fischer, *Scots in Germany*.

95. Fascinating glimpses of Dundee during the occupation of 1547-8 are available through *CSP Scot.*, i, 21ff, and *The Scottish Correspondence of Mary of Lorraine* (SHS, 1927), 274ff.

96. The case of debt acknowledged by Walter Bull to his mother in Kirkintilloch in 1664 is typical of such actions in burgh courts over the previous two hundred years (see *Kirkintilloch Court Book*, 7ff.). An unusual case of contract can be found in Dundee during the French occupation: 'Mareschall de la Foye, Frensche man hes tane to preif upon Fryday nixt to cum, that George Blak, wricht, condicionit to mak the liddis to his pres . . .' (MS Dundee Burgh Court book, 12 Dec. 1554).

97. An everyday story of 'trublance' can be seen in Paisley in 1596, when one spouse hit another spouse on the head with a stone 'to the effusion of her bluid in greit quantatie . . .', followed by the complainer's son rearranging the market booth of the accused, whereby both sides were bound over for £40 for good behaviour (*Paisley Burgh Chrs.*, 170). Penalties varied from payment by expensive altar candle wax before the Reformation to public penance or reconciliation after it.

98. The dean of guild was an obvious target for disaffection; in Stirling in 1597 Thomas Forester was fined £20 for calling the dean of guild 'ane nastie dessaver' (*Extracts from the Records of the Merchant Guild of Stirling 1592-1846*, edd. W. B. Cook & D. B. Morris (Glasgow, 1916), 10). Cases of 'mispersoning' (defaming) or 'sclandering' bailies are a good indicator of popular unrest, both during the Reformation period and in the recurrent disputes between merchants and craftsmen which characterised the sixteenth century; see Lynch, Ch. 15, below.

99. *Abdn. Recs.*, p. xliv n.; P. Hume Brown, *Scotland in the Time of Queen Mary* (London, 1904), 160.

100. During the dearth of 1596 Dundee Town Council banned the baking of oaten bread after the 'puir inhabitantis received grite skayth and hurt' by this practice (DA, MS Dundee Town Council minutes, 30 Nov. 1596). For an examination of fixing of ale and bread prices, see Maxwell, *Old Dundee*, 93-9.

101. S. G. E. Lythe & J. Butt, *An Economic History of Scotland 1100-1939* (Glasgow, 1975), 37.

102. The licence for Dundee to use the former Greyfriars orchard as a burying ground in 1564 states that through the over-use of St Clements 'pest and uther contagius seikness is ingenerit' (DA, MS Dundee Town Charter Chest 1, no. 60).

103. T. C. Smout, 'Coping with plague in sixteenth- and seventeenth-century Scotland', *Scotia*, ii (1978), 19-33.

104. Many trades looked after their own poor and sick (see Lythe and Butt, *Economic History*, 36ff.). Although burghs had made provision for the casual poor, the influence of

The First Book of Discipline was to be seen in increased acts on behalf of the deserving poor (see *The First Book of Discipline*, ed. J. K. Cameron (Edin., 1972) and *The Second Book of Discipline*, ed. J. Kirk (Edin., 1980)).

105. For an examination of political conflict caused by attempts to influence education in Dundee, see Flett, 'Thesis', 148ff.

106. For Dundee see Flett, 'Thesis'.

107. See Lynch, Ch. 15, below.

108. Mackenzie, *Scottish Burghs*, 107–08.

109. *Dundee Chrs.*, 18.

110. *Edin. Chrs.*, 210.

111. Lythe and Butt, *Economic History*, 31.

112. Lynch, *Early Modern Town*, 19–23.

113. See *Roll of Edinburgh Burgesses and Guild-Brethren 1406–1700*, ed. C. B. B. Watson (SRS, 1929).

114. The 'Lockit Buik' of Dundee, containing the freedom roll of Dundee, was commenced partly as the register of 'Brether of Guild' (see *Roll of Eminent Burgesses of Dundee 1513–1886*, ed. A. H. Millar (Dundee, 1887)). The separate proceedings of the Guildry commence in 1570.

115. For Ayr see *Ayr Burgh Accts.*, p. lxxxviii, and for Edinburgh, *Edinburgh Records: The Burgh Accounts*, ed. R. Adam (Edinburgh, 1899), vol. ii.

116. In Dundee the MS 'Book of the Church' is presumed to have been compiled by the kirkmaster for reference (Maxwell, *Old Dundee*, 556).

117. Although committals for death by burning tend to have brief mention in minutes, the accounts dwell on the details of execution in painstaking detail (see *Ayr Burgh Accts.*, 156; *Edin. Accts.*, i, p. xxi); and DA, MS Dundee Burgh Treasurer's Accounts 1590, included disbursements on four fathoms of rope, one oak beam, a creel of coals, two tar barrels, an iron chain, and ten shillings to the 'Wiche hanger'.

118. In the litigation of 1850–60 between Dundee Town Council and Dundee Presbytery about stipend payments, attempts were made to disentangle the historical accounts, and a useful product of this litigation is the printed edition by Cosmo Innes of relevant documents (Town Charter Chest 14, no. 32).

119. For a general survey see *Ayr Burgh Accts.*, pp. lxii ff.; the income for altar lights and chaplainry duties is still described as such in the Glasgow accounts by 1573 (*Extracts from the Records of the Burgh of Glasgow, 1573–1642*, (SBRS, 1876), 447); the Dundee burgess roll was also used in 1582 to record pre-Reformation rental lists payable to the treasurer, kirkmaster, and hospitalmaster respectively (MS Dundee Burgh Lockit Buik).

120. Mr John Preston, burgess of Edinburgh and collector for funds to send an ambassador to Denmark, noted in his accounts the contributions of Dundee, Edinburgh, Aberdeen and Perth (*Edin. Accts.*, i, 41).

121. See *Dundee Chrs., Edin. Chrs., Glasgow Chrs.* For forms see *Formulary of Old Scots Legal Documents*, ed. P. Gouldesbrough (Stair Society, 1985).

122. See MS Dundee Burgh Cartularies, 2 vols., c. 1820; Mollisone's catalogue of Aberdeen registers, 1591, printed in *Report to Aberdeen District Council* 29 June 1981; and *Extracts from the Records of the Royal Burgh of Stirling*, ed. R. Renwick (Glasgow, 1887), 60.

123. See above, n. 79.

124. See Pryde, *Burghs*, 54ff.

125. See Lynch, *Edinburgh*, 373–92, and Ch. 15, below.

126. See above, n. 79.

127. These can range from an udal law decree of the Lawting at Kirkwall in 1514

(*Facsimiles of the National Manuscripts of Scotland* (London, 1867–71), iii, no. xi) to printed secular fragments in Dundee surviving from the first Scottish printing press (R. Donaldson, 'An early printed fragment of the "Buke of the Howlat" – addendum', *Edinburgh Bibliog. Trans.* (1983), 27–8; and MS Dundee Protocol Book 1526–28).

128. *APS*, iii, 44.

129. *APS*, iii, 448; iv, 549.

130. *Sources of Scots Law*, 289; Durkan, 'The early Scottish notary', 22–40.

131. *Sources of Scots Law*, 290.

132. Only a few incorporations predated 1500, but some papers of the Edinburgh skinners going back to 1474 are in Merchant Maiden Hospital, Edinburgh.

133. See *First Book of Discipline*, 16, 55: cf. B. Moeller, *Imperial Cities and the Reformation* (Philadelphia, 1972), 92.

134. 17 & 18 Victoria, c. 80. Kirk session records for the sixteenth century have been collected under the superintendence of the Keeper of the Records of Scotland, although some have been placed in local record offices under supervision agreements. Covering dates for baptismal and marriage registers are given in *Detailed List of the Old Parochial Registers of Scotland* (Edinburgh, 1872). Those for Aberdeen date from 1562, and for Dunfermline from 1561.

135. See M. H. B. Sanderson, 'The Edinburgh merchants in society, 1570–1603', 183–99; Donaldson, *Sources*, 28–9.

136. Sheriff Court records have now been transferred to the Keeper of the Records of Scotland, but the early survivals are noted in C. A. Malcolm, 'Sheriff and other local court records', *Sources of Scots Law*, 111–32; for town and country links see Lynch, *Early Modern Town*, 12, 23–6, and Booton, Ch. 9, and Ewan, Ch. 13, below.

137. For major collections see Donaldson, *Sources*, 32; SRO *Lists of Gifts and Deposits* (HMSO, 1971–6); NLS *Summary Catalogue of the Advocates' Manuscripts* (HMSO, 1971) and NLS *Catalogues of Manuscripts, Charters and other Formal Documents acquired since 1925* (HMSO, 1966): for title and date descriptions of large and small collections see SRA Datasheet no. 6 and central lists maintained in SRO.

138. See *The Compt Buik of David Wedderburn, 1587–1630*, ed. A. H. Millar (SHS, 1898); *Halyburton's Ledger* is a fund of information on the activities of a wool and fell merchant following the yearly cycle of fairs in Flanders and Brabant, 1493–1504; it is analysed in detail in Stevenson, 'Thesis', 298–316. Only the fragment of an earlier similar book, of c. 1400, survives; see A. Hanham, 'A medieval Scots merchant's handbook', *SHR*, 1 (1971), 107–20.

139. *Burghs Conv. Recs.*; (MS in ECA).

140. See J. D. Mackie and G. S. Pryde, *The Estate of the Burgesses in the Scots Parliament* (St Andrews Univ. Publication, xvii, 1923); Donaldson, *Sources*, 15ff.

141. See e.g. *Ancient Burgh Laws*.

142. Donaldson, *Sources*, 16.

143. *RPC*, v, 238, 505, 513, 61, 214, 251; the text includes complete inventories of *The Great Jonas of Danzig*.

144. See *The Warrender Papers*, ed. A. I. Cameron (SHS, 1931–2).

145. See *Foreign Correspondence with Marie de Lorraine Queen of Scotland, from the Originals in the Balcarres Papers* (SHS, 1923–5).

146. Donaldson, *Sources*, 19.

147. *Ibid.*, 19.

148. *Ibid.*, 19.

149. See above, n.95; M. H. Merriman, 'The "Rough Wooing" of 1544–50', *Historical Atlas*, 83, 194–5.

150. Donaldson, *Sources*, 19.

151. *Ibid.*, 19.

152. J. Dow, 'A comparative note on the Sound Toll Registers, Stockholm Customs Accounts, and Dundee Shipping Lists, 1589, 1613–1622', *Scandinavian Economic History Review* (1964), 79–85; and 'Scottish trade with Sweden 1512–1622', *SHR* xlviii (1969), 64–79, 124–50.

153. Donaldson, *Sources*, 19; T. L. Christensen, 'Scoto-Danish relations in the sixteenth century'; see also n.46, above.

154. Robert Howie, born the son of an Aberdeen merchant burgess, served in the burgh churches at Aberdeen and Dundee. His foreign correspondence can be found in Basel and Frankfurt (see *Letters of John Johnston and Robert Howie*, ed. J. K. Cameron (St Andrews University Publications, liv, 1963), 265).

155. *Ibid.*

156. See Donaldson, *Sources*, 27; A. I. Cameron, 'Vatican Archives, 1073–1560', *Sources of Scots Law*, 274–81; I. B. Cowan, 'The Vatican Archives: a report on pre-Reformation Scottish material', *SHR* xlviii (1969), 227–42.

157. *Nat. MSS. Scot.*, i, no. xlvii.

158. Abdn. Chrs., p. vii.

3

The Medieval Townscape of Perth

R. M. Spearman

It is some twenty-five years since Conzen published his seminal work on town-plan analysis based on Alnwick, Northumberland.[1] His study established the guiding principles and terminology of historic town-plan analysis that have been followed, to a greater or lesser extent, in subsequent studies throughout Britain. In Scotland there are regrettably few detailed studies of historic town-plans, but work has been undertaken on Ayr, Perth, St Andrews, Stirling, and Glasgow.[2] There has in addition been some limited general synthesis of Scottish town-plans and there is a substantial series of reports by the Burgh Survey dealing with basic topography, history and archaeology.[3] The resulting corpus of work gives varied impressions of what can be said of any medieval component in Scottish townscapes. Yet the structure and layout of those Scottish towns that can boast a medieval origin is very much a product of their ancient roots. It is therefore the purpose of this chapter to examine in greater detail the medieval aspects of townscapes and specifically to consider the value of detailed cartographic study for urban historians and archaeologists.

In Conzen's study of Alnwick the medieval townscape is seen in geographical rather than historical or archaeological terms. The medieval component in that town-plan is dealt with within the first two sections or 'morphological periods'. The first deals with the Anglian nucleus (c. seventh century to c. 1070) while the second deals with the Norman to Georgian town (c. 1070 to c. 1750). These two medieval sections are substantial and rich in methodology, but they lack detailed subdivision. This contrasts with the following three sections, including four sub-sections, which are devoted to the remaining two hundred years of Alnwick's development. The difficulty of subdividing some 700 years of Alnwick's development underlines a basic problem for historians and archaeologists examining any medieval townscape. The distinctive pattern of long narrow burgage plots fronting, at approximately right angles, onto their street is readily recognisable and has, as Conzen demonstrates, considerable geographical importance. But for the historian and archaeologist there is a need for careful sub-phasing of such a protracted and popular pattern of land use.

The cartographic methodology of any such study is essentially that devised by Conzen, although it is important to note the point at which subjective decisions replace objective measurement. The topography of streets, properties and buildings is used to distinguish progressively smaller divisions of land. The largest of these are the 'street-blocks', areas of land defined by the street lines, which are in turn divided into 'plots' of land, generally separate properties, and finally into individual building 'block-plans'. Thus far the process should be objective, although in practice it is often difficult to define exactly individual properties and buildings from early plans. The patterns formed by these various divisions of land are at the general level defined as major 'morphological periods', each of which may include several smaller 'plan-units'. The recognition of both types of topographic pattern is essentially subjective, although in the case of any morphological period the differences should be so gross as to be indisputable. The recognition of plan-units can, however, be extremely subjective, and what constitutes a significant change in layout for one researcher may be either too general or too elaborate for another. Conzen's own preference would seem to be for well-defined large plan-units. Nevertheless, it is in the correct identification of smaller plan-units within the medieval and post-medieval morphological period of burgage plot settlement that hopes for any detailed analysis of the medieval townscape must lie.

The medieval burgh of Perth provides an extremely useful case study of both the advantages and disadvantages of such detailed analysis. The medieval town has been the subject of some of the most detailed and extensive urban excavations in Scotland.[4] Its medieval topography is reasonably well documented and there are good seventeenth-century rentals for the town.[5] Cartographic sources begin in the early eighteenth century and are of a high standard from 1765.[6] The first 1:500 Ordnance Survey plan of Perth was published in 1863 and this has been used to check measurements and, wherever possible, for place and street names used in this chapter. By a combination of these sources it is relatively easy to define the extent of Perth's morphological period of burgage plot settlement.

Essentially the main late medieval and post-medieval street system is that of Buist's 'Plan of the Town of Perth' drawn in 1765 at a scale of 1:2400 and Rutherford's 'Town Plan of Perth' published in 1774, scale 1:63360. However, eighteenth-century additions to the earlier street system mean that it is necessary to remove Princes Street from Buist's plan and also George Street and Smeaton's Tay Bridge from Rutherford's 'Town Plan'. As Buist illustrates, the site of the various medieval bridges and fords across the Tay had been at the east end of High Street. It is immediately apparent that the developed medieval street system of Perth consisted of two main streets aligned east-west, with subsidiary north-south gates and vennels. Such parallel-street systems have a marked concentration around the Firths of Forth and Tay, many of which are early (pre-1250) royal foundations.[7]

Some of the smaller closes and rows which connect with the larger streets, gates and vennels are also marked by Buist and Rutherford, although few are named. These are rarely recorded in the documentary sources and it may be that many were private closes which, even when used as public rights of way, may have had quite mixed histories and no permanent names. The main cartographic problem with these closes is therefore not in the recognition of street-blocks but in the identification of their common ownership between plots and the subsequent definition of plot widths. Moreover, these smaller closes occasionally pose strictly interpretative problems as, for instance, when they are situated at the boundaries of plan-units or conversely when they appear to have interrupted the regular layout of plots. Each case has to be treated on its merits but it is clear that these smaller closes hold part of the solution to any more detailed analysis of medieval townscapes.

The other ingredient in such a solution is the careful evaluation of complete burgage plots. Burgage plots are not only the most striking feature of the medieval morphological period; they are the basic topographic unit of both burgh documentation and, along with building plans, excavation. They represent a crucial spatial link between excavation on the ground and any documentary evidence for individual burgesses and their land. Fortunately, the continuity of plot boundaries is now well attested from excavations in Perth and many other medieval towns. There are examples of plot boundaries being replaced and repaired on the same alignment for centuries and also of regular plot amalgamations and subdivisions. There is, then, a causal relationship between earlier medieval plot boundaries and those surveyed in the eighteenth and even twentieth centuries. However, after hundreds of years of boundary replacement, and on occasions deliberate alteration, the correspondence is unlikely to be simple or absolute. Any successful analysis must therefore take into account changes in layout which may have occurred between the original establishment of the plots and the eighteenth-century plan of their successors.

The location of numerous eighteenth-century plots and building blocks is apparent from Rutherford's plan. Moreover, the detail and accuracy of Rutherford's work is confirmed by comparison with the 1:500 scale Ordnance Survey plan of 1863. Individual plots are not recorded on

Buist's plan, although he does identify many of Perth's principal buildings, thereby providing useful townscape information. It is possible, then, to measure the length and width of most of the eighteenth-century plots surveyed by Rutherford from the larger-scale Ordnance Survey plan. Individual problems occur where new roads and major building changes have taken place, and in these cases Rutherford's plan has been used with cross-checks to fixed points on the Ordnance Survey plan. A further problem has been the frequent division of plots into building blocks, gardens and yards, many of which cut across the backlands of several plots. This is a characteristic feature of burgh townscapes with cross-plot divisions being documented in Perth from at least the sixteenth century. Fortunately, an equally firm characteristic of such townscapes is that the principal building of any plot is located at the street frontage. It is then extremely rare that both frontage buildings and backlands were so amalgamated as to destroy all trace of plot divisions. Wherever possible, plot-width measurements have been taken at street frontages, although these retain an inevitable error of measurement which when scaled up gives a probable accuracy of plus or minus 1 ft (350 mm).

A major problem with plot widths is how to determine their history of amalgamation and subdivision. Conzen's approach was to distinguish the most frequently occurring, or modal, widths of plots in each street-block. He then went on to note any fractions or multiples of modal widths using 0.5, 0.75, 1.25, 1.5, 1.75, or 2 × the modal width. Such fractions or multiples were taken to indicate the subdivision or amalgamation of plots. However, these measurements will only relate to changes in plots of modal width. In order to highlight any subdivision or amalgamation of non-standard plots an additional, but less satisfactory, approach is suggested: that all plots which are more than twice the average width of plots in their plan-unit are divided into two or more plots as appropriate. Generally, it is not possible to define the exact positions of plots lost through amalgamation. The only occasions where this can be convincingly done is when contiguous plots with fractional and multiple modal widths can be paired to reproduce dismembered plots. For instance, two adjacent plots, each 1.5 × the modal width, would imply the original existence of three plots of modal width. In most other cases the interpretation of the original layout of plots is more tenuous although certain changes can often be explained by, for instance, the insertion or enlargement of a close.

The various plot measurements also have a direct influence on the definition of plan-units in this analysis. An addition to Conzen's recognition of modal plot widths within street-blocks is to check whether or not these widths have any geographical distributions within their street-block. Where this can be demonstrated to coincide with other topographic features such as changes in plot lengths or the existence of a right of way, street-blocks have been divided into plan-units. In the absence of such topographic detail, intact street-blocks define the plan-unit. A total of twenty plan-units have been identified in this way from Rutherford's plan, including the Castlegable/Curfew Row and New Row/Mill Wynd suburbs but excluding the buildings at Bridge End on the north-east side of the River Tay (see Map G).

Having helped to define the plan-units, plot widths and lengths can be used to provide additional information about patterns of settlement within the burgh. The chronological relationship between plan-units is essentially one of horizontal stratigraphy: it is generally possible to identify the process of urban growth by examining the lengths of plots from different plan-units at street junctions and other boundaries where there is a restricted amount of land available. Plan-units with the longest plots are invariably the earliest, having restricted the room available for later plan-units. Using these techniques it is possible to examine in detail the morphology of medieval town-plans, including that of Perth.

The earliest settlement

The site of the first occupation at Perth is generally accepted to have been in what is now Watergate and this is confirmed by plan analysis.[8] Plan-unit

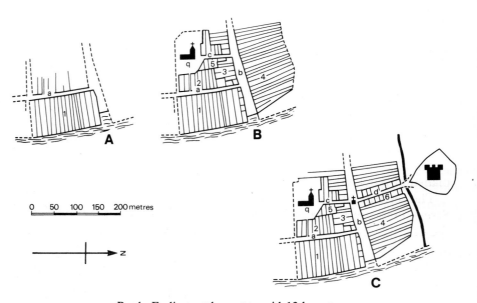

Perth: Earliest settlement to mid-12th century

1 lies on the east side of Watergate running back to the Tay between High Street and Glen Close. (For key to Maps A–G, see p. 58.) The northern plots of plan-unit 1 face onto the river and Watergate but at some later date they were broken up to provide additional very short High Street plots, indicating that Watergate does indeed pre-date High Street. The development of Perth at the lowest fording point on the Tay and the subsequent dominance of High Street underlines the importance of land transport, but it was river trade which attracted the first permanent settlement along the banks of the Tay. This early settlement may well have been established on an area of dry ground sited between the North and South Inches of Perth. The only archaeological work to have been carried out in this area to date was during a building-site inspection where natural sands and gravels were noted only some 1.5 m below present ground level, that is, about 2 m above the modern water table.

Watergate is undocumented until the thirteenth century. It is clear, though, that Perth was a thriving port and agricultural centre by at least the first quarter of the twelfth century – from when the earliest references to Perth survive. Alexander I wrote to all English merchants c. 1124 promising a safe passage to Scone, and from at least David I's time there was an organised cain from shipping at Perth.[9] The east side of Watergate would have played an essential part in this maritime trade with the shores of the Tay being used to beach vessels and for early wharfage.

Initial growth and the church

There is no indication of any street or vennel continuing the line of Watergate northwards. Either the ground there was impassable, perhaps marsh, or early settlement along the north side of High Street (plan-unit 4) foreclosed any possible expansion of Watergate north. There is no indication of how far westwards this early High Street settlement extended. Plots within plan-units 4 and 8 have the same modal width and Skinnergate, which for convenience is taken as the point of division between plan-units 4 and 8, is almost certainly a later intrusion (see plan-unit 6 below).

The settlement of land to the west of Watergate's junction with High Street, plan-units 2, 3 and 5, contrasts markedly with that of plan-unit 1 to the east. There would seem to be a more or less equal division of land between plots along the west side of Watergate, plan-unit 2, and the south side of High Street, plan-unit 3. Although for convenience Kirkgate is taken to mark a division between plan-units 3 and 7, settlement along the south side of High Street would seem to be a continuous process of occupation. Plots along both sides of Kirkgate, plan-unit 5, share the area equally not only with those in plan-units 2 and 3 but also 7 to the west. Moreover, this equal division of land between the various plan-units makes it likely that both kirk and Kirkgate were also an original feature of settlement in the area.

The first documentary evidence of this area is for c. 1128 when the income and rights of the already established parish church were confirmed to Dunfermline Abbey.[10] The earliest surviving documents provide only a *terminus ante quem* for this period of settlement. The precinct of the church is defined to the west and east by High Street and Watergate plots respectively. The southern boundary is marked by the line of Baxter's Vennel, which, along with Oliphants Vennel, provided access from the church to Watergate. It was, however, Kirkgate which provided the main approach to the church. The two southernmost plots on the west side of Kirkgate are unusually long and may well be later encroachments upon the church precinct. If so, then the precinct's northern boundary may be to the rear of the High Street plots.

Defended market

The establishment of a castle at Perth has major economic and social implications. The site of the castle has been convincingly identified as the sub-circular area of land north-east of Castlegable to the north end of Skinnergate.[11] Its relationship to the rest of the town-plan is therefore determined by Skinnergate, plan-unit 6, rather than its own precinct. Although Skinnergate meets Kirkgate across High Street, it does not in fact align with it. Moreover, the pattern of settlement along Skinnergate is quite different from that along Kirkgate. Instead of merging with the High Street plots on an equal basis, as in the case of those on either side of Kirkgate, Skinnergate plots are extremely short, giving the appearance of having been carved out of the pre-existing High Street plots of plan-units 4 and 8. The plots are in many cases little more than booths, making their cartographic identification extremely difficult.

Skinnergate and by implication the castle seem therefore to be later than settlement in plan-units 4 and 8. The first surviving documentary references to the castle and Skinnergate provide a *terminus ante quem* for this plan-unit of c. 1160.[12] Skinnergate may be seen, then, as an intrusive right of way connecting the castle to an existing town and church. In so doing, a market cross-road was added to the town which dominated its subsequent economic development. The construction of the castle on the north side of the town may also have involved the coursing of a stank along that side of the town. Such a stank might not have been purely defensive for it would have helped in the drainage of this low-lying area and may even have been used to power the royal mills at Perth.[13]

Gradual expansion and definition

These two plan-units would seem to be part of a gradual expansion of the town along High Street which is hardly distinct from that represented by plan-units 3 and 4. For statistical convenience this sequence of settlement has been divided at Skinnergate on the north and Kirkgate on the south. The significance of both these gates has been described in detail above. On the south side of High Street plan-unit 7 extends from Kirkgate on the east to Meal Vennel. On the north side of the street, plan-unit 8 extends from Skinnergate on the east to Roger's Close, opposite Meal Vennel, on the west.

Four excavations have taken place in plan-units 7 and 8, three of which have reached the underlying natural subsoil. Quantities of twelfth-century or earlier pottery have been recovered from wattle and timber buildings from two of these deeper excavations.[14] By the twelfth century, then, settlement existed as far west along High Street as Parliament Close on the north and what is now King Edward Street near Meal Vennel on the south.

These plan-units were enclosed by the first clear topographic boundary around the town. There is a continuous route leading from the castle

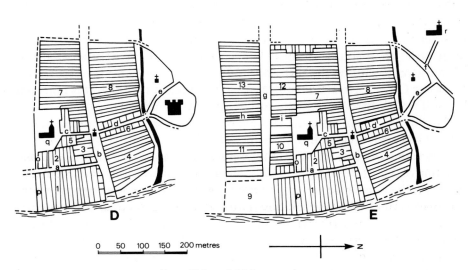

Late 12th and 13th centuries

along Curfew Row and Roger's Close to Meal Vennel. On the southern side of the town there was almost certainly a back lane to the High Street plots of plan-unit 7, the church precinct and Baxter's Vennel/Glen Close. It is not clear to what extent this circuit was a functional product of the town's size or a deliberate attempt to define the area of the burgh. That this boundary was marked by a substantial ditch has been indicated by excavations on the west side of Meal Vennel where traces of an early north-south ditch were found just emerging from under Meal Vennel. Unfortunately, the lower levels of this ditch lay outwith the excavation so that the ditch is not precisely dated.[15] The first documentary reference to some form of burgh boundary or *claustura* comes in 1153 x 58 for which this line is a good but unproven contender.[16] Whatever the exact line of this *claustura*, it seems significant that the mid-twelfth century marks not only the existence of a burgh boundary, but also of a royal castle and the planned construction of a street, Skinnergate, and market cross-roads. Moreover, documentary evidence of Perth's development only begins to survive from about this time.

The addition of South Street

That South Street was secondary to High Street has already been widely accepted.[17] The relationship between South Street and the southern end of Watergate with its continuation, Speygate, is less certain. The southern end of Watergate, plan-unit 9, is distinguished from the remainder of Watergate by the abrupt change in plot widths which occurs south of Baxter's Vennel and Glen Close. Plots along the west side of plan-unit 9 are shorter than their South Street (plan-units 10 and 11) neighbours, indicating that South Street was occupied before the southern end of Watergate. Events on the east side of Watergate/Speygate are obscured by the later Gowrie House. Disturbance of this area is such that it is not even clear if South Street originally reached the River Tay.

East of Meal Vennel and Candlemaker's Close, settlement along South Street has been divided into plan-units 10–13, each consisting of plots of a distinctive modal width. These four plan-units are also differentiated by the line of Flesh Vennel/Cow Vennel which runs south from the church. Plots on the north side of South Street are shorter than their counterparts on High Street. This is particularly the case in plan-unit 10 where they were restricted by the pre-existing boundary to the town and church precinct. With the extension of South Street as far as Meal Vennel any back lane to the southern High Street plots must have become less important, much of its traffic being carried by South Street. No such lane is recorded in documentary or cartographic sources and its ground is likely to have been incorporated into the plots of plan-unit 12. The new boundary around the town would therefore run from the castle along Curfew Row, Rogers Close, Meal Vennel, Candlemakers Close and then along the back lane to the southern plots of South Street, later known as Canal Street.

The surviving first documentary reference to South Street is not until 1214 x 49, by which time the street was well established.[18] However, in 1178 x 87 a charter of William I confirmed a plot to Cambuskenneth Abbey which was described as 'outside the burgh as defined by the two ports'.[19] There has been some debate about the location of these two ports, including a suggestion that they were on the site of the later fourteenth-century Turretbrig and Southgate ports.[20] The town-plan analysis presented in this chapter makes this identification extremely doubtful. It seems likely, though, that there were indeed ports on High Street and South Street, but at either end of Meal Vennel. Two archaeological excavations have taken place within plan-unit 13 and one within plan-unit 10. The largest of these was situated in the backlands of plan-unit 13. This uncovered a carefully laid-out sequence of property divisions beginning in the thirteenth century. These divisions overlaid earlier activity, and it would seem that occupation of the area had begun, perhaps at the South Street frontages, during the late twelfth century.[21]

A further charter of William I, dated 1178 x 95, refers to William's 'new burgh of Perth'.[22] The site of this 'new burgh' is even more enigmatic than those of the two ports; but given the sequence of development suggested by the topography and the remarkable regularity with which South Street east of Meal Vennel was laid out, there seems every possibility that South Street and its settlement was a deliberate creation of William I.

The defended burgh

The next expansion of the town is defined by the line of Perth's main medieval defences. High Street and South Street settlement extended west to Turretbrig and Southgate Ports respectively. The land between High Street and South Street was a little more evenly shared between the plots running back between these two streets, plan-units 15 and 17. Nevertheless, the High Street plots were still longer and perhaps slightly earlier than their southern neighbours. That the boundary between the two plan-units varied back and forth a little adds to the generally haphazard appearance of settlement along these two streets west of Meal Vennel.

At some stage after this westward extension, plots were also established

along the eastern and western sides of Meal Vennel, plan-unit 14. Plots on
the eastern side of the vennel were severely restricted by the pre-existing
plots running back from High Street and South Street. Excavation of a
number of plots on the west side of Meal Vennel has indicated a sequence
of major changes in the property holdings of High Street and Meal Vennel
plots.[23]

Documentary evidence for this phase of the town's growth makes it clear
that High Street and South Street reached Turretbrig and Southgate Ports
by at least 1336 when there was major work on the town's defences.[24] It is
likely, though, that these defences were on the line of those ordered by
Edward I in the first years of the fourteenth century.[25] What is less clear is
whether the area enclosed by these defences was already occupied by
burgesses or whether the intention was to defend an additional area to
provide a military compound. The irregular line taken by the western
defences of the town may provide a limited indication of the extent of any
settlement that it enclosed. The main anomalous feature is undoubtedly
the right-angled junction between the western and northern lades.
Excavation in this area would suggest that this stretch of lade was indeed
fourteenth century, although dateable finds from the town ditch were
scarce.[26] The angle of the lade may therefore have been determined by
extant features such as burgage plots on the north side of High Street.
Conversely the gentle curve of the lade round the south-west corner of the
town may indicate that that area was relatively undeveloped.

Suburban growth

There are two suburbs of the medieval town: Castlegable/Curfew Row to
the north, plan-unit 19, and New Row/Mill Wynd to the west, plan-unit
20. The variety of settlement in both these suburbs makes it extremely
difficult to estimate the number of plots that had existed in them. Unlike
plots within the burgh, suburban plots were not a legal part of the burgage
system. Functionally they tended to be used for agriculture and industry
with any residential use being purely an overflow from the burgh. It is a
remarkable testament to the popularity of strip plots, as well as to the
conservatism of suburban landowners, that there was such similarity
between suburban and burghal land division, especially in the Castlegable
area.

As has been noted, use of the Castlegable/Curfew Row suburb dates to
the establishment of the castle there by at least the mid-twelfth century.
Beside the castle and enclosed within the line of Curfew Row was an open
area later known as Horse Cross. It does not seem to have been subdivided

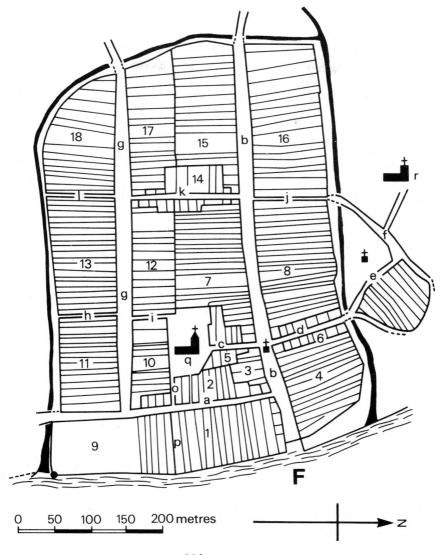

| 0 | 50 | 100 | 150 | 200 metres |

14th century

for settlement and its medieval function is undocumented. In post-medieval times it was used as a livestock market and fairground. It would have been a convenient fairground and military muster point during the middle ages. The abandonment of the possibly flood-damaged castle followed by the establishment of a Dominican friary there in the early thirteenth century marks just one of the major changes that had effected this plan-unit. The site of the friary has been located by excavation at the

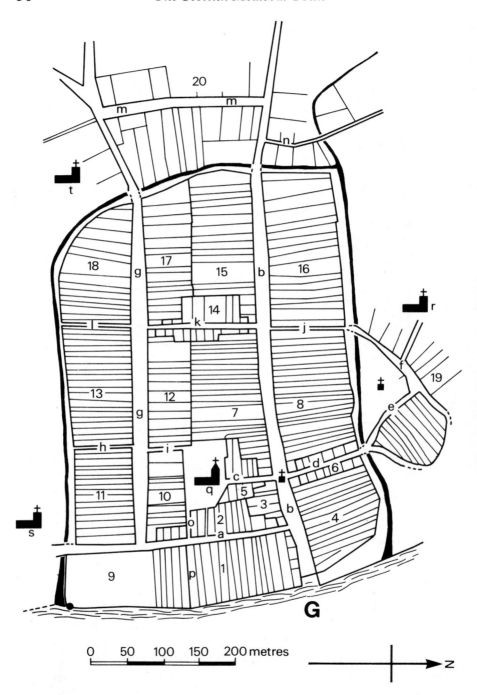

0   50   100   150   200 metres

15th and 16th centuries

junction of Carpenter Street and Kinnoull Street, south-west of Rutherford's place mark.[27] The difficulty that existed in locating the friary underlines the very great changes that have taken place in this area. The basic street system mapped in the eighteenth century is however confirmed from charters issued by the Dominicans when they began to feu out their substantial holdings in the area in the late fifteenth and early sixteenth centuries.

Like the Castlegable/Curfew Row area, some settlement may well have taken place in the New Row/Mill Wynd area prior to its development as a suburb of Perth. The area would certainly have been used for farming and perhaps also industrial activities such as tanning, giving rise to the name Barker Row, and perhaps potteries in the area of Claypots. However, full suburban settlement in this area must largely post-date the western defences of the fourteenth-century town. Excavation on the east side of Mill Wynd indicated the existence of fifteenth-century buildings constructed over traces of earlier activity and this is also the date of most early documentary references to the suburb.[28] It is likely that the town mills at the north end of the suburb also post-date these defences, as it is hard to see them being left outside in the fourteenth century. At the south end of New Row was the Carthusian monastery founded in 1429.

Conclusion

A summary of the various plan-units' modal widths, the number of plots and the proportion at the modal widths is presented in the appended table. It will be apparent from this table that there is normally little regularity in plot widths; even the modal widths range from 18–29 ft (6.3–10.15 m). However, certain districts of the town, most notably the eastern half of South Street (plan-units 10–13) and the west side of Meal Vennel (plan-unit 14W), do achieve exceptional regularity. The contrast between these plan-units and the rest of the town is such, for the east end of South Street, that the layout of plots may have been part of a planned expansion. For at least part of plan-unit 13 this has been confirmed by excavation.[29] It is noticeable that, rather than a single modal width for the whole district, there are in fact different modes for each of the constituent plan-units. These modes are so pronounced that they may well be the result of an expansion conceived and executed as a series of steps. Although at first glance the regularity of plots along the west side of Meal Vennel might suggest a similar interpretation, there is a need for caution in such work. Excavation west of Meal Vennel has indicated that the eighteenth-century

C

layout of plots there was the result of late medieval and even post-medieval reorganisation of the frontages.[30]

Although there is no overall modal plot width for the town, it is significant that there are no plan-unit modes below eighteen feet, and indeed there are only some nine plots in the whole town less than eighteen feet wide. This almost certainly relates to the fact that burgess status and taxation in the medieval and post-medieval burgh was based on the holding of one particate or rude of land, a rude being either a quarter of a Scottish acre or six ells in length.[31] It is this latter definition which is the more important, for six Scots ells are eighteen and a half feet. That many plots are in fact slightly wider than eighteen feet is also consistent with the documentary evidence, for it would seem that in burghs a rood may be taken as twenty feet.[32] The popularity of widths around 18–21 ft (6.5–7.35 m) may also be a reflection of building traditions in Scottish burghs. If so, the secondary concentration of widths around twenty-six feet may represent a building width plus plot access.

This analysis also identifies the maximum number of plots that could have existed between fixed points in Perth's plan (Table at chapter end). Such a figure is of considerable interest in determining potential burgess numbers and burgh size. It must be emphasised, though, that the maximum figure is just that, and it is highly unlikely that all the plots defined in this study were ever independently owned or even occupied at the same time. Nevertheless, this provides a guide to the changing scale of settlement. There were only sixteen plots in the original settlement beside the Tay (Map A), which had risen to around 150 by the mid-twelfth-century (Map D). The date of the original settlement remains unknown but it is clear that the town-plan had undergone at least two major changes before the mid-twelfth century. In the early thirteenth century South Street added a further hundred plots to the burgh (Map E), with room for yet another hundred being enclosed by the early fourteenth-century defences (Map F). Having achieved quite a remarkable growth, the fourteenth-century burgh of some 370 burgage plots had reached its burghal limits. There would seem to have then been a slow suburban expansion during the fifteenth century which tailed off leaving the town without significant physical growth until the end of the eighteenth century.[33]

An important aspect of this type of town-plan analysis is its ability to provide models which can be related to not only archaeological evidence, but documentary sources as well. It is possible to locate excavated or potential archaeological sites on historic town-plans which are sufficiently detailed as to permit the identification of individual burgage plots. At the same time documents, especially sasines and rentals, which also provide topographic detail, can be built up into what is in effect a descriptive plan of streets, plots and the distribution of burgesses.[34] Cartographic models such as the one for Perth presented here may therefore be checked not only by excavation but also by documentary analysis of property registers, protocol books and sasines. Indeed, detailed analysis of the cartographic evidence may provide a framework for the plot by plot comparison of both documentary and archaeological evidence.

Table. Plot-width distribution by Plan-Unit

Plan Unit	Modal Width	No. of plots from plan	No. at Mode	Multiples at Mode	Other Multiples	Notional Max. No.
1	28 ft	14	5		1 @ ×2	16
2	26 ft	11	7	2 @ ×2	1 @ ×2	17
3	28 ft	7	3			7
4	23 ft	15?	6			15
5 E.	c. 23 ft	7	0		1 @ ×2	9
5 W.	c. 26 ft	7	0		1 @ ×2	9
6 E.	21 ft	13	5		1 @ ×3	15
6 W.	18 ft	11	6	1 @ ×2	1 @ ×2	15
7	a 21 ft	25	10	1 @ ×2		
	b 18 ft		10	2 @ ×2	1 @ ×2	30
8	23 ft	21	7	2 @ ×1.5		22
9 E.	c. 22 ft	5+	0			5+
9 W.	21 ft	6	5	2 @ ×2		8
10	20 ft	12	10	2 @ ×2	1 @ ×3	17
11	26 ft	13?		1 @ ×2		
			16	1 @ ×3		16
12	19 ft	17	15	4 @ ×2	1 @ ×2	23
13	18 ft	20	16	5 @ ×2		25
14E.	25–31 ft	14?	0			14+
14W.	36 ft	10?		2 @ ×1.5		
			10	1 @ ×2		12
15	18 ft	22		4 @ ×1.5		
			17	4 @ ×2	1 @ ×2	30
16	29 ft	23	5			23
17	23 ft	16		2 @ ×2		
			10	1 @ ×3		20
18	23 ft	17	3		2 @ ×2	21
19	28 ft	29	4		1 @ ×2	31
20	18–31 ft	34?	0			34+

Key to maps A - G

All numbers relate to Plan-Units described in text

a — Watergate
b — High Street
c — Kirkgate
d — Skinnergate
e — Castlegable
f — Curfew Row
g — South Street
h — Cow Vennel
i — Flesher's Close
j — Roger's Close
k — Meal Vennel
l — Candlemakers Close
m — New Row
n — Mill Wynd
o — Baxter's Vennel
p — Glen Close
q — St John's Church
r — Dominican Friary
s — Franciscan Friary
t — Carthusian Monastery

NOTES

1. Conzen, 'Alnwick, Northumberland – a study in town plan analysis'.

2. Dodd, 'Ayr: a study in urban growth'; Duncan, 'Perth'; Brooks & Whittington, 'Planning and growth in the medieval Scottish burgh: the example of St Andrews'; Gibb, *Glasgow, The Making of a City*; Fox, 'Stirling, 1550–1700'; Gourlay, Simpson & Stevenson, *Scottish Burgh Survey*.

3. Houston, 'The Scottish burgh', 114; Whitehand & Alauddin, 'The town plans of Scotland: some preliminary considerations'; Adams, *The Making of Urban Scotland*: Fox 'Urban Development, 1100–1700', in Whittington & Whyte (eds.), *A Historical Geography of Scotland*.

4. Much information is as yet unpublished. Interim Reports for excavations after 1982 are available from Scottish Urban Archaeological Trust Ltd, 55 South Methven Street, Perth. Prior to that date the Perth High Street Excavation 1972–75 awaits publication. Publications include: Bogdan & Wordsworth, *The Medieval Excavation at the High Street, Perth*; Thoms, *Perth, St Ann's Lane Exc.*; Blanchard, *Perth, Canal St Exc.;* Holdsworth, *Perth Excavns.*

5. Milne, *The Rental Books of the King James VI Hospital, Perth*.

6. McLaren, 'Early Plans of Perth'.

7. Whitehand & Alauddin, '*Town plans of Scot.*', 111.

8. Duncan, *Scotland*, 467.

9. Duncan, 'Perth', 32.

10. *ESC*, no. lxxiv.

11. Duncan, 'Perth', 33.

12. *RRS*, i, nos. 157, 171; *St Andrews Liber*, 142.

13. *RRS*, i, no. 57.

14. Bogdan & Wordsworth, *Perth High Street Interim*, 20; Blanchard, *Perth, King Edwards St Exc.*

15. Blanchard, *Perth, Meal Vennel Exc.*

16. *RRS*, i, no. 121.

17. Duncan, *Scotland*, 468.

18. *Scone Liber*, no. 97.

19. *RRS*, ii, no. 233.

20. Duncan, 'Perth', 33.

21. Spearman, *Perth, Canal Street Exc.*

22. *RRS*, ii, no. 278.

23. Blanchard, *Perth, Meal Vennel Exc.*

24. *Chron. Pluscarden*, ix, 219.

25. *CDS*, no. 1912.; Colvin, *History of the King's Works*, 1205, 419.

26. Spearman, *Perth, Methven St Exc.*

27. Hall, 'Blackfriars Excavation Interim' (SUAT).

28. Spearman, *Perth, Methven St Exc.*

29. Spearman, *Perth, Canal Street Exc.*

30. Blanchard, *Perth, Meal Vennel Exc.*

31. *Ancient Burgh Laws*, 4, 24 *Leges Burgorum*, nos. 1, 49.

32. *Ancient Burgh Laws*, 186; *Fragmenta Collecta*, no. 54.

33. In 1712 there were still only 404 households recorded in the burgh (Sanderson Library, 1359/25/2/29).

34. Verschuur, '*Thesis*', Ch. 1.

4

Urban Buildings

Geoffrey Stell

Except for churches and castles, there are few standing buildings in Scottish towns that antedate the Reformation, and virtually none earlier than the sixteenth century. However, these urban churches and castles themselves remain relatively untapped as sources of historical evidence, and the more numerous domestic and public buildings that date from the immediate post-Reformation era between 1560 and 1603 are also under-utilised as guides to their medieval antecedents.[1] In addition, archaeological surveys and excavations carried out in recent decades have placed further evidence of buildings and building activity at the disposal of the Scottish medieval urban historian.[2] The total amount of available information is not as slight as has sometimes been suggested, although it is admittedly much less than that which has been derived from the regions of England, especially when compared with the surviving structural evidence of, for example, medieval York and Norwich. The main purpose of this essay is simply to bring together and review the Scottish evidence, and to consider its implications for further historical and archaeological research.

Most, but, as the cases of Haddington and Inverkeithing demonstrate, not all early Scottish burghs lay within the immediate vicinity of a castle or strongpoint. Forfar even had a royal castle which was described as 'old' as early as the reign of William I when, redundant as a fortification, it was being subdivided into private lots.[3] It is in fact noticeable that many of the mottes associated with early burgh foundations appear to have remained comparatively undeveloped beyond their first earth–and–timber phases, and to have atrophied in the later middle ages. Archaeological excavations have shown that the histories of the castles of Elgin and Lanark conform to this pattern, and, after the mottes of Perth and Annan had been physically eroded within the first century of their existences, there was apparently no pressing need to rebuild or replace them.[4]

Indeed, few urban castle-sites preserve stone-built and mortared remains of structures known to have been erected before the middle decades of the fourteenth century. St Margaret's Chapel obviously provides clear evidence of twelfth-century masonwork in Edinburgh Castle, but the earliest extant secular remains of the major royal strongholds of Edinburgh and Stirling otherwise date from the 1360s and the 1380s respectively.[5] Because of its front-line position and rival attentions on the part of the English, Berwick Castle (and possibly Roxburgh, although now only a slight remnant), retains defensive works of late thirteenth- and early fourteenth-century origin.[6] Elsewhere, however, the pattern is patchy and inconclusive, and the vestiges of early stone castles at, for example, Crail, Dunfermline and Kirkcudbright, may partly be an accident of survival.[7] Rothesay, the most spectacular and substantial early stone castle in an urban context, long preceded the formal creation of the royal burgh in 1400, but it had probably always been closely associated with a proto-urban community.[8]

The urban castle of the later middle ages was characteristically the tower house in its several variant forms. These multi-storeyed dwellings of the principal patrons became the dominant physical nuclei around which, or at a short distance from which, urban communities grouped themselves. At Alloa the massive fifteenth-century tower of the lords Erskine was, architecturally and institutionally, parent to the burgh of regality established in 1497.[9] At Mauchline, which in 1510 was erected into a burgh of barony dependent on the abbots of Melrose, the mid-fifteenth-century tower built by Abbot Hunter (1444–71) served as the administrative centre of the burgh and of the monastery's lordship of Kylesmure.[10] The Campbells of Loudoun, who later acquired Mauchline, were responsible for promoting Newmilns to the same status in 1491 and for building a tower there, which still survives, probably early in the sixteenth century.[11] In 'Chapel', one of two constituent settlements that made up Stranraer, a tower was built by the Adairs of Kinhilt almost a century before the formal creation of the burgh of barony in 1595, subsequently made a royal burgh in 1617.[12] Clearance and landscaping has once again brought this tower fully into view in the centre of Stranraer. Fordyce also conveys a particularly good visual impression of the physical setting of a tower house at the centre of a small burgh of barony, although the nucleus of its tower, dated 1592, is almost a century later than the foundation of the burgh in 1499.[13]

Various factors appear to have governed the disposition of the gateways and routes that linked or separated a castle and its associated urban community, but the present state of archaeological and topographical research does not permit any generalisations. At Stirling, for example, the oldest surviving portion of the castle includes a postern gateway which provided direct access to the castle from the river crossing over the Forth; the route skirted but did not penetrate the town itself which lay some distance south-east of the main gateway of the castle. At Linlithgow, the approach routes from the town to the royal palace may have been slightly reorganised in the 1530s, but the reasons for the reconstruction of the southern gateway, and its effects on traffic in the adjacent Kirkgate, are imperfectly understood.[14]

The boundaries of the larger burghs were generally defined by garden walls or dykes, and the roads were controlled by 'ports' or gates, which were designed as much for fiscal and social purposes as for military security. The West Port (1589) at St Andrews is the only surviving early town gateway in Scotland, its (altered) dimensions being closely comparable to those which gave access to the medieval city of York.[15] However, formal urban defences, always a matter of considerable cost and organisation, were probably not as common as has been alleged.[16] It is known that Inverness, Selkirk and Perth, for example, possessed earthwork defences comprising ditches, ramparts and palisades, and there are indications that at least one of Perth's gates may have been stone-built. However, except for the White Wall at Berwick upon Tweed, originally put up by the English in 1297–8, substantial visible traces of town defences in stone and lime are confined to Edinburgh and Stirling, where they date mainly from the sixteenth century.[17]

For those burghs which grew up alongside river crossings, fords, ferries and bridges served as means of controlling military and civilian traffic and as toll-collection points. The bridges themselves, however, were major burdens of burgh expenditure, as the records of destruction, reconstruction and maintenance testify. The crossing of the Tay at Perth proved particularly troublesome, and the struggle to maintain a bridge was abandoned after a major destructive flood in 1621.[18] Although timber, or stone and timber in combination, is known to have been much used in Scottish medieval bridge-building, surviving urban bridges are of arched masonry construction, and usually slightly wider than their rural counterparts; none now preserves traces of an associated gateway.[19] The most complete examples are the multiple-arched structures of fifteenth-century origin at Ayr, Dumfries, Haddington and Stirling, while less obvious medieval remains still survive at, for example, Peebles and Brechin.[20]

Harbour works constituted another major item of public expenditure, not only for coastal and riverside settlements but also for those landlocked royal burghs that enjoyed the benefits of foreign trade. In Lothian, for example, Haddington, Edinburgh, and Linlithgow had their outlets on the Forth estuary at Aberlady, Leith and Blackness, $5\frac{1}{4}$, $1\frac{1}{2}$ and $3\frac{3}{4}$ miles distant respectively. On the Moray Firth, Elgin had its port at Lossiemouth, where its rights conflicted with those of the bishops of

Moray who had access to the open sea from the Loch of Spynie via the River Lossie. Whether their maritime connections were direct or indirect, however, few urban centres have preserved or revealed early evidence of waterfront structures. The agreement made in 1394 between the abbot and townsmen of Arbroath for the building of a harbour at the mouth of the Brothock Water is probably the earliest known detailed account of harbour construction in Scotland.[21] What seems to have been envisaged was a breakwater-pier constructed of boulders contained within framed timber cages, and a harbour of that form, doubtless repaired, was shown in Captain Slezer's late seventeenth-century engraving of the town. All-stone quay construction, possibly in combination with wooden fenders, is known to have been used at North Berwick and at Aberdeen, where short stretches of a late medieval harbour wall were excavated at Shore Brae in 1974.[22] The harbour at Fraserburgh was probably constructed in a similar manner in the second half of the sixteenth century, and the near-contemporary 'Wine Tower' there is one of the few surviving harbourside buildings of sixteenth-century origin.[23] Other early storehouses are also to be found in the north-east at Stonehaven and Peterhead, and in non-urban contexts at Limekilns, Fife, and on Whalsay, Shetland.[24] Lanterns in St Ninian's Chapel, Aberdeen, are known to have served as navigation beacons,[25] but there are no surviving improvised sea-marks of pre-seventeenth-century date. Nor, it might be added, are there any other recognisable standing monuments of medieval trade and industry, although it seems reasonable to suppose that water-courses in, for example, Elgin, Perth and Paisley have probably served a succession of millsteads since the middle ages.

Another major item of public expenditure among the common works section of the burgh accounts was the tolbooth, its cost and its position in the layout of the town usually reflecting its central role in civic administration.[26] By the sixteenth century the building to which the vernacular term 'tolbooth' was applied, literally the office at which the tolls and customs were collected, had absorbed the wider functions of municipal council chamber and court, implied by the Latin term *praetorium*. However, it is likely that only the larger and richer burghs such as Edinburgh and Aberdeen enjoyed regular use of such purpose-built town-houses in the later middle ages; elsewhere, other buildings were adapted as circumstances permitted. With the possible exception of the lower part of the tolbooth tower in Crail, for which a date of 1517 has been claimed,[27] the earliest surviving structures of this type date from the second half of the sixteenth century when there was increased pressure on royal burghs to provide judicial courts and prisons. The tolbooths of Canongate (1591) and Musselburgh (c.1590) are probably the most complete of this early group,[28] and display to good effect the three major functional and symbolic elements in town-house design: the conspicuous tower or steeple which served as a civic bell-house; the council chamber block which contained the public meeting-rooms and offices; and the prison cells on the upper and lower floors.

Like the tolbooth forestair, the mercat cross was a regular venue for public assembly and proclamations. However, surviving medieval mercat crosses are comparatively few and fragmentary, and most of these have had an eventful and mobile history. The most complete authentic specimens which survive wholly or in part are those of Edinburgh, Peebles, Inverkeithing and Banff.[29] Sadly, none of the early halls and meeting-places associated with medieval guilds remains standing and intact, the earliest surviving trades incorporation building being the much-altered and heightened Tailors' Hall in Edinburgh which dates from 1621 and later.[30]

Given the relative paucity of other categories of building, there can be no doubt that churches are the richest single source of architectural evidence for pre-Reformation Scottish towns, parish churches in particular being especially informative about the communities that they served. However, not all burghs possessed separate purpose-built parish churches, for many of the greater urban ecclesiastical establishments of regular or secular clergy also included provision for parochial worship. The parish altar of the Canongate, for instance, stood within the nave of Holyrood Abbey until the late seventeenth century.[31] By 1220 the parishioners of Jedburgh had also acquired for their use an altar in the nave of the Augustinian abbey in their town, parochial use of part of this abbey church persisting for more than three centuries after the Reformation.[32] Similar arrangements obtained at Melrose, Kelso, Forfar (Restenneth Priory), and probably Paisley, Dunfermline and elsewhere, but the actual location or nature of the parish altar is not often clearly deducible. According to a detailed description of 1517,[33] the Tironensian abbey of Kelso had a stone screen-wall that closed off the inner monastic or conventual portion of the church: 'the outer part is open to all, especially parishioners both women and men, who there hear masses and receive all sacraments from their parochial vicar'; the wall itself bore a wooden platform on which was mounted the Holy Rood and a tin organ.

At Arbroath, on the other hand, parochial needs were served, not within the greatest of the Scottish Tironensian houses which was also the feudal superior of the burgh, but at the ancient sacred site of St Vigeans, about one mile away to the north. Cathedral churches varied likewise in their parochial arrangements: some, such as those of Glasgow and Old Aberdeen, accommodated parish altars, but others such as Elgin did not, Elgin being an established community with its own parish church of St

Giles when the church of the diocese of Moray was finally re-located near to it in 1224. In the first half of the thirteenth century St Andrews also acquired its own parish church, a free-standing structure evidently situated close to the east end of the cathedral-priory, but in 1412 the church of the Holy Trinity was re-sited nearer the centre of the burgh.[34]

Among those towns that possessed separate, purpose-built parish churches, only a few retain, or are known to have had, ecclesiastical remains that date from the twelfth or early thirteenth centuries. Convincing evidence of Romanesque or Transitional architecture has indeed been noted in Ayr, Crail, Edinburgh, Rutherglen and St Vigeans, but it is not easy to ascertain the character and size of these early urban churches.[35] Those at St Vigeans, Rutherglen, and, as recent excavations have shown, St John's, Ayr, acquired aisled naves, but the earliest evidence of a fully developed cruciform plan with aisled nave and probably aisled choir is the Transitional work in the transepts and crossing, later called the Drum and Collison Aisles, of St Nicholas' Church, New Aberdeen.[36] In about 1200 this church measured about 27.5 m in maximum width over the transepts, and was probably already close to its later medieval length of 71.3 m. The parish church of Crail also survives substantially in the form in which it was enlarged in the early thirteenth century when a simple Romanesque structure was expanded on each side to create a six-bay aisled nave. The east end of the present parish church at Kinghorn retains indications of an aisled chancel, possibly of thirteenth-century date, and, although the ruins of the six-bay arcade of the old parish church at Lanark were rebuilt in the nineteenth century, it seems reasonably certain that it too had had an aisled nave in the thirteenth and fourteenth centuries.[37]

As reconstructed upon an enlarged aisled and cruciform plan in about the third quarter of the fourteenth century, St Giles', Edinburgh, became the first of a series of large burgh churches, mainly of central and eastern Scotland, which were rebuilt or substantially repaired in the later middle ages.[38] Its subsequent organic growth between 1387 and 1560 also reflected, more fully and dramatically than any other, the effects of endowments, either by individual burgesses and lairds or by corporate groups such as trade guilds and confraternities, upon the architecture of the single urban parish churches characteristic of Scotland. A building contract for the erection of five chapels on the south side of the nave, presumably recently completed, was agreed upon in 1387, and other lateral stone-built chapels distended the structure even further in the course of the fifteenth and sixteenth centuries. The extension and heightening of the eastern limb in the middle decades of the fifteenth century marked a prelude to a final and successful petition on the part of the magistrates and community of Edinburgh to attain collegiate status for their church in

1468-9. By the Reformation the collegiate establishment included a provost and fourteen prebendaries, as well as numerous chaplains serving more than forty altars that are known to have been founded or re-dedicated in the church by that time.

No other major burgh parish church achieved formal collegiate status before the sixteenth century, although some were developing an architectural and institutional character broadly similar to St Giles', Edinburgh, from the second quarter of the fifteenth century onwards. Agreements with their monastic proprietors record the intentions of the

Fig. 1: St Mary's Church tower, Dundee (from R. W. Billings, *The Baronial and Ecclesiastical Antiquities of Scotland* (1845-52), II, plate 13).

burgh magistrates of Perth, Dundee and Stirling, for example, to reconstruct the choirs of their parish churches in 1440, 1442–3 and 1507 respectively.[39] Their endeavours and investment are well reflected in the scale and refinement of the surviving architecture at Perth (1440–8) and Stirling (1507–20), while the massiveness and Netherlands-inspired 'telescopic' design of the extant 50 m-high western tower of St Mary's, Dundee (Fig. 1), provides some measures of the grandiose nature of the church to which it was added in the later fifteenth century, a structure that, like St Giles' in Edinburgh, was large enough to accommodate no less than three congregations at the Reformation.[40]

On stylistic grounds, the completion of the central-towered cruciform church of St Mary's, Haddington, which achieved an overall length of more than 62 m and possesses some homogeneity of design, can probably be ascribed to the mid-fifteenth century.[41] The structural components of the slightly smaller church of St Michael's, Linlithgow, represent episodes of building effort protracted over a century after 1424, and probably comparable to Linlithgow in their original sizes were the parish churches re-erected in the centres of St Andrews (1412–) and Cupar (c. 1415–29).[42] Like the larger churches, however, Holy Trinity, St Andrews, is known to have accommodated more than thirty altars, although practically all of its altars and chaplainries were founded by churchmen, not by burgesses. A provisional analysis[43] suggests that they were founded in three main phases — in the 1430s, the 1460s, and 1490–1510 — but it remains to be tested whether there was a similar chronology in other burghs, and whether such foundations conceivably embody indirect effects of other aspects of town life such as the incidence of heresy or plague.

Whatever the share of architectural patronage exercised by churchmen, by the lay nobility, and by the townspeople themselves, the construction and development of these major burgh churches appear to pinpoint phases of investment on the part of their urban communities, and to show, if material demonstration were needed, precisely where the growth-points of late medieval urban Scotland were located. Among the lesser burghs too, the remains of the medieval churches of Dalkeith and Dysart, for example, reflect the promotions of their associated communities to burghal status at the hands of Sir James Douglas and Lord Sinclair respectively in the early fifteenth and early sixteenth centuries.[44] The case of Dalkeith is unusual, if not unique, for not only did the vill become a burgh of barony in 1401, but its church, a chapel dependent on Lasswade, became collegiate five years later, and in 1467 a parish church in its own right. Its elaborately detailed choir remains clearly visible, and enough has survived a reconstruction of 1851 to show that the church also had a fifteenth-century aisled nave. On the other hand, the chapel around which the eastern part of Stranraer grew up in the sixteenth and seventeenth centuries remained a pendicle of the distant parish church of Inch, three miles to the east, while the western half of the town continued to pertain to Leswalt, situated a similar distance to the north-west. Unlike Dalkeith, Stranraer failed to establish a separate parish for itself, and the late medieval chapel building no longer survives, having been removed in the late seventeenth or early eighteenth centuries.[45]

Urban and suburban parochial chapels are well enough attested from documentary sources: in and around Glasgow, for example, there were in existence at different times as many as half a dozen chapels dependent on the 'greater church' (the cathedral), many of which were founded by burgesses;[46] more typically perhaps, Linlithgow probably had a couple situated at the main entrances to the town;[47] and at Lanark, where the parish church lay a short distance away, there was apparently a chapel of convenience at the centre, close to the burgh cross.[48] Few such chapels have remained structurally evident, the two most complete pre-Reformation urban chapels having been associated with hospital foundations. The better known is the Magdalen Chapel in the Cowgate, Edinburgh, part of a hospital founded by a burgess of Edinburgh about 1537 and conveyed by his wife to the Edinburgh hammermen in 1547–8;[49] the hospital chapel was substantially altered in 1614–15 to serve as a meeting-hall, but the tomb of the foundress (d. 1553) and four roundels of stained glass, probably the most important collection of pre-Reformation stained glass in Scotland, still survive. Less renowned, but of much earlier date and greater architectural distinction, is the surviving Gothic frontage of the chapel of the Maison Dieu poors' hospital in Brechin, founded in 1261 x 7 by William of Brechin, the son of one of Earl David of Huntingdon's bastards.[50]

Being products of an essentially urban mission in Scotland, as elsewhere, the most numerous of the lesser religious houses in the towns were those of the mendicant friars, but, partly because of their later unpopularity and the fact that they bore the main brunt of Reformation violence, Scottish friaries have not experienced a high survival rate. Of the Dominican (Black) Friars, the principal surviving buildings are the ruins of the 1525 north aisle of the friary-church in St Andrews, and possibly part of the present parish church of St Monance, although it is not clear just how much alteration or addition was undertaken after 1477 when James III was granted papal authorisation to refound David II's royal chapel as a house of Friars Preacher.[51] Also in Fife is the most substantial surviving relic of the Friars Minor, a former *hospitium* of fourteenth-century date in Inverkeithing, the church of the Greyfriars in Kirkcudbright retaining very little of its medieval origins.[52] The restored friary-church of the house of Reformed Franciscans, or Observants, founded in Elgin by John Innes of Innes some time before 1494, is the only standing building of that order, although excavation has revealed some remains, including fragments of traceried windows, of the near-contemporary Franciscan friary in Ayr.[53] Archaeological excavations in Aberdeen, Perth and Linlithgow have also shed much light on the physical aspects of urban and suburban Carmelite (White) friaries, of which the former friary-church in South Queensferry (1441–), despite the loss of its nave, remains the most complete upstanding specimen.[54] Remains of the few urban establishments of the non-mendicant Trinitarians or so-called Red Friars comprise traces of the conventual buildings added to the Cross Kirk in Peebles after 1474, and excavation has confirmed that the later dovecot in Friarscroft, Dunbar, was the central tower of an unaisled thirteenth-century Trinitarian church, the chancel of which contained the greater part of a late medieval tiled floor.[55]

The earliest domestic urban residences to survive in reasonably complete and recognisable form date from the second half of the sixteenth century. The main groups are to be found in Edinburgh and Stirling, principal seats of the royal court before the Union of Crowns in 1603, but examples can still be seen in the ancient administrative and commercial centres throughout the country. Particularly in burghs associated with medieval cathedrals and major religious houses, a few buildings retain evidence of pre-Reformation origins. Although much altered in the seventeenth century, Provand's Lordship in Glasgow probably originated in about 1470 as the manse of Barlanark, one of the prebendaries of Glasgow Cathedral.[56] Tankerness House in Kirkwall also appears to represent a seventeenth-century remodelling of a group of manses originally associated with the medieval cathedral chapter of Orkney.[57] The most substantial unaltered structure of this category is the building identifiable as the Precentor's Manse in Elgin, the upstanding wing, which is dated 1557, possibly being a later addition to what is now a much-reduced main block.[58] There are also altered vestiges of at least two other manses of the College of the Cathedral Chanonry in Elgin, those of the canon of Inverkeithny and of the archdeacon.

Although the cathedral-priory of St Andrews was staffed mainly, but not exclusively, by regular clergy, one effect of the general clerical and academic activity within the burgh in the later middle ages was to stimulate urban house-building in much the same way as secular cathedrals; it is thus not surprising that St Andrews lays claim to town houses of fifteenth-century origin, the earliest surviving in Scotland.[59] Town lodgings and guest houses were also associated with major religious establishments, such hostries or hostelries being located outside the conventual layouts for the accommodation of ordinary visitors. Surviving urban examples include the former *hospitium* of the Grey Friars in Inverkeithing, the earliest nucleus of the buildings on the north side of Abbey Strand outside Holyrood Abbey, probably the extensive west gatehouse range of Arbroath Abbey, and the much smaller gatehouse of Whithorn Cathedral-Priory, object of frequent pilgrimages by James IV.[60]

By the sixteenth century the wider, ripple-like effects of regular royal presence and activity were undoubtedly being felt in Edinburgh and Stirling where the lodgings of the greater nobility were erected as close as conveniently possible to the royal buildings. Argyll's Lodging, although much added to after 1603, and its neighbour, the incomplete but grandiose Mar's Wark, are two such courtier residences in Stirling, and in position and size these large sub-medieval town houses stood as physical intermediaries between the royal castle and the burgh.[61] In Linlithgow the progressive rebuilding of the royal palace between 1424 and 1539, a major undertaking by any standards, probably had a direct and indirect effect upon much of the town over a long period. In architectural terms, the design and detailing of the largest known of Linlithgow's late medieval houses, which probably belonged to the Knights Hospitallers of Torphichen and was demolished in the late nineteenth century, appear to have been closely comparable to parts of the nearby palace, particularly with regard to their respective hall fireplaces and oriel windows (Fig. 2).[62] Late medieval features, including fireplaces, exposed in the course of demolition in the centre of Linlithgow in the 1960s, displayed similar affinities, and it seems reasonable to suggest that the pattern and character of building in and around the small burgh of Falkland was influenced by royal works at its palace, especially during the intense activity of James V's reign.[63]

The architecture of non-royal lordship, represented by the urban castles that have already been reviewed, likewise dominated and perhaps to some extent determined the forms of the lesser town houses within their spheres of influence, although it is usually difficult to gauge the extent to which such building practices may have permeated the middle and lesser ranks of urban society. Given the town and country interests of most of their builders, it is not surprising that the late medieval and early modern tower houses of the urban aristocracy and gentry show only few variations in design from their rural counterparts, and many make virtually no concession to the restrictions of an urban environment, MacLellan's Castle (1582) in Kirkcudbright being a classic case in point.[64] Terraced or semi-detached treatment is, however, detectable among buildings in, for example, Abbey Strand, Edinburgh and the Shiprow, Aberdeen. Towers are also believed to have been erected in some numbers in smaller towns

Fig. 2: Town house of the Knights Hospitallers, Linlithgow; tower block prior to demolition *c*. 1886. By courtesy of Edinburgh City Libraries.

such as Maybole and Peebles, but is now difficult to assess their individual or collective character largely on the random evidence of vaulted cellars and architectural fragments.[65] The indications are that most such urban towers or bastles were relatively small-scale affairs; only a few medieval towns in Scotland are likely to have possessed more than one sizeable tower and to have borne even a remote resemblance to those in northern Italy where, as at San Gimignano, lofty seigneurial towers are still prominent in their townscapes.

Nevertheless, to foreign visitors in the later sixteenth and seventeenth centuries, Scotland and Edinburgh in particular was a land of impressive urban 'skyscrapers' rising to four or more storeys in height. Sheer height was not their only special characteristic, however, for whilst some of these multi-storeyed tenement-buildings were self-contained dwellings in single ownership, others were of multiple occupation and ownership. To an English observer in the early eighteenth century, for example, it seemed that 'every staircase may contain 28 familyes, for the Scotch houses are built after the manner of the Inns of Court in England, and every apartment is call'd a house',[66] or what we would now call a flat. The ways in which many buildings in central Edinburgh were subdivided into houses of various sizes, with rooms arranged over one or two floors and providing household accommodation for owner-occupiers and tenants alike, first emerge clearly in an annuity tax roll of 1635.[67]

By 1635, however, such arrangements were clearly an accepted and probably long-established mode of urban life, at least in Edinburgh, but when, how and why the practice of flatting and multiple ownership over a single solum emerged are fundamental questions which have not yet been satisfactorily answered. To suggest that such practices resulted from the pressure of overcrowding within a comparatively secure and advantageous area defined by a town's defences is insufficient,[68] for it does not explain why similar conditions in major walled cities in England such as London, Norwich and York did not provoke a similar response. Whether horizontally divided ownership obtained further north in England in the houses of medieval Newcastle or Carlisle, or even in the numerous, large and frequently turbulent towns of the Low Countries, has not been clearly established. It thus remains to be seen whether flatting is a specially distinctive, or possibly even unique, aspect of early Scottish urban society.

Structural evidence for its occurrence at an early date in Edinburgh can be detected in the disposition of original stairs (usually circular newel stairs, known as turnpikes), partitions and doorways. By the later sixteenth century the upper floors of the so-called 'John Knox's House', for example, formed a separate dwelling which was reached by its own newel stair in the front corner of the building.[69] And although later usage makes it difficult to work out the original arrangements in detail, Gladstone's Land in the Lawnmarket appears to conform to this general pattern, Thomas Gledstanes himself probably occupying one of its four 'houses' after his acquisition and reconstruction of the property in 1617–20.[70] Various historical sources attest the physical density of buildings in pre-Reformation Edinburgh, but the extent to which they were designed or modified to suit divided ownership or tenancy is not easy to determine. However, in notarial instruments involving three-way subdivisions of urban properties in the Canongate between 1501 and 1506, for example, the divisions agreed upon by the co-parcenors appear to have been horizontal as well as vertical, much importance being attached to the 'forebooths' and 'forelofts'.[71]

Not quite so tall nor so complex, two-storeyed flatted or 'stacked' cottages are a characteristic feature of the towns and villages of south-eastern Scotland, especially Fife, and in the early eighteenth century Defoe also found them in Northumberland: 'houses with the stairs to the second [that is, first] floor, going up on the outside of the house, so that one family may live below, and another above, without going in at the same door; which is the Scots way of living, and which we see in Alnwick and Warkworth, and several other towns . . .'.[72] In Fife, this type of dwelling dates back to at least the last quarter of the sixteenth century, but the existence of a forestair can point to any of several functional variations on the same basic building design; surviving examples include an inn, and a house over a shop.

From the evidence of archaeology and historical sources it is reasonably clear that early town houses, as well as structures of all periods in the backlands, were built mainly of wood, thatch, wattle and other perishable and potentially combustible materials. Urban excavations have recovered traces of buildings of timber box-frame construction that display varieties of technique in the uses of, for example, earth-fast posts and stone dwarf-walls, the outbuildings behind the street frontages generally having been small in scale and primitive in character.[73]

The earliest known illustration of Scottish town houses, a fifteenth-century view of Stirling burgh and castle in the background to an animated depiction of the battle of Bannockburn (Fig. 3), also shows jettied buildings, presumably of timber, and, although the sixteenth-century panoramic views of Edinburgh (1544) and St Andrews (?c.1580) are insufficiently clear to permit firm conclusions on the prevailing building materials, all-stone construction is likely to have been the exception rather than the rule in the centres of even these major towns at the time of the Reformation.[74] By this period, however, a few houses of stone and lime, a mark of better-class secular building practices in the country as a whole, had made an appearance in most towns, such atypical structures having been disproportionately the subjects of contemporary remark and modern architectural record.[75]

However, as some visitors observed, many apparently timber-built town houses were essentially stone buildings with frontages or galleries of timber. 'John Knox's House' in Edinburgh is a surviving case in point: the main part of the restored timber frontage, which dates from about 1570, is jettied in two stages, and incorporates small galleries set wholly in front of a main load-bearing stone wall. A similar wall did not lie immediately

Fig. 3: Stirling Castle and town in the background to the Battle of Bannockburn (from a fifteenth-century version of *Scotichronicon*, Corpus Christi College, Cambridge, MS 171, f. 165). The earliest known illustration of Scottish town houses. By permission of the Master and Fellows of Corpus Christi College, Cambridge.

behind the two-storeyed galleried frontage of the erstwhile Kinnoull Lodging in Perth (c. 1600), recorded prior to its demolition in 1966, but there the timber frame was set above a masonry screen at ground level and encased part of a stone stair turret; the three remaining load-bearing walls were also of stone (Fig. 4).[76]

Superficially, these timber-fronted houses of the later sixteenth and early seventeenth centuries thus appear to represent a late, hybrid stage in

Fig. 4: Kinnoull Lodging, 84 Watergate, Perth; in course of demolition 1968. Crown Copyright, Royal Commission on Ancient Monuments, Scotland.

a transition from timber to stone in the domestic urban buildings of late medieval and early modern Scotland. However, architectural 'evolution' is rarely so logical, progressive, and free of inconsistencies and anomalies. In England, a temporary reversion from stone to timber has been remarked upon in relation to the richer houses of Winchester and Southampton.[77] Similarly, despite the difficulties of obtaining domestic and foreign supplies of timber, large houses that are known to have been completely or substantially timber-framed were erected in Edinburgh

Lawnmarket in the last decades of the sixteenth century.[78] In this instance it is not too facile to suggest that English or continental architectural fashion lies at the root of these expensive and aberrant structures, tangible symbols perhaps of Scotland's outward-looking mercantile and urban communities?

NOTES

1. For general surveys of the architectural evidence, see I. G. Lindsay, 'The Scottish burgh', in G. Scott-Moncrieff (ed.), *The Stones of Scotland* (1938), 77–102; J. G. Dunbar, *The Historic Architecture of Scotland* (1966), 170–209; G. Stell, 'Architecture: the changing needs of society', in Brown, *Scottish Society*, 165–9; and *idem*, 'Scottish burgh houses 1560–1707', in A. T. Simpson and S. Stevenson (eds.), *Town Houses and Structures in Medieval Scotland: a Seminar* (1980), 1–31.

2. For general reviews of urban archaeology and survey in Scotland, see G. G. Simpson (ed.), *Scotland's Medieval Burghs, an archaeological heritage in danger* (1972); N. P. Brooks, 'Urban archaeology in Scotland', in M. W. Barley (ed.), *European Towns, their archaeology and early history* (1977), 19–33; G. G. Simpson, 'A viewpoint from Scotland', in 'The use of documentary sources by the archaeologist', *Archives*, xiii, no. 60 (Autumn 1978), 206–10; E. J. Talbot, 'Scottish medieval burghs', in P. Riden (ed.), *The Medieval Town in Britain* (1980), 15–21; and J. C. Murray, 'The Scottish Burgh Survey – a review', *PSAS*, cxiii (1983), 1–10.

3. *RRS*, ii, 479, no. 572.

4. *Discovery and Excavation 1973*, 38–9; J. H. Lewis, 'Excavations at Lanark Castle', *TDGAS*, 3rd series, liii (1977–8), 129–32; *Chron. Bower*, i, 528; Duncan, 'Perth', 39–40; R. C. Reid, 'The caput of Annandale or the curse of St Malachy', *TDGAS*, 3rd series, xxxii (1953–4), 155–66.

5. RCAHMS, *Inventory of monuments in the City of Edinburgh*, no. 1; *ibid., Stirlingshire*, i, no. 192. See also J. Gifford *et al.*, *The Buildings of Scotland, Edinburgh* (1984), 85–102; and R. Fawcett, *Edinburgh Castle* (Official guide, 1986 ed.).

6. H. M. Colvin (ed.), *The History of the King's Works*, ii (1963), 563–71; RCAHMS, *Roxburghshire*, ii, no. 905.

7. E. Beveridge, *The Churchyard Memorials of Crail* (1893), 5–6n, 8–9; RCAHMS, *Fife*, no. 200; *ibid., Kirkcudbright*, no. 262 (see also reports on excavation and excavated material in *PSAS*, xlviii (1914–15), 381–94, and *ibid.*, xci (1957–8), 117–38).

8. W. D. Simpson, 'The architectural history of Rothesay Castle', *TGAS* new series, ix (1939), 152–83, and *ibid.*, x (1941), 78–9.

9. *Cast. and Dom. Arch.*, i, 155–6; RCAHMS, *Fife*, no. 588.

10. *Cast. and Dom. Arch.*, iii, 202–4; R. C. Reid, 'Mauchline Castle', *TDGAS*, 3rd series, xvi (1929–30), 166–71; see also G. Stell, 'Castles and towers in south-western Scotland, some recent surveys', *ibid.*, lvii (1982), 65–77 at 71–2.

11. *Cast. and Dom. Arch.*, iii, 377–8.

12. *Ibid.*, iii, 561–3; RCAHMS, *Wigtown*, no. 461; and Stell in *TDGAS*, lvii (1982), 76.

13. *Cast. and Dom. Arch.*, iii, 606–8; Pryde, *Burghs*, no. 175. See also e.g. the Tower

Hotel, Hawick, rebuilt in 1677 out of the 'hous and tower of Hawick', which was on record at the end of the sixteenth century, RCAHMS, *Roxburghshire*, i, no. 234.

14. J. Ferguson, *Linlithgow Palace; its history and traditions* (1910), 114–17; RCAHMS, *West Lothian*, no. 356.

15. RCAHMS, *Fife*, no. 469; Royal Commission on Historical Monuments (England), *Inventory of monuments in the City of York*, ii (1972), The Defences, 95–100, 116–21, 125–32, 142–9, and 151–2.

16. Mackenzie, *Scottish Burghs*, 38–44. In the words of T. C. Smout, 'Much more use was made of town walls and town gates in the sixteenth and seventeenth centuries as defences against plague than as defences against armies' (T. C. Smout, 'Coping with plague in sixteenth and seventeenth century Scotland', *Scotia*, ii (1978), 19–33 at 24).

17. Colvin, *King's Works*, ii, 563–71; RCAHMS, *Edinburgh*, lxii–lxvi, nos. 59 and 60; a suggested identification of the fifteenth-century 'King's Wall' is made by J. Schofield *et al.*, 'Excavations south of Edinburgh High Street 1973–4', *PSAS*, cvii (1975–6), 155–241; RCAHMS, *Stirlingshire*, ii, no. 249; and see also *ibid.*, *Peeblesshire*, ii, no. 544.

18. *Chron. Perth*, 22; see also *APS*, v, 688–9, for a petition for its rebuilding in 1641. The history of the medieval bridge is summarised by H. R. G. Inglis, 'The roads and bridges in the early history of Scotland', *PSAS*, xlvii (1912–13), 303–33 at 322–4, and *idem*, 'The most ancient bridges in Britain', *PSAS*, xlix (1914–15), 256–74 at 259.

19. Timber construction proved unequal to the force of the River Ness, and the bridge at Inverness was rebuilt in stone in 1685. For a general review of the structural characteristics of late medieval bridges, see E. C. Ruddock, 'Bridges and roads in Scotland: 1400–1750', in A. Fenton and G. Stell (eds.), *Loads and Roads in Scotland and Beyond* (1984), 67–91, and for evidence of timber and timber/stone bridges, see G. Stell, 'By land and sea in medieval and early modern Scotland', in *ROSC*, iv (forthcoming). Bridge gateways at Glasgow and Dumfries are illustrated in J. Slezer, *Theatrum Scotiae* (1693 and later eds), pl. 16, and F. Grose, *The Antiquities of Scotland*, i (1789), 158–9.

20. RCAHMS, *Dumfries*, no. 131; *ibid.*, *East Lothian*, no. 75 (see also no. 76); *ibid.*, *Stirlingshire*, ii, no. 455; *ibid.*, *Peeblesshire*, ii, no. 630; J. A. Morris, *The brig of Ayr* (1912).

21. *Arbroath Liber*, ii, 40–42, no. 42, discussed by G. Hay, *The History of Arbroath* (1876), 314–15, and A. Graham, 'Old harbours and landing places on the east coast of Scotland', *PSAS*, cviii (1976–7), 332–65 at 335–6.

22. A. Graham, 'Archaeological notes on some harbours in eastern Scotland', *PSAS*, ci (1968–9), 200–85 at 257–9; *idem*, 'Old harbours', 340–43, citing J. Robertson, *The Book of Bon-Accord* (1839), 275–6; C. Brooks in *Abdn. Excavns.*, 37–45.

23. *Cast. and Dom. Arch.*, ii, 31–4; National Monuments Record of Scotland, report ABR/24/1 (1976); *Geog. Coll.*, ii, 236 and 297 (translation); Graham, 'Old harbours', 348–50.

24. J. Anderson, *The Black Book of Kincardineshire* (1844), 49–50, 60 (and *APS*, iv, 246, c 51); R. Neish, *Old Peterhead* (1950), 11; RCAHMS, *Fife*, no. 206; *ibid.*, *Orkney*, i, 56–7.

25. R. W. Munro, *Scottish Lighthouses* (1979), 23–4.

26. G. Stell, 'The earliest tolbooths: a preliminary account', *PSAS*, cxi (1981), 445–53.

27. RCAHMS, *Fife*, no. 124.

28. RCAHMS, *Midlothian*, no. 114; *ibid.*, *Edinburgh*, no. 105; Stell, 'Tolbooths', 449, 452 and refs cited.

29. J. W. Small, *Scottish Market Crosses* (1900), plates 19, 45, 50, 88, 102; RCAHMS, *Fife*, no. 285; *ibid.*, *Edinburgh*, nos. 61 and 119; *ibid.*, *Stirlingshire*, ii, no. 401; *ibid.*, *Peeblesshire*, ii, no. 541.

30. T. Ross *et al*, 'The Tailors' Hall, Cowgate', *BOEC*, xi (1922), 125–72; RCAHMS,

Edinburgh, no. 54. However, Magdalen Chapel, also in Cowgate, was used as a meeting-place by the Edinburgh hammermen even before 1560; see below and n. 49.

31. Cowan, *Parishes*, 26; *Prot. Bk. Young*, no. 55; RCAHMS, *Edinburgh*, nos. 86 and 89.

32. *Glas. Reg.*, i, 97–8, no. 114; RCAHMS, *Roxburghshire*, i, no. 414.

33. *Vet. Mon.*, 527, cited in RCAHMS, *Roxburghshire*, i, no. 504 at 240–41.

34. W. E. K. Rankin, *The Parish Church of the Holy Trinity St Andrews* (1955), 14–29.

35. W. J. Dillon, 'Pre-Reformation church', in A. I. Dunlop (ed.), *The Royal Burgh of Ayr* (1953), 88–96; R. G. Cant, 'The medieval kirk of Crail', in A. C. O'Connor and D. V. Clarke (eds.), *From the Stone Age to the Forty-Five* (1983), 368–83; RCAHMS, *Fife*, no. 121; J. Grant, *Old and New Edinburgh* (1882), i, 139, 141; D. Ure, *The History of Rutherglen and East-Kilbride* (1793), 80–81; W. Duke, 'Notice of the fabric of St Vigean's Church, Forfarshire . . .', *PSAS*, ix (1870–2), 481–98.

36. J. Hunter, 'The Church of St Nicholas, Aberdeen', *PSAS*, cv (1972–4), 236–47; see also *St. Nich. Cart., passim*.

37. RCAHMS, *Fife*, no. 339; *Eccles. Arch.*, ii, 266–9; and J. M. Davidson, 'St Kentigern's Church, Lanark', *PSAS*, xlvi (1911–12), 133–9.

38. G. Hay, 'The late medieval development of the High Kirk of St Giles, Edinburgh', *PSAS*, cvii (1975–6), 242–60. For a general review of late medieval town churches, see e.g. W. E. K. Rankin, 'Scottish burgh churches in the 15th century', *RSCHS*, vii (1941), 63–75; and Stell, 'Architecture', in Brown, *Scottish Society*, 167–71.

39. *Dunf. Reg.*, 291–3, no. 413 (see also *ibid.*, 293–301, nos. 414–17); *Dundee Chrs.*, 19–23; *Stirling Chrs.*, 71–3, no. 37.

40. W. D. Simpson, *A History of Saint John's Kirk of Perth* (1958); RCAHMS, *Stirlingshire*, i, no. 131; *Eccles. Arch.*, iii, 123–32; see also R. Fawcett, 'Late Gothic architecture in Scotland: considerations on the influence of the Low Countries', *PSAS*, cxii (1982), 477–96.

41. RCAHMS, *East Lothian*, no. 68.

42. Ferguson 1905; RCAHMS, *West Lothian*, no. 352; RCAHMS, *Fife*, no. 168; and Rankin, *Holy Trinity*.

43. Rankin, *Holy Trinity*, 52–3; altar foundations described in *ibid.*, 54–99.

44. RCAHMS, *Midlothian*, no. 75; *ibid.*, *Fife*, no. 224; Cowan, *Parishes*, 44; Cowan and Easson, *Religious Houses*, 218.

45. For the chapel of St John, Stranraer, see e.g. *Geog. Coll.*, ii, 92, and P. H. M'Kerlie, *History of the Lands and their Owners in Galloway*, i (1870), 130, 144.

46. J. Durkan, 'The bishop's barony of Glasgow in pre-Reformation times', *RSCHS*, xxii (1986), 277–301 at 296 ff.

47. J. Ferguson, *Ecclesia Antiqua* (1905), 139, 328–9.

48. *Lanark Recs.*, xxiv–xxvi and refs cited. Similarly, medieval Forfar was served by a chapel, its parish altar being in Restenneth Priory 1½ miles to the east. A surviving portion of this chapel was evidently incorporated in a later church and was said in 1760 to have possessed 'a Saxon door and small narrow windows'; this was the usual description applied to a Romanesque or Transitional structure, the tower of Restenneth itself being similarly described. D. W. Kemp (ed.), *Tours in Scotland . . . by Richard Pococke, Bishop of Meath* (SHS, 1st series i, 1887), 217–18.

49. RCAHMS, *Edinburgh*, no. 6; Cowan and Easson, *Religious Houses*, 176–7.

50. *Eccles. Arch.*, ii, 215–17; Cowan and Easson, *Religious Houses*, 172.

51. RCAHMS, *Fife*, nos. 464 and 485; Cowan and Easson, *Religious Houses*, 119–21.

52. RCAHMS, *Fife*, no. 276; RCAHMS, *Kirkcudbright*, no. 216.

53. J. Cooper, 'The church and convent of the Grey Friars, Elgin', *Trans. Aberdeen*

Ecclesiol. Soc., ii (1890–3), part v, 45–53; *Eccles. Arch.*, iii, 356–8; H. B. Mackintosh, *Elgin Past and Present* (1914), 134–44; W. J. Lindsay, 'Digging up auld Ayr, an excavation at 102–104 High Street', *Ayrshire Coll.*, xiv, no. v (1985).

54. *Eccles. Arch.*, iii, 296–309; RCAHMS, *West Lothian*, no. 321; Cowan and Easson, *Religious Houses*, 137–8, and refs cited. See also Ferguson, *Ecclesia Antiqua*, 332–4.

55. RCAHMS, *Peeblesshire*, ii, no. 480; and J. Wordsworth, 'Friarscroft and the Trinitarians in Dunbar', *PSAS*, cxiii (1983), 478–88.

56. J. D. Duncan, 'House, Nos 3–7 Castle Street', *The Regality Club*, i (1889), 45–53; W. Gemmell, *The Oldest House in Glasgow* (1910); J. A. Brown, 'Provand's Lordship . . .', *TSES*, ix (1927–30), 13–22; and J. L. Mackie, *Provand's Lordship* (n.d.).

57. RCAHMS, *Orkney*, ii, no. 403.

58. *Cast. and Dom. Arch.*, ii, 58–60; *ibid.*, v, 91–3; R. G. Cant, *Old Elgin* (1954), 12–13.

59. N. P. Brooks, ' "St John's House": its history and archaeology', *St Andrews Preservation Trust Annual Report* (1976), 11–16; R. G. Cant, *The College of St Salvator* (1950), 82–3; and RCAHMS, *Fife*, nos. 467–8 *passim*.

60. RCAHMS, *Fife*, no. 276; *ibid.*, *Edinburgh*, no. 90; R. L. Mackie *et al*, *Arbroath Abbey* (Official guide, revised ed. 1982), 15, 19; RCAHMS, *Wigtown*, no. 462.

61. RCAHMS; *Stirlingshire*, ii, nos. 227, 230.

62. *Cast. and Dom. Arch.*, i, 508–14; *Edinburgh Architectural Association Sketch Book*, ii (1878–9), plates 35–7; Stell, 'Architecture', in Brown, *Scottish Society*, 163–7; RCAHMS, *West Lothian*, no. 356; and C. McWilliam, *The Buildings of Scotland, Lothian except Edinburgh* (1978), 291–301.

63. NMRS, photographs (1958 and later). For building activity at Falkland Palace, see e.g. *Works Accts.*, i, p. xiii, and refs cited; RCAHMS, *Fife*, nos. 238, 239 and 49.

64. RCAHMS, *Kirkcudbright*, no. 218.

65. E.g. RCAHMS, *Edinburgh*, no. 90; NMRS, drawings of 48–50 Shiprow and Provost Ross's House, Aberdeen; RCAHMS, *Roxburghshire*, i, no. 234; *ibid.*, *Peeblesshire*, ii, no. 540; *Peebles Chrs.*, lix; *Geog. Coll.*, ii, 17.

66. J. Taylor, *A Journey to Edenborough in Scotland* (1903), 107.

67. ECA, MS Extent Roll for the Annuity Tax, 1635, used by C. B. B. Watson, 'List of owners of property in Edinburgh, 1635', *BOEC*, xiii (1924), 93–146; M. Ash in Schofield, 'High Street excavations', 162–8; and discussed by W. Makey, 'Edinburgh in mid-seventeenth century' in Lynch, *Early Modern Town*, 206–15. The roll provides details of some 4,000 households and over 900 businesses, the geographical zones and probably the size and quality of housing being reflected in the differences in rent levels between the centre of the burgh and its outskirts.

68. P. Robinson, 'Tenements: a pre-industrial urban tradition', *ROSC*, i (1984), 52–64.

69. RCAHMS, *Edinburgh*, no. 39 and refs cited; Gifford, *Edinburgh*, 206–8.

70. RCAHMS, *Edinburgh*, no. 14; R. Hurd, *Gladstone's Land* (1966 ed.), 6–9; Robinson, 'Tenements', 58–9.

71. *Prot. Bk. Young*, nos. 1120, 1251, 1388 and 1653.

72. Daniel Defoe, *A Tour through the Whole Island of Great Britain* (1724–6; 1968 reprint), ii, 693.

73. e.g. H. K. Murray, 'Medieval wooden and wattle buildings excavated in Perth and Aberdeen', in Simpson and Stevenson, *Town Houses*, 39–52; *idem*, in *Abdn. Excavns.*, 224–8.

74. Cambridge, Corpus Christi College, MS 171, f. 265 (reproduced in G. W. S. Barrow, *Robert Bruce* (1965), frontispiece); British Library, Cotton MSS, Augustus I, ii, 56 (reproduced in *Bannatyne Misc*, i, opp. 184 and in this volume as jacket illustration); NLS,

MS Acc. 2887 (reproduced and discussed by D. McRoberts (ed.), *The Medieval Church of St Andrews* (1976), 151–2 and frontispiece).

75. e.g. *Abdn. Recs.*, pp. lix–lx, n., and 14; *C.A. Chrs.*, i, no. 13; *St Giles. Reg.*, 57, no. 42; *Prot. Bk. Carruthers*, 39; and *Scone Liber*, no. 80. For architectural records, see e.g. *Cast. and Dom. Arch.*, i, 508–14, and F. C. Mears, 'Notes on a medieval burgess's house at Inverkeithing', *PSAS*, xlvii (1912–13), 343–8.

76. Stell, 'Burgh houses', 17–18.

77. Reynolds, *English Towns*, 196 and refs cited.

78. J. M. D. Peddie, 'Description of an old timber building in the Lawnmarket, Edinburgh', *PSAS*, xviii (1883–4), 465–76.

Part Two

The Ecclesiastical Setting

5

The Emergence of the Urban Parish

Ian B. Cowan

The emergence of the urban parish cannot be dissociated from that of parochial origins in general. Indeed, it may be doubted whether many truly urban parishes existed in medieval Scotland. Burghs acted as a catalyst and frequently, but not invariably, contained the church of the parish in which they stood. Whether a church initially stood within a town is often debatable; it is certain it did not always do so. The parish itself was seldom only co-extensive with the burgh and usually extended far beyond its limits. To this extent the origins of the urban parish must be sought not in the town, but rather in the countryside surrounding it, in which parishes recognisably antedate the appearance of towns.

Initially the term *parochia* was applied to describe the particular area covered by the jurisdiction of any religious institution.[1] On occasions it might denote a bishop's or abbot's sphere of authority, and even in the twelfth century it was still being used in that sense. In the 'Glasgow Inquest', c. 1114, the terminology *parochia Cumbrensis* is used to denote the sphere of influence of the bishops of Glasgow throughout Cumbria, while by the mid-twelfth century *parochia* can be equated with the territorial limits of the bishopric of Glasgow.[2] In quite a different context, however, David I confirmed to the abbey of Dunfermline the *parochiam totam Fotherif*, an area which can neither be equated with a diocese nor with a strictly delimited parish, but rather with a sphere of ecclesiastical influence which may have pertained at one period to some religious institution.[3]

Even in the first half of the twelfth century, when the term is used in connection with a church which undoubtedly became parochial, its use is characterised by a lack of precision, and it would appear to be equatable with areas of jurisdiction enjoyed by a mother church. It would seem to be in this sense that the church of Old Roxburgh in *capellis et parochiis* was granted to the bishopric of Glasgow, and the church of Mow, *cum parochiis*, was confirmed to Kelso.[4] It was only gradually that these diversities disappeared and the term *parochia* assumed its present connotation as an area within the jurisdiction of a baptismal church. Nevertheless, it is occasionally found in this precise sense even in twelfth-century records, as in a reference which occurs between 1185 and 1187 to the *parochia ecclesia de Libertun* in Lanarkshire.[5] It is rash to assume that parishes which do not bear this precise designation are parochial rather than proprietorial, and it is not until the thirteenth century that the use of *parochia* and *parochia ecclesia* become commonplace.[6]

The question of terminology, while important, is not, however, conclusive, as it is apparent that throughout the twelfth century a parochial system was gradually taking shape under Anglo-Norman influence, the principal steps in this direction being taken during the reign of David I (1124–53), although constant progress had been made towards such a system from the beginning of the century. These developments were not entirely innovatory, but owed much to earlier ecclesiastical organisation. In Scotland, as in England, parishes were at first mostly large districts served by clergy resident at central churches, known to early writers as *monasteria* or ministers, but while these clergy shared a communal life, they were not necessarily bound by any rule; they were rather a body of secular clergy who were frequently married and held hereditary prebends.[7] South of the Forth-Clyde line, such institutions are readily identifiable at Whithorn, Kirkcudbright, Applegarth, Hoddam and Govan; north of that line, communities of Culdees who, whatever their origins, had by the eleventh century become little more than colleges of secular priests, performed a similar function at most of their known centres.[8]

Originally these clergy, or clerks appointed by them, held services within certain areas which were frequently quite extensive and not necessarily geographically compact. Gradually, however, new churches were founded within these bounds, sometimes by the king or bishop but more frequently by the local landowner who appointed a resident priest and so assumed the patronage of the church. This church – the proprietary church – was already discernible in the eleventh century, the founder and his heirs providing for the service of the church while for the sustenance of the *curatus* or priest in charge a tract of land was usually attached to the church.[9] With these developments, which ended the necessity for a community of secular priests, the minister either declined in status, itself assuming the form of a parish church, or retained its community status by its personnel either entering one of the orders of canons regular or continuing to serve a bishop as his *familia*, their previous existence revealed only by the survival of various dues or rights.[10]

The Norman penetration of Scotland, and the subsequent re-allocation of land into feudal fiefs, continued to obscure these earlier arrangements even further, and the coincidence of parish, fief and vill, although the latter was far from normal, became an observable part of feudal development in the twelfth century.[11] The identification between parish, fief and vill was made closer, moreover, by an 'assize' of David which made compulsory the exaction of teind.[12] Earlier churches had possibly been supported by certain dues and certainly by an allotment of land, the extent of which seems to have varied. The appropriation of definite dues to a particular church was new, however, and this levying of teinds from the estate upon which the church was built undoubtedly had the effect of territorially and legally creating the parochial unit.[13]

The creation of parishes was not, however, confined to the creation of feudal fiefs and several new parishes resulted from the erection of burghs which went on apace during the reign of David I and his successors. Burghs in the twelfth century were founded by the king or with royal permission by bishops, abbots and later by secular lords.[14] All in their own ways played some part in the creation of the parochial system, a process which can be most clearly seen in burghs which were ecclesiastically inspired. Hence, eleven of the thirteen Scottish cathedral sites attracted urban settlements.[15] Only the Isles, which possessed no recognised diocesan centre for much of its existence, and Lismore, which although described in the fifteenth century as a *civitas*, remained poverty-stricken and rural, understandably failed to generate a community.[16] In most cases the emergence of a cathedral was the governing factor in this development. At Elgin, however, the establishment of the burgh owed little or nothing to the establishment of the cathedral, for of all the Scottish cathedrals, this was one of the last to find a permanent site, the bishop ending a previous peripatetic existence only when he settled at Elgin in 1224.[17] By that date, both burgh and parish church, which remained independent of the cathedral, were of fairly long-standing origin, the former having been erected by David I between 1130 and his death in 1153 while the patronage of the church with its associated chapels of St Andrews and Manbeen, the existence of which may indicate the prior appearance of a wider *parochia*, was also acquired by that king who conferred them upon his clerk, Richard de Prebenda. Subsequently, however, William the Lion, having protected the life interests of Richard and his clerk Walter to the benefice, granted them to the bishopric of Moray between 1187 and 1189.[18] In all probability this church, which subsequently became parochial, antedated the erection of the burgh, but this must remain conjectural.

With the exception of Elgin, the existence of a cathedral was a dominant feature, if not always the primary factor in the creation of ten burghs in which the superiority pertained to the bishops of their respective dioceses. Nevertheless, where the bishopric was of considerable antiquity the emergence of the church long preceded the appearance of the burgh. At Brechin a community of Culdees with a prior at their head served a church with which a bishop was associated from an early period, possibly much earlier than the reign of David I when proof of its existence is first conclusively found; this ecclesiastical community formed the focal point around which an urban community grew.[19] David himself granted the bishop the right of holding a weekly market in the *villa* of Brechin. Subsequently the town was usually referred to as a *civitas*, not formally appearing as a burgh until 28 April 1488.[20]

If the evidence for the existence of a pre-burghal religious community is less conclusive at other cathedral sites, a strong case for their existence can be mounted at both Dunblane and Dunkeld. Here too the existence of clerks who acted as the bishops' *familia* led in the thirteenth century to the establishment of cathedrals which in turn stimulated the erection of burghs or *civitates* dependent upon their respective bishops.[21] Evidence is unfortunately lacking for the existence of a pre-cathedral church at Dunblane, but the church of the Holy Trinity, Dunkeld, which was granted to Dunfermline Abbey c. 1150, may have formed the mother church of a widespread *parochia* which, when reduced in status, served Dunkeld alone until it was superseded c. 1234 by the foundation of the cathedral church of St Columba.[22] Parochial service thereafter was provided within each of the cathedrals, but the status of their burghs is for long uncertain.[23] Dunblane had certainly attained burghal status in the course of the thirteenth and fourteenth centuries, but thereafter appears to have enjoyed the standing of a *civitas*. Dunkeld, on the other hand, was certainly a burgh by 1511/12, but may equally have been equated with a *civitas* from an early period.[24]

If the evidence for developments at Brechin, Dunblane and Dunkeld is tenuous, facts about the materialisation of Old Aberdeen and Glasgow are virtually non-existent. The site of the north-eastern see is said to have been transferred from Mortlach to Aberdeen by David I in 1125.[25] The clergy who served this church only gradually acquired a corporate identity, and the church which they served in turn acted not only as a cathedral and the fulcrum of a *civitas* but also as a church which was both 'baptismal and parochial'.[26] The community served by a vicar pensioner did not, however, attain full burghal status until 1489 when the township of Old Aberdeen was erected as a burgh of barony in favour of the bishop of Aberdeen.[27] Nine years later the erection of the parish of Snow to serve a new suburb of Old Aberdeen resulted in a duality of parishes within the burgh, but this unique arrangement was not to survive the Reformation.[28] The early history of Glasgow is no less obscure, and until the Glasgow Inquest of c. 1114 during the episcopate of Bishop John (c. 1114 x 1118–47) and the consecration of the cathedral on 7 July 1136, there is no evidence for the existence of either a church or a community of clerks.[29] This was quickly changed with the creation of a small chapter by Bishop John who 'assigned the parish of Glasgow, with its whole rights and liberties' to form one of the prebends of the cathedral. The original limits of this parish appear to have been confined to the vill of Glasgow and several adjacent properties, including Shettleston, to which Barlanark was added at a later date.[30] A parish was thus constituted before the community was given formal burghal status between 1175 and 1178 when William the Lion granted to the bishop the right to erect a burgh at Glasgow with a weekly market and all the liberties of a king's burgh.[31]

In all these instances with the exception of Elgin the cathedral acted in a dual capacity as cathedral and parish church; an arrangement which could cause problems of service, but was resolved at Glasgow which embraced both burgh and barony by the appointment of a vicar *in burgo* and a vicar *in rure*.[32] This problem had been avoided at Elgin by the separation of parochial and diocesan responsibilities, and so too at Kirkwall, which is not perhaps typical as Orkney only became part of the kingdom of Scotland in 1469; here the parish church of St Olaf founded by Earl Ragnvald in the eleventh century contained the cathedral of St Magnus, begun in 1137, within its bounds.[33] The circumstances which led to this arrangement are uncertain and the charter of 31 March 1486 which recognised Kirkwall as a city and royal burgh is equally unhelpful as to the town's previous status, although almost certainly it possessed urban privileges.[34] Kirkwall is not alone in providing evidence which is comparatively late, for even on the Scottish mainland the town of Dornoch, which housed the cathedral church of Caithness, is not mentioned as a burgh holding from the bishop of that diocese until 1607.[35] Nevertheless, the town appears on record as early as 1127 x 53 when David I commanded Reinwald, earl of Orkney, to respect the monks dwelling at 'Durnach in Ceiteneis'.[36] It is styled the city of Dornoch in Bishop Gilbert's erection of the chapter, while in 1275 Bishop Archibald calls it his town of Dornoch.[37] This town clearly possessed a church before the foundation of Bishop Gilbert's cathedral: this in turn can be identified with the church of St Bar which was contiguous to the cathedral and apparently continued to act as the parish church after its erection, as its buildings existed until the seventeenth century; notice of the cemetery of St Finbar occurs in several boundary charters.[38]

These cathedrals were all staffed by secular canons, but two Scottish cathedrals, Whithorn and St Andrews, consisted of regular clergy and these equally gave rise to burghs. Of the two, Whithorn is relatively straightforward as, whatever the antecedents of the religious community situated there, its foundation led ultimately to the creation of a burgh of barony dependent upon the prior and canons of Whithorn.[39] Little is known of its early history after Robert I granted the *villa* of Whithorn as a free burgh to the prior and convent in 1325; it may not have prospered as a re-erection took place in 1511.[40] St Andrews, on the other hand, presents a wealth of early material which is not easy of interpretation. It is clear, however, that the church of St Andrews or Kilrimont was the mother church of a *parochia* of considerable extent, one version (B) of the foundation legend claiming that the original *parochia* consisted of the whole of Fife east of a line drawn from Largo on the Firth of Forth through Ceres to Naughton on the Firth of Tay.[41] Two groups of clergy served this church (the present St Rule's Church), which also acted as the bishop's cathedral, but no regular service was provided at the high altar in 1124, although its revenues were divided into seven portions, five of which supported 'personages' held by married clergy (*personae*) who did not lead a communal life and whose only duty lay in providing hospitality to pilgrims and strangers.[42] The community of Celi Dé, who numbered thirteen c. 1114, held their prebends hereditarily, and though they had no rights connected with the church of St Andrew at this date and celebrated their offices at a side altar of the church, their position may be compared with the Celi Dé at Armagh who were responsible for the choral and other services in that church.[43] Robert, bishop of St Andrews, undertook the re-building of St Rule's c. 1126 x 27, and this work was almost completed in 1144 when by the foundation of the priory of St Andrews in that year the church passed into the hands of the Augustinian canons.[44] It was, however, only after a long struggle over rights in the election of the bishops that the Culdees eventually departed in the mid-thirteenth century and entered the neighbouring church of St Mary.[45]

The foundation of the burgh between 1124 and 1144, probably c. 1114, just to the west of the older ecclesiastical settlement of Kilrimont, appears to have antedated the creation of the priory; this, and the uncertain relationship of the bishop to his monastic cathedral, may explain why the priory church did not provide parochial services, these being instead undertaken by the church of the Holy Trinity which appears as the parish church of St Andrews in the 1144 charter.[46] The origins of this church whose bounds included the whole 'shire' of Kilrimont are uncertain; it probably antedates the erection of the burgh even though its first known parson, Matthew, archdeacon of St Andrews, does not appear on record until a date between 1147–52 and 1172.[57] Significantly, when Richard, bishop-elect of St Andrews, granted to the priory the parish church, with the chapels of the whole 'shire' of Kilrimont, the grant included not only its teinds and oblations but also all rights belonging to the parish church –

which unusually for this period is designated as such – from Scots, Flemish, English, both within and without the burgh.[48]

If the interconnection between the foundation of cathedrals and the establishment of parishes is complex, and particularly so when the bishop's cathedral was also a religious house, the relationship between the foundation of religious houses and the emergence of an urban parish is correspondingly straightforward. In some cases, however, the king pre-empted the possible aspirations of a religious house by establishing a king's burgh. Dunfermline, for example, was founded by David I between 1124 and 1127.[49] The presence of the priory (which became an abbey in 1128), to which an already existing church had been granted to the monks by David, probably encouraged the early decay of the king's burgh and its replacement by a community dependent upon the abbey which provided the parochial services; the abbey eventually attained its own burgh apparently on the opposite bank of the Tower Burn from that on which the king's burgh had probably been situated.[50]

A similar situation might have arisen at Selkirk after David I founded a Tironensian house there in 1113 on what may have been an earlier site at what became subsequently known as Selkirk Monachorum or Selkirk Abbatis.[51] The monks, however, were transferred to Kelso in 1128, leaving behind a church which continued to act as parochial until c. 1300 when it became merged with the church of Selkirk Regis, which in earlier confirmations of both churches to Kelso is referred to as the church of the other Selkirk.[52] The origins of this site are obscure, but may represent an attempt to found a king's burgh, for William the Lion refers on one occasion to the 'parish of his town of Selkirk'.[53] It is not, however, until 1328 that definite proof of a king's burgh is forthcoming.[54] By that date the two parishes had effectively merged, but it is clear that for two centuries the dual effect of an abortive monastic foundation and an attempt to found a community dependent upon the crown had resulted in the evolution of two distinct, but nevertheless essentially rural, parishes.[55]

A few king's burghs situated at religious houses did, however, manage to preserve their status. Haddington was erected by David I between 1124 and 1153 and, if temporarily assigned to Ada, wife of Earl Henry, who founded the Cistercian priory or nunnery there before 1159, fell to the crown on Ada's death in 1178.[56] The church with its chapels had, however, been granted to the priory of St Andrews by David I c. 1139.[57] To this extent the nunnery had little control over the burgh or its church. Nevertheless, certain revenues of the church had been granted to the priory by Richard, bishop of St Andrews (1163–78), and this in turn may have been the origin of, or included, the chapel of St Martin in the Nungate.[58]

In terms of the date of the priory's foundation and status, the maintenance of the king's burgh at Haddington is understandable. More surprisingly, the same situation arose at Jedburgh which, although a priory had been founded c. 1138, was given the status of a king's burgh by Malcolm IV, 1159 x 65, created within what might have been justly regarded as the priory's own sphere of interest.[59] Parochial bounds in this case were not determined by the foundation of the burgh but by a much older ecclesiastical organisation. The *mansiones* of the two 'Geddevrd' which then belonged to the see of Lindisfarne are recorded as early as c. 854, but the first distinct notice of a church is not until c. 1080.[60] This church probably stood at Old Jedburgh, about five miles from the site of the priory, to which David I confirmed the *monasterium* Jeddewrde.[61] Thus the original mother church was thereafter apparently superseded by the priory which became responsible for all parochial services for both the burgh and its rural hinterland, one of the canons acting as a parochial chaplain.[62] In this instance the creation of the burgh seems to have added little to the emergence of the parish, although the burgh eventually acted as host to the parish church.

This was not always the case and the foundation of a religious house could lead to the growth of an urban community and subsequent creation of a burgh. Most religious communities did, however, desire solitude and in this respect did not encourage urban growth. In consequence the process is surprisingly relatively limited. As has been noted, Dunfermline ultimately achieved its own burgh, but few religious houses possessed the privilege from an early date. Indeed, only Holyrood and Arbroath appear to have achieved their own burghs within a few years of their foundations.[63] The former received, on or shortly after its foundation in 1128, permission to build and enclose the burgh which came to be known as Canongate.[64] Between 1178 and 1182 Arbroath received a similar privilege. In both instances a new urban parish appears to have been carved out of the existing parish in which the abbeys lay.[65]

Canongate was detached from the widespread *parochia* of St Cuthbert under the castle, which was itself annexed to Holyrood at its foundation.[66] As far as the burgh was concerned, service was provided at the parochial aisle within the nave of the abbey at which one of the canons served.[67] Such a solution was not so easily attained at the abbey of Arbroath. Here, the church of the vill, known as St Vigeans, situated some one and a half miles distant from the abbey, passed to the abbey on its foundation and apparently continued to serve its previous bounds which now included the abbey and its burgh.[68] So too at Kelso, first mentioned as a burgh with the abbot and convent as its superior in 1237,[69] for a church which was confirmed to the abbey on its transference from Selkirk in 1128 was in existence before that event; thereafter the history of the church becomes one with that of the abbey, the cure being served by a vicar pensioner responsible to the abbot.[70]

With the exception of these four burghs, evidence for burghs of which the superior was head of a religious house is lacking until the erection of Whithorn in 1325.[71] Thereafter, Paisley in 1488, Culross in 1490, Kinloss in 1497, Pittenweem in 1526 and Dryburgh in 1526/7 constitute the remaining pre-Reformation abbatial burghs.[72] In most, if not in all cases, a pre-burghal community can be surmised, but the effect of such a community on the emergence of parishes must have been slight. These houses and others which did not attain burgh status of their own, but nevertheless may have possessed small communities at their gates, appear instead to have formed the focal point of an essentially rural parish. In some cases, as at Blantyre (1598/9), Melrose (x 1605) and Coupar Angus (1607), burgh status came only after the Reformation when with the secularisation of religious houses lords of erection sought increased prestige for themselves and their newly acquired communities.[73]

Even after their inception the majority of such burghs remained essentially rural and in consequence very few of their associated parishes were urban in character. Those which were so were invariably creations of the crown. Edinburgh is the outstanding example of such a parish, bounded by the Canongate at one extremity and surrounded by St Cuthbert under the castle and its pendicles of Corstorphine and Liberton on the other three sides. In this respect it is clear that the parish of St Giles which served the burgh of Edinburgh was carved out of the ancient *parochia* of St Cuthbert which may date back to the ninth century. The first documentary evidence comes, however, in a charter which preceded the foundation of Holyrood in 1128. In this charter the king endows the church with lands which were later transferred with the church itself in the abbey's foundation charter. In these early grants there is no mention of the later parish church of Edinburgh – St Giles. David did, however, grant the church of the castle with all its rights to the abbey of Holyrood. In all probability at Edinburgh, as in other early Scottish burghs such as Peebles and Stirling, it was this church which initially served the community. Nevertheless, it would appear that a church dedicated to St Giles had been erected by the early twelfth century. This may not as yet have been the church of the community or burgh which had been created by David 1124 x 27, and with which the lands subsequently known as the grange of St Giles came to be associated. The history of the burgh church remains hazy until the early fourteenth century, but it is clear that in this case at least the emergence of the parish was brought about solely by the erection of the burgh.[74]

So too was the case at Berwick where, of the three churches associated with the town, St Laurence, St Mary and Holy Trinity, the first two appear to antedate the last which became the parish church of the burgh only on or after its foundation by earl David between 1119 and 1124.[75] Thereafter the churches of St Mary, granted to the priory of Durham 1130 x 1133, and St Laurence, also granted to Durham 1147 x 1150, continued to serve the area adjoining Berwick.[76] For a time they may also have served the burgh, for the parish church of Holy Trinity in Berwick, like that of St Giles, Edinburgh, does not appear on record until the thirteenth century, and may or may not have been included among the churches of Berwick confirmed to Durham by Richard, bishop of St Andrews, 1163 x 1178.[77] Only with the passage of time was a more rational solution to emerge. By the thirteenth century the two landward parishes had combined to form the parish of Bondington, which in turn, and probably precipitated by the expansion of the burgh, was merged by the end of the century with that of Holy Trinity.[78]

To what extent other burghal parishes emerged as a result of similar developments is less clear-cut, but this appears to have been the case at New Aberdeen which became a burgh by a grant of David I between 1124 and 1153, and confirmed by William the Lion, 1173 x 84.[79] Following upon the erection of the burgh, which as elsewhere was undoubtedly influenced by its proximity to a river and the sea, the parish of St Nicholas appears to have been carved from the vill of Old Aberdeen with the safeguard that the newly erected church was annexed to the bishopric of Aberdeen and subsequently became the prebend of the bishop.[80]

Elsewhere the erection of an urban parish in this manner is less certain. Dundee, a town 1178 x 82, not yet designated as a burgh, had attained burghal status by the early 1190s when David, earl of Huntingdon, as superior granted to his newly founded abbey of Lindores a toft in his burgh of Dundee.[81] The church of St Mary which the earl reputedly built in the field which was called the wheat field was granted to the abbey at the same time, 1191 x 95, and thereafter was apparently accounted the parish church of the burgh, although lying outwith its bounds and serving the hinterland around it. Nevertheless, an earlier church dedicated to St Clement, which had almost certainly served the earlier township, continued to act in this capacity, and according to Boece this ancient church was attended by the greater part of the townspeople. In all probability St Mary's only began to fulfil its role as the parish church of Dundee with the westward expansion of the burgh from the thirteenth century, but even then St Clement's remained in service until the period of the Reformation.[82] Equal uncertainty as to the identity of the earliest urban church surrounds most other major burghs. At Stirling, however, Alexander I caused the chapel of the castle to be dedicated and granted to it the teinds of all his demesnes in the soke of Stirling.[83] However, not until the reign of his successor, David I, does Stirling appear as a burgh within the vill of Stirling.[84] Its *parochia* contained at least two churches, both of which were annexed to Dunfermline c. 1150.[85] One of these chapels may have been the church of the castle, but the other undoubtedly was the later burgh church of the Holy Rude. Whether this was an existing church or erected *de novo* to serve the burgh cannot be ascertained, but as its parochial boundaries transcended that of the burgh, the existence of a pre-burghal church may be the preferable of the two possibilities.[86]

Similarly, at Perth, where the burgh was created by David I between 1124 and 1127, the church of St John the Baptist was confirmed to Dunfermline abbey in 1128 by the same king. In the same period between 1126 and 1159, Robert, bishop of St Andrews, confirmed to the abbey the church of Perth and its pendicle of St Leonards.[87] The relationship between the two churches is obscure, but the early ecclesiastical history of most Scottish burghs is equally obscure. If anything can be ascertained, it does appear that churches often pre-dated the formal erection of a burgh. This was certainly the case at Roxburgh, where the burgh was created by Earl David between 1119 and 1124.[88] The original church was held, significantly, by Ascelin, archdeacon of Glasgow (1126 x 27–1153 x 56), and granted only after his death in chapels and in parishes to the church of Glasgow by Malcolm IV (1153 x 56).[89]

Ascelin had also held the churches of the burgh.[90] Of these the church of St James, dedicated on 7 April 1134, appears to have been a new erection, as was the church of the Holy Sepulchre also situated within the burgh which may have been connected with the Knights of St John.[91] The church of the castle, dedicated to St John the Evangelist, of which one of its two chaplains had the status of parson, may as elsewhere have originally served the community.[92] Initially, however, all three churches appear to have been accounted as part of the *parochia* of Old Roxburgh and hence their possession by Ascelin. Only after his death did the burgh's churches secure their own identities; this freedom allowed David I to grant them to his abbey of Kelso, although even then Herbert, bishop of Glasgow, managed to retain until c. 1160 a portion of their land in his own hands.[93]

If Roxburgh St James is a clear example of a burgh church usurping the functions of an earlier mother church, other burghs present a mixed picture. At Dumfries the church may have been in existence by the 1150s when Radulf, sub-king of Strathnith, granted land in 'Dronfres' to the hospital of St Peter at York.[94] The burgh there was created in July x August 1186 and the church was subsequently granted to Kelso by William the Lion between 1183 and 1188. This grant did not pass unchallenged and the unsuccessful action by Ralph, dean of Dumfries, who attempted to annul the abbey's right, would seem to have rested on an anterior right to a pre-burghal church.[95] At Inverness likewise the grant by William the Lion (1165 x 1171) of one ploughgate of arable to Thomas the priest would suggest, despite the erection of the burgh between 1130 and 1153, a church which was still proprietorial rather than parochial, and it was not until sometime later that the church was granted by the same king to Arbroath Abbey.[96]

A clearer example of a pre-burghal church occurs, however, at Lanark where the burgh was apparently created by Malcolm IV between 1153 and 1159.[97] Somewhat earlier, between 1150 and 1153, David I had granted to the newly founded abbey of Dryburgh the church of Lanark with its lands, teinds and other rights, and the church of Pettinain with all its pertinents and the carucate of land in the vill or kirktoun which had previously been held by Nicholas, the king's clerk.[98] The church which stood about a quarter of a mile to the south-west of Lanark had obviously been the mother church of a considerable *parochia* as a series of legal actions in the thirteenth century involving dues owed to the church clearly indicates.[99] At Peebles likewise the mother church appears in the Glasgow Inquest of c. 1114 and thus precedes the burgh founded in 1152/3 by almost forty years.[100] The original church may not, however, have been situated within the burgh, and the chapel of the castle of Peebles which was confirmed to the monks of Kelso by William the Lion c. 1193, saving the rights of the mother church of Peebles, may have as in other burghs served the community.[101] The dedication to St Andrew the Apostle on 29 October 1195 of a church within the burgh may, however, mark the transference of the original church to a site within the burghal boundaries.[102] Such a move was not unknown elsewhere and is clearly demonstrated over two centuries later at Cupar in Fife where shortly before 1429 the burgesses rebuilt their church, formerly outside the town, within their burgh in order to enhance its dignity.[103] This was not an isolated example and the building of churches at more convenient centres can be authenticated. Thus the parish church of Abdie is described in 1473 as sited in an almost uninhabited place and was in consequence to be rebuilt in the neighbouring town of Newburgh in Fife in which the parishioners commonly assembled.[104]

Such moves were clearly not unknown in the twelfth and thirteenth centuries, although in some cases such as at Linlithgow in 1242 the dedication of a church cannot be taken as indicative of a new building or site.[105] Only in a handful of instances is a church unquestionably erected *de novo* after the creation of a burgh. The classic case is undoubtedly at Ayr which was founded as a burgh between 1203 and 1206.[106] It appears that Ayr provides the clearest of all records of the close relationship between early castle, burgh and sheriffdom.[107] To this assumption might be added the emergence of a parish church, for the urban parish of Ayr appears to have been created at the same time, the place names in the foundation charter laying out in fine detail the lands which may have initially formed part of the ancient parish of Alloway (Carcleuien of the Glasgow Inquest) and henceforth were to form the parish of Ayr.[108] Whether a chapel of any kind had existed previously is uncertain, but at Nairn, where a similar policy of 'planting' an associated castle and burgh took place c. 1190, it is nevertheless clear that an existing chapel, dependent upon the church of the short-lived neighbouring burgh of Auldearn, provided the nucleus of the operation and in this case remained as the mother church, although the burgh which it had originally served had disappeared.[109]

In terms of burghs not dependent on the king, patterns are more difficult to discern as evidence is more sparse. It is safe to assume, however, that in common with other burghs those founded after the early thirteenth century were erected within already existing parishes and had no influence upon their formation, although the site of the parish church itself may have influenced the location of the burgh, or alternatively the church may have been re-located within the bounds of the new township. The evidence is not conclusive but at Prestwick, founded as a burgh by Walter FitzAlan 1165–1174, the parish of St Nicholas may have been carved from the existing parish of Prestwick St Cuthbert, on the erection of the burgh.[110] At Renfrew, however, the church certainly antedated the acquisition of the burgh by Walter FitzAlan and in all probability its foundation by David I 1124 x 1147.[111] No conclusions can be drawn in relation to other early burghs and parishes such as Annan and Dunbar, but at Inverurie the burgh was associated with a chapel within the existing parish of Rothket.[112] The foundation of this burgh led, however, to parochial status being acquired by the chapel which thereafter superseded the original parish church.[113] At Kirkintilloch (or Lenzie) on the other hand where the church was granted to Cambuskenneth Abbey at the end of the twelfth century by William, son of Thorald, sheriff of Stirling and lord of Kirkintilloch, the parish clearly pre-dated the burgh's foundation in 1211 x 1214.[114] The church, which was not in the burgh, continued, moreover, to be sited at the west end of the parish with a chapel serving the burgh itself.[115]

Whatever a burgh's origins, the parishes in which they lay had, with few exceptions, deeper roots than the burghs which they served. The creation of burghs was not so crucial to the evolution of the parochial system as has sometimes been supposed. The creation of burghs, however, provided a new stability for the whole system. Towns meant more substantial churches and a more generous endowment of their clergy in terms of parochial service and associated chaplaincies than could ever have been possible in a purely rural society. The initial steps in the evolution of the parochial system and subsequent developments in the middle ages were, nevertheless, rural rather than urban phenomena.

NOTES

1. I. B. Cowan, 'The development of the parochial system in medieval Scotland', *SHR*, xl (1961), 43–55.

2. *Glas. Reg.*, 7, 43, 50.

3. *Dunf. Reg.*, 6.

4. *Glas. Reg.*, no. 12; *Kelso Liber*, no. 416.

5. *Glas. Reg.*, no. 53.

6. *Ibid.*, no. 114; *Kelso Liber*, no. 179.

7. Cowan, 'Parochial system', 44.

8. *Ibid.*, 45.

9. *Ibid.*, 47–8.

10. *Lindores Cartulary*, no. xcix; *St A. Lib.*, 188–9, 362. Examples of early clergy becoming canons regular, or continuing to serve as a bishop as his *familia* are clearly observable at Abernethy, Brechin and Monymusk (Cowan and Easson, *Medieval Religious Houses Scotland*, 46–7, 51.

11. Cowan, 'Parochial system', 50–51; a few examples of proprietary churches may be observed at Covington (Villa Colbani), Dolphinton (Dolfinston), Lamington (Lambinistun), Livingstone (Villa Leving), Symington (villa Symonis Lockard), Wiston (villa Withce) (*Origines Parochiales Scotiae* [*OPS*] (Bannatyne Club, 1851–5), 130, 140, 144, 171, 173; *Liber Cartarum Sancte Crucis* [*Holy Lib.*] (Bannatyne Club, 1840), no. 2.

12. *Moray Reg.*, no. 5.

13. Cowan, 'Parochial system', 51.

14. Pryde, *Burghs*, 1ff.

15. Cowan and Easson, *Medieval Religious Houses*, 201–12; Pryde, *Burghs*, nos. 7, 13, 52–3, 64, 70, 72–3, 77, 81, 83, 87, 90, 96, 98, 108, 120, 140, 202, 232, 243, 294.

16. Vatican Archives, Registra Supplicationum [Reg. Supp.] 884, fo. 74v; the designation 'civitas' which denotes a centre of civilised living was equally applied to all the cathedral 'cities' within the kingdom (ibid., 885, fo. 40).

17. Cowan and Easson, *Medieval Religious Houses*, 206.

18. Pryde, *Burghs*, no. 13; *Moray Reg.*, nos. 6, 18, 24, 42; *RRS*, ii, nos. 272, 465.

19. Cowan and Easson, *Medieval Religious Houses*, 203; Pryde, *Burghs*, no. 87.

20. *Ibid.*, no. 87.

21. Cowan and Easson, *Medieval Religious Houses*, 204–6; Pryde, *Burghs*, nos. 96, 202.

22. Cowan, *Parishes*, 53.

23. *Ibid.*, 51, 53.

24. Pryde, *Burghs*, nos. 96, 202.

25. *Abdn. Reg.*, ii, 227.

26. Cowan and Easson, *Medieval Religious Houses*, 202–3; Cowan, *Parishes*, 2.

27. *Ibid.*, 2; Pryde, *Burghs*, no. 169.

28. Cowan, *Parishes*, 2.

29. *ESC*, 44–7; Watt, *Fasti*, 43–5; Cowan and Easson, *Medieval Religious Houses*, 207–8; *Chronicle of Holyrood*, ed. M. O. Anderson (SHS, 1938), 119.

30. *Glas. Reg.*, nos. 7, 28, 66; *OPS*, I, 11–12.

31. Pryde, *Burghs*, no. 90.

32. *Abstracts of Protocols of Town Clerks of Glasgow*, ed. R. Renwick (Glasgow, 1894–1900), iv, 117, 119, 122n.

33. Cowan and Easson, *Medieval Religious Houses*, 209–10; Cowan, *Parishes*, 125; R. G. Cant, 'The church in Orkney and Shetland in the middle ages', in *Northern Scotland*, i (1972), 4–5; D. McGibbon and T. Ross, *The Ecclesiastical Architecture of Scotland*, 3 vols. (Edin., 1817), i, 109.

34. Pryde, *Burghs*, no. 52.

35. *Ibid.*, no. 73.

36. *Dunf. Reg.*, no. 23.

37. Sutherland Charters cited *OPS*, II², 636; *Bannatyne Miscellany*, iii, 17–21.

38. *Ibid.*, II², 597, 623.

39. Cowan and Easson, *Medieval Religious Houses*, 212.

40. *Ibid.*, nos. 53, 120.

41. M. O. Anderson, 'St Andrews before Alexander I', in *The Scottish Tradition*, ed. G. W. S. Barrow (Edinburgh, 1974), 5–6.

42. Cowan and Easson, *Medieval Religious Houses*, 49–50.

43. *Ibid.*, 49–50.

44. R. G. Cant, 'The building of St Andrews Cathedral', in *Innes Review*, xxv (1974), 77–8, 83; *St A. Lib.*, 122–3.

45. G. W. S. Barrow, 'The clergy of St Andrews', in *The Kingdom of the Scots* (London, 1973), 212–32.

46. Pryde, *Burghs*, no. 72; Cowan, *Parishes*, 176.

47. Watt, *Fasti*, 304; M. O. Anderson, 'The Celtic church in Kinrimund', in *Innes Review*, xxv (1974), 72–3; Cant, 'The building of St Andrews Cathedral', *ibid.*, 77–8.

48. *St A. Lib.*, 55, 58, 63, 132–3. For the Scottish settlement outside the burgh see R. G. Cant, 'Historical notes: Western St Andrews, Argyle, Rathelpie, Kinburn', in *St Andrews Preservation Trust Report and Year Book, 1984*, 15.

49. *Dunf. Reg.*, no. 26.

50. Cowan and Easson, *Medieval Religious Houses*, 58–9; *Dunf. Reg.*, no. 2; Pryde, *Burghs*, nos. 2, 106, 157.

51. Cowan and Easson, *Medieval Religious Houses*, 70; Cowan, *Parishes*, 181.

52. Cowan and Easson, *Medieval Religious Houses*, 68–70; Cowan, *Parishes*, 181–2; *RRS*, ii, 167, 373.

53. *Kelso Liber*, i, 16; *RRS*, ii, 363.

54. Pryde, *Burghs*, no. 41.

55. Cowan, *Parishes*, 181–2.

56. Pryde, *Burghs*, nos. 9, 85.

57. *St A. Lib.*, 135, 153, 180.

58. Cowan, *Parishes*, 79.

59. Cowan and Easson, *Medieval Religious Houses*, 92; Pryde, *Burghs*, no. 17.

60. Cowan and Easson, *Medieval Religious Houses*, 49.

61. *Ibid.*, 49.

62. Cowan, *Parishes*, 91. Canons regular could act as parochial chaplains, but this was not true of other orders. Paisley, for example, a Cluniac house, had, from the start, secular

chaplains serving its appropriated churches (Ian B. Cowan, 'The religious and the cure of souls in medieval Scotland', in *RSCHS*, xiv (1962), 215–30; *Pais. Reg.*, 318–23).

63. Cowan and Easson, *Medieval Religious Houses*, 66–7, 90; Pryde, *Burghs*, nos. 69, 84, 91, 159.

64. *Ibid.*, no. 84.

65. *Ibid.*, nos. 84, 91.

66. I. B. Cowan, 'The early ecclesiastical history of Edinburgh', in *Innes Review*, xxxiii (1972), 16–18; *Holy. Lib.*, nos. 1–2.

67. Cowan, *Parishes*, 26.

68. *Ibid.*, 178–9.

69. Pryde, *Burghs*, no. 100.

70. Cowan, *Parishes*, 82–3.

71. Pryde, *Burghs*, no. 120.

72. *Ibid.*, nos. 156, 164, 172, 206, 209.

73. *Ibid.*, nos. 259, 276, 281.

74. Cowan, 'Early ecclesiastical history of Edinburgh', 17–19.

75. Cowan, *Parishes*, 17; Pryde, *Burghs*, no. 1.

76. Cowan, *Parishes*, 17.

77. *Ibid.*, 17; J. Raine, *The History and Antiquities of North Durham* (London, 1852), no. cccclvi.

78. Cowan, *Parishes*, 17, 20.

79. Pryde, *Burghs*, no. 7; *RRS*, ii, 223.

80. Cowan, *Parishes*, 2.

81. Pryde, *Burghs*, nos. 29, 94.

82. Cowan, *Parishes*, 51; H. Boece, *Scotorum Historiae a prima gestis origine . . .* (Paris, 1527), fo. cclxxxvi; *Lind. Cart.* 22, 95; *Liber Sancte Marie de Lundoris*, (Abbotsford Club, 1841), 13, 17; A. C. Lamb, *Dundee: Its Quaint and Historic Buildings* (Dundee, 1895), xvii. The above references were kindly supplied by Dr E. P. D. Torrie.

83. *Dunf. Reg.*, no. 4.

84. Pryde, *Burghs*, no. 6.

85. *Dunf. Reg.*, nos. 2, 6, 237.

86. Cowan, *Parishes*, 187–8.

87. Pryde, *Burghs*, no. 5; Cowan, *Parishes*, 163–4.

88. Pryde, *Burghs*, no. 2.

89. Cowan, *Parishes*, 159; *RRS*, i, 179–80; Watt, *Fasti*, 170.

90. *RRS*, i, 193.

91. Cowan, *Parishes*, 175; *OPS*, I, 455.

92. *Ibid.*, I, 461–2; *Glas. Reg.*, i, 9–10, 146.

93. *Kelso Lib.*, ii, 320; *RRS*, i, 179–80.

94. R. Gourlay and A. Turner, *Historic Dumfries: the archaeological implications of its development* (Scottish Burgh Survey, 1977), 1.

95. Pryde, *Burghs*, no. 24; Cowan, *Parishes*, 50; *RRS*, ii, 289; *Kelso Liber*, nos. 4, 11, 13, 279, 324.

96. *RRS* ii, 199, 353–4; Pryde, *Burghs*, no. 20.

97. *Ibid.*, no. 18.

98. *Liber S. Marie de Dryburgh [Dryburgh Liber.]* (Bannatyne Club, 1847), nos. 43–5, 52, 209–10.

99. *OPS*, I, 117–19; *Dryburgh Liber*, nos. 50–2, 230–4, 271.

100. *ESC*, 46; Pryde, *Burghs*, no. 18.

101. *RRS*, ii, 362.

102. *The Chronicle of Melrose*, edd. A. O. Anderson *et al* (London, 1936), 49.

103. *Calendar of Scottish Supplications to Rome, iii, 1428–32*, ed. I. B. Cowan and A. I. Dunlop (SHS, 1970), 27, 140, 176.

104. Reg. Supp. 691 fo. 273.

105. *St A. Lib.*, 348.

106. Pryde, *Burghs*, no. 31.

107. *The Sheriff Court Book of Fife*, ed. W. C. Dickinson (SHS, 1928), xix.

108. *The Royal Burgh of Ayr*, ed. A. I. Dunlop (Edinburgh, 1953), 1–18; *RRS*, ii, 426–8; *ESC*, 46.

109. Pryde, *Burghs*, nos. 22, 25; Cowan, *Parishes*, 11, 89.

110. Pryde, *Burghs*, no. 89; Cowan, *Parishes*, 150, 167.

111. Pryde, *Burghs*, nos. 11, 86; Cowan, *Parishes*, 170.

112. Pryde, *Burghs*, nos. 30, 50, 55, 82, 93, 95; Cowan, *Parishes*, 7, 50, 90, 174.

113. *Ibid.*, 90, 174.

114. *Registrum Monasterii S. Marie de Cambuskenneth* (Grampian Club, 1872), nos. 25, 132.

115. *OPS*, I, 48.

6

The Monastic Presence:
Berwick in the Twelfth and Thirteenth Centuries

Wendy B. Stevenson

It has recently been shown that, although elsewhere in Western Europe religious houses were often prevented from holding urban property, the monastic stake in Scottish burghs in the twelfth and thirteenth centuries was very considerable. Not only were Scottish monasteries in receipt of grants of urban property from all ranks of society from the king down, but in the thirteenth century they were purchasing additional holdings for themselves. By the end of the thirteenth century some twenty-four religious houses had property in all of the fifty or so burghs then in existence. Some burghs had only one or two monastic tenants with one property apiece but in other burghs the monastic presence was very much stronger. It was strongest of all in Berwick[1] which was the leading burgh in Scotland in the twelfth and thirteenth centuries. Since an important aspect of urban growth in this period was the development of a new kind of society outwith the feudal order, of which the monasteries were very much a part, it is worth examining the role of the monasteries in the life of Berwick in as much detail as possible.

Table 1 shows that by the end of the thirteenth century a total of fifteen religious houses are known to have held property in Berwick. The houses concerned are all located in the eastern half of Scotland and range from Kinloss in Moray, which is not known to have had any estates in the neighbourhood of Berwick, to Coldstream in the south-east, most of whose property was in Berwickshire. The table also shows that a majority of these monasteries held more than one property in Berwick and that Melrose and Kelso had a particularly large stake in the burgh.

What was the attraction of Berwick to the monasteries? It has been stated that the main purpose of the monasteries' acquisitions in the various burghs was 'to victual the monastic community, which in many cases was not provided with adequate supplies of grain for bread and ale from its own estates'.[2] However, all fifteen monasteries with property in Berwick were nearer to some other burgh, and at least nine of them had more than one

Table 1. Monastic acquisitions in Berwick by c.1296

Monastery	Number of acquisitions (purchases in brackets)	References
Arbroath	2	*RRS*, ii, no. 197; *Arb. Lib.*, no. 256.
Coldstream	3	*Cold. Cart.*, nos. 14, 49, 51.
Coupar Angus	1	*Newb. Reg.*, no. 190.
Dryburgh	2	*Dryb. Lib.*, nos. 153, 154.
Dunfermline	2 (1)	*RRS*, i, no. 118; *Dunf. Reg.*, no. 120.
Holyrood	1	*RRS*, ii, no. 39.
Jedburgh	2 or more	*RRS*, ii, no. 62; Stevenson, *Documents*, ii, 153.
Kelso	9 (2)	*ESC*, no. cxciii; *RRS*, i, no. 131; *Kel. Lib.*, nos. 36, 44–7, 50, 354.
Kinloss	1	*RRS*, ii, no. 543.
Lindores	1	*RRS*, ii, no. 366.
May	2	*RRS*, ii, no. 8; *May Recs.*, no. 31.
Melrose	10 (3)	*RRS*, ii, nos. 97–8; *Melr. Lib.*, nos. 28, 180, 181–2, 312, 313, 315.
Newbattle	3 (1)	*Newb. Reg.*, nos. 186, 188, 189.
St Andrews	2	*RRS*, i, no. 174; *St A. Lib.*, 272–3.
St Bothan's	1	Stevenson, *Documents*, ii, 152.

property in Berwick. In some burghs, such as Perth, a town house also gave the monastery's abbot somewhere to lodge when the king required his presence there,[3] but in the case of Berwick the presence of the royal court was a fairly rare event.[4] Clearly, there were other factors which attracted the monasteries to Berwick.

An examination of the properties acquired by the monasteries in Berwick shows that the situation whereby tenants held a single toft direct from the king for a fixed customary rent soon ceased to pertain. In a number of cases, it is true, the property acquired by a monastery did consist of a single toft,[5] and this is particularly true of royal grants. In many other cases, however, especially in the thirteenth century, the extent and nature of the property acquired is not clear. By this time the original plan of burgage tofts and tenements had become much disturbed, both by the division of holdings[6] and by the consolidation of adjoining properties into larger properties,[7] and it is not safe to assume that when someone granted his 'land' or 'property' in Berwick it was necessarily an original burgage tenement. The subdivision of tofts suggests, of course, that there was a considerable demand for property in Berwick.

Not only does the size of the acquisition vary from one transaction to another, but so does the status of the property concerned. In some cases the

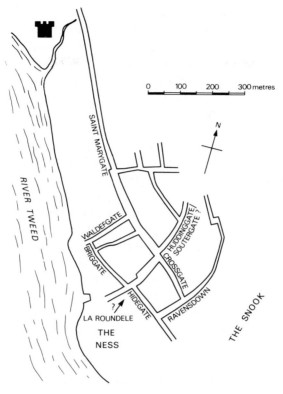

Berwick in 12th and 13th centuries

property acquired was henceforth to be held by the monastery directly of the king for the customary rent of sixpence *per annum*.[8] In other cases someone else held directly from the king but the monastery concerned gained possession of the property and paid rent to the intermediary between itself and the king.[9] In yet other cases the monastery became the intermediary and someone else remained in possession of the holding and paid rent to the monastery.[10] In one case the abbot of Kelso was an intermediary and the abbot of Dunfermline actually held the property, having purchased it from William de Doway.[11] Again, the fact that monasteries acquired rights in properties held by someone else suggests that their interest in such holdings was primarily fiscal, although it is true that they sometimes subsequently purchased direct control over properties held of them.[12]

In some cases the document recording a grant or purchase gives no indication at all of the location of the property concerned.[13] This is especially true of royal grants. Other documents provide information which would have identified the property to contemporaries but is of little use to the historian unless supplementary information is available from elsewhere. For example, it is quite common for a document to record the name of the previous tenant of a property as well as the name of the tenant granting or selling it to a monastery.[14] Similarly, the names of the tenants holding properties on either side of the property concerned are often recorded.[15] Sometimes, however, the location of the property is given in terms much more useful to the historian. In a few cases, for example, a property is described as being next to some identifiable building such as the churches of St Laurence and Holy Trinity.[16] In quite a number of cases the street name is given and in a very few cases a more detailed description of the location in relation to a particular street.[17]

The street-name information provided by monastic charters is worth further comment as it provides almost the only contemporary documentary evidence of street names in Berwick in the twelfth and thirteenth centuries.[18] It also shows that Berwick had, for the time, an unusually large number of street names. Finally, it shows that the property of the monasteries in Berwick was not restricted to a particular street or a particular corner of the medieval burgh. On the other hand, some street names occur more frequently than others and some monasteries seem to have had groups of holdings in particular areas. For example, Melrose and Kelso had a number of properties respectively in Briggate and around the junction of Briggate and the adjoining Waldesgate. Table 2 lists the streets in which monastic holdings are known to have been located.[19]

It is tempting to assume that the streets in which monasteries purchased property were the streets in which it was most desirable to have holdings. Three of the purchased properties were in Briggate, two in Waldesgate and one 'super Nes'. However, the choice of property to be purchased might have largely depended on what became available or perhaps reflected a desire to extend an existing property.[20]

It has been noted above that by the thirteenth century both the division and consolidation of holdings in Berwick were becoming commonplace. The monasteries, of course, never divested themselves of property in this period (except perhaps in an exchange[21]) but at least two monasteries, Melrose and Kelso, acquired properties adjacent to existing holdings.[22] Thus, while the monastic presence was spread throughout the burgh, Melrose and Kelso probably had at least one very substantial property each. This is confirmed in the case of the former by a reference to some land granted to Newbattle which is described as being *iuxta magnas domos de Melrose*.[23]

The documents recording purchases of Berwick property supply

Table 2. Streets and districts with a monastic presence by c.1296

Medieval Name	Modern Location	Monastery	References
Briggate	Bridge St & Love Lane	Kelso May Melrose	*Kel. Lib.*, no. 47. *May Recs.*, nos. 31, 32, 36. *Melr. Lib.*, nos. 180, 312, 313.
Crossgate Hidegate	Woolmarket Silver St	Coldstream Jedburgh St Bothan's	*Cold. Cart.*, nos. 49, 50. Stevenson, *Documents*, ii, 152–3.
Huddinggate/ Uddinggate	Church St	Coldstream Kelso	*Cold. Cart.*, no. 48. *Kel. Lib.*, no. 46 & p. 467.
The Ness	'An area contained by modern Ness St, Silver St, Sandgate, Quay Walls and Wellington Terrace round to Ness St'	Melrose Newbattle St Andrews	*Melr. Lib.*, no. 181. *Newb. Reg.*, nos. 186, 188, 189. *St A. Lib.*, 272.
vicus de Rammisden super le Nesse	Probably an error for Ravensdowne	Coldstream	*Cold. Cart.*, no. 14.
Revenysden la Roundele	Ravensdowne ?	Dryburgh Jedburgh Melrose	*Dryb. Lib.*, no. 154. Stevenson, *Documents*, ii, 153. *Melr. Lib.*, no. 182.
The Snook	'Fields outside Eastern Wall'	Melrose	*Melr. Lib.*, no. 182.
stratam regiam	?	Melrose	*Melr. Lib.*, no. 182.
Sutergath/*vicus sutorum*	'Probably in area of Castlegate'/ Soutergate	Newburgh Coldstream	*Newb. Reg.*, no. 187. *Cold. Cart.*, no. 52.
Waldesgate	'Probably including West St and extending to water front'	Kelso	*Kel. Lib.*, nos. 35, 44, 47.

information of a kind not found in the charters recording gifts. However, analysis of the seven acquisitions which were acknowledged to be purchases[24] is rather unrewarding, partly because of the small number of transactions involved and partly because the relevant documents do not all give the same sort of information. The charters relating to the seven purchases cannot all be dated precisely but the earliest dates from c. 1226, another from the reign of Alexander II (1214–1249), another from between about 1240 and 1300, two from 1250–51, another from c. 1266 and the last from 1290.[25] However, the sample is too small to allow the inference that the property market was active throughout the thirteenth century. Purchase prices are given for only four of the seven transactions. In descending order these are: (i) 100 merks plus an annual payment of ten bolls of marketable corn, one chalder of marketable barley and half a merk to whomsoever survived the longer, the vendor or his wife (1250); (ii) 100 merks (c. 1251); (iii) £60 (1290); and (iv) half a merk (1226).[26] Unfortunately, too little is known about the size, type and location of the properties concerned to enable any conclusions to be drawn from these figures. Although they reveal nothing about price fluctuations in Berwick, they do suggest that prices in Berwick were higher than elsewhere. The two highest recorded prices paid by monasteries for property in other burghs were £33 6s 8d paid by Melrose during the reign of Alexander II for half a carucate of land in the 'villa' of Edingham, plus two burgages in Roxburgh,[27] and forty merks paid by St Andrews between 1239 and 1253 for the possession of some land previously held of them in St Andrews itself.[28] In 1244 the bishop of Moray purchased a full toft in Elgin for four and a half merks and later in the same century paid £100 for some property in Berwick.[29] These transactions support the impression that prices were higher in the more important burghs and highest of all in Berwick.

From the moment a monastery acquired property in Berwick it had a role to play, however limited, in burgh affairs. Indeed, where the property was acquired by purchase rather than by gift, the monastery must have played a part in the burgh land market even before the property was formally acquired. In fact, but for monastic charters, nothing at all would be known about the land market in Berwick in the twelfth and thirteenth centuries. These charters, whether concerned with monastic purchases or not, sometimes record in passing a past lay purchase. For example, one of the seven charters recording monastic purchases in Berwick mentions that land next to the Trinitarians' hospital purchased by Dunfermline from William de Doway had previously been purchased by William from the heirs of Salomon de Norham.[30] Similarly, a charter recording a gift of urban property to Kelso contains a reference to land purchased by Adam, son of Hudding of Berwick, from his father and elder brother,[31] while a

Melrose charter contains references to two pieces of land in Berwick which Adam le Vilure and his wife had purchased from William Mirihild and William de Bernam respectively.[32]

Once they had acquired properties in Berwick, how did the monasteries exploit them? In some cases the monasteries only acquired superior rights over properties already occupied by tenants, and in these cases the only role for the monasteries, at least until the leases expired or were surrendered, was that of rent collector. In most cases, however, the monasteries acquired immediate possession of their Berwick properties and were therefore able to exploit them as they chose. Even then, a number of monasteries were content merely to be rent collectors and farmed out their properties. Although quite a number of documents recording farming out agreements in respect of urban property have survived for the thirteenth century, only a small proportion of them relate to Berwick. The monasteries concerned are Coupar Angus, Newbattle and May.

In the case of May, the farming out arrangements emerged as the settlement of disputes between the monastery and third parties who disputed its right to the properties in question. For example, between 1219 and 1240 there was a dispute between May and Thomas, son of Eustace of Berwick, over certain land in Briggate which the monks said had been bequeathed to them by Waldo Ruffus. Agreement was reached that Thomas should give up all claims to the land and recognise the rights of the monks but that he should hold it from the monks, together with other land which Waldo had held of the monks during his lifetime, in return for two merks of silver *per annum*.[33] In the other two May cases, the annual rents were twenty pence and two merks *per annum* respectively.[34] In none of the three cases is a precise description given of the property involved, so the figures are of little use for comparative purposes. On the other hand, one of the rents of two merks is for a property which was valued at 'about 50 merks', which gives some idea of the return expected on capital in one isolated transaction. The possibility that rents agreed as part of the settlement of a dispute are not necessarily at normal current rates must, of course, be borne in mind.

In the cases of Newbattle and Coupar Angus there is no record of any dispute being involved. When Coupar Angus farmed out land in Berwick given to the monastery by Thomas de Colville, the tenant was Newbattle Abbey.[35] This is the only example which has come to light of one monastic house farming out urban property to another. This agreement is also interesting because the rent was not the usual money rent, which was typical in burghs, but was 3 lbs of cumin or 1 lb of pepper *per annum*. Other examples of rents in kind can be found in other burghs[36] but this appears to be the only surviving example in Berwick.[37] It was probably an attempt to cope with the inflation which accompanied the economic expansion of the thirteenth century.

In 1297, according to a survey of parts of Berwick made when the town was captured by the English, the abbot of Jedburgh held two burgages with their buildings in Hidegate and *placea rotunda dicta la Roundele* with its buildings. The rents for the two former properties were half a merk *per annum* each and for the latter property twenty merks *per annum*. The nuns of St Bothan's had one burgage, also in Hidegate, which was farmed out with its buildings for two merks *per annum*.[38]

Apart from the farming out agreements and the 1297 partial survey of Berwick, there are three surviving monastic rentals from the late thirteenth century. These are interesting for a number of reasons. Two of them give rents in Berwick and in other burghs for the same years. Although one cannot be sure that the properties are comparable in size and situation, the Kelso rental seems to support the hypothesis that Berwick rents were generally higher than the amounts obtainable in other burghs. In Berwick, Kelso received £10 3s 5½d from property 'in Briggate, Waldesgate and elsewhere' and ten merks from property in 'Uddinget'.[39] These figures can be compared with 8d from some land in Jedburgh and 12d, 16d, 20d and 40d from tenements in Haddington, Edinburgh, Stirling and Renfrew respectively. Although Kelso is known to have had at least nine properties in Berwick (of which at least one was retained for the monastery's own use),[40] the level of rents was obviously still much higher than in these other burghs. On the other hand, Kelso also received just over £8 in annual rents in Roxburgh.[41] However, this figure almost certainly includes such items as 40s annual rent granted from the revenues of the burgh by Earl David.[42] A similar item of 40s from the farm of the burgh of Berwick is shown separately in the Berwick account and is not included in the figures quoted above. The document recording the value of Newbattle's Berwick properties when they were returned to the monastery by Edward I in January 1300 confirms the level of rents suggested by the Kelso rental and the figures supplied by the farming out agreements. Three properties were farmed out at rents of 46s 8d for one and 20s each for the other two.[43] However, the St Andrews rental, which dates from c. 1282, confuses the picture somewhat. St Andrews received 9d each from three tenants, 11d from another, and 18d and certain benefits in kind from another, while larger sums than these were received from some of the monastery's properties in Linlithgow, Crail and Haddington.[44] But this does not necessarily affect the hypothesis that rents were generally higher in Berwick than elsewhere. St Andrews may have subdivided its Berwick properties to a high degree or fixed the rents in perpetuity before inflation made this an unwise policy.

Rent levels almost certainly fluctuated during the course of the period under review. The most likely general trend is an upward one, for the thirteenth century was a period of general economic expansion and there are some indications that landholders in Berwick were having to cope with price inflation. The occurrence of rents in kind has already been noted. The agreement between Melrose and Nicholas the weaver whereby the former purchased part of the latter's Berwick property for a hundred merks plus annual payments of half a merk and specified amounts of marketable grain looks like another attempt to beat inflation.[45] In some circumstances rents could fall. The register of Newbattle contains a charter of Lawrence Stater dated c. 1264 which records his quitclaim to the abbey of certain land in Berwick *que ante captam villam per Anglicos reddidit domui xlvis. viiid. nunc vero funditus dillapidata esse et demembrata et quasi nullius valoris.*[46]

These rentals also allow comparison between the general level of rents received from urban tenements and the general level of income from other sources. The St Andrews rental shows, for example, that the revenues the monastery received from various mills in Linlithgow were higher than those received from most of its urban tenements.[47] Similarly, the Kelso rental shows that the revenues received from each of two churches[48] were considerably higher than the sums accruing from either St Andrews' mills or the urban tenements of both St Andrews and Kelso.

Finally, the rentals are important because they provide positive evidence that, although many of the monastic properties in Berwick were farmed out, others were not. Newbattle and Kelso are both described as having a tenement *in proprio usu*[49] and it seems likely that they were not alone. It has been noted above that some land granted to Newbattle was described as being *iuxta magnas domos de Melrose*,[50] which perhaps suggests that the property concerned was actually in Melrose's possession. St Andrews appears to have farmed out all its Berwick properties but retained the right of lodging in one of them.[51] A number of similar cases occur in other burghs and it may well be that there were other cases in Berwick. The St Andrews rental names the tenant of the property concerned, states the rent paid, and adds the bare statement *et est hostilagium nostrum*; in other cases in other burghs more details are sometimes given of what such arrangements involved.[52] Jedburgh also appears to have had the use of a house in Berwick but it is not clear whether the house was in its own hands or the monastery merely retained the right of lodging there.[53]

The question now arises as to why some monasteries retained urban properties in their own hands, or at least retained the right of lodging in them, and others did not. It is possible that the property would have been used, or the right to lodging exercised, when the king required the presence of the abbot or his representative in Berwick. It is more likely, however, that the properties were used mainly as a base for the commercial activities of the monasteries concerned. Little is known about such activities on the part of the monasteries in the twelfth and thirteenth centuries but the numerous grants of trading privileges suggest that they were not negligible.[54] The earliest surviving grants of freedom from tolls and customs date from the reign of David I and were made to Cambuskenneth, Dryburgh, Dunfermline, May, Melrose and all Cistercian houses, and St Andrews.[55] Malcolm IV made grants to Coldingham and Coupar Angus,[56] and Alexander II to Inchaffray.[57] They generally specified that the king granted the freedom throughout all his lands and that the freedom applied only to the monks' own goods. Clearly, from their earliest days, some monasteries either had surplus produce for sale or were able to purchase goods which they could not provide for themselves. At least four monasteries had their own ships[58] and there is direct evidence that the monks of Scone used their vessel for buying and selling goods for their own needs. However, there is very little other direct evidence of the trading activities of the monks within Scotland. Of the monasteries with property in Berwick, Melrose and Newbattle are known to have regularly sent carts to the burgh, for both houses claimed the right to a night's free grazing for the animals pulling their carts.[59] Malcolm IV granted Jedburgh 'such liberty in the houses which the abbey has in Berwick that none of the king's servants may presume to demand tonnels of wine brought thither and emptied on the premises'.[60] This suggests that Jedburgh purchased wine in Berwick, possibly for consumption in its houses there but more likely for dispatch to the monastery itself. It is the Kelso rental that provides the best evidence of a regular traffic in goods between the burgh of Berwick and monastic estates elsewhere. At Redden, Kelso's eight husbandmen all owed regular carrying services from Berwick. Every week in summer each had to bring from the burgh, one pack-horse laden with three bolls of corn, or two of salt, or one and a half of coal. In winter the load was reduced to two bolls of corn, or one and a half of salt, or one and a quarter of coal. At Bowden all twenty-eight husbandmen and at Selkirk Abbatis two out of fifteen husbandmen had to bring one pack-horse from Berwick just once a year but the nature of the load is not specified.[61]

Paradoxically, there is more evidence – although still lamentably little – for monastic trade with England and the continent than there is for trade within Scotland, and it suggests that the monopoly of the professional merchant was by no means complete in this period. The growth of towns, trade and industry which characterized the general economic revival enjoyed by much of Western Christendom in the eleventh, twelfth and thirteenth centuries was accompanied by the emergence or revival of a professional merchant class; it tends to be assumed that most inter-regional and foreign trade was in the hands of members of this class, which was based in the towns. In the case of Scotland, Professor Duncan has pointed out in the course of a discussion on the grain trade that in the thirteenth century some western monasteries purchased grain directly from Ireland and England, but he sees this as exceptional

> 'it is striking that there is little trace of similar purchases by the religious houses of eastern Scotland, where grain was imported from England by sea to the larger towns not by monastic agents but by merchants of the two kingdoms. King John of England gave permission to Arbroath Abbey to trade in England quit of tolls in 1207, but he also gave his protection to the merchants of Perth and Dundee whose ships would carry the goods of the abbey; professional merchants were the past and the future of inter-regional trade'.[62]

It is certainly true that professional merchants from east coast ports were active in Scotland's overseas trade in this period. It is also true that numerous foreign merchants visited Scotland. However, the seven references to three western monasteries trading directly with other countries can be more than matched by references to monasteries in eastern Scotland trading abroad on their own accounts. Indeed, Professor Duncan has himself noted some of these in connection with his discussion of Scotland's wool trade but does not follow the story beyond 1230. He concludes that in the twelfth and early thirteenth centuries the Cistercians may have had a system of collecting wool for export under the control of Melrose and Coupar Angus.[63] It is thus worth examining in more detail and beyond 1230 the activities of those monasteries that were directly involved in overseas trade, for they were all monasteries with property in Berwick.

In the 1180s the count of Flanders, at that time the most important textile-producing region of north-west Europe, granted Melrose freedom from tolls in his country.[65] In 1224 Henry III of England granted letters of protection until the following Pentecost to the men of the abbot of Melrose and Coupar going to 'parts beyond the sea'.[65] In April 1225 the same king granted permission to the abbot of Melrose to send a vessel to Flanders, laden with wool and other merchandise, in charge of William de Led and Brother Thomas of Boulden.[66] This licence and a similar licence granted at the same time to the abbot of Coupar were to last until Michaelmas 1225. In April 1230 the English king, at the request of the Scots king, granted the abbot of Melrose leave for his ship in charge of Brother William of Boulden and 'laden with the abbot's goods and merchandise' to come and go freely in the king's dominions for a year.[67] Normally, of course, there were no restrictions on trade between Scotland and England in this period, but in these years England and France were at war and goods from other countries were liable to arrest in England. In August 1290 Edward I granted the abbot of Melrose 'freedom from distraint except by his special precept'[68] and this grant may have related to Melrose's trading activities in England. In June and August 1291 the abbot of Melrose was granted Edwards's protection for a year along with a number of other persons, mainly merchants of Berwick.[69] Some time before 1240 Melrose acquired a base for her trade in England when Thomas de Multon granted the monastery a piece of land in St Botolph (Boston), Lincolnshire 'upon which to build houses'.[70] Between then and 1243 Melrose granted to her daughter house of Holm Cultram in Cumberland 'that in their houses on the ground they hold in the vill of St Botulf by gift of Sir Thomas Multon, they [the monks of Holm] may stay with them at fair-times and whenever necessary, and because Holm has borne half the expense of building these, they may have half the profits accruing from the houses and lands at fair-times and other times. But no one is to live in these houses at fair-times without the consent of both parties'.[71] Subsequently, Abbot Patrick (fl. 1296) of Melrose granted to Holm Cultram the land in Boston which Thomas de Multon had granted them,[72] presumably because of the strife between England and Scotland. If further confirmation is needed that the monks of Melrose or their representatives were regular attenders at the famous St Botolph Fair, it should be noted that in 1223 the monks of Vaudrey in Lincolnshire farmed to Melrose some land they held in Scotland for a perpetual farm of four merks annually, to be paid at St Botolph.[73]

Two other monasteries which traded directly both with England and the continent were Newbattle and Arbroath. In 1292 Edward I confirmed the charter 'of King Henry his great-grandfather, freeing the abbot and monks of Newbattle, their men, horses and goods, of all toll and other customs at certain ports in England and Normandy'.[74] Edward's great-grandfather was Henry II who died in 1189, so Newbattle was apparently trading with both England and Normandy as early as the twelfth century. The grant in respect of Normandy had ceased to be relevant after the loss of that duchy to the French king in 1204 but the fact that the charter was confirmed in 1292 suggests that Newbattle continued to trade directly with England during the thirteenth century. It has already been noted that the abbot and monks of Arbroath were granted freedom from tolls and customs in England by King John in 1207. This grant was confirmed by Henry III in 1260,[75] which again suggests that it was still valuable to the monks.

It seems clear that there was a small group of important monasteries in eastern Scotland which were trading outwith Scotland on their own behalf in the late twelfth century and throughout the thirteenth century. Three of the four houses whose activities are documented above were Cistercian abbeys – Melrose, Coupar Angus and Newbattle. Because of the nature of their rule,[76] the Cistercians tended to be given uncultivated land which was often ideal for sheep farming, and in time many of their houses became important wool producers. Indeed, Melrose was probably the largest producer of wool in Scotland.[77] The fourth house, Arbroath, was not founded until 1178 but rapidly became one of the wealthiest in Scotland.[78] No doubt its extensive estates included many pastures suitable for sheep. Presumably it was only practicable and profitable for the largest producers to export their own wool, for some houses certainly sold their wool at the point of production to foreign merchants.[79]

Although Professor Duncan in his consideration of the overseas trading activities of Melrose and Coupar Angus before 1230 suggests that 'the Cistercians may have had a system of collecting wool for export from these and other houses in stores at Berwick and Perth', it seems that Berwick has a stronger claim than Perth to be the port used by monastic exporters. Melrose, Coupar Angus, Newbattle and Arbroath all had property in Berwick; Melrose and Newbattle retained some of their Berwick property in their own hands while Arbroath may or may not have done so. The case of Coupar Angus is especially interesting. At some date between 1212 and 1240 it leased its only known Berwick property to Newbattle. Whereas there is evidence of Coupar trading abroad on its own behalf until 1225, there is none to indicate that it continued to do so after that date. What probably happened was that Melrose, which was Coupar's mother house, exported Coupar's wool along with her own once Coupar parted with possession of its Berwick property. There are arguments against the use of Perth in the case of three of the four houses under consideration; Melrose and Newbattle are not known to have had any property in Perth[80] and were in any case geographically closer to Berwick. Coupar Angus did hold property in Perth and was nearer to Perth than Berwick, but the association of Coupar and Melrose in the English king's grants of 1224 and 1225 perhaps suggests that they were in close contact over their trading activities. The fact that Melrose was Coupar's mother house may well have decided the latter to organise its trading activities from Berwick. In the case of Arbroath there are no particular grounds for arguing that it used the port of Berwick: it had property in Perth also and was nearer to Perth; moreover, it was also unique in having access to the sea via its own burgh of Arbroath. Nevertheless, these factors do not preclude the use of Berwick which as the leading port of Scotland would have had many facilities to offer.

As well as their roles as occupiers or superiors of urban property and as traders, monasteries made their presence felt in Berwick in other ways. At least one monastery acted as a moneylender within the burgh. In 1275 an agreement was made between the abbot of Kelso and Roger Lawird of Berwick, his wife and son, that in return for a sum of money paid to Roger 'in his great need', the abbot should receive 20s *per annum* for twelve years from the rents of Roger's land in Waldesgate.[81] The monks may also have actively exploited the fishing rights which some of them were granted in Berwick, but no evidence survives to show whether this was so or whether the fish caught were just for their own use.[82] Only Kelso seems to have had a role in the spiritual life of the burgh and that was a very minor one. For a short time that monastery held the revenues of the church of St Laurence and would have had to make arrangements for the provision of services.[83]

The acquisition of urban property inevitably gave the monasteries a place in the legal life of the burgh. It also led to a conflict of jurisdictions because the burghs and the monasteries each had their own courts. It has been shown elsewhere that in Scotland as a whole no standard practice had yet evolved for dealing with cases arising in the burghs and involving laymen and the monasteries.[84] Burgh courts and ecclesiastical courts both heard such cases, apparently haphazardly. The evidence from Berwick does not appear to accord with this generalisation but this probably reflects the paucity of the sources rather than a real difference.

The occasions when the monasteries became involved in the legal life of the burgh fall into two categories: the transfer of property, and the settlement of disputes. Normally burgh property was resigned and re-granted in the burgh court but the abbot or prior with burgh land regarded it as part of his fief and hence subject to his feudal court. In Berwick, as elsewhere, evidence can be found of property transfers involving a monastery (either as superior, recipient or purchaser of the property) taking place sometimes in the burgh court,[85] sometimes in the abbot's court[86] and, on at least one occasion, in both.[87] In the case of disputes between monasteries and laymen, the monasteries appear to have been more successful in pressing the claims of their own courts. All five recorded cases involving Berwick property were dealt with in ecclesiastical courts.[88] It is possible that this represents established practice but it seems unlikely, for in Perth, which also had a strong monastic presence and was the second most important burgh in Scotland, such cases were sometimes heard in the burgh court.[89] Three charters recording the transfer of Berwick property to Kelso also contain clauses committing the grantor to ecclesiastical jurisdiction if the terms of the transfer were not kept.[90] Such clauses are also found in two Paisley charters relating to property in Glasgow[91] but cannot be regarded as common form. They seem rather to represent attempts by these monasteries to ensure that ecclesiastical courts would be preferred to the burgh court in any future dispute. The need for the insertion of such clauses suggests that what Kelso and Paisley stipulated was not necessarily standard practice. There, perhaps, the matter must rest.

It seems clear that Berwick had a particularly large monastic presence in the twelfth and thirteenth centuries because of her position as the leading burgh in Scotland, an eminence which she owed to her predominance in Scotland's overseas trade. Property prices and rents were high and some monasteries remained content with the role of landlord. However, a small but important group of monasteries were involved in the commercial activities of the burgh, including overseas trade. The acquisition of property gave the monasteries an active role in the life of the burgh. They came into contact with the donors of their property before or when the gift was made, or became involved in the burgh land market when they purchased land for themselves. Those monasteries which rented out their holdings entered into a continuing relationship with their tenants, while those that retained houses in their own possession must have made their presence felt more widely. As a result of the monastic presence representatives of the monasteries sometimes appeared in the burgh court and the townsfolk were sometimes obliged to attend the abbot's court. The monasteries also played a part in the life of Berwick of which they were unaware at the time. In recording details of their acquisitions in the burgh and noting the settlement of disputes connected with them, the monasteries supplied the modern historian with the sources of most of his knowledge about Berwick in the twelfth and thirteenth centuries. Apart from supplying almost all known information about the land market and street names of Berwick, monastic charters are also a fruitful source of other information such as the names of provosts,[92] mayors,[93] burgesses[94] and other residents of the burgh.[95] Finally, it is clear that unlike the parish clergy and the friars, who ministered to the spiritual needs of the townsfolk, the monks had a role in the affairs of Berwick which was entirely secular, except perhaps for a brief time in the case of Kelso.

NOTES

1. Stevenson, 'The monastic presence in Scottish burghs in the twelfth and thirteenth centuries', 109–18.

2. Duncan, *Scotland*, 504.

3. *Ibid.*, 468.

4. *RRS*, i, 113–15; ii, 96–105; *Handlist of the Acts of Alexander II*, ed. J. Scoular (1959), *passim; Handlist of the Acts of Alexander III, the Guardians and John*, ed. G. G. Simpson (1960), *passim*.

5. *RRS*, ii, nos. 8, 366.

6. *Kel. Lib.*, no. 46.

7. *Melr. Lib.*, no. 181.

8. *Cold. Cart.*, nos. 49, 51.

9. *Kel. Lib.*, no. 47; *Melr. Lib.*, no. 313.

10. *May Recs.*, no. 31.

11. *Dunf. Reg.*, no. 120.

12. *Newb. Reg.*, no. 186.

13. *RRS*, i, no. 118.

14. *Kel. Lib.*, no. 354; *Melr. Lib.*, no. 181.

15. *Cold. Cart.*, no. 49; *Kel. Lib.*, no. 354.

16. *RRS*, i, no. 131; *St A. Lib.*, 343; M. Ellison, 'An archaeological survey of Berwick-upon-Tweed', *Archaeology in the North*, eds. P. A. G. Clack and P. F. Gosling (1976), 152, 157.

17. *RRS*, ii, nos. 97–8; *St A. Lib.*, 272–3.

18. A membrane recording part of a survey of Berwick in 1297 contains references to Hidegate, Segate and *vicus piscatorum* (Stevenson, *Documents*, ii, 152–6).

19. See Table 2; the modern street locations are based on Ellison, 'Archaeological survey', 152, 156–7.

20. *Melr. Lib.*, nos. 180, 312, 313; *Kel. Lib.*, nos. 44, 47; *Newb. Reg.*, no. 186.

21. *RRS*, i, no. 130.

22. *Kel. Lib.*, no. 47; *Melr. Lib.*, no. 315.

23. *Newb. Reg.*, no. 189.

24. Stevenson, 'Monastic presence', 101.

25. *Dunf. Reg.*, no. 120; *Kel. Lib.*, nos. 44, 47; *Melr. Lib.*, nos. 180, 312, 313; *Newb. Reg.*, no. 186.

26. *Melr. Lib.*, nos. 312, 313; *Kel. Lib.*, no. 44; *Newb. Reg.*, no. 186.

27. *Melr. Lib.*, no. 239.

28. *St A. Lib.*, 281.

29. *Moray Reg.*, nos. 98, 129.

30. *Dunf. Reg.*, no. 120.

31. *Kel. Lib.*, no. 46.

32. *Melr. Lib.*, no. 181.

33. *May Recs.*, no. 31.

34. *Ibid.*, nos. 32, 36.

35. *Newb. Reg.*, no. 190.

36. *C.A. Chrs.*, no. xx.

37. *Newb. Reg.*, no. 187. The Newbattle agreement gives no other information except that the rent payable to Newbattle by a Berwick burgess for a burgage in *Sutergath* was 21s. 4d. sterling.

38. Stevenson, *Documents*, ii, 153, 152.

39. *Kel. Lib.*, 467.

40. *Ibid.*

41. *Ibid.*, 470.

42. ESC, no. xxxv.

43. *Newb. Reg.*, no. 191.

44. *St A. Lib.*, 343–4.

45. *Melr. Lib.*, no. 312.

46. *Newb. Reg.*, no. 188.

47. *St A. Lib.*, 343–5.

48. *Kel. Lib.*, 470, 471.

49. *Newb. Reg.*, no. 191; *Kel. Lib.*, 467.

50. *Newb. Reg.*, no. 189.
51. *St A. Lib.*, 343.
52. *Arbroath Liber*, no. 321; *Kel. Lib.*, 468.
53. *RRS*, i, no. 278.
54. Duncan, *Scotland*, 504.
55. *ESC*, nos. cliii, clxviii, cci, ccix, ccx; *RRS*, ii, nos. 65, 177.
56. *RRS*, i, nos. 200, 222.
57. *Inchaff. Chrs.*, no. xxxv.
58. ESC, no. lxxxviii; *Holyrood Liber*, no. 28; *RRS*, i, no. 279; *Scone Liber*, no. 73.
59. *Melr. Lib.*, no. 309; *Newb. Reg.*, no. 205.
60. *RRS*, i, no. 278.
61. *Kel. Lib.*, 456, 461, 462.
62. Duncan, *Scotland*, 505.
63. *Ibid.*, 513.
64. *Melr. Lib.*, nos. 14, 15.
65. *CDS*, i, no. 880.
66. *Ibid.*, i, no. 904.
67. *Ibid.*, i, no. 1086.
68. *Ibid.*, ii, no. 452.
69. *Ibid.*, ii, no. 535.
70. *The Register and Records of Holm Cultram* [*H.C. Reg.*], edd. F. Grainger and W. G. Collingwood (Cumberland and Westmorland Antiquarian and Archaeological Society, 1929), no. 256. See also no. 258.
71. *Ibid.*, no. 258.
72. *Ibid.*, no. 257.
73. *Melr. Lib.*, no. 195.
74. *CDS*, ii, no. 624.
75. *Ibid.*, i, no. 2231.
76. Duncan, *Scotland*, 147–8.
77. *Ibid.*, 507.
78. *Ibid.*, 175; *Arb. Lib.*, xv.
79. Raine, *North Durham*, Appendix no. lxxii.
80. Stevenson, 'Monastic presence', 109–18.
81. *Kel. Lib.*, no. 35.
82. *ESC*, no. clxviii; *RRS*, i, no. 235; ii, nos. 39, 63.
83. Cowan, *Parishes*, 17. These revenues were ceded to the priory of Durham in the 1170s. Durham also held the revenues of the churches of Holy Trinity and St Mary's.
84. Stevenson, 'Monastic presence', 105–08.
85. *Newb. Reg.*, no. 186; *Melr. Lib.*, no. 315.
86. *Kel. Lib.*, no. 44.
87. *Ibid.*, no. 34.
88. *May Recs.*, nos. 31, 32, 36.
89. *Inchaff. Chrs.*, no. 110; *Balmerino Lib.*, no. 30; *Scone Lib.*, no. 95.
90. *Kel. Lib.*, nos. 36, 44, 45.
91. *Paisley Registrum*, 386, 400.
92. E.g. *Cold. Cart.*, no. 50; *Newb. Reg.*, no. 186.
93. E.g. *Melr. Lib.*, no. 314; *Newb. Reg.*, no. 188.
94. E.g. *Melr. Lib.*, no. 312; *Dryburgh Lib.*, no. 154.
95. E.g. *Cold. Cart.*, no. 49; *Kel. Lib.*, no. 354; *Melr. Lib.*, no. 181.

7

Glasgow: An Ecclesiastical Burgh[1]

Norman F. Shead

It is easy enough to categorise Glasgow as an ecclesiastical burgh since the burgh charter (1175 x 1178) was granted to Bishop Jocelin.[2] It is, however, now commonly understood that a charter grants legal definition to a community, and the search for urban origins must look back to the time before the granting of a charter. It is not necessary to enter into the controversy about the seat of the bishop of the Strathclyde Britons, whether Govan or Glasgow, but it is salutary to be reminded that the connection of St Kentigern with Glasgow in written sources depends on Jocelin of Furness's identification of 'Cathures' with Glasgow in his life of the saint, written in the later twelfth century.[3]

What can be gleaned from Jocelin's life of St Kentigern is that in the later twelfth century there existed a cross, a tomb and a cemetery, all of which, of course, Jocelin connected with the saint's career, and which presumably pre-dated the cathedral. A stone ram's head, also associated by Jocelin with the saint, was presumably a piece of Romanesque sculpture, perhaps from the cathedral of 1136.[4] To these must be added the well, for which there is no documentary evidence, but which was incorporated into the south wall of the lower church when the cathedral was extended eastwards in the thirteenth century.

When David I drew up the famous statement of the possessions of this see (1113/14 x 1124) he referred to the founding of the church of Glasgow as the seat of the bishop.[5] The first recorded cathedral was dedicated in 1136, the earliest firm date for Glasgow itself and some forty years before the burgh charter.[6] It is unlikely that a cathedral would be built in the middle of nowhere, and presumably some tradition dictated that the chosen site had been that of Kentigern's church; it is an awkwardly sloping site, not at all an obvious one, since the cathedral could have been built at a higher level. Once it had been decided to build a cathedral, any existing settlement is likely to have been expanded by the demands of the workmen building it, by those of the clergy, and later of a chapter. Certainly by 1164 there were inhabitants, since it is reported that they fled on the approach of Somerled.[7] Jocelin declares that 'in the cemetery of the church of that city, as the inhabitants assert, six hundred and sixty-five saints rest'.[8] Even though this almost certainly dates from after the creation of the burgh by charter, it would have been pointless to seek the opinion of newcomers, and Jocelin presumably refers to 'original' inhabitants. If such a settlement existed to serve the cathedral, its shrine and its clergy, it is not improbable that it lay close to the cathedral rather than down the hill. There may perhaps be corroboration of this in the earliest town plan, dating from 1773,[9] which seems to show market colonisation due south of the bishop's castle: perhaps this filled triangle indicates the site of the informal market of pre-burghal times.[10] However, the origin and function of Glasgow before David I's time are matters of informed speculation; as far as recorded history is concerned, Glasgow's *raison d'être* was ecclesisastical.

From an early date St Kentigern's tomb was probably the centre of a cult, and the lives of the saint commissioned by Bishops Herbert and Jocelin were presumably connected with the development of that cult. It would have attracted pilgrims, and attention has been drawn to the importance of pilgrimage in stimulating buying and selling.[11] Thus the grant of a weekly market on a Thursday by King William in 1175 x 1178,[12] the first recorded formal grant of a market to a burgh,[13] may have merely formalised an existing arrangement. As late as 1324 Robert I's confirmation of the burgh to the bishop refers to Thursday as the market day, but in 1397 Robert III authorised the burgesses to alter the market day from Sunday to Monday.[14] What had brought about the change from Thursday to Sunday, and when it had taken place, is not known: Sunday was, however, a day when most people would be free to attend an event more important to the life of the community than the fair; and J. D. Marwick suggested tentatively that this might be a second market day, additional to Thursday, but pointed out that there was no evidence to support this suggestion.[15]

An annual fair, which presupposes rather wider trade, was also granted to Bishop Jocelin,[16] and was presumably prompted by the profits which any lord would expect from toll, stallage and other taxes. Unhappily, it is difficult to produce direct evidence of wider Scottish or international involvement in the fair. What evidence there is concerns transactions made at the time of the fair rather than buying and selling: the payment of money by Paisley Abbey to end a lawsuit; the payment of rent from Renfrew to Coupar Angus Abbey; payments from Argyll to the Dominican friars; the reddendo of a pair of Parisian gloves from Archibald Campbell of Lochawe to the countess of Menteith for the lands of Kilmun; and the delivery to the cathedral canons of two separate consignments of wax for lights.[17] There is

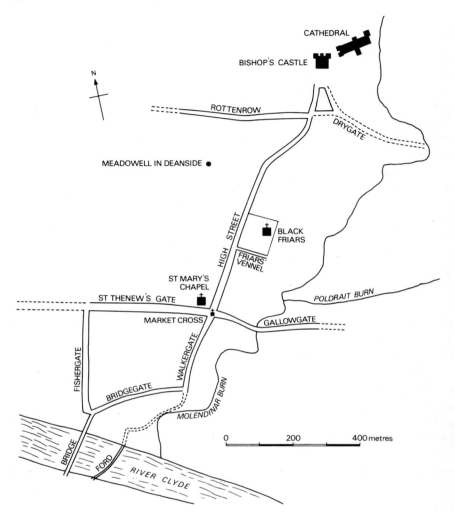

Medieval Glasgow: cathedral and burgh

also abundant evidence that the earls and others in Lennox found the fair an appropriate occasion for paying and receiving rent.[18]

Before 1240 the bishop and the dean and chapter contracted a debt to Florentine merchants,[19] an arrangement which may well have been entered into at Glasgow fair. In the 1320s the dean was a member of the famous Florentine banking family, the Bardi,[20] and was apparently in residence for at least part of the time;[21] it would have been surprising if his presence had not brought other members of the family to the fair. Edward

I of England acquired timber from the wood of Glasgow, and ordered the buying of tools, coal and iron at Glasgow.[22] The sources of the coal and iron are not known, but excavation on a High Street site has brought to light a furnace for forging iron which may be medieval. These transactions and numerous excavated pieces of pottery and the base and part of the stem of a glass drinking vessel may[23] reflect the business of the market or the fair. There is thus little to connect the clerical community in Glasgow directly with the fair; even the payments made to the bishop as lord of the fair have to be assumed for lack of evidence.[24]

The burgesses, however, were certainly engaged in trade by the 1220s, when Alexander II granted them freedom of movement and protection throughout the kingdom and also forbade the men of Rutherglen to collect toll in Glasgow: that was to be done at the customary place, Shettleston Cross.[25] By 1304, however, Bishop Robert Wishart, petitioning Edward I to allow the men of Glasgow to distrain the men of Rutherglen on all goods bought or sold in Glasgow, was able to claim that it had long been Glasgow's right to take toll from them.[26] Trade with Argyll and Lennox brought the burgesses into conflict with Dumbarton.[27] These troubles did not go away: Alexander III and Robert I both had to repeat the warning to Dumbarton,[28] and in the fifteenth century there were disputes with Renfrew, Rutherglen and Paisley.[29]

The earliest trades to be named include those of miller, baker and cobbler,[30] necessary to the whole community; archaeological excavation allows the addition of blacksmith. The appearance of a painter and a goldsmith[31] indicates that there was room for less necessary activities, perhaps made possible by clerical patronage. The textile and leather industries are revealed by references to a skinner, a dyer, a fuller, a weaver, and apparently a female weaver.[32] The existence of fullers is confirmed by the street name *vicus fullorum* (Walkergate), though the earliest references seem to be as late as the mid-fifteenth century, and by that date it would not be certain that even a majority of the street's inhabitants was engaged in fulling.[33] However, in the sixteenth century tanning was being carried on in the backlands of Walkergate and High Street using water from the Molendinar Burn, and it is not impossible that both tanning and fulling had been practised there at an earlier date.[34] Another street name, the thirteenth-century *vicus pischatorum*[35] (Fishergate), reveals another activity important to both cleric and layman. Finally, although it is acknowledged that occupational names may have become simply hereditary surnames, the fascinating name Hangpudyng[36] must surely refer to the process of smoking something like black puddings.

Another activity which existed, though perhaps intermittently, in the thirteenth and fourteenth centuries was the minting of coins. The main

E

period of activity for which there is good evidence is the reign of Alexander III. Glasgow seems to have been used as a mint for a longish period during Alexander's reign, and since its moneyer, Walter, was shared with a number of royal burghs, the initiative may have been the government's, perhaps as part of the re-coinages of 1250 and 1280 when a larger number of mints, more widely spread geographically, was used. It seems unlikely that the purpose was to benefit Bishop Bondington as chancellor, since he had demitted office in 1249, although the bishop may have had some profit from the mint. Given that there is no evidence at this date that any Scottish mint occupied a special building of its own,[37] and that security was necessary, it might be suggested that the obvious place for minting in Glasgow was the bishop's castle.

It would be difficult to overestimate the importance of the cathedral community in stimulating local trade. There was obviously the matter of supplying the canons, vicars choral, choir boys and others with the necessities of life. Also, throughout the middle ages the cathedral area must have resembled a permanent building site. The construction of a cathedral church began before 1136, and there seems to have been a sequence of building and rebuilding which lasted until at least the mid-fourteenth century. The fire at the end of the fourteenth century led to a long process of reconstruction which seems to have lasted into the early sixteenth century. The spire was replaced in stone, a rood screen and pulpitum were built, the nave was furnished with stone altars, and canopies were provided for the canons' stalls. A proposal to move the shrine of St Kentigern and reference to its jewels in the 1430s are reminders of the need for specialised craftsmen.[38] Like any cathedral, Glasgow's would have provided employment for 'masons, glaziers, sawyers, carpenters, joiners, plasterers, smiths, plumbers, coopers, carriers, painters, lime-burners and other specialists, as well as labourers'.[39]

The street-plan of later medieval Glasgow has been aptly compared to a cross of Lorraine, its layout formed by a long street ascending from the River Clyde to the cathedral and intersected at right angles by two pairs of streets, namely Trongate and Gallowgate nearer the river, and Rottenrow and Drygate further up the hill towards the cathedral.[40] An objection to using this as a description of Glasgow at an earlier period is that Drygate first appears on record only in 1410.[41] It is, however, possible that Drygate followed the line of an earlier track which would have been necessary to form one side of that triangular space of the market colonisation suggested above.[42] The evidence is scanty: Rottenrow is recorded before 1321[43] and Gallowgate at much the same time.[44] Even the existence of St Thenew's Gate (the later Trongate) can be inferred only from references to the chapel of St Mary which from later evidence is known to have stood in that street.[45] To these can be added Fishergate[46] and Friars' Vennel.[47] The street running from the river to the cathedral went by a variety of names: *via regia*; *strata regia*; *via regalis*; *commune vicus*; and 'le Weynde'.[48] The site of the market cross has to be inferred from its later position.

It is reasonable to suppose that the granting of the burgh charter encouraged the laying out of plots and the construction of buildings on them; Bishop Jocelin's grant of a toft to Melrose Abbey refers to 'the first building of the burgh'.[49] The new burgh at Glasgow may have been set apart from the cathedral area, as later occurred at Elgin where a burgh already existed. In Glasgow, access to a ford, river and a route along the river's north bank might suggest an earlier huddle of huts, but not a settlement of an overall size likely to determine the layout of the new burgh. The map of 1773 suggests that the main development lay south-west of the intersection of High Street with St Thenew's Gate and Gallowgate; the positions of the chapels lying west of the cross suggest the same. The map also shows a ribbon development along High Street, so Glasgow, like many Scottish towns, had two distinct centres: the cathedral with its associated buildings, and the burgh.

The line of the High Street was rendered obsolete by the building of a bridge; presumably the southern end (later Walkergate, and later still Saltmarket) communicated originally with the ford, but the bridge necessitated a route south-west from it. This need was presumably the origin of the street later called Bridgegate. Archaeological evidence shows that it was laid out after the delineation of the Walkergate plots; and if it is accepted that Walkergate ended roughly where the flood-plain began,[50] Bridgegate could have been built from the southern end of Walkergate, leaving a track continuing the line of Walkergate to the ford. There are, however, serious difficulties in dating the construction of Bridgegate, for references to it are late, and the name even later.[51] Who took the initiative in building the bridge, whether urban community or bishop, is not known, but it was in existence by March 1286.[52] There is no evidence to support the contentions that the original bridge was built of wood and that it was replaced in stone by Bishop William Rae in the mid-fourteenth century.[53]

Apart from the streets and the bridge, few sites can be placed on a map. The cathedral, of course, occupied its present site, and slightly to the south-west lay the bishop's castle. At least in the thirteenth century there was also a separate residence for the bishop, the *pallacium quod est extra castrum*, perhaps a hall or a courtyard group rather than a 'palace'. There were also houses for the canons 'round the church'. By the mid-thirteenth century the canons were finding them unsatisfactory, for in 1258 and again in 1268 they agreed that if one of their number were elected bishop he would pull down the *pallacium* and give the area over to houses for the canons.[54] It seems unlikely that this agreement was carried out, as no canon succeeded in becoming bishop on either of these occasions.

The parish organisation of Glasgow was centred upon the cathedral, part of which constituted the parish church.[55] There were also three chapels in the burgh, two of them much more conveniently placed for the burgesses than the cathedral up the hill. These may have been provided by the burgesses themselves, since a petition to the pope by the citizens in 1490 claimed that St Mary's had been founded by the townspeople and that the right of presentation belonged to them. St Mary's was certainly in existence by 1293, and St Thomas the Martyr's by 1320,[56] the latter dedication probably reflecting King William's devotion to Becket and thus dating back to the very early days of the burgh.[57] A reference in 1295 to the 'service of St Enock'[58] suggests that the chapel of St Thenew was already in existence, since there is no evidence of an altar of St Thenew in the cathedral. It also suggests that if Enoch is a corruption of Thenew, that change had taken place before 1295.

Earlier in the century the Dominican friars had arrived in Glasgow, and by 1246 were engaged in building their church.[59] A carved architectural fragment, probably from a doorway or fireplace-surround (and possibly thirteenth century in date) was recovered during excavation of this site, and may be from the conventual buildings. The site acquired for the community is likely to have been on the edge of the town (there is also a reference to vacant land opposite the friars),[60] indicating perhaps the extent to which building had crept up the hill towards the cathedral by the 1240s.[61] The friary had a precinct wall.[62] Later, Bishop Robert Wishart granted the friars the spring called Meadowell in Deanside to be channelled into their cloister, which must have meant piping the water under the High Street.[63]

There are scattered references in the sources to tofts: presumably the houses fronted the street and the gardens lay behind them. Archaeological excavations have shown that a variety of activities such as iron-forging took place in these backlands, and these investigations, together with historical sources, also suggest that the normal building materials were wood, wattle and clay:[64] excavated ironwork appears to have been used in wooden buildings; and a reference to stone houses in 1478[65] can be taken to mean that stone was still an unusual material at that date, although there were two sources of stone available to the burgh (the Necropolis and the site of Queen Street Station). It has been possible to identify oak, hazel and cherry as woods used in the construction of the mill on the Poldrait Burn which had a brief existence in the thirteenth or early fourteenth century,[66] but it was not necessarily typical of burgh structures. Historical references to trees and gardens include, for example, the granting of part of the bishop's garden to one of the canons.[67] References to town walls and ports all date from the fifteenth and sixteenth centuries, the 'walls' being a physical barrier or mere boundary created by contiguous back walls or fences of tenements. It would be surprising if the well-organised urban community of the late thirteenth century had no means of closing off access to the burgh at night by ports across the main streets, but what form they took and whether they were built of stone, as some later ports certainly were, is a matter of speculation.[68]

Corporate property owners in the burgh included the Templars, and the abbeys of Kilwinning, Melrose, Newbattle and Paisley.[69] Possession of a single property would suggest that it was used as a base for buying and selling or as a town residence; those prelates whose abbeys lay within the diocese of Glasgow might well have felt the need for a town house for ecclesiastical business. The grants to the Cistercian abbeys of Melrose and Newbattle by the Cistercian Bishop Jocelin may have been intended not merely as benefactions to his own order but also as a way of stimulating the economy of the new burgh by attracting business: the abbot of Newbattle is not likely to have had ecclesiastical or political reasons for lodging in Glasgow. Where an abbey acquired additional burgh properties, as Paisley and Newbattle did in the thirteenth century, one explanation is likely to have been investment in the form of revenue from rents.[70]

It is not possible to discover much about the origins of Glaswegians in the first century or so of the burgh. While it is clear that there were surnames in the modern sense,[71] even apparently established surnames could be set aside,[72] and there are several examples of simple patronymics.[73] An early inhabitant was William Gley, granted along with his toft by Bishop Jocelin to the Templars; in these circumstances, William can hardly be reckoned a free man, but the Templars' re-grant of the same toft to him made him their tenant.[74] Men bearing the name Gley were prominent in Glasgow a century later, and also appear to have been in the following of the Steward.[75] The origin of Ralph of Haddington is clear enough (since the toft which he had built was granted by Bishop Jocelin to Melrose Abbey,[76] it might be conjectured that Ralph had died and the land had reverted to the bishop). The name Mithyngby seems to derive from Miningsby (Lincolnshire), which is recorded as Mithingesbia in the mid-twelfth century.[77] Smalhy is perhaps from Smalley (Derbyshire), and Coupland from one of the places of that name in Northumberland and Cumberland.[78] Tyndale[79] suggests north-eastern England or Lothian. Dunidovir is a form of Dunnydeer (Aberdeenshire), Ra seems to be Rae (Dumfriesshire) and Roule Rule in Roxburghshire.[80] Local names are those of the bailie John de Govan, the knight John de Erskine, and the burgess William de Bonkel. The latter seems from his surname to come from Lanarkshire rather than Berwickshire; his father-in-law, the burgess Nicholas Sproull, bore a name known in Lanarkshire and Dunbartonshire in the late thirteenth century.[81] Finlay Jager's surname may be the same as Jagger, common in the West Riding of Yorkshire, but his first name seems to be Gaelic, though one does not have to look further afield than Lennox or Carrick for Gaelic-speaking families in the thirteenth century; his father's name was Ralph, so the Gaelic name is presumably from his mother.[82] The surnames Ivet (also recorded as 'son of Iveta') and Garland suggest an English origin on linguistic grounds,[83] although that might mean Lothian as readily as England itself. From such a small sample it is impossible to draw hard and fast conclusions. If English experience were applicable to Scotland, the population ought to have been recruited from areas adjacent to the burgh;[84] it is not known if it was, but it would probably be safe to conclude that thirteenth-century Glasgow, like south-west Scotland as a whole, was a 'melting-pot of races and languages'.[85]

Evidence for burghal administration does not appear until about a century after the burgh's founding, and then only thanks to the fortunate survival of a group of thirteen documents, probably spanning a period of some sixty years: the earliest can be dated 1245 x 1268 and the latest 1321.[86] As a result, 'Glasgow is as well documented as any early Scottish burgh, and much better than most'.[87] These documents show a well-organised burgh community, not only with its own officials and court, but also with its own seal.[88] Other evidence suggests that the burgh had its own writing office which could issue an *inspeximus* and demonstrate a terse style, indicating some experience in this kind of work.[89] However, many of these documents also carry the seal of the bishop's official,[90] and the main feature of the earliest surviving burgh seal is a mitred head, presumably representing St Kentigern.[91]

There is no evidence as to how burgh officials were chosen or what influence, if any, the bishop had in their appointment. The chief men of the burgh were provosts or bailies, though how many held office together cannot be deduced. There is evidence of three provosts at the same time,[92] and evidence which suggests more by naming two and referring to 'the rest of the provosts'.[93] It has been pointed out that *prepositus* and *ballivus* were probably interchangeable.[94] Although both provosts and bailies are mentioned together in documents,[95] there is nothing to indicate differentiation, and 'provosts and bailies' might be taken as a collective phrase for the leading men. This may be supported by comparing the use of *ballivus* for the official who gave formal sasine in Finlay Jager's charter with the use of *prepositus* in a similar context in the *Laws of the Four Burghs*.[96] The office of sergeant is also known, and although there is no evidence for the sergeant's functions, it can be assumed that he was an official of the burgh court.[97] There is also mention of a constable, who may be the same as a *nuntius*: *Alexander filius quondam Ricardi nuntii de Glasgw* and *terram Alexandri filii Ricardi quondam constabularii de Glasgw*.[98] It seems to be stretching coincidence to have two Alexanders, son of Richard, at the same time, even if it is odd to have different descriptions of the same man in one document, and even when there is the difficulty of knowing to which name *constabularii* is attached. Nonetheless, as far as the constable is concerned, 'the nature and authority of the office varied in various burghs',[99] and if constable and *nuntius* are to be equated, perhaps the constable was a general factotum for the burgh. It is inconceivable that there were no liners for measuring land, especially as a reference to three particates[100] shows that land in the burgh certainly was measured, but liners do not appear in the record till the early sixteenth century.[101]

There is no direct record of a guild merchant as the forerunner or partner of the burgh government, but there is a faint clue. It has been argued that in Perth one provost was also alderman, that is, head of the guild 'so that one provost by virtue of being alderman outranked his fellow provosts and was perhaps accorded the courtesy of *dominus* before his name ...'[102]. The occurrence of three provosts as witnesses, and only the first designated *dominus*,[103] perhaps points to the same situation in Glasgow, though as the provost in question is nowhere referred to as alderman, corroborating evidence is lacking.

The first clear reference to a sole provost is a reference to the provost and bailies in a grant of privileges to the university in 1453;[104] in the following year John Stewart was described as 'the first provest that was in the cite of Glasgow'.[105] Presumably the modern provostship had emerged in the 1450s, perhaps as a result of the creation of the regality in 1450;[106] however, the bishop was not granted the right to create a provost, bailies and other officials till 1476 when James III confirmed the grant of regality.[107] Did the king merely confirm what had come to be established practice, or did the bishop use the opportunity of the confirmation to control the appointment of civic officials?

By the later thirteenth century, the burgh court shows every sign of being well established, though in the surviving evidence it is seen primarily as a public occasion when land transactions could be carried out. In Robert of Mithingby's charter (1245 x 1268) sasine was given *coram prepositis et ballivis de Glasgu et xii burgensibus et aliis eiusdem civitatis*,[108] and sasine was given by a provost or a bailie;[109] the use of twelve burgesses is found in other burghs.[110] Transfer of sasine was accompanied by *intol* and *outtol*, the payment of money by buyer and seller to the officiating bailie or provost.[111] There were three head courts in the year, and lesser courts were held on a

Tuesday every fortnight.[112] By the fifteenth century, the head courts met in the tolbooth, and their proceedings were recorded on rolls in the vernacular.[113]

It is difficult to say what law was administered in the burgh court. Some documents use the term *ut moris est*, some *secundum legem burgi*, and others *secundum legem et consuetudinem burgorum* and *lex burgorum*;[114] unhappily, the evidence for the plural form *burgorum* depends on the unreliable register of Paisley Abbey, and the third form quoted above is suspiciously like *secundum legem et consuetudinem burgi* in Robert of Mithingby's charter. It is not wholly clear, therefore, if this is a reference to a set of burgh laws of general application in the manner of the *Burgh Laws*. It can be shown, however, that some parts of that collection were known and used in late thirteenth-century Glasgow: the three head courts in the year (the dates, Michaelmas, Christmas and Easter, cannot be confirmed, though October, January and April recorded in the late fifteenth century are not far out);[115] the offering of land for sale at the three head courts because of the vendor's poverty; the fortnightly courts; the twelve burgesses; the transfer of land by an official of the burgh; the payment of *intol* and *outtol*; holding sasine of purchased land unchallenged for a year and a day, and the calling in of neighbours to witness it; the accepting of sasine at a lawful time of day.[116] Finlay Jager might have been acting in accordance with the statute which lays down the procedure for the heir of a debtor who cannot pay his father's debts, since he refers to himself as heir of the late Ralph Jager, burgess of Glasgow, and declares that he has made the triple offering of his property in the three courts of the burgh.[117] On the other hand, the cases of Robert of Mithingby and Gilbert de Camera seem to follow the *Fragmenta . . . Vetera Legum*: both refer to offering their land *propinquioribus, parentibus meis et amicis* and to the presence of twelve burgesses.[118]

Despite the ability to sell, exchange and feu burgage holdings,[119] the burgesses held of the bishop in heredity and were liable to a variety of payments — an annual render of 10d to the bishop, a contribution to the burgh ferm, and services and aids to the bishop.[120] Land left without an heir presumably reverted to the bishop, and he made grants of land in the burgh: perhaps one of the earliest was the toft granted to Newbattle Abbey, since there seemed to be no need to define its boundaries.[121] A grant to Gilbert de Camera by Bishop Robert Wishart was presumably made in return for past services, since Gilbert's name is glossed as *de camera domini R. dei gratia episcopi*.[122] Earlier in the century, the names Nicholas, David and Coyn appear in witness lists, twice as *servientes* of the bishop and twice as burgesses,[123] perhaps reflecting a progression in their status, although the chronology of the four documents cannot be completely established.

Thus, although Glasgow had by the thirteenth century emerged as a 'trading fellowship with a communal life and a corporate sense',[124] it seems that the bishop remained an all-pervading and ever-present figure. Even if the ecclesiastical origin of the bulk of the sources is allowed for, the clerical element in Glasgow continued to be strong;[125] it must have been intensified rather than reduced over the course of the next three centuries, with the series of fifteenth- and sixteenth-century foundations such as the University, the Greyfriars, St Roche with its cemetery, and three hospitals.[126] Emerging late by the standards of Edinburgh but belonging to much the same period as those of Aberdeen and Dundee,[127] Glasgow's craft incorporations were granted seals of cause between 1516 and 1559 by the civic authorities, and all but one were expressly approved by the archbishop; each craft had its own altar, and there was a strong religious element in the craft regulations.[128] When a single provost appeared in the mid-fifteenth century, his appointment was in the hands of the bishop, and in 1553 the archbishop nominated two bailies to be elected for the following year.[129] The use of a burgh seal bearing a bishop's head as the principal feature continued beyond 1560 and even into the early seventeenth century.[130] In 1510 three bailies and other citizens incurred excommunication for dealing in the burgh court with a matter which properly pertained to an ecclesiastical court; despite having the earl of Lennox as provost, the citizens were obliged to renounce any laws made by them against the jurisdiction of the Church.[131] It seems clear that the Church continued to watch civic activity with a jealous eye up to the very eve of the Reformation.

NOTES

1. The origin of this study was a short article, 'Glasgow in 12th and 13th centuries: evidence other than excavation', *Glas. Arch. Soc. Bull.*, new series, xiii (1982). The evidence used is basically for the period up to the early fourteenth century, but in several instances it has been necessary to carry the story further. Between c.1320 and c.1440 there is a considerable dearth of evidence for the burgh. I should like to express my gratitude to Mr Brian Kerr who showed me slides of the High Street goods yard excavation and artefacts from several excavations carried out by SUAT in Glasgow, and to Mr Kerr and Mr Hugh McBrien for discussing this evidence with me. It has to be stressed that conclusions must remain largely tentative pending scientific analysis of the finds. A summary by McBrien and Kerr of recent excavations is 'Recent work in Glasgow by the Scottish Urban Archaeological Trust', *Glas. Arch. Soc. Bull.*, xx (1985). A foretaste of what may be revealed about diet and domestic use of plant material is contained in W. E. Boyd, 'Botanical fossils from medieval and post-medieval Glasgow', *ibid.*, xxii (1986).

2. *Glas. Reg.*, i, no. 40 (=*RRS*, ii, no. 190).

3. J. MacQueen, *St Nynia* (Edinburgh & London, 1961), 68.

4. A. P. Forbes (ed.), *Lives of St Ninian and St Kentigern* (Edinburgh, 1874), 52, 108, 110. I have not been able to find a parallel to this sculpture in either P. and F. Sharrat, *Écosse romane* (St. Leger-Vauban, 1985) or J. S. Richardson, *The Medieval Stone Carver in Scotland* (Edinburgh, 1964), but cf. the external corbels in the shape of rams' heads on St Peter's Church, Kilpeck (Hereford and Worcester) and Adel Parish Church (West Yorkshire), and the ram's head occupying one corner of a capital in the chapel at Drüggelte (Kreis Soest, Nord-Rhein Westfalen). I am grateful to Hans-Jürgen and Renate Vogt who showed me the chapel.

5. *Glas. Reg.*, i, no. 1. A recent identification of names in this document is in J. Durkan, 'The bishop's barony of Glasgow in pre-Reformation times', *RSCHS*, xxii (1986), 277–301.

6. *Chron. Melr.*, s.a. 1136.

7. Lawrie, *Annals*, 81.

8. Forbes, *Lives*, 118.

9. From Ross's map of the shire of Lanark, reproduced as the frontispiece to *Glas Recs., 1573–1642*.

10. D. C. Pollock, 'Recent excavations under Glasgow', *Glas. Arch. Soc. Bull.*, xiv (1982).

11. Reynolds, *English Towns*, 64.

12. *Glas. Reg.*, i, no. 40 (=*RRS*, ii, no. 190).

13. *Kirkintilloch Court Book*, p. xxxiii.

14. *Glas. Chrs.*, i, part II, nos. xvi, xviii.

15. *Ibid.*, i, part I, p. xxv.

16. *Glas. Reg.*, i, no. 42 (=*RRS*, ii, no. 308).

17. *Pais. Reg.*, 189–90; *C.A. Chrs.*, i, 229; *Glas. Friars*, no. 9; *RRS*, vi, no. 304; *Glas. Reg.*, i, nos. 49, 117.

18. *Lenn. Cart.*, 30, 60, 72, 80, 84–6; *Pais. Reg.*, 217.

19. *Glas. Reg.*, i, no. 176.

20. Watt, *Fasti*, 153.

21. *Glas. Reg.*, i, no. 273.

22. *CDS*, ii, 1271; iv, 452.

23. The pottery which has been excavated does not seem to have travelled far. There are only a few scraps of Scarborough ware among them. The glass has been identified as early fourteenth century in date and north European in type, but these identifications are very tentative.

24. McUre asserted that Bishop John Cameron obtained the grant of a second fair from the king; it was held in January in association with the feast of St Kentigern. It was still in existence when McUre was writing in the 1730s, and was referred to in the Town Council minutes in 1744 (J. McUre, *A View of the City of Glasgow* (Glasgow, 1736), 56; R. Renwick, *Glasgow Memorials* (Glasgow, 1908), 206). The royal grant does not survive, but McUre had information from the records then kept in the Scots College in Paris, and so his information may be correct. If this fair was held at the junction of Rottenrow and Drygate with High Street (*Glas. Chrs.*, i, part I, p. xxviii, n.), it might explain a reference to the 'two crosses' in 1477 (*Glas. Reg.*, ii, no. 412).

25. *Glas. Chrs.*, i, part II, nos. vii, viii.

26. *CDS*, ii, 1627.

27. *Glas. Chrs.*, i, part II, no. x.

28. *Ibid.*, nos. xii, xvii.

29. *Ibid.*, no. xx; *Pais. Reg.*, 274; G. S. Pryde, 'The city and burgh of Glasgow, 1100–1750', in R. Miller and J. Tivy (eds.), *The Glasgow Region* (Glasgow, 1958), 137.

30. *Glas. Reg.*, i, nos. 236, 254; *Glas. Friars*, no. 14.

31. *Newb. Reg.*, no. 177; *Glas. Reg.*, i, no. 237.

32. *Glas. Reg.*, i, nos. 220, 236, 237; *Glas. Friars*, no. 14.

33. *Glas. Reg.*, ii, no. 386; *Glas. Chrs.*, i, part II, no. xxvi; V. W. Walker, 'Medieval Nottingham: a topographical survey', *Trans. Thoroton Soc.*, lxvii (1963), 44–5.

34. I owe this point to Messrs McBrien and Kerr.

35. *Pais. Reg.*, 399–400. There is no evidence for the existence of a society of fishermen in 1201, as claimed by G. MacGregor, *The History of Glasgow* (Glasgow and London, 1881), 37. I have not been able to identify MacGregor's source: it is not McUre.

36. *Glas. Reg.*, i, no. 248.

37. I. Stewart, 'Scottish mints', in R. A. G. Carson (ed.), *Mints, Dies and Currency: Essays in Memory of Albert Baldwin* (London, 1971), 170, 172, 186, 212. The assertion that there was a mint house in Glasgow (McUre, *View*, 95) is simply derived from the knowledge that coins were struck in the burgh.

38. C. A. Ralegh Radford, *Glasgow Cathedral* (HMSO, 1970), 16–25; J. Durkan, 'The great fire at Glasgow Cathedral', *Innes Review*, xxvi (1975), 89–92, and 'Notes on Glasgow Cathedral', *ibid.*, xxi (1970), 51–69 (the medieval altars).

39. M. Biddle (ed.), *Winchester in the Early Middle Ages* (Oxford, 1976), 477.

40. Gibb, *Glasgow*, 11.

41. Renwick, *Memorials*, 15.

42. This would be the track postulated by Gibb (*Glasgow*, 14) as leading towards Lanark. Cf. the view that the street plan in the centre of Alnwick was determined by older roads (M. R. G. Conzen, 'Alnwick, Northumberland: a study in town-plan analysis'). I am grateful to Messrs McBrien and Kerr for drawing my attention to this parallel.

43. *Pais. Reg.*, 382, 384, 386.

44. *Glas. Friars*, no. 14 (dated by the ref. to John de Govan).

45. *St Mary Lib.*, 87, 244.

46. *Newb. Reg.*, no. 177; *Pais. Reg.*, 400.

47. *Glas. Reg.*, i, no. 254.

48. *Pais. Reg.*, 382, 384, 385 (twice).

49. *Melr. Lib.*, i, no. 43.

50. Gibb, *Glasgow*, 12, map of Glasgow c.1325. This map does not, however, allow for the existence of Fishergate.

51. In 1487 still described as 'the street leading to Glasgow Bridge' (*Glas. Chrs.*, i, part II, 75).

52. *Pais. Reg.*, 400.

53. McUre, *View*, 17; this was pointed out by R. Renwick and J. Lindsay, *History of Glasgow*, (Glasgow, 1921), i, 160–1. The idea that Rae built the bridge goes back to the early seventeenth century (J. Spottiswoode, *History of the Church of Scotland* (Bannatyne Club, 1850), i, 223). It was certainly possible to have a stone bridge in the later thirteenth century since there was one in Strathspey (*Moray Reg.*, no. 128). I owe this reference to Mr W. W. Scott.

54. *Glas. Reg.*, i, nos. 208, 213.

55. Cowan, *Parishes*, 74.

56. Durkan, 'Bishop's barony', 296; *Glas. Reg.*, i, nos. 248, 267.

57. *RRS*, ii, p. 11; the suggestion was made by Renwick, *Memorials*, 232–3. It is clear that by the early fifteenth century there were two chapels dedicated to St Thomas the Martyr, one at the north end of the city, and the other west of the cross (J. Durkan and J. Kirk, *The University of Glasgow, 1451–1577* (Glasgow, 1977), 26). It may be that both date back to the

late twelfth century, but Dr Durkan believes that the former is the one mentioned in 1320; 'Bishop's barony', 298. I am grateful to Dr Durkan for discussing this point with me.

58. *Newb. Reg.*, no. 177.

59. *Glas. Friars*, no. 2.

60. *Glas. Reg.*, i, 254.

61. It seems to me more likely that this marks the northern limit of the urban community's expansion, rather than an extension southwards of the clerical community associated with the cathedral. Cf. Gibb, *Glasgow*, 11.

62. *Glas. Reg.*, i, no. 237.

63. *Glas. Friars*, no. 6.

64. H. Murray, 'Medieval wooden and wattle buildings excavated in Perth and Aberdeen', in A. T. Simpson and S. Stevenson (eds.), *Town Houses and Structures in Medieval Scotland* (Scottish Burgh Survey, Glasgow, 1980); *Perth: the archaeology of the medieval town* (SUAT, 1984), 12.

65. *Glas. Reg.*, ii, no. 420.

66. D. C. Pollock, 'The Saracen Head excavation 1980/81', *Glas. Arch. Soc. Bull.*, xii (1981).

67. *Glas. Reg.*, i, no. 217.

68. *Glas. Chrs.*, part I, p. dcxxv.

69. *Glas. Reg.*, i, nos. 41, 237; *Melr. Lib.*, i, no. 43; *Newb. Reg.*, nos. 175–7; *Pais. Reg.*, 382–7, 399–401.

70. W. Stevenson 'Monastic presence', 99, 103.

71. Peter de Castro, son of Alexander de Castro (*Pais. Reg.*, 384).

72. Richard called Bruning, son of William Gley (*Glas. Reg.*, i, no. 77).

73. E.g. Nicholas, son of Germanus (*Glas. Reg.*, i, no. 236).

74. *Glas. Reg.*, i, no. 41.

75. *Ibid.*, i, no. 236; *Newb. Reg.*, nos. 176, 177; G. F. Black, *The Surnames of Scotland* (New York, 1946), 312.

76. *Melr. Lib.*, i, no. 43.

77. *Glas. Reg.*, i, no. 236; E. Ekwall, *The Concise Oxford Dictionary of English Place Names* (4th edn., 1960), 327; D. M. Smith, *English Episcopal Acta*, i, *Lincoln, 1067–1185* (London, 1980), no. 252.

78. *Glas. Reg.*, i, nos. 236, 248; Black, *Surnames*, 169–70, 733.

79. *Glas. Reg.*, i, no. 236.

80. *Ibid.*, i, nos. 236, 237; D. E. R. Watt, *A Biographical Dictionary of Scottish Graduates to A.D. 1410* (Oxford, 1977), 151; *Glas. Friars*, no. 14; Black, *Surnames*, 679, 703.

81. *Pais. Reg.*, 382–7; *Glas. Reg.*, i, no. 236; Black, *Surnames*, 743.

82. *Glas. Reg.*, i, no. 236; Black, *Surnames*, 264–5, 382; Barrow, *Anglo-Norman Era*, 49.

83. *Newb. Reg.*, no. 177; *Glas. Reg.*, i, nos. 254, 236; Black, *Surnames*, 288–9, 380.

84. Reynolds, *English Towns*, 70.

85. Barrow, *Kingship*, 12.

86. *Glas. Reg.*, i, nos. 236, 237, 248, 254; *Newb. Reg.*, nos. 176, 177; *Pais. Reg.*, 382–7, 399–400. I am unhappy about the date 1321, so easily mistranscribed, which occurs in the unreliable register of Paisley Abbey.

87. Pryde, 'Glasgow, 1100-1750', 136.

88. The earliest reference to the seal seems to be in 1270 (*Glas. Reg.*, i, no. 220).

89. *Glas. Friars*, 155; *Melr. Lib.*, ii, no. 392. It is of course possible that these documents were drawn up by the beneficiaries: the friars were on the spot, and the abbey of Melrose had property in Glasgow.

90. E.g. *Newb. Reg.*, no. 177; *Pais. Reg.*, 383, 386.

91. J. H. Stevenson and M. Wood, *Scottish Heraldic Seals* (Glasgow, 1940), i, 64; illustrated in *Melr. Lib.*, ii, plate VI, no. 3.

92. *Glas. Reg.*, i, no. 236.

93. *Ibid.*, i, no. 248; *Newb. Reg.*, no. 177.

94. Murray, *Early Burgh Organisation*, i, 33 and n.2.

95. E.g. *Pais. Reg.*, 385–6; *Glas. Reg.*, i, no. 236.

96. *Glas. Reg.*, i, no. 236; *APS*, i, 242–3.

97. *Glas. Reg.*, i, no. 248; *Newb. Reg.*, no. 177; *Abdn. Recs.*, p. xcviii, n.4.

98. *Pais. Reg.*, 384–5.

99. *Abdn. Recs.*, p. xxiii.

100. *Pais. Reg.*, 384.

101. *Glas. Rent.*, no. 606.

102. Duncan, *Scotland*, 494.

103. *Glas. Reg.*, i, no. 236.

104. *Glas. Chrs.*, i, part I, p. lxxiv; part II, 40.

105. *Ibid.*, Part II, 43.

106. *Glas. Reg.*, ii, no. 356.

107. *Ibid.*, ii, no. 410.

108. *Glas. Reg.*, i, no. 236; The dates are provided by the period of office of Archdeacon Reginald de Irvine.

109. *Ibid.*, i, no. 237; *Pais. Reg.*, 385–6.

110. *Abdn. Recs.*, pp. lxxxv–lxxxvi.

111. *Pais. Reg.*, 385–6; *Newb. Reg.*, no. 177; *Glas. Chrs.*, i, part I, p. xviii, n.2.

112. *Pais. Reg.*, 385–6; *Newb. Reg.*, no. 177; *Glas. Reg.*, i, no. 236. In Aberdeen they were held on Mondays (*Abdn. Recs.*, pp. cxvii–cxxi).

113. *Glas. Reg.*, ii, no. 453.

114. E.g. *ibid.*, i, no. 237; *Newb. Reg.*, 176; *Pais Reg.*, 382–3, 385–6.

115. *Glas. Reg.*, ii, no. 453.

116. *Leges Quatuor Burgorum*, xl, xlii, xlvii, cxii, lii, x, lxxv in *APS*, i, 334ff.

117. *Glas. Reg.*, i, no. 237; *APS*, i, 349, c.lxxix.

118. *Glas. Reg.*, i, no. 236; *Pais. Reg.*, 382–3, 385–6; cf. *APS*, i, 720–1, c.10.

119. *Newb. Reg.*, no. 176; *Pais. Reg.*, 382–4, 399–401; *Glas. Reg.*, i, no. 237.

120. *Pais. Reg.*, 382–5; *Newb. Reg.*, no. 176.

121. *Newb. Reg.*, no. 175.

122. *Pais. Reg.*, 384–5.

123. *Glas. Reg.*, i, nos. 120, 141, 108; *Pais. Reg.*, 217, where the names are reduced to Nicholdave Comyn.

124. Pryde, 'Glasgow, 1100–1750', 137.

125. The importance of the church in later medieval Glasgow is emphasised by J. N. Miner, 'Church and community in later medieval Glasgow: an introductory essay', *Histoire Sociale/Social History*, xv (1982).

126. The later medieval foundations are as follows: (1) The University, 1450 (*Glas. Reg.*, ii, no. 360); (2) The Grammar School, first reference 1460/61 (*Glas. Chrs.*, i, part II, 436); (3) St Roche's, new in 1508 (*ibid.*, i, part II, 97–9); St Roche was the patron of those suffering from the plague (*ibid.*, p. xlviii, n.1), and in 1504 there had been plague in Glasgow (*Glas. Rent.*, no. 87); (4) Little St Kentigern's, 1500 (*Glas. Reg.*, ii, no. 481); (5) Greyfriars (1473 x 1479), the site provided by Bishop John Laing (*MRHS*, 131); (6) The collegiate church of Our Lady and St Anne, by 1525 (*ibid.*, 221); (7) St Nicholas' Hospital, new in 1464 (*ibid.*,

180); (8) St Ninian's Hospital, first reference 1485 (*ibid.*, 180); (9) Blackadder's Hospital, 1524/5 (*ibid.*, 179).

127. Murray, *Early Burgh Organization*, i, 359; Wormald, *Scotland*, 49; see Lynch, Ch. 15, below, n.1. for further refs.

128. *Glas. Chrs.*, i, part I, 12, 14–19.

129. *Glas. Reg.*, ii, no. 523.

130. *Glas. Chrs.*, ii, frontispiece.

131. *Glas. Rent.*, nos. 498, 503, 504.

Part Three

Trade and Industry

8

Workshops, Materials and Debris – Evidence of Early Industries

R. M. Spearman

Industry is not a subject that is normally associated with the medieval towns of Scotland and it would be quite wrong to imply that Scotland ever had any massive manufacturing centres comparable to the great cities of northern Europe such as Bruges, Nürnberg, or Lübeck. In the whole of the British Isles the only city which might be classed alongside such great settlements was London. Nevertheless, the towns of Scotland, like the vast majority of urban settlements throughout medieval Europe, were industriously catering for the needs of their surrounding rural communities. Through their manufacturing skill burgesses converted the surplus produce of their hinterland either directly into artefacts or into other tradeable commodities. It is these various processing and manufacturing skills which are of concern here, for without a grasp of some of the practical aspects of medieval material culture it is all too easy to lose sight of the social and economic value of settlements whose size to modern eyes might suggest little more than rural villages and hamlets.

Documentary evidence provides an important source of information for any study of the manufacturing and trading abilities of Scottish burgesses, as other chapters of this book amply demonstrate. However, documentary sources, as a result of the very methods and purposes of both their compilation and survival, tend to be biased towards those materials and processes which were of interest to the great and powerful of the land. Inevitably, therefore, the majority of the surviving documents are concerned with large-scale trade in cash crops, such as wool and hides, and the services or luxuries that such crops could be used to buy. Although there are a few valuable exceptions, such as the *Ancient Burgh Laws*, it is not really until the explosion of documentation in the sixteenth century that the wide range of urban manufacturing activities was recorded in writing.

To understand more fully the diversity of the original manufacturing base of Scottish towns it is necessary to consider also the physical remains of medieval life in the burghs. The addition of evidence from material remains to that which can be gleaned from documentary sources is not, unfortunately, the historical equivalent of $2 + 2 = 4$. Before they are brought together archaeological artefacts and written documents will have been the subject of radically different levels and processes of recovery and interpretation. Any searches for a lowest common denominator which have permitted such calculations to be made in the past, invariably lead to the skill of individual historians (archaeologist or documentary) in striking a subjective balance between the two forms of evidence. It is, therefore, as well to remember what is going on. Archaeological excavations produce a great variety of 'evidence' which, at the same time, is of variable quality. The main evidence for manufacturing comes from the discovery of actual raw materials, tools and structures or half-finished goods and waste debris. However, it is very rare indeed that a tidy sequence of remains is recovered. Even if all the different parts of a process took place in the one area, it is unlikely that each stage of the work would leave some trace in the soil; those that will do so vary according to the preservative qualities of the soil. Moreover, should some diagnostic evidence of a process be initially preserved, later activities in the same area, such as the digging of pits, clearing of middens, erection of new buildings, or even other manufacturing processes, all conspire to fragment and confuse the remains of earlier industries. Thus, instead of having a logical group of manufacturing features and artefacts, what is normally recovered is the partial remains of several manufacturing processes, all of which may have been taking place on or near the area of excavation at different times.

There is, therefore, a need to sort information from archaeological excavations so that due weight is given to the different indicators of what was being manufactured in towns. First in importance are those structural and artefactual remains which are indicative of specific manufacturing activities having taken place on the excavation site itself. In this category are workshops and yards which may contain diagnostic structural remains or retain the remains of sufficient raw materials, tools, rough-outs, half-finished artefacts or waste to indicate what processes had indeed been carried out on the site. At the other end of the scale, dumps of waste material are often reasonable indicators of manufacturing processes having taken place in the vicinity, but isolated stockpiles of raw materials are a less reliable proof of manufacturing activity. Such goods could have been traded in their own right and may have been brought to the town for working or further trading. The same is true of finished artefacts which may well have been imports retailed in the town's market. The need in both cases is to demonstrate the origin of the goods in question, and this can be extremely difficult. These are but a few of the possible categories of archaeological evidence for urban manufacturing. Each piece of debris, structure or artefact needs to be considered in the light of both its archaeological context and its place in manufacturing. Indeed, documentary references to raw materials, tools, craftsmen or manufacturing ought to be treated in the same manner.

The sheer complexity of urban manufacturing rapidly becomes apparent in all such assessments. One craftsman's waste produce was more often than not another's raw material. Hence cattle slaughtered in towns became the raw material not only of fleshers, but tanners, cordwainers, cobblers, bone workers, ropemakers, horners, gutters, candlemakers and others. This was one of the many reasons for the success of Scotland's early towns: craftsmen who in isolated rural communities would not have had sufficient raw materials or large enough markets to support any development of specialist skills found that they could do so when working as a community. As a result of communal manufacturing, rural produce could be more fully and competently utilised in the towns than if it were worked, with greater wastage, at home. There were of course many social and political pressures, in addition to these economic ones, which ensured that cash crops such as wool and hide or surplus foodstuffs reached a market. Regional monopolies in trade and the manufacture of staple goods all had their part to play in concentrating agricultural wealth in a number of regional centres. Whatever the geographical or social reasons for the concentration of agricultural produce on certain settlements, it was this concentration of produce which stimulated the development of towns and manufacturing. The steady supplies of rural produce attracted and permitted the development of smiths, coopers, wrights, salters and merchants who found it worthwhile to manufacture and trade directly from these market settlements rather than merely to conduct their business at seasonal fairs.

The towns were essential to the efficient conversion of agricultural produce into the tools of better farming and the luxuries of social status. The clearest way to examine how this agricultural produce was transformed into cash and goods is to loosely divide urban manufacturing into the ancient categories of animal, vegetable and mineral. The first two categories have obvious connections with Scottish agriculture, but many of the minerals available in the towns, such as salt and iron, were also essential to the smooth running of farming communities.

Animal-based industries may be subdivided into those dealing with the produce of live animals and those based on the various parts of carcasses. Even in the largest Scottish burghs the townsfolk were directly involved in farming their surrounding countryside, as well as any vacant plots within their town. Byres, pens and other structures together with skeletal remains indicate that cattle, horses, pigs, sheep, goats and fowl were commonly kept (or allowed to scavenge) within towns. They variously provided milk, cheese, butter and eggs, as well as motive power for mills and transport, before finally being consigned to the pot. However, the main urban industries based on the produce of live animals were connected with wool trading and working. Burgesses were not directly involved in the farming of sheep for wool. The age/kill-off pattern deduced from sheep and/or goat bones recovered from sites in Perth, Aberdeen and Elgin indicates that these animals were being slaughtered for their meat, skins and woolfells. Only a small proportion of the sheep being kept in or brought to the towns were of a sufficient age at death to suggest that they had been left for their wool crop.[1] Despite a taste for mutton, then, urban communities would seem to have been primarily concerned with the working and trading of wool from flocks kept by rural, not urban, communities.

The great value of wool, even as a raw material, meant that the wool trade attracted considerable taxation and documentation. The documentation of this trade is discussed in some detail in subsequent chapters of this book but archaeology provides various insights into the actual technology and production of woollen cloth in the burghs.[2] All of the produce and most of the tools of the textile industry are of organic composition and as such are preserved only in exceptional soil conditions. Fortunately, under the centre of modern Perth, Scotland has some of the best-preserved organic remains in Europe. Several hundred pieces of medieval textile have now been recovered from excavations in Perth, to which may be added a number of fragments from Aberdeen and Elgin.[3] Most of these pieces are of animal hair, usually wool, but there are occasional examples of coarse cloth made from goat-hair and threads, cords and yarns of cow-, horse-, and goat-hair. A few threads and textiles of silk have been found but vegetable fabrics such as linen are very rare as they do not survive well once buried. Evidence of linen is, however, indicated by empty stitch holes and linen working tools such as glass smoothers and a possible flax-breaking mallet from Perth.[4] These discarded rags provide firm evidence of at least some of the textiles that were available in the major medieval burghs. Such finds avoid the problems of translation and definition inherent in descriptions of cloth in the documentary sources. There is, however, a major problem in identifying which of these fabrics may have been woven and finished in the burghs, as opposed to the surrounding countryside or abroad.

That cloth of some form or another had been woven, dyed and otherwise finished in the medieval burghs is clear from the documentary evidence.[5] It is impossible to tell what volume of cloth was manufactured, but to judge from the proportion of different textiles recovered from medieval contexts, it seems likely that the common cloth of the burghs was a 2/1 twill. The wool was often of fairly poor quality, with perhaps the better parts of the fleece going for export. As it had been prepared for spinning by combing rather than carding, the resulting cloth would have been like a type of coarse worsted. The yarn does not show whether the spinning had been undertaken professionally or that spinning wheels had been employed.[6] A few spindles and many spindle whorls testify to the continued popularity of drop spinning throughout the medieval period. Spinning wheels, of the type known in Scotland as the 'muckle wheel', were in use in England during the fourteenth century and they are likely to have been introduced into Scotland at about this time.

There is some debate about the type of looms used, for although much of this cloth is thought to have been produced on horizontal looms the various weaves and selvedges cannot positively confirm this; to date no parts of a medieval horizontal loom have been recovered through excavation. In contrast, several pieces of cloth from Perth have starting edges of the type found on cloth produced on vertical looms and there are weaving swords and pin beaters for use with such looms from Aberdeen and Perth.[7] It is apparent that the vertical loom was still in use in the burghs during the medieval period. Once woven, the cloth was often fulled but did not normally have a raised nap. There are problems in identifying the presence of dyestuffs on these pieces of textile and the number of pieces forwarded for testing has been small. However, a sample of pieces from Perth suggests that only some 30% had been dyed although almost 60% of the remainder had a certain amount of natural pigmentation.[8]

Little can be deduced of the tailor's craft from these scraps of well-used cloth. However, the recovery of a wide range of bone, copper alloy and iron needles as well as occasional iron scissors and shears from Perth and elsewhere testifies to both amateur and professional cloth working. A few fragments of felt, one from Perth being of good quality,[9] indicate another dimension to the working of wool which perhaps extended to hatting. Bone and metal dress pins, buttons and buckles provide further clues to the range of clothes produced.

More diverse than the crafts using live animal produce were those based on the various parts of carcasses. The cattle, although small by modern standards, provided for greater quantities of meat and skin, plus lard, bones, guts, horn and many other serviceable raw materials per head than sheep, goats or pigs. As industrial raw material cattle were by far the most important breeds of animal. This is reflected in the bone assemblages from urban sites which indicate that cattle were consistently the most commonly slaughtered of the commercial animals. The overwhelming majority of these cattle were of the age of five to six, which would suggest that the primary requirement was for hides not meat.

After wool, hides were Scotland's most valuable raw material. Documentary sources provide, then, useful information on the taxation and export of hides, but it is archaeology that has demonstrated the importance of hide preparation and working in the towns.[10] Preparation of the hides depended upon whether they were for export or for home use. The drying and salting of hides for export required much less outlay of time, skill and investment than did actual tanning to produce serviceable leather. The organic materials involved in both these processes are not normally recovered by excavation. In addition, the sites of skinners' and tanners' yards were deemed noxious even by medieval standards so that they were located away from town centres and hence have largely avoided excavation. Nevertheless, the existence of medieval skinners' yards has been indicated by large quantities of cow-hair and scraps of leather as in the Gallowgate, Aberdeen, and also the High Street, Perth.[11] On another site in Aberdeen, the Queen Street midden area, a pit containing large quantities of animal hair and oak bark confirmed the existence of a medieval tanning industry in Aberdeen.[12] Elsewhere, trial excavations on the outskirts of medieval Linlithgow and Inverness have identified the remains of possible tanning pits.[13] The widespread working of leather in the towns is evidenced by the occurrence of leather offcuts on virtually all urban sites where the conditions have allowed leather to survive. At least some of this work must have been amateur, but concentrations of specific types of offcuts and leather-working tools indicate the existence of specialist cobbling and cordwaining workshops as at Perth, and perhaps the Gallowgate site in Aberdeen. The range and quality of leather goods that were produced in the towns in evidenced by the recovery of numerous decorated scabbards, belts and coverings, a wide variety of footwear, fragments of jerkins and leggings.[14]

Although the presence of so much beef in the burghs was largely a result of the leather trade, the starting point for all the carcass-related industries was the fleshers who obviously benefited from such a considerable traffic in cattle. By comparison with textiles and leather, skeletal remains are a robust and common find from medieval sites and demonstrate clearly that the basic butchering of carcasses was carried out with knives and cleavers. It seems that saws were mainly employed by bone, antler and horn workers. However, there are many problems in deriving detailed information about butchering and related industrial activity from bone assemblages. Eating habits and social divisions or the butchering of meat for salting and storage would all have affected the distribution of bones associated with the better cuts of meat. Conversely, the removal from the flesher's yard of low meat value toe and skull bones may be associated with horn working, the production of neatsfoot oil, the removal of skins for tanning or perhaps all three processes together. The complexity of skeletal assemblages recovered from urban excavations makes it clear that all these activities were being carried out. Moreover, in those towns where several excavations have taken place it is apparent that craftsmen involved in utilising the various parts of the carcass were, at different times, situated in different districts of the town.

The tallow, guts, sinews and other fragile organic by-products of butchery do not survive in even the most favourable soil conditions. Archaeology can provide little information, therefore, on candle and soap making or the use of gut and sinew. In the same way, hoof and horn does not usually survive, but toe bones and the bone cores from inside cattle, sheep and goat horns are a common find. Occasionally, as from sites in Perth, Inverness and Inverkeithing, saw-cuts on the horn-cores confirm that they are waste from horn working. The large number of horn-cores from Methven Street and High Street, Perth suggest an industry of considerable organisation. On the Perth High Street site 1,753 cattle and 722 goat horn-cores were recovered. Indeed, on these two sites the minimum number of individual animals indicated by the tally of horn-cores is far higher than that suggested by any other bones recovered. It would seem that horn on the cores was being gathered from around the town or even imported into towns for working. Some evidence of the utilisation of hooves, which have the same composition as horn, has been recovered from sites in Inverness and Inverkeithing where toe bones of cattle and horses have chop marks caused during the removal of the hooves.[15]

Another major raw material drived from animal carcasses was the bone itself. Not only was bone cheap and readily available, it was strong and capable of being finely worked. There is a wide range of objects and workmanship in bone. At the simplest level specific bones had virtually ready-made uses, such as pins or awls made from pig fibula, spindle whorls made from femur heads, or ice skates made from horse metapodials. Such finds are relatively common but there is also evidence, from unfinished objects and blanks prepared from bovine longbones and scapulae, of a more organised and skilful craft. The products of these skilled bone workers included pins and needles, gaming pieces, dice, knife handles, bobbins and toggles. Among the finest pieces of workmanship are five well-made bone plates with incised decoration from Perth which were most probably made locally for the decoration of caskets.[16]

These same skilled bone workers were probably responsible for high-quality work in another closely related medium, antler. A bone- or antler-working tool-kit, including two hammer heads made from antler burrs, and an antler tine wedge have been found from medieval contexts in Aberdeen.

Scrap pieces of waste red deer antler have been found on sites in Aberdeen, Perth, Elgin and Inverness. Excavations in Elgin and Perth High Street have also produced pieces of roe deer antler.[17] The principal produce made from these antlers was very fine single- and double-sided combs, several of which have been found in Perth, and there is also one single-sided comb from Aberdeen. Other artefacts made of antler in the burghs include knife handles and spindle whorls.[18]

The importing of antler to the burghs raises the question of venison and other wild animal produce reaching urban communities. The number of red and roe deer bones suggest that only occasional haunches of venison reached the towns. Documentary sources indicate that furs were also being brought to the towns either for home or foreign trade. However, perhaps because the techniques for preserving such skins were different from those used for tanning leather, no furs have been positively identified from excavation. In contrast, and despite their small size, fish bones are frequently found on excavation. The larger bones of larger fish, such as the head bones of salmon and cod, are more easily found and identified. Nevertheless, their incidence of recovery may also reflect how the different fish were preserved. The salting and barrelling of smaller fish such as herring might not even involve gutting, still less filleting. However, larger fish needed to have their guts and heads removed if they were to be preserved for any length of time. Shellfish such as oysters and both fresh and salt water mussels are an almost ubiquitous find on medieval sites and they must have been widely traded.

Of those industries that used either wild or domesticated vegetable matter as their basic raw material, the most commercially important were involved in the preparation of food and drink, the working of wood in all its various forms, and the production of cloth from bastic fibres such as flax. There is useful documentary evidence for these industries, but where preservation allows, archaeological evidence is of unique importance. The linen industry has been reviewed above but flax seeds also provided linseed oil, and a wide range of seeds, including those of flax, have been recovered from archaeological excavations. Seeds are generally the most robust part of a plant, and in a number of instances their identification throws some light on industrial activities in the towns. Flax seeds are frequently present in those soils with good preservation, and a concentration of them in a medieval building on the Kirk Close site in Perth may indicate the production of either linseed oil and/or flax fibres.[19] It is also worth noting that the seed remains of a few dye plants such as weld (dyer's rocket) have been identified from sites in Elgin, Aberdeen and Perth.[20] Originally dyer's rocket must have been introduced to the country for use as a source of pigment, but it is not possible to tell whether this plant was being grown commercially in the burghs.

Of the vegetable foodstuffs that have been identified within the burghs from their seed and other remains the most common are the cereals: oats, barley and wheat. Wheat was especially thought of as a cash crop for the production of bread, while oats and barley provided the porridge and ale of the masses. Less commonly found are brassica seeds such as turnips and kail, and legume seeds such as beans and peas which were most probably grown for private consumption.[21] The archaeological recovery of so much grain no doubt reflects the importance of cereal crops in the burgh economy, but it is also a result of the common preservation of grain or malt through its accidental carbonisation during drying. The damp Scottish weather has meant that grain was normally dried before milling, while in the production of malt for brewing germination was stopped by parching the sprouting barley. The drying furnaces were the same for both processes. Such furnaces are common on urban excavations in Scotland, and there are instances of their repair and replacement over many years. Appropriately, several large drying furnaces have been discovered along Meal Vennel and also the Mill Lade in Perth.[22]

The grinding of grain would normally have been carried out in the water-powered mills controlled by the burgh's feudal superior or latterly by the burghs themselves. Few medieval mills, rural or urban, have been excavated in Scotland although the likelihood is that most urban mills were powered by vertical wheels of the undershot type. The only example excavated to date is on the outskirts of Glasgow on the Poldrait.[23] A wooden cog wheel, most probably from the gearing of a water mill, was recovered from Perth.[24] In addition to the commercial powered mills, some limited grinding of grain for private use is indicated by the recovery of rotary hand querns from urban excavations.[25] Structural remains of ovens for the baking of bread in the burghs fall into two categories, single- and double-chambered. An example of the simplest type of oven was excavated in Aberdeen which consisted of a single chamber of wattle and clay constructed in the form of a beehive over a substantial hearthstone.[26] At Meal Vennel in Perth the stone base for such an oven was made from a reused rotary quern stone.[27] The oven was heated by lighting a fire on the hearthstone inside the chamber. Once the oven was hot enough the embers were raked out and the bread was placed inside on the hearthstone. The chamber was then sealed and as the oven cooled the bread baked. This is a fairly basic, small-scale oven which must normally have been for private use. A larger oven, which may have been more typical of the type used by baxters, was excavated at Kirk Close, Perth. In this type the oven was constructed from stones as well as wattle and clay set against the wall of an outbuilding with a paved working area around the oven itself.[28] A fire was kindled in a lower chamber below that of the actual oven so that heating could be continuous.

Wood was central to almost every aspect of medieval town life. Among the more important urban industries making use of wood, other than as a fuel, were house and boat builders, coopers, carpenters, and turners. The extent to which the simpler wattle houses in the backlands of properties were the result of specialist craftsmen is open to question. However, more substantial buildings on at least some street frontages and backlands have been recovered which demonstrate, along with various re-used timbers in other structures, much higher standards of craftsmanship.[29] The re-use of timbers has also provided a number of examples of ships' timbers, but while it is likely that at least some of the ferries, river-boats and coasters represented by these timbers were built by shipwrights in Scottish towns, this cannot be proven.[30]

The evidence of cooperage is quite common on those sites where wood has survived. Barrels were essential to the exporting by sea, and to the airtight preservation of many goods and foods; not surprisingly, fragments have been recovered from Aberdeen, Inverness, Elgin and Perth. At sites in the latter three towns barrels were re-used to line wells.[31] Some of these barrels would no doubt have been imported from abroad and no cooperages have been identified in Scottish towns. However, the range of vessel staves recovered from sites makes it likely that skilled coopers were working in the towns or more probably adjacent woodlands to produce a range of bowls, tankards, porringers, buckets, and barrels for urban markets. Alternatives to the smaller coopered vessels were wooden bowls and cups turned on simple pedal lathes. Several turned vessels have been recovered from Aberdeen and Perth, but as yet the characteristic waste blocks from inside these bowls have not been found within the burghs and wood turners serving urban communities may also have been based in neighbouring woodland.[32]

The third and final category of raw material used in the towns is the minerals. The documentary evidence for these industries is extremely variable. It is often only those parts of an industry which involved large-scale building or foreign trade that were recorded, while the local backbone of the industry is missed. Little, for instance, is written about the substantial pottery industries which developed beside Aberdeen, Inverness, Perth and other towns, to provide the inhabitants with their everyday cooking pots and jugs. The quarrying and purchase of building stone, in contrast, appears in the records of various institutions, and yet few domestic buildings made use of stone until the sixteenth century.[33]

Along with the simplest of materials, clay and stone, this section covers a very wide range of industries, several of which made highly skilled use of complex raw materials. The structures of these industries were often highly developed, with the sorting, refining or smelting of minerals often being carried out in the countryside, while any specialist finishing of the material normally took place in the towns. This pattern is seen most clearly in the metalworking industries. Waste from iron smithing is one of the most ubiquitous of finds from urban excavations and substantial smithies have been discovered at Inverness, Perth and Elgin.[34] It is clear from this ironworking waste that iron ore was not smelted in the towns. The origin of all the iron used in the towns is unknown but it included bloomery iron in an unsmithed state and probably scrap and imported iron. The most probable source for the former was the many moorland bloomeries of Scotland which utilised bog-iron.[35] On arrival in the towns these crude blooms were first worked into serviceable wrought iron and then all the multivarious iron nails, tools, weapons and implements that were required. Without more rural excavation it is unclear how the work of the urban and rural smiths differed, although it is likely that the urban smith was more skilled and had access to larger supplies of iron and steel than his rural counterpart.

Because of the value and craftsmanship of the products, non-ferrous metalwork was mainly the preserve of urban smiths. An exception was the lead used for roofing, windows and piping in large medieval buildings. Perhaps because it was such an easily worked metal and ore, leadworking furnaces are commonly excavated in and around castles and churches. However, a much larger open furnace associated with leadworking was discovered in Inverness. This would seem to have been for a more complex use of the metal, but it has not been possible to determine what that was.[36] Any lead that was worked for silver would have been taken abroad or to Scottish goldsmiths for cupellation. Precious metalworking sites are rare and no mint has been excavated, although one specialist metal workshop has been excavated in Perth.[37] Of more common occurrence are the remains of scrap copper, bronze and brass, often in sheet form, which confirm the availability of non-ferrous smithing. Fragments of debris from the casting of copper alloy jewellery and fittings, including small crucibles and a wide range of clay and occasionally stone moulds, have been found in Aberdeen, St Andrews, Elgin and Perth.[38] Moreover, clay moulds from Canal Street, Perth, indicate that a range of vessels had been cast near the site, while folded pieces of copper alloy sheet were clearly from the repair of such vessels. At least some of the raw material of this workshop consisted of broken pieces of vessels, fragments of which were also found.[39] Other important materials were closely connected with towns through trade and use, rather than manufacture. Some of these, such as salt for the preservation of fish, meat and hides, were brought to the towns in their refined state. Others, such as limestone, chalk, alum, saltpetre, and the ashes of various plants would have been brought to the towns as anything from ship's ballast to burnt lime, lyes, mordants and gunpowders. Although there are occasional finds of limestone and chalk, many of these materials are water soluble and are not recovered. Knowledge of their use comes, therefore, from related products and documentary records of their purchase. A more robust example of the importation and use of a prepared product is glass. Fine imported glassware has been found in the towns, and with this glass, almost certainly, would have come lumps of cullet, which are pieces of ready-made glass for working by local glassblowers. Although no pieces of cullet have been recovered from excavation, there are from Elgin offcuts of glass from the work of a glassblower repairing the windows of the cathedral.[40]

A wide range of Scottish urban industry using all categories of material, animal, vegetable and mineral, has been illuminated through excavation, and many aspects of manufacturing have been illustrated for the first time. However, it is important to realise that old and new techniques and equipment were being used alongside one another at the same time, such as vertical and horizontal looms. Changes in technology do not take effect immediately today and were even more gradual in the medieval period. In part this was a result of the great variety in size, business and function of Scottish burghs.[41] Also, with the exception of a few busy specialist craftsmen, the inhabitants of even the largest medieval burghs were still directly involved in farming. Most urban manufacturing was, therefore, tied to the farming cycle for labour as well as materials. Even if they had wanted to, very few craftsmen would have been able to stockpile sufficient raw materials to avoid seasonal working. Seasonal working should not, however, be equated with unskilled or simple manufacturing: for a blacksmith it might mean the difference between building up stocks of worked bloomery iron and the smithing of building materials and ploughing equipment; for a bone worker it might mean the opportunity to work in antler.

The restricted area of urban excavations means that archaeology has provided only a sample of the remains that exist and the activities that took place in different parts of a town. Much of the general framework that facilitates some understanding of the more fragmentary evidence comes from documentary sources. Without the written evidence for trade, manufacturing and many other aspects of urban life, the results of excavation would lose much of their impact. However, it is through the detailed archaeological examination of specific sites, features and materials that the true complexity of manufacturing resources and labour in the Scottish towns has begun to emerge. Moreover, when such information is set alongside documentary evidence for life and work in the towns the result is not simply a more complete picture of the past, it is a different way of looking at the primary evidence. We are brought firmly back to the materials of trade and subsistence. In the processing and marketing of these materials lies the economic function of the towns: the reason for their success or failure; the reason for their origin.

NOTES

1. Bone Reports in: Murray, *Abdn. Excavns.*, 234–6; Lindsay, *Elgin Excavns.*; Thoms, *Perth, St Ann's Lane Exc.*, 452; Blanchard, *Perth, Canal St Exc.*, 516; *PHSE bone*; Holdsworth, *Perth Excavns.*

2. See Ditchburn, Ch. 10, and Stevenson, Ch. 11, below.

3. Textile Reports in: Murray, *Abdn. Excavns.*, 197–200; Holdsworth, *Perth Excavns.*; *PHSE textiles*; Lindsay, *Elgin Excavns.*

4. *PHSE textile, wood, glass.*

5. See Ditchburn, Ch. 10, and Stevenson, Ch. 11, below.

6. *PHSE textile.*

7. Worked Bone and Wood Reports in: *PHSE textile, bone*; Murray, *Abdn. Excavns.*, 179, 182–3, Ills. 103.9, 105.27.

8. *PHSE, textile.*

9. Textile Report in: Holdsworth, *Perth Excavns.*; *PHSE textile, metalwork.*

10. See D. Ditchburn's & A. Stevenson's chapters below.

11. Leather Report in: Murray, *Abdn Gallowgate Exc.*; *PHSE leather.*

12. Greig, *Abdn., Queen St. Midden Exc.*, 22.

13. *D & E* 1974, 68; 1976, 37.

14. Leather Reports in: Murray, *Abdn. Excavns.*, 191–7; *PHSE leather, metalwork*; Holdsworth, *Perth Excavns.*

15. Bone Reports in Holdsworth, *Perth Excavns.*; Wordsworth, *Inverness Exc.*, 377; Wordsworth, *Inverkeithing Exc.*, 544; *PHSE bone.*

16. *PHSE worked bone.*

17. Bone Reports in: Murray, *Abdn. Excavns.*, 180–82; Holdsworth, *Perth Excavns.*; *PHSE bone, worked bone*; Lindsay, *Elgin Excavns.*; Wordsworth, *Inverness Exc.*, 377.

18. Worked Bone Report in: Murray, *Abdn. Excavns.*, 182, Ill. 105.30; Blanchard, *Perth King Edward St Exc.*

19. Blanchard, *Perth, Kirk Close Exc.*; *PHSE worked bone.*

20. Botanical Report in: Murray, *Abdn. Excavns.*, 239–43; Lindsay, *Elgin Excavns.*; Holdsworth, *Perth Excavns.*; *PHSE botanical.*

21. Botanical Report in: Blanchard, *Perth, King Edward St Exc.*; *PHSE botanical.*

22. McGavin, *Perth, Mill St Exc.*; Blanchard, *Perth, Meal Vennel Exc.*

23. *D & E* 1981, 36.

24. *PHSE wood.*

25. *PHSE stone*; Blanchard, *Perth, Meal Vennel Exc.*

26. Murray, *Abdn. Excavns.*, 54, Ill. 26.

27. Blanchard, *Perth, Meal Vennel Exc.*

28. Blanchard, *Perth, Kirk Close Exc.*

29. Worked wood in: Murray, *Abdn. Excavns.*, 224–9; *PHSE wood, buildings*; Holdsworth, *Perth Excavns.*

30. *PHSE wood.*

31. Murray, *Abdn. Excavns.*, 180, Ill. 102.3–6; Lindsay, *Elgin Excavns.*; Wordsworth, *Inverness Exc.*, 375, fig.

32. Murray, *Abdn. Excavns.*, 177–224; *PHSE wood*; Holdsworth, *Perth Excavns.*; Lindsay, *Elgin Excavns.*

33. See Stell, Ch. 4, above.

34. Metalworking debris Reports in: Wordsworth, *Inverness Exc.* 347–55; Blanchard, *Perth Meal Vennel*; Lindsay, *Elgin Excavns.*

35. Aitken, W. G., 'Excavation of bloomeries in Rannoch', 188–204.

36. Metalworking debris Reports in: Wordsworth, *Inverness Exc.*, 352.

37. Blanchard, *Perth, King Edward St Exc.* archive.

38. Metalworking debris Reports in: Murray, *Abdn. Gallowgate Exc.*; Wordsworth, *St Andrews, Kirkhill Exc.*; Lindsay, *Elgin Excavns.*; Holdsworth, *Perth Excavns.*

39. Metalworking debris Reports in: Holdsworth, *Perth Excavns.*

40. Lindsay, *Elgin Excavns.*

41. See Lynch, Ch. 15, below.

9

Inland Trade:
A Study of Aberdeen in the Later Middle Ages

Harold W. Booton

The internal and regional trade of Aberdeen in the later middle ages was created by both the geographical assets of the burgh and the produce and demands of its hinterland.[1] The first were of considerable importance. Trade in the medieval period tended to be seaborne and, situated as it was on the estuary of the River Dee, much of Aberdeen's regional as well as international commerce was via the sea.[2] The harbour area was an important and busy centre of trade with goods being moved from there to various parts of Aberdeen at different rates of charge. Aberdeen possessed a relatively rich agriculturally based hinterland and the burgh served this in a variety of ways: as an entrepôt, collection, distribution and manufacturing centre. Regional trade was not confined to the sea, for there were important overland communications which must have represented a substantial but unknown percentage of regional commerce centred on Aberdeen. To help such inland trade there was to the north of the burgh a bridge over the River Don by the fourteenth century and by 1529 a bridge over the River Dee to the south of Aberdeen.

Aberdeen in the later middle ages enjoyed a flourishing domestic trade which was sophisticated in its structure and functioned at three levels: Aberdeen burgh; north–east regional, and national. The map opposite sets out the main centres mentioned frequently in documentary sources. This chapter will consider each of the various types of trade in depth but a number of useful generalisations can be applied to all of them. It was a phenomenon based on or near the east coast of Scotland, and a considerable number of Scottish vessels must have been engaged in carrying commodities between Aberdeen and other Scottish burghs during the late medieval period. It is important to note how much of the trade was east-coast orientated and tended to be confined to lowland areas with urban development rather than the Highlands or western parts of Scotland. Given that at around 1500 twenty-three out of the thirty-six royal burghs were sited on or near the east coast, this characteristic of the

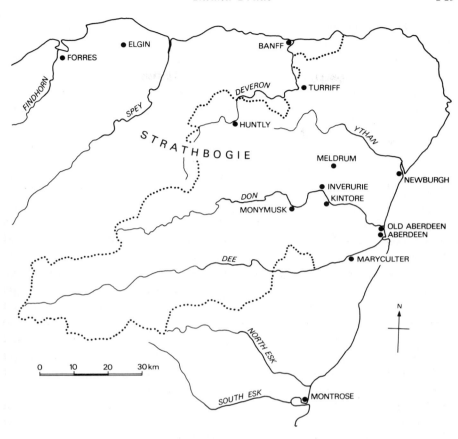

Aberdeen's trading hinterland

commerce is not surprising.[3] A variety of goods were traded internally at all of the respective levels, but foodstuffs and raw materials such as wool, skins and hides predominated.

The very sparse nature of the documentary evidence makes it difficult for the historian to be able to effectively identify the processes of Aberdeen burgh trade before 1400. Its early existence is indicated briefly in the texts of some of the first surviving Aberdeen burgh charters. For example, William I confirmed the trading privileges of Aberdeen burgesses as early as c.1171–85.[4] A weekly general market was held in the Castlegate, the main street of late medieval Aberdeen, and the right to hold this had been granted to the burgh in 1273. In the seventeenth century Parson Gordon described how the Castlegate was the town's 'mercat place and gives room abundantlie to the weeklie mercat which is made up by the confluence of the country people dwelling heir about the toune'.[5]

The Castlegate also contained the townhouse or tolbooth of Aberdeen and was itself an important focal point of burgh trade, for all goods entering the town were declared there for taxes to be levied on them. The Castlegate was not the only burgh market place. There was a flourishing business in the sale of fish on the seashore at Footdee by local fishermen. The council of Aberdeen disliked this activity as it was carried on without their permission, and periodic attempts were made to regulate the market to prevent unfair trading practices. Aside from the daily fish market and weekly burgh market much urban trade was carried on from the booths of both burgesses and craftsmen. The economic value of a well-located booth frontage was reflected in the high rents such units commanded. There was often considerable competition for the lease of prime booths and in particular those under the Aberdeen tolbooth.

Aberdeen was an important centre for livestock and meat trading. A brief indication of the trade can be seen in October 1485 when the Aberdeen town council received a letter from the crown ordering them to confiscate all beef and cattle that were being taken out of the burgh with the single exception of provisions for ships.[6] Unfortunately although the reference suggests the existence of a livestock trade, no reason is stipulated as to why the central government wished to prevent meat and cattle from leaving the burgh. Cattle and sheep needed pasture when brought to the burgh market and these matters were carefully administered by the town council. For example in May 1487 it was ordered that all outsiders bringing in livestock to the burgh market must pay 1d 'for ilk beast' that they put on the links of Aberdeen.[7] These animals were bought and sold in Aberdeen at 'the common oppin market'.[8] One interesting piece of evidence demonstrates a landed man buying sheep in the Aberdeen burgh market. In 1527 Thomas Lamintoun accused Thomas Scherar of withholding from him £3 16s. 'for xx scheip we sold togidder til ane gentilman til landwart'.[9] Apart from fish and meat, Aberdeen burgh saw trading in other foodstuffs such as butter, cheese, eggs and flour.[10] The burgh also acted as a centre for dealing in hides and skins on an extensive scale. Nearly every year from 1434 to 1535 saw men in Aberdeen convicted by the town authorities of buying and selling of hides and skins illegally. This suggests both the extent of the trade as well as the attempts of the Aberdeen council to control it. They were valuable commodities. In 1508 John Low promised to pay in silver for three oxhides and three cows: similarly in 1526 mention is made of the skins of John Murray in Aberdeen being worth over £200.[11]

Although the evidence is very sparse, there was some burgh trading in goods manufactured within Aberdeen. An interesting glimpse of this can be seen in the 1480s when one baronial customer demanded high standards for the manufactured goods he purchased in the burgh. Sir William Knollis, preceptor of Torphichen, was much involved in the export of salmon abroad from his lands at Maryculter, in Kincardineshire. To be able to do this he required a large number of good barrels for the secure despatch of his fish abroad. Sir William bought his barrels from the Aberdeen coupers and on 14 August 1486 he appeared in the burgh tolbooth and asked that 'the barrells that thai [the coupers] haid maid new for salmon pakking are of the same band and messur that thai wer of many yeris bigane'[12]

The value and importance of this particular baronial custom was reflected in the presence of seven coupers in the tolbooth that day who agreed to maintain high standards. Apart from this instance of burgh manufacturing, Aberdeen had a small luxury trade, met by specialised craftsmen, in particular gold and silversmiths. Evidence of their activities for the supply of the urban market is very sparse, but in 1520 a local laird commissioned work from an Aberdeen goldsmith. The laird of Meldrum bought silver from William Watson, an Aberdeen goldsmith, and ordered him to make it into a decorative bird.[13] In the spring of 1480 Sir Alexander Irvine of Drum visited an Aberdeen tailor to purchase new headgear.[14]

The considerable importance of trade in the economic life of later medieval Aberdeen was reflected in the attempts by the town council to manipulate and control the terms and processes of trading within the burgh. The urban authorities used various means to achieve effective economic intervention. The most frequent weapon was that of burgh statute with officers appointed by the town council to enforce local laws. Occasionally during periods of food shortage legislation was relaxed and normal codes of practice were suspended in the interests of promoting rapid supplies for the town market. The desire to prevent shortage led the burgh to attempt to control not only its immediate market but that of the supplying regions.[15] The statutes made by the council of Aberdeen to control burgh trade covered a very wide range of matters, and in particular the price of goods was a frequent item for town legislation. Indeed these price statutes reveal that between 1435 and 1531 the burgh market was affected by a degree of price inflation. For instance bread doubled in price during these years and mutton increased by two and a quarter times. Throughout this period the town bakers were unsuccessfully ordered to keep the price of bread to the levels set by the burgh council and bailies. The council also attempted to control the prices of other commodities which figured in Aberdeen burgh commerce. For example in 1445 the price of wool was set at a maximum of 5 shillings per stone.[16] Similarly in the 1440s ale was constantly set at 4d and 6d per gallon by the council.[17]

F

Meat was also subject to similar price controls by the authorities of Aberdeen.

Statutes were not only used in an attempt to control the prices of food in the Aberdeen market place. Strict controls were maintained on forestallers by the council with hides, skins and wool being the main commodities covered by burgh legislation. In 1438 five burgesses were found guilty of forestalling and four were fined 20 shillings and one 4 shillings.[18] That the burgh increased the fines for the offence of forestalling through the fifteenth century further suggests some level of inflation within the town economy. By 1482 66 shillings was the penalty for a first offence of forestalling.[19] The burgh authorities used their own officers to help enforce burgh legislation on the conduct of town trading. In 1489 reference is made to the council employing two officers to 'keip' the market and ensure adherence to burgh price and trading regulations every Wednesday and Saturday. The amount of work that these two burgh officials were expected to do was probably excessive, for in 1508 the council appointed two extra men to help regulate the processes and prices of the burgh market.[20]

Apart from legislation on prices and imposition of fines, the burgh council also attempted to profit from town trade. There were burgh taxes on urban trade and the council appointed an officer to collect the dues. On a regular basis the council fixed both the amount they wanted to raise and the fee of the collecting officer. For example in 1460 Alexander Rolland was set the right to levy burgh trade tolls for a period of five years and was to pay 24 shillings to the town authorities for the money he collected.[21] The town granted a special licence to one burgess to have a monopoly of the Sunday fish market of Aberdeen. This was a very valuable privilege and one which was much sought after. In 1493 John Chalmer received the right because he offered the council the highest rent for the licence: three barrels of salmon each year.[22]

During periods of food shortage the Aberdeen council waived the statutes it normally used to govern the burgh markets and the trading practices of dealers. For example in the winter of 1509 the town was short of basic foodstuffs so that the council stipulated that any persons from the regions of Scotland who had food to sell might bring it into the burgh market of Aberdeen and sell it free of all taxes and burgh regulations.[23] In normal circumstances the council carefully stipulated who could trade in Aberdeen. Usually such concessions were confined to 'freemen', that is craftsmen and burgesses of guild, and simple burgesses who were entitled to trade within the burgh.[24] Those who were not possessed of such privileges could only buy food or goods for themselves or their families. The council each year repeated these restrictions on who might participate in burgh commerce and levied heavy fines on 'unfreemen' found guilty of dealing in hides, skins and fish.[25]

It should not be thought that the trading life of the late medieval burgh of Aberdeen was so over-regulated and controlled by the council as to be stagnant and stifled. The urban authorities wanted trade to grow and prosper and tried to achieve this through beneficial intervention. For instance in 1456 the council set up a court of six members of the town council who were to sit each Monday and decide on 'small complaints'. These were specifically described as burgh trading disputes which involved sums of less than £5.[26] The burgh authorities of Aberdeen were also ambitious to increase their dominance and control not only of town trade, but also regional commerce. This trend is revealed in the early sixteenth century. For instance in November 1502 the burgh council obtained a royal letter stating that all those who bought or sold goods and food outwith the burgh gates and thereby avoided burgh regulations and taxes faced fines. This was not an idle threat for six months later in the spring of 1502 Robert Brown of Skene was found guilty of trading illegally outside Aberdeen and fined. The town council later tried to control trade with the regions by the use of licences. In 1519 a special licence was introduced for those who wanted to trade in the north-east with the approval of the burgh authorities.[27] Unfortunately it is impossible to determine if the licence system was applied vigorously or not. It is of interest to note that by the seventeenth century Gordon remarked on how the 'market tounes villedges and hamlets of the shyres and countrey neerest neighbouring to Aberdeine ... are ... subject to thame, that without the licence of Aberdeen they dare nather tradde in merchandice ather by sea or land'.[28]

What were the 'tounes' and 'villedges' trading regionally with Aberdeen in the late medieval period? In the context of the north-east Forres, Elgin, Newburgh, Banff, Pitcaple, Old Aberdeen (still a separate burgh), Turiff and Montrose all had regional trade links with Aberdeen.[29]

The bounds of this economic strength were Forres and Elgin in the north-west and Montrose to the south. A brief indication of the growing importance of regional trade can be seen as early as 1287 when the Guardians of Scotland set up a commission to adjudicate upon a dispute over fairs between the burgesses of Montrose and Aberdeen.[30] Similarly two years later in 1289 the burgesses of Banff requested the Guardians to give them a confirmation of the fairs held in Aberdeen 'for the benefit of us and of other burghs lying to the north of the mountains which fairs are obstructed and every year disturbed by burgesses of Montrose ... to the injury of Aberdeen and ... the whole northern province'.[31] This evidence suggests that by the 1280s Aberdeen was the premier north-east burgh whose fairs were of considerable economic importance to the other smaller urban centres in the region. In 1485 taxation figures for the burghs north of the Forth reveal how Aberdeen's regional economic pre-eminence within the north-east had grown even stronger by the late fifteenth century. Aberdeen was recorded by the burgh commissioners as being stented for £26 13s 4d, Forres for £6, Montrose £5 6s 8d, and Banff and Elgin both £3 respectively. By 1535 the regional importance of Aberdeen was even more pronounced. The burgh contributed nine times as much in royal taxation as Elgin, twelve times as much as Forres and nearly fourteen times as much as Banff.[32]

Apart from burgh-oriented trade, Aberdeen acted as the focal point for regional commerce, and it was the demands of the Aberdeen populace which helped create a profitable market for the agricultural produce of north-eastern Scotland. Some of the demand was met by the common lands of Aberdeen, which extended four miles to the west of the burgh. It is very probable that these were valuable agricultural areas by the late medieval period, for in the seventeenth century Parson Gordon noted how 'The fields nixt to the gaits of the citie [Aberdeen] are fruitful of corns such as oats beir quhet and abound with pastures'.[33] Foodstuffs were a particularly important element of regional commerce and especially grains such as wheat, rye, barley, malt and meal. One reference suggests the sending of malt from Elgin to Aberdeen in the fifteenth century. Grain was in constant demand by the burgh populace for the production of the important staple foodstuffs of bread and the brewing of ale. An interesting glimpse of this can be seen in 1495 when Patrick, Lord Ogilvy, supplied wheat to an Aberdeen baxter.[34] Apart from grain, fish figured in regional trade. For instance Jean, countess of Huntly, bought fish for her household whilst in Aberdeen in the early sixteenth century and ordered it to be sent from the burgh 'til her familiars [at] Girmouth in Murray'. Aberdeen acted as an entrepôt for Elgin and Banff by taking much of their salmon for re-export to other parts of Scotland and overseas. Similarly, at least two north-east barons sold fish to Aberdeen burgesses from their estates. The instance of William, Lord Sinclair, is of particular interest, for his estate overseer remarked on the problems of selling agricultural produce on a regional basis in the summer of 1511: 'ther was nocht slaine in the watter of ythane this xiiii dais by gain ii salmond it has bene euer su gret ane spait and sa gif your lordshipe thinkis to get reddy mone or ony price for vittall in thir partis . . . the silver is mair wer(k) to gett in orkney and shetland than it is in buchane'.[35]

Apart from foodstuffs, industrial raw materials flowed in and out of Aberdeen in the late middle ages. Wool was a particularly important commodity. One man from Turiff sent over 1000 lbs of wool to Aberdeen in the early sixteenth century.[36] William, Lord Sinclair, sent wool from the sheep on his Newburgh estates. Skins and hides also figured in regional trade although the evidence is more limited. In 1496 a Banff burgess bought hides and skins from an Aberdeen merchant and arranged for them to be shipped to Banff.[37] Timber was an important and valuable commodity used in Aberdeen as much for shipbuilding and repair as for domestic housing. One reference in June 1499 reveals seventy trees being delivered to John Fichet in Aberdeen by Gilbert Litster of Banff and valued at nineteen Scots crowns. John Fichet was a dealer in timber, for an earlier reference from 1490 mentions his purchase of 'hewin treis'.[38]

A large part of Aberdeen's domestic trade was with other Scottish burghs, but unfortunately this is the least well documented of the three trading zones. In the late middle ages Aberdeen had trading contacts with Dundee, Perth, Edinburgh, Leith, St Andrews, Dysart, Berwick upon Tweed (whilst in Scottish hands), Caithness and the Orkney Isles.[39] A strong general characteristic of this commerce was that it tended to consist of foreign goods or foodstuffs imported principally into Leith and shipped onward to other parts of Scotland. As early as 1447 a merchant of Aberdeen bought foreign wheat in Edinburgh and transported it by sea to Aberdeen and then sold it on the burgh harbourside.[40] The Menzies family of Aberdeen made large profits from this type of trade in the early sixteenth century. Foreign wheat, salt and wine were taken from Leith by Aberdeen merchants and retailed from Aberdeen to centres such as Elgin, Montrose, Forres and the Orkney Isles.

By contrast to this essentially entrepôt function Aberdeen merchant burgesses developed a thriving export trade in salmon. They added to this by also taking the fish of other north-east burghs and sending it from Aberdeen to other parts of Scotland, as well as abroad. There were regular shipments of salmon from Aberdeen to Scottish centres such as Edinburgh, Leith and St Andrews. The most lucrative domestic market for the Aberdeen merchants was that of Edinburgh and the royal court. By the 1480s James III was a major customer for Aberdeen salmon although he was expected to pay cash in advance before the fish were dispatched. Salmon were not the only produce sent from Aberdeen to other Scottish burghs. By the fifteenth century Aberdeen was an important national centre for the purchase of skins and hides. In 1471 skins were shipped to St Andrews after merchants from the Fife burgh had bought a consignment.[41] Both Dundee and Perth merchants also took considerable quantities of these commodities. The Aberdeen authorities did not discourage such trading, but at times of market shortages they attempted to exclude outside merchants from Perth and Dundee with the threat of fines.[42] Unfortunately no evidence remains to prove the impact of such statutes. The often contradictory attitude of the Aberdeen council to its Dundee trading partners can be seen in a burgh statute of 1531. This encouraged Dundee merchants to trade in Aberdeen by the removal of taxes on their goods.

Several pieces of fragmentary material help reveal the often varied commodities which figured in Aberdeen's trade linkages with other Scottish burghs. In 1498 James Guild of Dundee paid £20 for a cargo of wood he received from Andrew Cullen of Aberdeen. The reference suggests the timber was in a finished state, for it was described as being made up of planks. In another brief instance Aberdeen litsters sent a consignment of the dye woad to Dundee for colouring cloth to be manufactured there. One brief reference in the mid-1530s reveals the import of 'dross of the colis' by an Aberdeen smith from a merchant of Dysart in Fife.

Having identified and examined briefly the three levels of trade, burgh, regional and national, it is possible to discuss some of the problems and difficulties that were common to each. Plague could seriously curtail local commercial activities at all levels. On a north-east regional level the outbreak of plague in 1499 forced the Aberdeen council to order that craftsmen and burgesses must cease all further trading with Old Aberdeen, Monymusk, Strathbogy and other 'north partis' until such time as the council could be certain these regional trading partners were free of any infection.[43] At a national level but along very similar lines in 1529 the Aberdeen authorities refused to allow goods from St Andrews to enter Aberdeen because of what they termed the 'gret pestilance' in the Fife burgh.[44]

The early 1480s brought serious problems for both burgh and regional trade because of the debased coinage issued by James III's government.[45] Although the evidence is limited, it would appear that the poor coin had a severe impact on burgh trading and resulted in considerable upset of the economic life of the town, and this in turn affected regional commerce. At burgh level on 11 July 1482 the council ordered that all of the town fleshers, bakers and brewers must provide food at stable prices.[46] The burgh authorities also noted that: 'al gudis that the Kingis blak money is refusit for to be eschet and thame person's [who] refusit to be punist eftir the kingis proclamation And al blak mony til haf course unto the tyme it be anullit be open proclamation of the Kingis'.[47]

This attempt to prevent inflation of prices failed. There was a rush of court cases in the late summer of 1482 between merchants over the correct prices of goods being traded in Aberdeen. Each of the cases had a common theme in the refusal of one merchant to accept payment for his wares in 'blak' money. The Aberdeen council tried to calm the situation at burgh level on 10 October 1483 when it ordered that all town inhabitants must use the 'new' coinage and that 'blak mony suld be payt' so as to avoid further dislocation of burgh trading.[48] Those who refused to supply goods in return for 'blak mony' would have their produce confiscated. Unfortunately council legislation had little impact and some of the continuing problems caused by the debased coinage for town trade can be seen only five days later on 15 October 1483. Four men who bought ale from a lady called Ann were ordered to pay her in 'quhite silver' because 'blak' money was not acceptable.[49] The debasement of the Scottish coinage in 1482 also affected the regional trading partners of Aberdeen. On 7 October 1482 the laird of Johnstone, in West Aberdeenshire, insisted upon 'quhite silver' to the value of 37 shillings in payment for the malt he had sold to Margaret Scherar of Aberdeen. The council considered the case and found in favour of the laird and ordered that he was to be paid in good coin.[50]

Yet the inherent strength and vitality of the burgh and regional trade of Aberdeen and the north-east was revealed by the events of the 1480s. Despite the severe problems created by crown debasement of the coinage the trading pattern was not broken or destroyed. It resumed its normal flow and ebb as the crisis passed. Similarly other problems such as plague, bad debts or war never seriously threatened to end local commercial activities.

Inland trading at each of the various levels required credit to function in many instances. Unfortunately for a few traders this turned into the problem of bad debts. Judging by the many Aberdeen merchants who faced the difficulty, it was not uncommon. It is of further interest to see that a number of Aberdeen burgesses were in the position of owing money to north-east landed men through the interaction of trade at both burgh and regional level. For instance in the 1480s Sir William Knollis of Torphichen took action to receive payment of a debt owed to him by Alexander Howison of Aberdeen. This had been incurred through trading in salmon by Howison on behalf of Sir William.[51] Similarly, in the 1480s Elizabeth, countess of Huntly, was owed money from a burgess of Aberdeen for timber.[52]

Some important social points emerge from the study of the processes of burgh trading. They reveal a town council in late medieval Aberdeen which was attempting to regulate trade for the positive good of the burgh community as a whole. Their actions in this respect can be seen as an attempt to continue the work of the earlier *Burgh Laws*, to replace self-interest with common self-interest. For instance, in 1518, during a period of food shortage, limits were placed on the amount of food a person could purchase. He was to take only enough for himself and his family.[53]

Similarly in 1520 the council settled a dispute between the fishermen of the coastal suburbs of Torry and Footdee by arranging the hours of fishing to prevent the loss of nets by either side.[54] In the absence of systematic provision for the poor the social conscience of the burgh authorities was sensitive: in 1522 it fined a number of wealthy burgesses who were found guilty of selling food 'to puyr folkis derrar than it was sellit in the mercat quhilk causit gret dearth and herring of pris of vittalis within the burgh'.[55]

Nor was the burgh council devoid of information on economic conditions in other parts of Scotland when it made price legislation for burgh goods. For instance, in January 1517 the provost and bailies, knowing that a boll of wheat was 12 shillings in Aberdeen and 'also considering the wight of the bred of quheit in edinburgh dundee and uder partis in lowthane angus caus the twa penny breid weyand xxxv unces'.[56]

Aberdeen in the late medieval period had a flourishing inland trade which can be seen at three functioning levels: burgh, regional and national. The task of writing about the latter spheres is a difficult exercise compounded by the limited surviving evidence. For instance, in the regional context nothing remains to prove the trading interaction between Aberdeen and baronial burghs such as Inverurie. The later middle ages were a period of considerable importance for many such towns, with a large increase in their numbers, not just in the north-east but throughout Scotland.[57] This suggests both a certain dynamic in internal trade and a desire by both clerical and baronial interests to exploit regional commerce. In the context of the north-east, each of the levels of inland trade tended to deal in goods of great similarity with foodstuffs and raw materials predominating. It was a commerce which tended to overlap and interconnect at each of the respective levels. This was a trend reinforced by the role of Aberdeen as a focal point for much burgh and regional commerce. Aberdeen as the major entrepôt for north-east Scotland acted as a funnel for regional trade which became a complementary part of the foreign overseas commerce enjoyed by the town. Much of the local produce sent to Aberdeen was destined for overseas, and in particular salmon, hides, skins and wool were major exports. In turn, at least one north-east regional market by the 1530s saw foreign imports exchanged by Aberdeen merchants for agricultural produce.[58] Burgh, regional and even national Scottish trading by its extensive nature involved many more people than overseas commerce, which tended to be a minority activity (although a very important one) confined to the wealthiest burgesses of Aberdeen. It was such a vital part of medieval Aberdeen economic life that a decline of burgh or regional trade was of proportionally greater significance for the town authorities than overseas trade. Such a view helps explain the often extensive intervention and attempts to control local commercial activities made by the Aberdeen council.

NOTES

1. Houston, 'The Scottish burgh', 118.
2. For a discussion of the geographical site of medieval Aberdeen, see J. S. Smith, 'The physical site of historical Aberdeen', in J. S. Smith, ed., *New Light on Medieval Aberdeen* (Aberdeen, 1985), 1–9.
3. Nicholson, *Scotland*, 15.
4. *Abdn. Chrs.*, no. iii.
5. J. Gordon, *Aberdoniae utriusque descriptii: A description of both towns of Aberdeen* (Spalding Club, 1842), 12–13.
6. ACA, MS Council Register [CR], vi, 935.
7. CR, vii, 17.
8. CR, viii, 732.
9. CR, x, 152.
10. *Abdn. Counc.*, i, 16.
11. CR, viii, 909; xii, 16; it paid 8.8% of customs on hides in the 1440s; Lynch, 'Towns', 176.
12. CR, vi, 697, 717.
13. CR, x, 201.
14. CR, vi, 621.
15. See Torrie, Ch. 14, below.
16. CR, v(2), 702.
17. CR, v(2), 722.
18. CR, iv, 132.
19. CR, vi, 758.
20. CR, viii, 804.
21. CR, v, 410.
22. CR, vii, 405.
23. CR, viii, 924.
24. *Spalding Misc.*, i, pp. xvi–xxvii.
25. For example see CR, v/2, 782.
26. CR, v(2), 795.
27. CR, x, 56.
28. Gordon, *Description*, 5.
29. CR, iv, 316, 350; vi, 245, 815; xii, 502.
30. *Abdn. Chrs.*, 289–90.
31. Ibid., 290–91.
32. *Burghs Convention Recs.*, i, 543; Lynch, 'Towns', 188 n.
33. Gordon, *Description*, 147.
34. CR, vii, 689.
35. *A.B. ILL*, iii, 106–108.
36. CR, x, 24.
37. CR, vii, 470.

38. CR, vii, 215, 959.
39. CR, iv, 461; v, 572,828; v(2)702,, vi, 146, 750; xi, 372.
40. CR, v(2), 498; x, 194.
41. CR, vi, 146; Lynch, 'Towns', 176-7.
42. CR, v(2), 702.
43. CR, vi, 963.
44. CR, xii, 689.
45. N. Macdougall, *James III: A Political Study* (Edinburgh, 1982), 160-61.
46. CR, vi, 742.
47. CR, vi, 743.
48. CR, vi, 806.
49. CR, vi, 762.
50. CR, vi, 760.
51. CR, vi, 797.
52. CR, vi, 690.
53. CR, x, 227.
54. CR, x, 227.
55. CR, ix, 659.
56. CR, xiii, 197.
57. Nicholson, *Scotland*, 562.
58. CR, xiii, 197.

10

Trade with Northern Europe, 1297–1540

David Ditchburn

In 1297 Andrew Moray and William Wallace, leaders of the community of the realm, wrote to Lübeck and Hamburg.[1] They thanked the towns for past assistance and advised them that Scottish ports were open again for business. This letter, though one of the earliest indications of Scottish trade with Germany, leaves a number of questions unanswered. It does not elaborate on which Scottish burghs participated in German trade. It is not known whether German towns other than Lübeck and Hamburg received similar letters. There is no indication of the commodities being traded. Other than two named Scottish merchants, there is no evidence about who traded and, indeed, how they traded. Finally, it is not clear whether

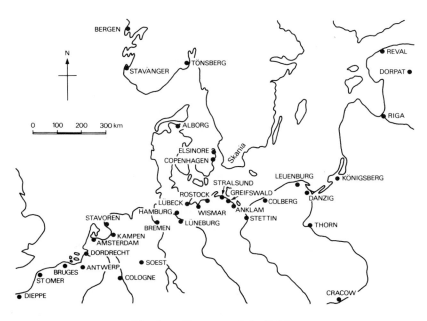

Northern Europe and the Baltic

161

national government normally took such an interest in trade or whether, in more settled times, the conduct of commerce was left to the burghs and merchants. Such questions can be raised not only about the state of trade with northern Europe in 1297, but about trade during the following two centuries as well.

By the end of the thirteenth century at least Dundee and Berwick participated in trade with northern Europe. Three Lübeck merchants left Dundee in 1297 without payment of £80 in customs duties.[2] At Berwick, Scotland's largest contemporary burgh, it has been suggested that German merchants, like their Flemish counterparts, had a commercial base or 'factory' at the White Hall.[3] Nevertheless, although a James of Cologne possessed the White Hall in the early fourteenth century, there is no evidence that it was ever a factory.[4] Berwick did, however, have contact with Germany and possibly a resident German community. Before 1297 both Alexander of Cologne and Christiana, widow of Gotschalk of Cologne, had land in the town.[5] A letter sent from Alv Erlingson to James the Steward, concerning the seizure of a Norwegian ship at Berwick, also indicates contact with Scandinavia.[6]

Both Dundee and Berwick remained active in north European trade during the early fourteenth century. In 1310 the bailiffs at Boston in England arrested nine Germans for trading at Dundee, and Berwick merchants had contact with German and Norwegian traders both during the town's English occupation (1296–1318) and Scottish reoccupation (1318–1333).[7] Surviving evidence indicates that other burghs by now also participated in the trade. In 1312 St Andrews merchants had their goods seized in Norway, while Aberdeen was regarded as a friendly haven for Germans selling goods pirated from English vessels, following German assistance in ousting the burgh's English garrison in 1308.[8] The second War of Independence, however, witnessed the ravaging and wasting of several towns, adversely effecting their trade. Berwick, cut off from its hinterland again in 1333, was especially badly effected, and the town's German community perhaps disappeared. By 1334 James of Cologne had lost possession of the White Hall, while at least one of the town's German-born burgesses, Christopher of Cologne, was imprisoned from 1333 to 1335 in Newcastle for his Scottish sympathies.[9] Although more stable political conditions conducive to trade resumed in the mid-fourteenth century, there is little evidence of Germans or Scandinavians continuing to visit Scottish ports.[10] This may reflect the paucity of the sources, but it is more likely to reflect a growth in Scottish merchants' share of foreign trade. When, from 1331 to 1333, foreign merchants paid double the normal customs duties (save at Berwick), the Scottish share of foreign trade (elsewhere) was approximately five-sixths of the total. It was even higher in the few subsequent years of the fourteenth century when similar calculations can be made.[11] During this period most Scottish-German contact was probably in the Low Countries, with even smaller burghs such as Cupar, Inverness and St Andrews involved.[12]

By the 1380s, however, Germans were again visiting Scotland. In 1385 the earl of March wrote to Danzig requesting the resumption of trade with his burgh of Dunbar.[13] Prussians were at Edinburgh in 1388 and Linlithgow in 1393.[14] Scottish merchants were also visiting the Baltic. In 1382 John Dugude of Perth journeyed to Prussia *in servicio regis*.[15] Thus by the end of the fourteenth century the important eastcoast burghs all had trading links with German merchants. Due to the fragmentary source material, only guesses can be made at the relative importance of the burghs in this trade. Since, however, there is no reason to suppose that any particular burgh specialised in German trade, the Scottish customs accounts probably reflect, at least for staple goods, the importance of each burgh in Germanic, as well as general European, trade. By the 1390s Edinburgh's exports were easily the largest, roughly double those of her nearest rival. Linlithgow, trading through Blackness, normally came second. This is somewhat surprising, since her feu-ferme was much lower than that of the other major exporting burghs. Aberdeen's share had temporarily slipped behind that of Dundee, to about the same level as Perth's.[16] During the fifteenth century the east-coast burghs still held a virtual monopoly of this trade, though a Danish ship appeared at Ayr in 1488.[17] Smaller burghs, however, were apparently more active. Merchants from Cupar, Dunfermline, Dysart, Haddington, Inverkeithing, Lanark, Peebles and Selkirk were trading with Danzig in 1444, probably through Edinburgh.[18] Danish merchants were at Stirling in 1488, and by the later fifteenth century Orkney and in particular Shetland attracted German merchants.[19]

Nonetheless, except for Haddington the links of these burghs with the Baltic during the fifteenth century were probably small. The bulk of northern European trade remained in the hands of the larger burghs. As in the fourteenth century there are problems in assessing each burgh's share in the trade. The only firm evidence to survive is for 1497. One of the Sound Toll Registers lists for that year the origin of shipping passing in and out of the Baltic. Twenty-one Scots ships are recorded, seven from Dundee, five from Leith, four each from Aberdeen and St Andrews and one from an unknown port.[20] Otherwise the customs accounts are again the only evidence to reflect the proportions of Scottish burgal trade. Edinburgh's share of a diminishing total grew steadily during the fifteenth century; by James IV's reign it contributed about two thirds of total customs. Aberdeen followed with roughly a sixth share, though her Baltic trade probably declined for a time from the 1480s. Dundee, Berwick (when in Scottish hands), Haddington and Perth followed. Linlithgow had seen her share fall considerably since the late fourteenth century.[21]

This picture of Scotland's Baltic trade as almost exclusively belonging to east-coast ports and predominantly the preserve of the larger burghs is also, with some modifications, true of the early sixteenth century. Before 1540, 41.3% of Scottish ships passing through the Sound came from Edinburgh or Leith. Dundee, apparently specialising somewhat in Baltic trade, had 31.3%, St Andrews 9.1% and Dysart 3.9%. Aberdeen's share was a lowly 2.6%.[22] Perth, Linlithgow and Haddington are not recorded as sending any ships. All the smaller burghs recorded in the Sound Toll Register over this period, with the exception of Montrose, were situated in Fife or the Forth estuary: Cupar, Dunfermline, Dysart, Inverkeithing, Kinghorn, Kirkcaldy and Queensferry. It was not until the later sixteenth century that direct voyages between the Baltic and the burghs of the East Neuk of Fife or the west coast are recorded. The Sound Toll Register does not, of course, record Scottish trade with either Norway or north-western Germany. For geographic reasons the northern burghs perhaps had stronger ties with Norway. Orkney and Shetland were most frequented not by Baltic merchants but by those of Bremen and Hamburg. Nonetheless Edinburgh, its port of Leith and Dundee had, by the sixteenth century, come to dominate Scotland's trade with northern Europe.

The destination of trade changed fundamentally over the period. The earliest Scottish-German contacts were probably with the Rhineland and Westphalia. The presence of several merchants at Berwick styled 'of Cologne' has already been noted. Topographical evidence from thirteenth-century Cologne also suggests strong ties with Scotland.[23] Other western German cities too had Scottish connections. The Schotte family, whose name is thought to have arisen from the family's mercantile contact with Scotland, were prominent in Soest from the late thirteenth century.[24] A Dortmund merchant, Herman Clipping, assisted in the Scottish recapture of Aberdeen in 1308. Four other Dortmund merchants and one from Cologne had their goods arrested in 1320 for complicity in attacking an English ship and selling its wares in Scotland.[25] Merchants from Osnabrück and Münster also found their goods liable for arrest in England because of suspected dealings with Scots.[26] From the 1340s, however, Rhenish and Westphalian merchants no longer played an important role in Scottish trade. Some Scots, probably emigrants, were in Cologne from the mid-fifteenth century, but Cologne's British trade was increasingly focused on southern England, while Scotland's direct trade with the western Hansa was confined to the Dutch towns of Kampen, Nijmegen, Stavoren and possibly Deventer.[27]

The towns of north-western Germany enjoyed a more sustained trade with Scotland. When this began is uncertain, but the 1297 letter from Moray and Wallace to Lübeck and Hamburg points to the revival of an established trade, not the commencement of a new one. During the Wars of Independence merchants from Lübeck, Hamburg, Greifswald, Stralsund and, to a lesser extent, Bremen participated in trade with Scotland, though probably not from their home ports. Edward II of England never apparently requested these towns to cease trade with Scotland. Rather, German merchants were supplying Scotland from England and the Low Countries. John le Witte of Lübeck was found guilty in 1315 of freighting a ship at Boston for Scotland, while an English ship coming from Sluys and seized by Germans in 1316 was taken to Scotland.[28] Little, however, is heard of merchants from north-western Germany in Scotland in the mid-fourteenth century, though an ordinance of the Hanseatic Diet in 1358 suggests trade did not cease completely.[29] It continued, with some structural changes, for the remainder of the period. Some trade was still conducted in the Low Countries, but by the mid-fourteenth century there was also direct trade. Merchants from some of the region's other towns (Rostock, Wismar and, by the early sixteenth century, Anklam) also began to participate, while Scots started to visit the area, in sufficiently large numbers for Anklam in 1330 and 1335 and Stralsund in 1370 to regulate their activity.[30] In the mid-fifteenth century there was considerable contact with Bremen, culminating in James II's grant of special privileges to the city's merchants in 1454.[31] Nevertheless this was not maintained and, save for Bremen's interest in Shetland's fisheries, trade again declined. Of all the region's towns, however, Scotland's closest ties were with Stralsund. Scots traded and, in the later fifteenth century, settled there, while Stralsunders regularly visited Scotland, one in 1489 even attempting to sell Holy Island goose feathers in Aberdeen.[32] More significantly, in 1428, the closure of the Sound during a Danish-Hanseatic dispute sparked off discontent among Stralsund's brewers. They complained that Scotland, one of their most important markets, was closed to them.[33]

Nonetheless Scotland's links with north-western Germany were latterly less important than those with the eastern Baltic. Encouraged by the opening of the Sound route in the 1380s, Prussians from Danzig and Königsberg began to take an interest in Scottish trade. By the early fifteenth century their stake outstripped that of the more westerly towns. This can be gauged from reactions to the embargo on Scottish trade imposed by the Hansa in 1412, following Scottish piracy on Hanseatic shipping. Danzig led the opposition, while among the north-western towns, Stralsund and Hamburg alone showed reluctance to toe the line.[34]

The embargo remained in force until 1436 but Prussians visited Scotland undeterred. Despite periodic friction over piracy and trading privileges, links with Danzig and Königsberg grew steadily and Scottish settlements developed there in the fifteenth century.[35] Though Danzig was the port with the greatest Scottish contact, other eastern Baltic towns developed minor trading links with Scotland — such as Stettin by the fifteenth century and Colberg by the early sixteenth century. Dorpat, Reval and Riga, all took a keen interest in the Hanseatic trading embargo.[36] From the 1470s Scots also traded in Danzig's hinterland, at Leuenburg, Thorn and even Cracow, forshadowing an even greater Scottish presence in the area from the later sixteenth century.[37]

Among the Scandinavian countries, Scotland's traditional links were with Norway. Increasingly, however, in the fourteenth and fifteenth centuries, Norwegian commerce fell under the domination of the Hansa. As German influence grew, commerce with other foreigners declined. Only in the early sixteenth century did Norway again open up to non-Germans. Merchants from Dysart and Kinghorn were in Bergen in 1525, and a Scottish community living precariously alongside the Germans had emerged there by 1524.[38] German commercial domination of Denmark was never as great as in Norway. Nonetheless only in the later fifteenth century did trade with Denmark develop. Copenhagen was the main centre of Scottish activity and by 1539 Scottish merchants were sufficiently numerous to maintain their own altar there. There was also contact with Aalborg, Elsinore and Roskilde.[39]

Trade with Sweden, except in Skania, only became important in the later sixteenth century. Skania's herring fairs, however, attracted Scots from the fourteenth century. Restrictions on Scottish activity at these fairs were imposed by the Hansa in 1369, 1370 and 1378.[40] There is little indication of the Scots visiting the fairs in the fifteenth century, but by the early sixteenth century they could be found at Malmo, Falsterbo and Hälsingborg.[41] Yet despite these growing ties with Scandinavia, Prussia remained the region of northern Europe with which the Scottish burghs had their strongest trading links. A variety of reasons explain the shift in Scottish trading patterns from the North Sea in the early part of the period to the eastern Baltic. Political factors played a part; most markedly Hanseatic dominance of Norway reduced Scottish contact with that country from the mid-fourteenth century. The opening up of the Sound route to shipping in the 1380s made direct contact with eastern Europe possible. The chief reason for shifts in trade, however, is to be found in the commodities of that trade.

Throughout the middle ages, Scotland's main exports, as reflected in the customs accounts, were wool, fells and hides. In addition some cloth, fish, skins and salt were exported. Germans trading with the Low Countries would deal in all these commodities — and a few others. Lübeck merchants took grain, a very rare export, to Flanders in 1476.[42] There was not, however, the same demand for Scottish goods in the Baltic and Scandinavia. Wool in particular was not wanted in any great quantity, since no great cloth-manufacturing centres existed there. Yet wool, despite the decline in its quality and price from the 1390s, remained the most important Scottish export throughout the middle ages. Exports to Germany and Scandinavia were therefore composed of the more peripheral Scottish produce.

The only Baltic port for which firm data survive regarding Scottish imports is Danzig. The proportionate share of imported Scottish goods there in the late fifteenth and early sixteenth centuries has been calculated as follows: small packs (*Krämerwaren*), which probably consisted of a mixture of Scottish staple goods, 52%; hides 3%; cloth 17%; salt 27%; and other goods 1%.[43] It was for *Krämerwaren* that the Scots traders in Danzig's hinterland were renowned. Scottish cloth, compared to the produce of the Low Countries and England, was of poor quality, but doubtless found a market among the poorer sections of Baltic society. Scottish salt, exported from the Forth ports, competed with that of the Baltic's principal supplier, western France, especially once the general worsening of Anglo-Hanseatic relations in the fifteenth century meant that the Hansa's salt fleets to France became increasingly susceptible to attack by English pirates.

Scottish imports may have varied somewhat at the more westerly Hanseatic ports. Where there was no settled community of small-time Scottish traders, *Krämerwaren* may have been less important. Scottish salt, though not unknown, may have been less common in the Wendish towns, since supplies of a better quality were available locally from Lüneburg. Moreover, in addition to the main goods identified at Danzig, a few other Scottish goods also found their way to northern Europe. Precious stones, possibly pearls, were bound for Danzig in 1444. Shetland's supplies of stockfish were sought by Bremen and Hamburg merchants from the later fifteenth century.[44] Coal was sent from Dysart to Denmark in 1507, and other early sixteenth-century consignments suggest that a small market for Scottish coal had developed there. Some goods imported to Scotland were also re-exported. Wine and alum were sent from Leith to Copenhagen and Elsinore in 1479.[45] English goods too were probably exported to the Baltic in years of Anglo-Hanseatic tension. Large amounts of cloth which do not appear in the Scottish customs accounts and which may well have come from England, were sent by Scottish merchants to Danzig in 1444.[46] Similarly Anglo-Hanseatic friction may explain the increase in Scottish ships, coupled with a decrease in English ones, arriving at Danzig in the 1470s.[47]

If Scotland's exports were peripheral, her German imports were more mainstream. During the first War of Independence Germans brought victuals and arms from England and the Low Countries.[48] Cologne cloth, recorded in the 1330s and 1340s, may also have come from the Low Countries, while Rhenish wine, imported throughout the middle ages, probably came from Cologne's wine staple at Dordrecht, rather than direct from source.[49] Indeed, just as Germans sailing to the Low Countries took any available Scottish produce, so, on return journeys, they could be expected to ship all those goods available in the Low Countries, including Baltic produce.

From the 1380s, however, most Scottish-German trade was conducted with the eastern Baltic, which could most readily supply the food and raw materials which Scotland required. Grain from Prussia and Poland was one of the earliest and most important commodities of trade. The Teutonic Order's Scottish factors dealt in wheat, rye, malt, and flour.[50] A few other food articles, such as honey and ale, were traded in, though these were not nearly as important. Of the raw materials, flax and linen were the most significant. A Perth merchant bought flax in Danzig as early as 1428 and latterly this became a mainstay of trade with Prussia. Flax is recorded among the cargoes of every ship leaving Danzig for Scotland in 1477.[51] The other major raw material shipped to Scotland from Baltic ports was wood. 'Eastland boards', used for building, are regularly referred to in Scottish sources, along with wainscot, clapholt, *bogenholz*, masts, barrel staves, ship blocks and oars. Among the sylvan by-products which were needed in Scotland were pitch, tar and ash. A few other raw materials and by-products, such as wax, hemp, yarn and sail cloth, were also sought by Scots. Iron was the principal mineral traded in. Though not a major item of trade, it did find occasional demands in Scotland, and was used for example at Dalkeith Castle in 1444.[52]

As with Scottish imports, Danzig alone provides any long-term data for Scottish exports from the Baltic. The proportionate share of these exports has been assessed as follows: *Krämerwaren* 3%; grain 18%; linen (and flax) 60%; wood 1%; sylvan by-products 14%; iron 3%; and other goods 1%.[53] The small amount of wood is the main surprise in these figures. The explanation for this discrepancy with the known widespread use of Baltic timber in Scotland, may be that Baltic wood found its way to Scotland largely via the Low Countries.

Trade with northern Germany was generally less important than that with the Low Countries and the eastern Baltic, though it tended to be in similar commodities. Thus Bremen merchants visiting Scotland in 1404 dealt in barley, wheat, flour, beans, linen, wax, swine carcases, steel, ale and mead.[54] In addition salt, possibly from Lüneburg, came westward, as did a few re-exported goods, such as Skanian herring brought by Hamburg merchants in 1402. Nevertheless most of these goods, save beer and ale, were more readily available elsewhere.[55]

The basis for trade with Scandinavia was similarly weak. Norway required grain, which Scotland could rarely provide. Only with the growing Scottish demand for Norwegian timber, used for shipbuilding, did trade revive from the later fifteenth century.[56] Skania's economic prosperity was based on its herring fairs. Eastland herring, probably from Skania, could be found in Scotland by 1329, but by the fifteenth century the fairs were in decline.[57] In so far as other Swedish exports (agricultural produce, copper and iron) came to Scotland, they came via Danzig. Denmark's traditional exports were also agricultural and Scots certainly purchased some grain there. By the early sixteenth century ship masts, copper and arms were also bought.[58]

Since Danzig is the only Baltic port for which figures relating to Scottish imports and exports survive, it is difficult to come to general conclusions about the importance of Scotland in Baltic trade and its balance of trade with the Baltic. Even for Danzig, import and export figures do not always exist for the same years. Yet some broad conclusions can be made. Scottish wool was not wanted in the Baltic and other Scottish exports were small. The cargoes of many ships arriving at Danzig were minimal and some apparently arrived in ballast.[59] The value of Scottish imports in the later fifteenth century averaged only just over 3% of Danzig's total imports.[60] Conversely many goods were exported to Scotland, as is reflected in the long list of cargoes recorded in the Danzig customs accounts. The value of these exports in relation to Danzig's total exports from 1490 to 1492 was just over 12% of the total.[61] Meanwhile, ordinances against the drain of bullion from Scotland became frequent again in the later fifteenth century.[62] Bullion was doubtless used to pay for imports. The probability is that Scotland's stake in overall Baltic trade was minimal and her trade was heavily in deficit.

By the fifteenth century a fairly vivid picture exists of those burghs trading, where they traded and what they traded in. Rather less information exists on who traded and how they traded. The problem of who from the Scottish burghs traded with northern Europe is largely one of sources. Save for Aberdeen, it is almost impossible to check merchants known to be active in the trade with burgh records. At Aberdeen, wealthier merchants were certainly involved in Baltic trade. Thomas Pratt, Patrick Leslie and Andrew Cullen were just three prominent burgesses and council members trading at Danzig in the later fifteenth and early sixteenth centuries.[63] It must also be assumed that those Scots merchants who acquired citizenship in Baltic towns (as opposed to those merely resident) were men of substance: men such as Thomas Smith, a *doppelbürger* of Edinburgh and Stralsund prior to 1464.[64] Nonetheless, a parliamentary statute of 1467 decreed that only the 'famous and worshipfull' could trade abroad. Limitations on lesser men visiting the Baltic specifically were imposed at Aberdeen in 1503.[65] Such restriction points to participation in foreign trade from the fifteenth century by lesser men. This is supported by a stream of complaint and legislation against itinerant Scottish pedlars from all over Germany. Though 'the Scots' of these edicts may have come to mean any pedlar, regardless of nationality, they surely originally had a Scottish connection. Both lesser and more important men probably had an interest in Baltic trade.[66]

There was no equivalent to the pedlars among the Germans visiting Scotland. During the Wars of Independence, German traders were among the most prominent merchants active in trade with England.[67] Prominent Germans, such as Danzig's Reinhold Niederhof in the 1440s, continued to have a stake in Scottish trade. An immigrant into Danzig in 1416, he quickly established himself as one of the city's leading merchants and politicians. He had a share in at least five ships and ultimately became *Bürgermeister* of the city.[68] Niederhof was not unique. Nonetheless, there is little evidence to suggest that the elite of Baltic mercantile society as a whole found it worth their while trading with Scotland, and such trade was probably left largely to the lesser merchants.

The problem of how trade with northern Europe was conducted encompasses a whole series of points: mercantile partnerships, the sale of goods at their destination, and financial arrangements. Again, conclusions are hampered by a lack of evidence. Mercantile partnerships, between two or four merchants, were common in the Hanseatic cities.[69] They brought greater capital into a venture and spread the risk. How far this convinced medieval Scottish merchants is another matter. Scots frequently sent cargoes to the Baltic, owned apparently only by themselves. They would, however, normally join together to charter a ship, not only with other Scots, but also with Germans.

Scots do not seem to have had any qualms about using foreign ships, and an act of 1428 permitted them to do so.[70] As far as German trade is concerned, this merely recognised a *de facto* situation, and after 1428 there is evidence of German, Norwegian, Low Countries and French shipping being used to send goods to northern Europe. German ships were also used for taking goods to the Low Countries. Similarly, Germans trading in Scotland showed no aversion to using Scottish ships.[71] The ships ranged from *holks*, capable of loading 150 lasts (300 tons), to very much smaller ships such as *kraier* (25–50 lasts) and the even smaller *balinger, budsen* and barges.

Medieval skippers did not like to sail too far away from the coast. Nonetheless avoidance of the open seas between Scotland and Norway or the Sound was a practical impossibility. For reasons of safety, however, ships sailed in convoy. It is difficult to tell how long sea voyages took, because of the scarcity of detailed port books. By the late sixteenth century, it has been argued, two trips to Norway, but only one to Danzig, were possible in a season (February to November).[72] Still, Hans Dertholt is recorded twice in the Danzig custom account of 1471 for skippering a ship from Scotland, so more than one return journey per season was possible.[73] Some Scottish merchants travelled with their goods to sell them at their destination. By the later middle ages, however, selling and buying was usually left to factors. In the early fifteenth century the Teutonic Order and Danzig's von dem Walde family even stationed resident factors in Edinburgh while in 1490 David White acted as factor in Aberdeen for his brother in Danzig.[74]

Theoretically money obtained for goods sold could be used to purchase other goods. In practice, however, this had limitations. It depended on selling and buying in that order, which was not always advantageous. Scots in the Baltic also wanted to buy more than they sold. They needed therefore to have ready cash at hand, develop credit arrangements or borrow. In their transactions, Scots and Germans used a variety of currency. There are references to the use of Scots, Prussian, Rhenish, Wendish and, because it was one of the few medieval currencies not heavily debased, English money. Credit was used by Hanseatic merchants from the thirteenth century.[75] Not surprisingly there are indications of its use in Scottish-Hanseatic relations. Most evidence emanates from the existence of debts, which indicate either money loans or the receipt without payment of goods. A list of forty-one Scots in debt to the Teutonic Order was compiled in 1417. Some may have been for money loans, but some were clearly for grain and other goods.[76] Rather less information, however, survives about repayments. Two Danzig merchants trading at Aberdeen in 1489 sent factors to collect their dues. Baltic merchants ('Easterlings') also left money for repayment to Scots with the Scottish factors in the Netherlands.[77] It is not, however, clear whether interest was included in such repayments.

Scottish merchants thus possessed methods of facilitating trade, although none of them, in the context of Europe as a whole, were innovative. They could not, however, guard against every eventuality. Formal and informal hostilities were a constant threat to trade. It was due to the seizure of a Danzig ship bound for the Low Countries during a truce that James I fell into English hands. The situation in the Baltic was equally perilous. During the Hanseatic dispute with Denmark in the early sixteenth century, several Scottish vessels were arrested by Lübeck.[78] The threat from pirates was equally great. Scotland produced her fair share of pirates, most notably Alexander Stewart, earl of Mar, who operated from Aberdeen in the early fifteenth century. Scottish ports also welcomed pirates and their illicit goods, and this was true not only during the Wars of Independence. Edinburgh, Dundee and St Andrews were accused of just this by Danzig in the 1490s.[79] Scots were not, however, the only medieval pirates. Bremen pirates seized the goods of Edinburgh merchants aboard two ships in 1446, while Cologne merchants in the 1490s resorted to reciprocated piracy following their failure to get justice from Scots for their attacks.[80] Weather was the third major threat to Scottish-Baltic trade. Storms drove ships off course and could wreck them.[81] Just such meteorological problems, and the danger of ice, prompted the Hanseatic prohibition of winter sailings.

Other trading irritants also existed. Failure to meet debts, and payment in 'black' (debased) coinage, were behind Aberdeen's decline in trade with Danzig in the 1480s and 1490s. This even threatened to lead to the arrest of the burgh's merchants in Danzig in 1489.[82] Disputes arose over other matters too. In 1478 ten Scots merchants fell out with a Danzig skipper over the chartering of a ship to Scotland, while many Scots appeared before courts in Danzig charged with various crimes, including murder.[83] Yet the greatest threat to Scottish merchants in the Baltic was ironically, their success. The greater their presence, the greater their obvious challenge to established interests and the greater the tendency in the Hanseatic cities to restrict their trade. Such restrictions affected small-time pedlars most, but it was also, on occasions, directed against merchants trading directly from Scotland. The controls imposed from 1369 on Scots visiting the Skanian fairs were a classic expression of Hanseatic suspicion of foreign competition.

Merchants trading in northern Europe were not, however, left completely to their own devices. They looked to the burgh for assistance when things went wrong. Conversely they had to accept that the burgh had a rôle in determining what was in the best interests of the burgh and its merchants as a whole. A third force also came into play: the crown and its agents. Revenue from customs was an important source of royal income. If for no other reason than expediency the crown could not ignore mercantile activity.

The burgh had a positive rôle, in settling mercantile disputes and interceding on behalf of its burgesses abroad. It also had a more negative rôle, regulating how trade was conducted. The settling of mercantile disputes came within the jurisdiction of local courts. Cases could involve foreigners who visited the burghs as well as Scots. Frequently they concerned debts or the ownership of goods. In February 1475 a Danzig skipper, Paul Simonson, claimed in Aberdeen that he was owed one Scottish crown from John Rutherford and William Robertson. In 1447 Thomas Forman asked the aldermen of Aberdeen to seize Prussian wheat which he claimed was being withheld from him.[84] Occasionally the burghs can also be found recording officially details of business transactions. In 1444 Mathew Crukin requested the Aberdeen council to certify that he had sold all the rye from a ship which he had skippered from Stralsund.[85]

Burghs also intervened abroad on behalf of both individual merchants and the community. In the Baltic this rôle was especially important. Unlike the Low Countries, where a resident Scottish Conservator was established in 1407 to oversee and protect Scots, the Scottish community in the Baltic rarely acted as a unit.[86] It is clear from a letter sent to Danzig from Aberdeen in 1410 that interventions by burghs were common from an early date. Interceding for two alleged pirates, Aberdeen stated it did so, since its seal, it claimed, was already well known in Danzig.[87] Allegations of piracy, as in this case, were frequent, but they were not the only charges from which burghs sought to defend their burgesses. Questions regarding debt, ownership of goods and broken agreements were common course. The spirit behind such intervention was the desire to maintain stable trade and ensure that the wrongs of one merchant should not be held against the burgh and its merchants as a whole. Hence in 1487 Aberdeen, specifically because of the decline in its trade with Danzig, promised to honour the debts of its burgesses to Danzigers.[88]

Burghs also displayed their powers over northern European trade in a restrictive sense. Ordinances preserving the burghs' and burgesses' privileged trading status, ensuring that incoming goods were sold fairly and openly, and regulating weights, measures and prices were common. The medieval suspicion of strangers was reflected in a list of do's and don'ts for foreign merchants. Such xenophobia was not totally groundless. From the early sixteenth century attempts were made, for example at Aberdeen in 1500, to limit the spread of plague from foreign ships and men.[89] Merchants were also affected by local imposts on shipping. Again this was not always negative. The proceeds from a levy on ships arriving at Dundee in 1447 were earmarked for improving the safety of the harbour.[90]

On occasions, however, it made more sense for the burghs to act in unison. The Court of the Four Burghs, and latterly parliament, both provided a forum for coordinating action. Coordination was particularly important in the case of foreign diplomacy, when the interests of more than one burgh were at stake. In 1348 Aberdeen, Edinburgh, Dundee and Perth jointly guaranteed an agreement with the German community at Bruges following a dispute over piracy. In 1445 coordinated pressure from Edinburgh, Linlithgow, Perth, Cupar and Dundee, following an act of Bremen piracy, resulted in Bremen's acceding to peace terms. It was at the instigation of the burghs that an embassy was dispatched to Cologne in 1487 to settle another dispute over piracy. Edinburgh was the burgh responsible for the piracy, but all the burghs agreed to meet the cost of the embassy.[91] Legislation was another area in which the burghs found it useful to work together. It is probable that some commercial statutes were promoted by the burghs. An act of 1467, stipulating that written contracts be made between merchants and skippers to ensure the safe handling of goods was a repeat of a law enforced in Edinburgh since 1438.[92]

The crown also made encroachments into north European trade. There are indications that these were growing in the later fifteenth century. The two major issues of foreign trade which the crown had traditionally controlled were the imposition of customs duties and the granting of privilege and protection to foreign merchants. During the later middle ages old customs duties were increased, new ones levied and higher rates periodically imposed on foreign merchants.[93] Such tampering was not, however, conducted with any long-term vision of its effect on trade. Rather it was an attempt to increase royal revenues. The granting of privilege and protection to foreign merchants had also long been the prerogative of the crown. Robert I wrote to Lübeck in 1321, promising the same privileges *usi sunt temporibus predesessorum nostrorum*. Grants to other towns followed: Wismar (1440), Bremen (1454), Danzig (1475), Stavoren (1499 and 1525) and Colberg (1520).[94] These grants were, however, minimal compared to those won by Hanseatic merchants in Scandinavia and England. The profits from trade in Scotland were not sufficient for the Hansa to press for similar privileges. The effect was beneficial to Scots merchants. There were no major disputes with the Hansa over parity of privilege, which so damaged English trade to the Baltic in the fifteenth century.

The crown's tentacles, however, extended further, into both the positive and restrictive nature of burghal interests in trade. Mercantile disputes were not only settled in burgh courts. In 1451 Aberdeen bailies referred a dispute between Hans Lübeck of Stralsund and John Gismot of Dieppe to the Admiral's Court.[95] Maritime cases, such as this one involving the seizure of a ship, were, from the fifteenth century, normally the preserve of the Admiral's (or his depute's) Court, or another national court, the Lords of Council. Other cases involving strictly commercial matters also found their way to the Lords of Council. Thus in 1491 the Lords deliberated over a dispute about goods bought in Danzig by Haddington merchants.[96]

As well as its interest in judicial matters, the crown also gradually developed an interest in commercial diplomacy. Initial involvement in this sphere was largely in time of crisis. The letter from Moray and Wallace to Lübeck and Hamburg was not unique. Governor Albany, for example, made attempts to have the Hanseatic embargo on Scotland lifted.[97] By the fifteenth century, however, the crown was interceding increasingly on behalf of individual merchants. In 1475 James III recommended an Edinburgh merchant, John Fowls, to Danzig. In 1512 James IV wrote to the duke of Holstein and to Hamburg about attacks on the ships of David Gourlay of Dysart and Edward Cockburn of Leith.[98] Moreover it was to the crown that foreign powers turned increasingly, though not exclusively, for settlement of their commercial grievances in northern trade. Cologne wrote to Governor Albany in 1422 and 1423, regarding Scottish attacks on their citizen Dietrich Polych, and not to Aberdeen where Polych's goods were taken.[99] Foreign powers perceived that they were more likely to receive justice from the crown, while the crown's interventions in trade paralleled an increasing involvement in European political affairs during the fifteenth century.

Central government, through parliament, also involved itself in the regulative side of trade. Some parliamentary legislation, as already stated, was probably sponsored by the burghs themselves. Other statutes, however, clearly point to royal instigation. The new customs duties can be ascribed to financial expediency, but this was not the only reason for new legislation. During the reign of James I in particular the crown pursued 'an economic policy that was both mercantilist and nationalistic'.[100] This expressed itself in other legislation, such as the attempt to limit foreign merchants selling goods but not buying any (1424), the regulation of Scottish merchants going overseas (1425), and the stream of prohibitions on the drain of bullion.[101] By the early sixteenth century foreign trade was not just a matter for merchants. Burghs, groups of burghs and increasingly the crown also wanted to take a part in its regulation.

In 1297 Moray and Wallace wrote to Lübeck and Hamburg for assistance. By 1513 James IV was in conflict with Lübeck and Hamburg over his political support for Denmark and attacks on Scottish shipping. There were many changes over this period in Scotland's commercial relations with northern Europe too. Edinburgh and Dundee came to dominate the Baltic trade, though smaller burghs also became involved. The focus of trade shifted from the North Sea to the eastern Baltic. Whereas arms and victuals had been the key commodities of Scottish-German trade during the Wars of Independence, latterly other Baltic goods found their way to Scotland. While there were few innovations in trading techniques, German domination of the trade had given way to Scottish pre-eminence. And merchants were left less to their own devices as the rôle of the burghs and crown in trade developed. It is perhaps not surprising that there were so many changes in Scottish trade with northern Europe in three centuries, but one crucial factor remained the same: throughout the period Scotland's trade balance remained heavily in deficit.

NOTES

1. *HUB*, i, no. 1251.
2. K. Kunze (ed.), *Hanseakten aus England 1275 bis 1412* (Halle, 1891), no. 21.
3. J. Dilley, 'German merchants in Scotland 1297–1327', *SHR* xxvii (1948), 154.
4. *CDS*, iii, nos. 1128, 1129; *CPR* (1330–34), 554.
5. Stevenson, *Documents*, ii, 96, 154.
6. *Regesta Norvegica*, ii (Oslo, 1978), no. 444. I am grateful to Mrs. K. W. Tyson for translating this document.
7. *CCR* (1307–18); 451;(1318–23), 284, 297; *CDS*, iii, no. 500.
8. *Diplomatarium Norvegicum (DN)* (Kristiana, 1848–1919), ii, no. 114, J. M. Lappenberg, *et al* (eds.), *Hamburgisches Urkundenbuch (HHUB)* (Hamburg 1842–1933), ii, no. 206.
9. C. Fraser (ed.), *Northern Petitions* (Surtees Society, cxciv, 1981), 54. On James of Cologne, see n.4 above.
10. For exceptions, see *ER*, i, 474, 531.
11. *Ibid.*, i, 365–74, 419–28, 529–41; ii, 7–24, 64–70, 84–99.
12. *HUB*, iii, nos. 117, 127.
13. *HUB*, iv, no. 778.
14. *ER*, iii, 186; Wojewodzkie Archiwum Panstwowe Gdańsk, 300/59/2, fo. 258 (235).
15. *ER*, iii, 99.
16. *ER*, iii, 246–58, 283–304, 319–31, 350–64, 378–91, 405–18, 433–46, 462–75, 486–501.
17. *ER*, x, 47.
18. Staatarchiv Bremen, 1/Bc/1445, Juli 15; 1/Bc/1445, August 10.
19. *TA*, i, 89; K. Friedland, 'Hanseatic merchants and their trade with Shetland', *Shetland and the Outside World 1469–1969*, ed. D. J. Withrington (Aberdeen, 1983), 88–90.
20. N. Bang (ed.), *Tabeller over Skibsfart og Varetransport gennem Øresund 1497–1660* [*STR*] (Copenhagen, 1906–33), i, 2.
21. *ER*, x, 295–306, 352–64, 380–89, 454–64, 528–39, 604–15; xi, 46–56, 113–24, 218–35, 261–77.
22. *STR*, i, 3–8. Registers survive for 1503, 1528 and 1536–9. See also D. Ditchburn, 'Scottish shipping at the Sound', *Historical Atlas II*, for the later sixteenth century.
23. H. Keussen, *Köln im Mittelalter. Topographie und Verfassung* (Bonn 1918), esp. 275.
24. F. von Klocke, *Alt Soester Bürgermeister aus sechs Jahrhunderten, ihre Familien und ihre Standesverhältnisse* (Soest, 1927), 101.
25. On Clipping, see Dilley, 'German merchants', 149–150; *CCR* (1318–23), 248.
26. *Ibid.*, 89.
27. Historisches Archiv der Stadt Köln, Brb. 34/35, fos. 99, 99v; ibid., Schreinsurk. Schoff. 2/548/37. There were of course also a number of Scottish students in Cologne, for whom see R. Lyall, 'Scottish students and masters at the universities of Louvain and

Cologne in the fifteenth century', *Innes Review*, xxxvi (1985), 55–73. *HUB*, vi, no. 319; vii(1), nos. 94, 574; xi, no. 1139; *Urkundenbuch der Stadt Lübeck* [*LUB*] (Lübeck, 1843–1905), vii, no. 808.

28. *CPR* (1313–17), 316; *HHUB*, ii, no. 366.

29. K. Koppmann *et al* (eds.), *Die Recesse und Andere Akten der Hansetage* [*HR*] (three series) (Leipzig etc, 1870–1913), I, i, no. 212. Merchants visiting Scotland were ordered to bring back evidence that they had been in Scotland and not Flanders.

30. T. A. Fischer, *The Scots in Eastern and Western Prussia* (Edinburgh, 1903), 4; O. Heinemann *et al* (eds.), *Pommerisches Urkundenbuch* (Stettin, 1868–), ix, no. 5324; *HUB*, iv, no. 335, n.5.

31. *HUB*, viii, no. 223.

32. I. von Wechmar and R. Biederstedt, 'Die schottische Einwanderung in Vorpommern im 16. und 17. Jahrhundert', *Greifswald-Stralsunder Jahrbuch*, v (1965), 7, 23–7; *Spalding Misc.*, iv, 329–30.

33. K. Fritze, *Am Wendepunkt der Hanse* (Berlin, 1967), 226.

34. *HR*, I, vi, nos. 76, 77, 118, 119; *HUB*, v, no. 1061.

35. On friction, see for example *HUB*, viii, nos. 172, 190, 235; on settlements, see K. H. Ruffmann, 'Engländer und Schotten in den Seestadten Ost- und Westpreussens', *Zeitschrift für Ostforschung*, vii (1958), 23–24.

36. *HUB*, vii(1), no. 112; xi, no. 302; R. K. Hannay and D. Hay (eds.), *The Letters of James V* (Edinburgh 1954), 81; F. G. von Bunge *et al* (eds.), *Liv-Esth-und Curlandisches Urkundenbuch* (Reval etc, 1853–1910), iv, nos. 1844, 1876, 1931; v, no. 1966; ix, no. 34.

37. WAP Gdańsk, 300D/36a/88; 300D/36a/96; 300D/69/32; 300D/69/34; 300D/8/69. See also D. Ditchburn, 'Scottish emigration to the Baltic', *Historical Atlas II*, and A. Biegańska, 'A note on the Scots in Poland, 1550–1800', in *Scotland and Europe, 1200–1850*, ed. T. C. Smout (1986), 157–65.

38. *DN*, vi, nos. 694, 695, 696; viii, no. 573. There was also some contact with Stavanger (*DN*, ii(2), no. 978) and Tönsberg (ACA, Sasine Register, i, 651).

39. T. Jexlev, 'Scottish history in the light of records in the Danish National Archives', *SHR*, xlviii (1969), 98–106; T. Riis, 'Scottish-Danish relations in the sixteenth century' in *Scotland and Europe, 1200–1850*, ed. T. C. Smout (1986), 82–96; G. Hay, 'A Scottish altarpiece in Copenhagen', *Innes Review*, vii (1956), 5–10.

40. *HR*, I,i, nos. 510, 522; ii, no. 158.

41. J. Dow, 'Scottish trade with Sweden 1512–1580', *SHR*, xlviii (1969), 64–79.

42. *HUB*, x, no. 472.

43. H. Samsonowicz, 'Engländer und Schotten in Danzig im Spätmittelalter', *Seehandel und Wirtschaftswege Nordeuropas im 17. und 18. Jahrhundert*. edd. K. Friedland and F. Irsigler (Ostfildern, 1981), 50.

44. SA Bremen, 1/Bc/1445 August 4; K. Friedland, 'Hanseatic merchants', 94.

45. *TA*, iv, 71–2; SRO, E71/29/3; *HUB*, x, no. 715.

46. SA Bremen, as n.18 above and 1/Bc/1445 August 4; 1/Bc/1445 August 12; 1/Bc/1445 August 13 I; 1/Bc/1445 August 13 II. James I's new duties on cloth did lapse after his death, but had this cloth come from Scotland it seems unlikely that the crown would have allowed such a profitable source of income to disappear.

47. H. Samsonowicz, 'Engländer und Schotten', 54.

48. See, for example, *HUB*, ii, nos. 254, 271, 324, 399, and J. Dilley, 'German merchants', *passim*.

49. *ER*, i, 433, 532; iv, 678.

50. C. Sattler (ed.), *Handelsrechnungen des Deutschen Ordens* (Leipzig, 1887) 20–22.

51. *HUB*, vi, no. 844; WAP Gdańsk, 300/19/2a. I am grateful to Dr. I. Blanchard for allowing me to use his microfilm copies of the Danzig customs accounts.

52. *ER*, v, 150.

53. H. Samsonowicz, 'Engländer und Schotten', 50.

54. K. Kunze, *Hanseakten*, no. 334.

55. *Edin. Recs.*, i, 148-9; K. Kunze, *Hanseakten*, no. 337.

56. See, for example, R. K. Hannay and R. Mackie (eds.), *The Letters of James the Fourth 1505-1513* (SHS, 1953), 236, 435, 436; *TA, iv*, 289; ACA, CR, ix, 721.

57. *ER*, i, 134, 135.

58. *James IV Letters*, 168, 326, 387; *TA*, i, 69; iv, 284.

59. WAP Gdańsk, 300/19/3, fos. 40, 123v.

60. H. Samsonowicz, 'Engländer und Schotten', 53; 3% is the average of the figures presented here.

61. H. Samsonowicz, 'Handel zagraniczny Gdańska w drugiej połowie XV wieku', *Przeglad Historyczny*, xlvii (1956), 337. I am grateful to Mr. A. Malkiewicz for his help in translating this article.

62. Nicholson, *Scotland*, 307, 431-8, 541.

63. ACA, CR, vii, 659; ix, 442; WAP Gdańsk, 300/19/1, fos. 3v, 99.

64. Archiv der Hansestadt Lübeck, Anglicana 155a, 155b.

65. *APS*, ii, 87; ACA, CR, viii, 231.

66. These complaints are too numerous to list. Examples can be found in W. Stein (ed.), *Akten zur Geschichte der Verfassung und Verwaltung der Stadt Köln im 14. und 15. Jahrhundert*, ii (Bonn, 1895), 331, 455 and E. V. K. Brill, 'A sixteenth-century complaint against the Scots', *SHR*, xxvii (1948), 187-91.

67. J. Dilley, 'German merchants', 154-5.

68. C. Brämer, 'Die Entwicklung der Danziger Reederei im Mittelalter', *Zeitschrift des Westpreussisches Geschichtsverein*, lxiii (1922), 50.

69. P. Dollinger, *Die Hanse* (3rd ed., Stuttgart, 1976), 219.

70. *APS*, ii, 16.

71. For examples, see ACA, CR, ix, 722, 769; *HUB*, vii(1), no. 469; x, nos. 472, 769.

72. S. G. E. Lythe, 'Scottish trade with the Baltic 1550-1650', *Economic Essays in Commemoration of the Dundee School of Economics 1931-1955*, ed. J. K. Eastham (Coupar Angus, 1955), 73. Winter sailings were banned by the Hansa (P. Dollinger, *Hanse*, 193-4).

73. WAP Gdańsk, 300/19/3, fos. 131v, 165.

74. C. Sattler, *Handelsrechnungen*, 11, 20, 23, 28; *HUB*, no. 618; ACA, CR, vii, 167.

75. P. Dollinger, *Hanse*, 267.

76. C. Sattler, *Handelsrechnungen*, 75-7.

77. *HUB*, xi, no. 147; *Halyburton's Ledger*, 85, 98, 128, 134.

78. *CPR* (1405-08), 167; *James IV Letters*, no. 537.

79. *HUB*, xi, no. 489. On Mar's piracy, see T. A. Fischer, *The Scots in Germany* (Edinburgh, 1902), 5.

80. SA Bremen, 1/Bc/1446, April 23; *HUB*, xi, nos. 359, 393, 550, 1021, 1039, 1063, 1139, 1173, 1174, 1176, 1177.

81. *CCR* (1318-23), 284, 297.

82. *HUB*, xi, nos. 115, 147, 236, 265, 302, 314; ACA, CR, vii, 57.

83. *HUB*, x, no. 681; T. A. Fischer, *The Scots in Eastern and Western Prussia* (Edinburgh, 1903), 10-12.

84. ACA, CR, iv, 498; vi, 346.

85. ACA, CR, v(2), 687.

86. Stevenson, 'Thesis', 185. For a rare example of the Scottish community acting together in the Baltic, see *HUB*, xi, no. 637.

87. WAP Toruń, Kat.I.686. I am grateful to Mrs. G. Majewska for obtaining a photograph of this document for me.

88. *HUB*, xi, no. 115.

89. ACA, CR, vii, 1067.

90. *Dundee Chrs.*, 24–6.

91. *HUB*, iii, no. 131; SA Bremen, 1/Bc/1445, Oktober 16; 1/Bc/1446, April 16; *APS*, ii, 147.

92. *APS*, ii, 87; *Edin. Recs.*, i, 5.

93. *ER*, ii, pp. xl–xli; *APS*, i, 502–04, 571; ii, 5, 6, 8, 9, 13, 23, 34. For higher rates on foreigners see n.11 above; *APS*, ii, 6, 8.

94. *LUB*, iii, no. 68; *HUB*, vii(1), no. 556; viii, no. 223; x, no. 395; xi, no. 1139; Historisches Archiv der Stadt Köln, HUA 1/16328; *James V Letters*, 81. It was the town council of Edinburgh, however, which granted privilege and protection to Kampen merchants in 1435; *HUB*, vii(1), no. 94.

95. ACA, CR, v(1), 127.

96. *Acts of Council*, 224.

97. J. Baxter (ed.), *Copiale Prioratus Sanctiandree* (Oxford, 1930), 237–8.

98. *HUB*, x, no. 395; *James IV Letters*, nos. 469, 470.

99. *HUB*, vi, nos. 478, 532.

100. Nicholson, *Scotland*, 307.

101. *APS*, ii, 5, 8. See also n.62 above.

11

Trade with the South, 1070–1513

Alexander Stevenson

Scotland emerges into economic history only after the marriage of its Celtic king, Malcolm Canmore (1057–1093), to the Saxon princess Margaret in about 1070. Any earlier international trade with the south seems to have been restricted. Archaeology has brought to light almost no foreign imports after the eighth century, other than along the Norse-occupied fringes and in the Anglian south-east. There was no monetary economy and there were no recognisable trading centres.[1] According to St Margaret's contemporary biographer it was she who first encouraged foreign merchants to come to Scotland from various regions (unspecified) by land and sea with a wide variety of precious wares. Cloth in many colours, silks, dress ornaments, gold and silver, were imported to furnish the court and to apparel an initially reluctant native aristocracy.[2] Independent support for this account is to be found in another twelfth-century hagiography, the *Life and Miracles of St Godric of Finchale*. This records how Godric rose from very poor beginnings in the last decades of the eleventh century by shipping to Scotland goods from England, and later also from Flanders, which he could exchange at great profit for costly items rare elsewhere.[3] What those items were is not recorded, but Scottish fresh water pearls were well known in England in the early 1100s, and pelts presumably also bulked large.[4] This trade had become sufficiently established before King Malcolm's death for fixed customs duties to be introduced, or so proclaims an assize attributed to his son, David I (1124–1153).[5] The *can* or *cain* of ships, as it is referred to in early Scottish charters, became an important source of royal revenue and was, apart from burgh rents, initially the only one expressed in monetary terms.[6] Detailed tables of customs duties were drawn up for ships and merchandise.[7] These amounted to no more than a shilling on a shipload of grain or salt, plus two bolls of the best; a shilling on a ship carrying merchandise, plus 4d per tun of wine, honey or oil; 4d per bale of dried fruit, nuts, spices, dye or alum; 2d per hundredweight of iron; 3d for a dozen brass pots; 3d for a dozen cauldrons, and so on. How early these scales of duty may be is impossible to

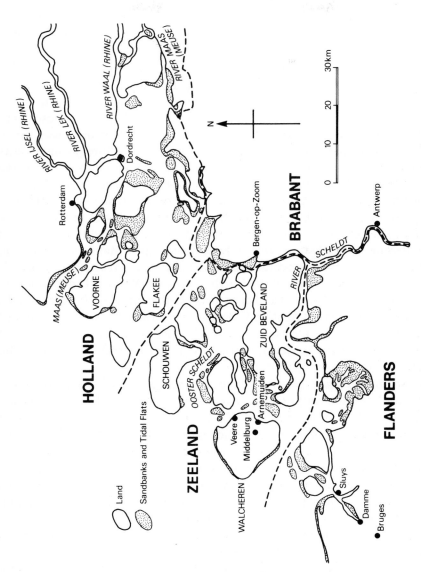

Scheldt, Meuse and Rhine delta in the late middle ages.

tell, but in the middle ages once such matters had been fixed custom was sufficiently rigid to prevent much change. Before 1153 the customs duties levied on ships entering the port of Perth were sufficiently large to support known endowments to three abbeys amounting to some 207s a year, to which were added in the 1160s two further endowments totalling 90s.[8]

Trade seems to have grown very rapidly in the course of the twelfth century. In Lothian all but one of the earliest identifiable towns, Berwick, lay inland; north of the Forth all but one of the earliest burghs (Dunfermline) were accessible from the sea. Late in the reign of Alexander I (1107–1124) only three trading communities were listed north of the Forth: Aberdeen, Perth and Inverkeithing.[9] At that time these were probably no more than authorised trading places. Not only was this a convenience to the crown, it also clearly indicated to foreign merchants where they could find both protection and a market, and it thus provided a focal point for the indigenous population to seek out foreign goods and to exchange their own. The restriction of overseas trade to a very few recognised trading points is a distinctive feature that was to have a long history. The schedule of customs duties on ships, ascribed to King David and current at Berwick in the thirteenth century, makes a fascinating allusion to three distinct economic regions: Lothian, Scotia and Moray.[10] The only major port south of the Forth, before the Wars of Independence, was Berwick. In the twelfth and early thirteenth centuries, Perth enjoyed a similar status in central Scotland. Beyond the Mounth Aberdeen fulfilled more or less the same role. Significantly both Aberdeen and Berwick lay at the south-eastern tip of their hinterlands – overseas traffic came from the south.

When burghs made their formal appearance, early in the reign of David I, they were foreign trading colonies (at least north of the Forth), occupied by *Franci et Angli*.[11] Some of these *Franci* were in fact Flemings,[12] indeed most of the more prominent early Scottish burgesses seem to have come from Flanders.[13] Flanders, already the most urbanised country north of the Alps, provided many skilled emigrants and Flemish merchants are known to have dominated English markets as well.[14] Scottish and English exports were very similar and all but the most limited kind could find an expanding market only in an urban environment.

To attract permanent settlers to these colonies the Scottish crown had to offer considerable inducements. The burghs therefore acquired at a very early date remarkably sweeping privileges.[15] So far as international trade is concerned, charter evidence is unhelpfully silent until the end of the twelfth century, but there are then several references that probably hark back to grants made in David's reign. Scottish merchant burgesses were given exclusive rights to trade in wool, hides and pelts, and rural producers might deal only with them. Alien merchants might deal only wholesale, with burgesses, except at fairtime. Alien merchants were permitted to trade only within the burghs, which in practice probably meant the port at which their goods were landed or in the case of overland trade those burghs situated along the English border, giving first option to the burgesses of that burgh.[16] Again presumably an exception was made for fairs but, unlike England or northern France, Scottish fairs have left little record to indicate their importance. In burghs without fairs, Aberdeen and Perth, alien merchants were permitted 'to cut cloth' only between Ascension Day and 1 August, which may perhaps be seen as a fair's substitute.[17] For the Flemings wool, for their burgeoning cloth manufactures, was Scotland's principal attraction. Flemish burgesses would have acted as agents for their non-resident countrymen and the process of colonisation would have been greatly accelerated by denying alien merchants access to wool producers – although such exclusion was never complete because certain monasteries and (possibly) barons acquired exemptions.[18]

Regrettably few records of international trade links have survived from the twelfth and early thirteenth centuries. Nonetheless circumstantial evidence suggests that Flemish demand for wool steadily increased and was to continue to do so for much of the thirteenth century while the Flemish cloth towns boomed.[19] Before the death of King William the Lion (1165–1214) vast tracts of the Scottish countryside were given over to sheepruns, leaving numerous dispossessed peasants in their wake. Or so indicates an assize transcribed in the early seventeenth century, usually dismissed as a forgery but to my mind genuine, which proclaimed that,

> earls, barons and freeholders of the realm should preserve the peace and do justice by their serfs. They should live as lords upon their lands, rents in kind and money rents, not as farmers, not as shepherds, devastating their domains and patrimony with a multitude of sheep and other beasts; bringing penury, poverty and destruction to God's people.[20]

A further assize to combat this social evil, by increasing the land under cultivation and if necessary empowering the peasantry to cultivate land without their lords' consent, was issued early in the reign of Alexander II (1214–1249). Unlike the earlier assize it is recorded in surviving medieval sources.[21] One consequence of this, highlighted in Alexander's assize, was an increasing need to import grain. It was England, particularly East Anglia, that made good the deficiency on the east coast and Ireland on the west. Ayr, Scotland's principal west coast port, seems not to have had regular supply lines to Ireland, or so suggest the safe conducts obtained by various western Scottish monasteries to seek grain in Ireland. West coast trade was limited and developed late: Ayr was the earliest established coastal burgh in the west but was founded only in about 1200.[22] By contrast, on the east coast a large-scale grain trade was early established, much of it in English hands.[23] English surnames become common in Scottish burghs during the thirteenth century. Some English settlers must have arrived earlier – no distinction was made between Lothian Angles and English Saxons or between Frenchmen and anglicised Normans – but it was after the time of England's occupation of the major southern burghs, between 1175 and 1189, that they became prominent.

A complication in considering trade at this time is the essentially coastal nature of seaborne traffic. Until the introduction of cogs late in the thirteenth century ship design had changed little since the time of the Vikings. Merchant ships were broader in the beam than Viking longships and were not usually equipped with oars but like them were shallow-draughted and open-decked.[24] Long sea voyages were avoided and merchants put into shore frequently. Direct trade across the North Sea was a rarity. In the Rolls of Oléron, the thirteenth-century customs of the sea used alike by Frenchmen and Flemings, ships sailing to Scotland were advised to take aboard a pilot at Yarmouth.[25] They might exchange part of their cargo there for English goods before proceeding north, possibly trading elsewhere on route. Further trade might take place on the way south. In 1242, when war broke out between England and France, French-owned goods impounded included twenty-eight sacks of Scottish wool seized at Yarmouth, forty-one at Dunwich and six, which had already been sold to Englishmen, at Ipswich.[26] English goods might be sold by Flemings or Frenchmen, French or Flemish goods by Englishmen. Wool was Scotland's main export to the French, and possibly to the English, as well as to the Flemings. Some of this wool would have been resold to Flemings, some would have been intended for the French cloth manufactures of Picardy and of Artois (the southern part of Flanders confiscated by the French king at the beginning of the thirteenth century and returned in the fourteenth century). Wine was France's main export to Scotland. Much may have come direct from Bordeaux and the Loire area, but some came via England and some may have come from the French wine staple established during the thirteenth century at Damme (an early port for Bruges).[27]

Numismatic studies suggest that the amount of coin circulating in Scotland remained very low until after the middle of the thirteenth century and the introduction of a sterling area in the Low Countries. Prior to that date English money was prevalent in Scotland. The Scots seem not to have accepted continental coin, and so foreign traders paying coin for Scottish goods were obliged to furnish themselves with English money.[28] However, the evidence of re-coinages in the 1250s and the 1280s, aimed at matching new English coin types, suggests that in the interim the amount of money circulating in Scotland had trebled.[29] Scotland seems to have moved into a dramatic trade surplus. Before that time imports and exports must hav been much more evenly matched. The restriction of trade with alien merchants to wholesale dealing with burgesses may disguise something approaching a barter economy – although the frequent mention in charters of money rents, and the ability of the crown to levy substantial taxes on occasion from 1190 onwards, indicates that money was available if required.[30] The royal assizes already quoted show that the economy was market-orientated by the beginning of the thirteenth century.

Further evidence of early prosperity is to be found in ecclesiastical records of the value of benefices throughout Scotland that may be as early as 1201 and are certainly considerably earlier than 1267. For parishes in south-eastern Scotland these can be compared with a valuation made in 1292, which indicates an overall increase in value of about 50 per cent. Perhaps significantly the lowest increase was in the immediate hinterland of Berwick; but the evidence of summary returns for the 1292 tax suggests that outside the catchment areas of the major towns the rise may have been fairly uniform.[31] Since church taxes on the same basis were also levied in the early 1290s in England, another significant conclusion that can be drawn is that, mile for mile, the Scottish Lowland dioceses (with the exception of Whithorn) were richer than Exeter or Lichfield and St Andrews was as wealthy as Winchester and poorer than only a handful of south-eastern English dioceses.[32] That much of this wealth was export-led is suggested by Flemish and Artesian cloth regulations surviving from the mid-thirteenth century onwards. These make it clear that careful quality control was exercised and that the wool of only a few countries was considered of sufficiently high standard to be used. The wools of different countries and districts might not be mixed – for Scotland in the later thirteenth century the separate districts recognised for this purpose at St Omer were the hinterlands of the ports of Aberdeen, Berwick, Montrose and Perth – and cloth made from different countries' wool was marked distinctively. The best English wool was accorded the highest grade, with Scottish and lesser English wools ranking next. In the earliest regulations these were followed by Irish and Welsh wools but, after its conquest by the English, Wales drops from view and Irish wool was banned before the end of the century. Last came Flemish and Zeeland wools. Except for Bruges, where use of Spanish wool was permitted for the most inferior cloth, no reference is made to the wools of other countries.[33]

Not only wool was in demand. Hides and pelts were also a major component of Scottish cargoes.[34] More problematic is the fish trade. Salmon was certainly exported in bulk but not in all cargoes. As in later times, it came mainly from Aberdeen. It has been suggested that Scotland was an importer of cod and herring but, patchy as the evidence is, it seems much more likely that it was a major exporter of both.[35] In the earliest rolls of the Exchequer large quantities of herring from Crail for the royal kitchens are a common item.[36] The impressive scale of Crail's twelfth-century town plan and its tradition as a fishing port are both indicative of the early wealth of its fisheries. In thirteenth-century Berwick the petty customs relating to herring were so extensive that trade in dry and fresh herring must have been of great importance to the town's economy.[37] On the west coast too the earliest rolls of the Exchequer show an important traffic in herring from Ayr and Dumbarton.[38] Herring was also fished in the Moray Firth and shipped from Inverness. Compared with later times its price was remarkably low: at Inverness in 1266 a thousand herring were selling for little more than the equivalent of a bushel of oats.[39] Cod too is a feature of the Berwick petty customs but was particularly associated with Aberdeen. In thirteenth-century Flanders cod was commonly known as *abberdaan*.[40] Scotland's fisheries must have been prolific indeed for the term *piscinata Scotia* to have become a byword for plenty in distant Spain, where it was still current but described as old at the end of the fifteenth century.[41]

Spanish merchants may well have bought fish at Scottish west coast ports. Spanish iron was imported at Ayr, as was red and white wine, which may have come from France.[42] But the most important group of southern Europeans trading in Scotland were probably Italians. Coming first as papal agents, they soon turned to a lucrative business as moneylenders. As early as 1240 Glasgow Cathedral was deeply in debt to a Florentine banker, and as the century wore on many Scottish religious houses borrowed heavily from Italians. Repayments were often made not in coin but in wool, thus enabling Italian merchants to bypass the usual Scottish middlemen.[43] This might explain a later Scottish chronicler's story of a Lombard proposal to build a factory on the Forth near Edinburgh if granted privileges by Alexander III (1249–1286), a proposal that the king was forced to refuse because of strong opposition, presumably from the burghs.[44] The Italians never managed to secure a strong presence in Scotland; they were resented by native merchants, and without special dispensation they could not hope to rival the well-established Flemish and Artesian connections. In England what gave the Italians and the Germans their major break was a rift with Flanders which occurred in 1270 and was never fully resolved.[45] No such rift occurred between Flanders and Scotland; indeed in 1282 the heir to the Scottish throne married a daughter of the count of Flanders.[46]

The death of that prince and the subsequent failure to honour an annuity settled on his widow has provided a unique insight into the extent of Scottish merchants' traffic in Flanders towards the end of the century. In April 1292 the arrears totalled £8,000 sterling, and to recoup that debt the count ordered the arrest of all Scots and the seizure of all Scottish goods and money in Flanders. The valuation placed on goods seized amounted to £1,459 sterling, a considerable sum at that time (when a sack of wool from some 270 sheep sold for less than £4).[47] A Scottish community was already well established in Bruges by the 1290s. Unique among foreign nations, a stretch of the main canal was named after it, the *Schottendyc*, and by that date there was an adjacent street called 'Scotland'.[48] Large numbers of Scots would, therefore, have been in Flanders in April to attend the Bruges Fair; but money rather than goods may have accounted for most of the count's gain. It would have been a time for Flemish wool merchants to settle debts and to place advance orders, as well as for Scots to spend profits accumulated the previous year – and the sum of money seized is not recorded.

What proportion of foreign trade belonged to Scottish merchants is difficult to tell. In the twelfth century little Scottish activity seems likely. Only in 1209 did a Scottish king seek to secure freedom of trade for his merchants in a treaty with England.[49] Yet from an early date Scottish burgesses had enjoyed considerable customs advantages over aliens – although apparently not favoured under the 'great' customs on wool, hides and woolfells, introduced in imitation of England and possibly at the same time (1275).[50] Scottish ships called regularly at English ports in the thirteenth century. Within the kingdom of France it is stated in a confirmation of Scottish trading privileges in 1295 that most Scottish trade was with Flanders.[51] In another document Normandy and Brittany are also mentioned as having extensive trade links.[52] But the bulk of Scotland's trade with these lands was probably passive. In a garbled eulogy, written over 150 years later, Abbot Bower narrated how Alexander III had banned Scottish merchants from trading overseas because of the inevitable risks involved. Thus, he claimed, foreign merchants had been persuaded to flock to Scotland from far and near, but permitted to trade only with Scottish burgesses,

> so that within a few years the realm abounded with all sorts of goods, both foodstuffs and money, sheep and cattle, merchandise and artefacts; in such manner that many came from east and west, and even from the ends of the earth.[53]

No such ban is known, but the tradition Bower records is indicative of a clear preponderance of foreign mercantile activity in Scotland and of a great trade boom.

That boom was shattered by the Wars of Independence which wracked

Scotland after the English invasion of March 1296, when Berwick was sacked and the Flemish guildhall – the Red Hall – was destroyed.[54] It is impossible to gauge the extent of the decline before the mid-fourteenth century because no quantifiable evidence survives, but the earliest surviving customs accounts, from 1327 to 1333, show a radically altered commercial network (Table 1). Berwick had been recovered from the English only in 1318 and had lost much of its former trade, as well as its old inhabitants – who had been butchered in 1296. Barely mentioned in thirteenth-century foreign records, Leith, as the port of Edinburgh, had become a serious rival for Berwick's export trade. Dundee, which may have become a royal burgh as late as the brief reign of John Balliol (1292–1296), had taken most of Perth's export trade and had completely overshadowed Montrose. Foreign merchants had largely disappeared, and at ports other than Berwick they accounted for no more than 15 per cent of wool, hides and woolfells exported between 1331 and 1333. The double duty levied on foreigners in these years was not collected at Berwick, but an import duty of 4d in the pound on English goods was in force, as at other ports, and indicates English imports there over a two-year period with a gross value of £1,731 10s sterling. At all other ports combined English imports were substantially less, although the sum cannot be computed because it is frequently indistinguishable from receipts of a tax of 12d in the pound on coin exports – a tax that was probably largely avoided.[55] Of foreign merchants mentioned by name in the *Exchequer Rolls* of this period three-quarters were Flemish and most of the rest were French.[56]

The Flemish connection had been maintained almost unbroken through the preceding years. It was through Flanders that money and munitions for the Scottish resistance had been mainly channelled in the years of the English occupation. All English attempts to prevent the Flemings from trafficking with the Scots were rebuffed, except during years of revolt against France when Flemings turned to England for support.[57] The city of Bruges was well to the fore in its support for the Scottish cause, and sometime in the first half of the fourteenth century it was rewarded by the establishment there of a Scottish Staple. Support for this supposition comes from a royal decree of 1347: that because of the seizure of all Scottish goods in Flanders, all Flemish goods in Scotland were to be confiscated; and at the request of the burghs negotiations were to proceed with Middelburg, on the island of Walcheren in Zeeland, for the transfer of 'our staple of merchandise' with the usual sanctions (unspecified) for non-observance.[58] That disruption had been caused by an English-backed revolt in Flanders against the Francophile establishment.[59] Its suppression brought the Scots back to Bruges and there they stayed, their position bolstered in 1359 by the first surviving Staple agreement.[60]

With the irreparable deterioration of relations with England, Bruges came to dominate Scottish overseas trade to a remarkable degree. Italian banking services that had earlier been supplied from England were now obtained at Bruges, and through Bruges passed almost all Scottish traffic with the papacy.[61] Bruges became the most important banking centre north of the Alps in the fourteenth century. It was also the principal north-European mart of the Venetians and the Genoese, and the principal foreign *Kontor* of the Hanseatic League. It was the main northern market of Spain and Portugal, and a major trading centre for the Normans and Bretons. Thus, besides the products of the Low Countries, at Bruges could be found the products of all the known world.[62] With Scotland's principal exports directed there by law, and almost all the imports Scotland needed readily obtainable in the city or in its satellite towns of Damme and Sluys, direct trade with other places withered.

After the thirteenth century the Scottish crafts seem to have been gravely weakened, and a wide variety of humble manufactured goods claimed a major place in the cargoes of most ships bound for Scotland. Froissart, who visited Scotland in 1365 and who discussed the problem with former members of a French expedition to Scotland in 1385, noted disparagingly that

> there was neither iron to shoe horses, nor leather to make harness, saddles or bridles: all these things came ready made from Flanders by sea; and should these fail, there was none to be had in the country.[63]

As discussed in Chapter 8, this was a gross exaggeration but the claim cannot have been unfounded. Native crafts must have been inadequate to meet domestic demand. The claim is echoed in a source dating from the 1430s, the anonymous *Libelle of Englyshe Polycye*, which remarks that

> The Scottes been chargede, knowene at the eye,
> Out of Flaundres wyth lytyll mercerye
> And grete plentee of haburdashers ware;
> And halfe here shippes wyth carte whelys bare
> And wyth barowes are laden as in substaunce.
> Thus moste rude ware be in here chevesaunce;
> So they may not forbere thys Flemyssh londe.[64]

As late as 1498 the *Ledger of Andrew Halyburton* testifies to the shipping of carts and wheelbarrows, although most of Halyburton's dealings were in much more valuable commodities.[65]

A slump in craft activity might help to explain an anomaly in the statistical records of this period. For the *Exchequer Rolls* show high export levels until the 1390s, while tax assessments, restrictions on the export of bullion and coin depreciation emphasise a catastrophic deterioration in the

Scottish economy, which cannot be attributable solely to the Black Death and intermittent payments to England (amounting in all to some £70,000 between 1328 and 1377 and mostly paid out of profits from the wool trade).[66] By 1366 the value of Scottish benefices had declined by a national average of nearly 37 per cent compared with their values in the first half of the thirteenth century, which would represent a decline of some 60 per cent of their value in 1292.[67] And this was but an early point in Scotland's economic decline. There appears to have been a flight of money from remoter areas, which presumably sank back into a subsistence economy. Scotland was running a serious trade deficit.

The vulnerability of most of Scotland's trade routes to English attack must have been a major factor in this financial decline. Ships sailing to and from Scottish ports in the late middle ages were few in number. In the later fourteenth century, even in a good year, no more than thirty vessels loaded with dutiable goods were cleared by the customs at Leith and the number was much less elsewhere.[68] By medieval standards many of these ships were large, they were probably heavily armed and they usually sailed in convoy. At some time in about 1455 an inventory was made of all ships in the port of Sluys, then still the most important port in northern Europe. Six of the seventy-two ships recorded were Scottish and these included the three largest for which tonnages are given. The largest was 'a very fine ship' of 500 tons belonging to the bishop of St Andrews (presumably Bishop Kennedy's renowned *Salvator*). The average Scottish size, at nearly 200 tons, was dramatically greater than the overall average of well under 100 tons.[69] There were, however, serious disadvantages in trading in few but large ships: the capital investment was high and loss through piracy or shipwreck could be crippling.

International trade was now concentrated on the east coast and increasingly in the south-east. Staple goods from western Scotland were brought overland for export from Leith or Blackness (the harbour for Linlithgow). The west coast ports are rarely mentioned in the fourteenth century. They seem to have had very little traffic and that mainly with Ireland. They had been relatively unimportant in the thirteenth century, when most western Scottish goods had probably been taken to Berwick, but the loss of Berwick in 1333 and the consequent rise of Linlithgow as an entrepôt for western trade highlights the extent of this traffic. The trade of the various Scottish ports in wool and woolfells, which together accounted for well over 90 per cent of customs receipts, and the economic trends are shown in Table 1. Woolfell figures have been converted into their wool equivalent, based on the fourteenth-century rate of duty of 240 fells: 1 woolsack of 157.46 kg. These figures should be treated with caution because the years are not typical. All the earliest customs returns are shown but they are not comprehensive because several nobles, prelates and monastic houses were exempted from paying duty to the crown. The first considerable period for which more or less comprehensive figures can be shown, 1372–6, is untypical because export levels were abnormally high. They had earlier been running at about 20 per cent less. Exports peaked in 1372 and by 1376 were already sharply down. They then levelled off at about 750 tonnes a year, including woolfells (with certain sharp dips, as in 1386 during a Flemish revolt). For much of the century Scottish wool and woolfell exports were probably running at about a fifth of English levels but in the early 1370s they were well over a quarter, and they remained at about a quarter thereafter (because the wool trade of both countries was in decline) until the bottom fell out of the Scottish export market at the end of the century.[70]

Table 1. Scottish Wool (and Woolfell) Exports 1327–1431 (Annual Averages in Tonnes)

	1327–33		1372–76		1400–06		1427–31	
Aberdeen	228	(8.8)	161	(2.6)	34	(1.2)	85	(4.3)
Arbroath	?		—		1.7	(0.2)	1	
Ayr	—		5	(0.5)	—		1.2	
Banff	—		—		—			(0.2)
Berwick	287	(18.5)	—		—		—	
Crail	—		—		—		0.5	
Cupar	4.5	(0.6)	—		13	(0.8)	14	(1.0)
Dunbar	?		20	(3.5)	0.2		7	(0.4)
Dundee	119	(7.3)	96	(4.1)	55	(1.6)	57	(2.9)
Edinburgh	172	(6.3)	328	(49.4)	64	(5.4)	294	(26.5)
Haddington	—		73	(12.5)	5.2	(0.7)	64	(4.7)
Inverkeithing	9	(0.2)	1.5	(1.5)	—		7	(0.8)
Inverness	?		13	(0.5)	—		—	
Kinghorn	—		—		6.2	(0.2)	—	
Linlithgow	11	(0.3)	138	(8.1)	30	(3.1)	72	(5.6)
Montrose	2		39	(2.1)	13	(0.6)	15	(1.3)
North Berwick	—		3	(1.5)	4.8	(0.3)	10	(1.3)
Perth	39	(1.3)	85	(3.3)	38	(1.8)	41	(4.0)
St Andrews	?		27	(4.8)	5	(0.5)	?	
Stirling	1		10	(0.6)	2.7	(0.2)	7	(0.5)
Total	872	(43.3)	999	(95.0)	274	(16.4)	676	(53.5)

While wool exports may have held up until the 1390s, their value had probably slumped, as was the case with northern English wool. In the early fourteenth century northern English wool consistently sold for about 90 per cent of the English mean price and as late as the 1360s it was selling a about 75 per cent. By the late 1380s Northumberland wool was selling for little more than half the English mean price and half its price of twenty years previously.[71] Before the end of the century the use of Scottish wool was banned in many of the principal Flemish cloth towns.[72] However, Scottish wool was still widely used in Flanders, particularly by the so-called *nouvelles drapèries*, which specialised in the manufacture of medium-quality cloth and which were perhaps most active in trade with the Hanseatic League.[73] Although the downturn in trade had begun in 1398, the cause of the great slump evident in Table 1 was not so much loss of demand in Flanders but an English naval blockade of Scotland from 1400 onwards.[74] This led to an upsurge in Scottish piracy. Scottish ships were perforce heavily armed and some sought to recoup trading losses at the expense of innocent merchant ships, often from neutral countries. War at sea caused a slump in Flanders and heavy losses by the Dutch and the Hanseatic League.[75] Since the Scottish government seemed unable to control the situation, it was the Scots who were mainly blamed.

There was war with the united counties of Holland and Zeeland until 1406, when a truce was hastily arranged because of a rupture with Flanders. The Scots were forced to abandon their Staple at Bruges but returned the following year, after the Flemings withdrew letters of marque issued earlier and promised to compensate the Scots for their losses. For the first time a resident Scottish governor, or Conservator of the Scottish Privileges as he was known, was appointed and given sweeping powers to regulate the large Scottish community in the city and to watch over Scottish interests generally in the Burgundian Netherlands.[76] Popular pressure seems to have been well to the fore. Under pressure from the deacons of the craft guilds, the Bruges council was persuaded to vote the Scottish ambassadors a gift of £3,000 *parisis* (more than twice the annual salary of senior Burgundian officers of state and nearly three times the pension of the Scottish regent).[77] This may be seen as a further indication of the variety and value of goods manufactured in Bruges and exported to Scotland. Scotland's only manufactured export also found its principal market in Flanders: cheap cloth for the urban poor, of low quality and sold at a fraction of the price of Flemish cloth.[78] Since it paid no duty the quantities exported are not recorded in the *Exchequer Rolls* but it seems to have been of considerable value to the Scottish economy – in various disputes with Scotland the exclusion of Scottish cloth was used as a weapon by the Flemings. Scotland also produced better-quality cloth but it was banned from Flanders, except for cloth shipped to Flanders for dyeing and finishing and then shipped back to Scotland.[79]

Apart from salmon, skins and salt, other Scottish commodities probably featured little in the export trade. In the late fourteenth century Scottish herring was still sold at Sluys,[80] but the Scottish sea fisheries seem to have eroded away in the fourteenth century. The price of herring soared far above the general rate of inflation from early in the century onwards.[81] As early as 1329 'eastland' herring (from the mouth of the Baltic) was purchased for the royal household, although much larger quantities of Scottish herring were still supplied.[82] Cod too became scarce. After the thirteenth century no more is heard of Aberdeen cod, and cod is rarely mentioned in fourteenth-century Scottish records.

With so few commodities available for general export it is perhaps not surprising that trade with countries other than Flanders was limited. Most important of these were the north German states, Poland and Prussia – the Hanseatic League – and with them a three-cornered trade seems to have developed, as indicated in the previous chapter. Baltic goods were shipped to Scotland, the ships were then loaded with cargoes partly destined for the Staple and sailed south to Sluys, whence they returned to the Baltic. It was, for example, aboard a Danzig ship laden with staple goods (wool, hides and woolfells) and presumably bound for Sluys that the young heir to the Scottish throne, later King James I (1406–1437), was seized by the English in 1406.[83] It was mainly the Hanseatic League that provided the grain Scotland needed, which in the thirteenth century had been obtained from England. Another important grain supplier was Normandy, particularly the port of Dieppe. There was a small Scottish colony at Dieppe by the beginning of the fifteenth century and trade with Scotland is also recorded at Rouen and Harfleur.[84] Further south there is little evidence of Scottish trade. French wine was as yet mainly shipped to Scotland from the French wine staple at Damme, and salt from the Bay of Bourgneuf likewise reached Scotland from Flanders. But there may have been some trade with the Basque country. In the thirteenth century iron was imported from Spain and some may also have come direct from Spain in the fourteenth century, although most came via Flanders. Spanish sailors are recorded at Blackness in 1384, and in 1398 gold lions of León were among the few foreign coins officially sanctioned by the Scottish parliament for use in Scotland (the other coins were from England, Flanders and France).[85] Trade with England was conducted in times of peace, but mutual antagonism restricted its scale; an exception was the cross-border traffic generated by the lower export duty levied in Scotland on English wool. Between 1363 and 1379 an annual average of ninety tonnes of English wool was exported through Haddington, Edinburgh, Dunbar and North Berwick (they have been excluded from Table 1).[86] But though for a town like Haddington the scale was substantial, in English terms it was minute apart from peak years between 1372 and 1376.

The trade with all these lands had collapsed by the early 1400s because of war at sea. This slump was to be the beginning of a long period of decline and instability. Hostilities between England and France from 1412 onwards and the subsequent English occupation of northern France destroyed the French economy and with it the trade of the Norman ports, which did not recover until the 1470s.[87] Scottish relations with the Hanseatic League deteriorated to the point that in 1412 the Hanseatic Diet imposed a general ban on the importation of cloth made from Scottish wool.[88] Since Scottish wool was a mainstay of many of the Flemish cloth centres that supplied the League, this decree plunged Flanders into confusion and increased hostility there towards the Scots.[89] A remedy widely adopted to retain Hanseatic custom was to switch from Scottish to Spanish wool. The Hanseatic ban was never fully effective (see previous chapter) but it was nominally in force until 1436, by which time Spanish wool had become firmly established in Flanders to Scotland's permanent loss.[90]

Deterioration in relations with Flanders led to the issue of letters of marque against the Scots in 1416. The Scottish government promptly made peace once more with the Dutch in order to secure alternative facilities in Middelburg; this caused such an outcry in Flanders that the Flemish authorities rapidly rescinded the letters, returned the money seized and paid off the aggrieved parties.[91] An uneasy peace then persisted until 1423, when letters of marque were again issued.[92] Again the Scots removed to Middelburg, having belatedly concluded a very disadvantageous peace treaty with the Dutch.[93] They returned to Bruges some months later but soon went back to Middelburg, at the insistence of the newly ransomed King James I, because the Flemings had failed to provide adequate compensation. Relations with Flanders were not restored until 1427, when the Flemings finally settled on James's terms.[94]

The years after James's return saw the restoration of strong government and were a time of considerable prosperity in Scotland by comparison with the preceding quarter-century. For a short period Scotland seems to have recovered many of its lost markets, or so the figures in Table 1 suggest. But to stimulate the wool trade King James felt obliged to cut the duty on wool by 19 per cent in 1426. The rate of duty per woolsack was not reduced as such but the statute weight on which duty was levied was increased from 157.46 kg to 187.58 kg.[95] To compensate for this loss of revenue duty was soon imposed on a wide variety of commodities.[96] For the first time it becomes possible to gauge the value of the cloth trade but not its scale (because the duty was levied *ad valorem*), so a direct equation with wool exports is impossible. All that can be said is that at 10 per cent the duty on cloth was far lower than the duty on wool, which was probably nearer 25 per cent, even after the reform of 1426. Receipts of the Scottish customs from the last surviving return of James's reign are shown in Table 2.

Table 2. Receipts of the Scottish Customs 1434/35 (in pounds Scots)

Commodity	Receipts	Rate of Duty	Percentage of Total
Wool	£3,379 9s 1d	£1 6s 8d per sack	68.0%
Woolfells	£ 437 4s 8d	13s 4d per 120	8.8%
Cloth	£ 349 14s 1d	2s in pound	7.0%
Shorn Sheepskins	£ 227 7s 4d	6s 8d per 120	4.6%
Hides	£ 216 3s 10d	£2 13s 4d per 200	4.4%
Salmon	£ 182 17s 6d	2s 6d per barrel	3.7%
Lambskins	£ 149 14s 1d	3s 4d per 120	3.0%
Salt	£ 22 16s 5d	1s per chalder*	0.5%
Pelts	14s 1d	various	

*chalder = approx 1.67 tonnes

Evidently, even with the wool trade in marked decline (down to 527 tonnes, including woolfells), the reliance on sheep for Scotland's export earnings was overwhelming. Notable also is the absence of cod or herring exports, although both were now subject to duty. The cloth returns are of particular importance both because of their scale and because they are our only documentary indication of the level of craft activity in and around the exporting burghs. The 1434/35 cloth returns are listed in Table 3.

Table 3. Cloth Exports — 1434/35

Burgh	Receipts	Percentage
Edinburgh	£206 19s 9d	59.2%
Kirkcudbright	£ 99 4s	28.4%
Linlithgow	£ 15 9s	4.4%
Aberdeen	£ 9 7s	2.7%
Dundee	£ 6 19s 8d	2.08%
Haddington	£ 2 18s 2d	0.8%
St Andrews	£ 2 6s 6d	0.7%
Perth	£ 2	0.6%
Stirling	£ 1	0.3%
Montrose	15s	0.2%
Dumbarton	12s 2d	0.2%
Arbroath	8s 6d	0.1%

As one might expect, Edinburgh predominates. But Kirkcudbright's level of cloth exports is remarkable and bears no relationship to its exports of other goods. Staple goods were mainly taken to the east coast and directed towards Flanders. Cloth exports were not so restricted and Kirkcudbright clearly had an extensive cloth trade, presumably with Brittany, La Rochelle and Spain. The poor standing of the other burghs is almost equally extraordinary. Either their cloth was of the wrong quality or Edinburgh merchants had cornered overseas markets. Ayr made no exchequer return that year but in earlier years duty on its cloth exports had been running between £11 16s 8d and 31s 1d, thus making it too, in Scottish terms, a substantial cloth exporter.

Such dramatic fluctuation is indicative of the reliance most western ports placed on the arrival of foreign ships, a reliance probably shared by all the smaller Scottish ports. If no ship came, the burgh merchants were forced to make a long trek overland or by boat to those burghs that possessed their own ships or at which a foreign ship was known to have called. Perhaps that was the secret of Kirkcudbright's success: under the patronage of the Douglases, who treated it as their personal fief for over a century, Kirkcudbright may have had one or more ships of its own to trade in. After the loss of Douglas patronage Kirkcudbright's export trade steeply declined (Table 4). Fewer and fewer foreign ships called as the value other states set by Scottish goods declined, and without adequate numbers of its own ships the Scottish economy was very vulnerable to such vagaries of fortune. Making a virtue of necessity, the crown tried to force reluctant burghs to purchase ships of their own by enacting at some unknown date in the mid-1420s that native merchants might only export goods in Scottish vessels. Good as the intention probably was, the inability of many burghs to comply, and their fears of domination by the few burghs that could, forced the government in 1428 to retreat from so rigid a policy.[97]

High-handed interference in economic affairs was a hallmark of James I's personal rule. On occasion they worked well but often his policies proved unenforceable or could be implemented only by offering bribes in return. The cut in the duty on wool may be seen as an offset for the introduction of a host of other customs duties. Another such bribe – aimed at counter-balancing hostility towards the removal of the Staple from Bruges to Middelburg – may have been the legislation in 1425 restricting overseas traffic to merchants with goods in their charge amounting to at least three sacks of wool or their equivalent in value.[98]

By excluding the more impecunious adventurers James I entrenched the position of the wealthier merchant burgesses and their families, on whose support he counted for financial assistance, in parliament and in the major burgh councils. This was to be the first of several such measures during the fifteenth century to make overseas trade the exclusive preserve of a small elite.[99] To a great extent it was a recognition that with overseas trade in decline the 'cake' was not big enough to go round. In a shrinking market there was much sense in restricting overseas traffic to those with established links, who could most readily clinch a sale and who were sufficiently respectable to enhance Scotland's image abroad. But there can have been no disguising the fact that this was an essentially reactionary measure. By denying an opening to poorly connected but ambitious young men, to whom 'wild adventures' had previously offered incomparable opportunities for advancement in an otherwise static society, the law must have forced many to rethink their careers. Many of the more able must have turned to the crafts, which a reduction in Scottish purchasing power abroad would have made more competitive and hence more profitable.

Table 4. Scottish Customs Receipts 1427–1505 (wool receipts in brackets) in pounds Scots

	1427–31		1455–60		1480–85		1500–05	
Aberdeen	762	(601)	252	(215)	412	(265)	418	(322)
Arbroath	10	(8)	—		7	(—)	7	(1)
Ayr	14	(9)	9	(—)	(?)		66	(3)
Banff	27	(26)	—		?		15	(1)
Crail	5	(5)	—		—		5	(—)
Cupar	108	(96)	40	(28)	30	(17)	18	(3)
Dumbarton	2	(—)	7	(—)	(?)		84	(—)
Dunbar	54	(49)	9	(6)	—		1	(—)
Dundee	451	(403)	151	(90)	153	(74)	127	(39)
Dysart*	—		—		15	(—)	19	(—)
Edinburgh	2327	(2085)	1262	(1033)	1399	(985)	1706	(1177)
Haddington	531	(454)	103	(80)	88	(41)	84	(38)
Inverkeithing	64	(49)	13	(5)	18	(9)	4	(2)
Inverness+	32	(—)	26	(—)	?		23	(—)
Irvine	—		4	(—)	(?)		16	(—)
Kinghorn	—		2	(1)	4	(—)	3	(—)
Kirkcudbright	?		61	(22)	(?)		(?)	
Linlithgow	661	(511)	55	(24)	18	(2)	33	(1)
Montrose	128	(105)	14	(7)	47	(10)	43	(2)
North Berwick	86	(73)	22	(13)	5	(—)	3	(—)
Perth	355	(289)	68	(43)	83	(37)	91	(46)
Stirling	76	(49)	28	(7)	17	(5)	59	(20)
Clyde Ports	[16	(9)]	[20	(—)]	117	(—)	[166	(3)]
Solway Ports	?		[61	(22)]	13	(—)	27	(—)
Total	5693	(4811)	2126	(1574)	2426	(1445)	2852	(1653)

*includes Pittenweem & Anstruther
+includes Elgin, Forres, Nairn & Caithness

Scottish overseas trade was particularly hard-hit by the renewal of hostilities with England in 1436. Open warfare between England and Burgundy between 1435 and 1438, and long trade wars throughout much of Western Europe thereafter, caused a dramatic downturn in Scottish trade that was to last until the mid 1440s, to be followed by a brief upturn and then a prolonged depression throughout the 1450s (Table 4).[100] The Scottish customs accounts are chaotic between 1436 and 1442.[101] Apart from that on salmon (and then only when exported by foreigners), the new customs duties enforced by James I were abandoned and not reintroduced until the early 1450s. The few ships that dared to trade with England were obliged to secure safe conducts in advance after 1435.[102]

All this was in marked contrast to the prosperous years following King James's ransom. Then trade with England had been extensive, particularly the salmon trade. English merchants were given first option on the purchase of salmon and were compelled by law to pay in gold for the privilege.[103] English-based Italian merchants had once more established strong Scottish connections and King James was heavily in their debt.[104] Despite the subsequent hostilities this Italian connection was not quite destroyed: in the 1450s, after Kirkcudbright was wrested from Douglas control, a Genoese merchant who had been based in London during the reign of James I, Lazarino Grello, reappears there as a prominent resident, acting as customs officer for the port.[105]

In these years of economic crisis the Scottish government sought to establish closer political ties with its principal trading partner, partly in the hope that this would expand the Netherlandish market for Scottish exports. In 1444 a sister of the Scottish king married the son and heir of Zeeland's premier lord and Burgundian Admiral, the Lord of Veere; and in 1449 James II (1437–1460) married a grand niece of the duke of Burgundy.[106] Yet whatever other political advantages there may have been, the immediate economic gain is not apparent. In the 1450s the wool trade was running at less than a third of its volume twenty-five years earlier and it was never to stage more than a temporary recovery thereafter (Table 4). The cloth trade had also suffered a steep decline from a gross value of about £3,000 a year in the early 1430s to about £1,000 a year in the 1450s – a volume of about 25,000 ells a year. The trade in other commodities seems to have declined less, although the extent of the trade in shorn sheepskins, lambskins and salmon cannot be gauged because duty was now levied only on foreigners.[107]

Economic failure led to growing disillusionment with restrictions imposed by the Staple arrangements. An increasing amount of international trade was now conducted at the four great Brabantine fairs of Antwerp and Bergen-op-Zoom, and the market at Middelburg was also much expanded by foreign traffic. Bruges's hegemony was already a thing of the past but the city authorities, fearing further loss of trade, imposed rigid restrictions on traffic passing through their satellite port at Sluys and held tenaciously to the letter of their Staple agreements. Not only that, the Scots felt they were treated with scant regard in the city and they found the harbour at Sluys increasingly unsatisfactory because of silting. The crisis came to a head in 1467 when the Scottish government closed the Staple and banned traffic with Bruges and its satellites.[108] A temporary embargo was placed on the departure of all ships from Scottish ports but this was soon relaxed to a ban on the export of staple goods. Trade in other goods with Middelburg, La Rochelle, Bordeaux, France (*sic*) and Norway was specifically permitted, presumably because ships were known to be preparing to sail there.[109] Middelburg became the *de facto* Staple until relations with Bruges were patched up in 1470,[110] but by then earlier trading patterns had been permanently broken. Scottish ships increasingly resorted to the deepwater harbour at Veere where – because of the close Scottish links with the ruling family – they enjoyed almost duty-free facilities, as well as a perfect location for transhipment to the major economic centres of Antwerp, Bruges, Middelburg and Bergen-op-Zoom.[111] The Bruges Staple lasted in name at least until 1477, but was then finally abandoned during the civil strife following the death of Charles the Bold, last Valois Duke of Burgundy.[112] A free trade policy took its place and traffic with the Netherlands inexorably declined.

Records from Dieppe suggest that after many years of inactivity trade with Scotland began to revive in the later 1440s; but direct trade with the British Isles was slight (except for the period between 1467 and 1472) until after the Scots had abandoned the Bruges Staple.[113] Scottish wool for the rapidly expanding cloth industry at Rouen was initially supplied mainly through Bruges,[114] and much trade between France, Brittany and Scotland was conducted through the Low Countries until the early sixteenth century.[115] First Sluys and after the 1460s Middelburg's port of Arnemuiden were the most frequent destinations of ships clearing most French ports.[116] Nonetheless there was sufficient direct exchange for a small Scottish colony to have become established at Dieppe: by 1486 twenty-three Scots-born burgesses had been admitted. By the end of the century Scottish settlers were also to be found at Rouen, Eu, Le Tréport and doubtless elsewhere.[117] Hides and cheap cloth (friezes and serge) had long been the major Scottish exports to France and Brittany from west coast ports, but it was the re-establishment of the Scottish fisheries that first stimulated a marked expansion of direct trade on both east and west coasts.

Deeply concerned about the erosion of overseas trade – and well aware of

the great profits Dutch seamen were making from the North Sea fisheries –
the Scottish parliament enacted in 1471 that

> for the common good of the realm and the great increase of riches to be brought
> within the realm from other countries, that certain lords spiritual and temporal and
> burghs have made or get ships, busses and other great pink boats with nets and
> equipment for fishing.[118]

Herring and cod fisheries were operating on a small scale before this date
but by the late 1470s relatively large exports from Montrose and the Forth
and Clyde ports are regularly recorded.[119] The Netherlandish and Baltic
markets were already fully supplied by their own fishermen, so this trade
was directed almost entirely towards France and Brittany. As Table 5
demonstrates, the value of these fisheries was not great (in 1511 herring
was being sold at Ayr for 16s 4d a barrel of c. 1,200 fish,[120] which suggests
that in 1504/05 herring exports may have been worth about £1,000). But
this was the main growth area in the Scottish export trade, although cloth
exports had also been flourishing over the previous decade by comparison
with the preceding half-century, as had the trade in hides.

Table 5. Receipts of the Scottish Customs 1504/05 (in pounds Scots)

Commodity	Receipts	Rate of Duty	Percentage of Toal
Wool	£1563 11s 4d	£1 6s 8d per sack	56.3%
Hides	£ 327 12s 8d	£2 13s 4d per 200	11.5%
Woolfells	£ 259 4s 1d	13s 4d per 120	9.3%
Cloth	£ 242 6s 11d[@]	2s in pound	8.7%
Salmon*	£ 178 4s	4s per barrel	6.4%
Herring	£ 59 19s	1s per barrel	2.2%
Tallow	£ 56 10s	5s per barrel	2.0%
Shorn Sheepskins+	£ 18 16s 6d	6s 8d per 120	0.7%
Cod	£ 18 16s	£1 per 1,200	0.7%
Lambskins+	£ 14	3s 4d per 120	0.7%
Salt	£ 8 3s	1s 4d per chalder	0.3%
Miscellaneous	£ 27 19s 11d	various	1.0%
[English Imports	£ 27 2s 9d	?1s 6d in pound]	

*Salmon exported by Aberdonians paid no duty
+Foreign exports only
@Approx 51,000 ells

The French economy was expanding rapidly from the 1470s onwards,
while the traditional industries of Flanders were in marked decline. The
Ledger of Andrew Halyburton, a Scottish merchant and factor resident in

the Low Countries at the end of the fifteenth century, shows that the Netherlandish market for Scottish goods was by then limited and wool sometimes remained in store for over a year before a buyer was found.[121] Cloth and hides sold better but the Norman market for hides was stronger still. Two 'cocket books' from Leith, listing cargoes and destinations of ships cleared by the Scottish customs, for the periods 1510/11 and 1512/13, show that by then sailings were almost equally divided between Normandy (mainly Dieppe) and Veere[122] – the compulsory Netherlandish port of entry for Scottish exports, by a decree of James IV (1488–1513) in 1508, and residence of the Scottish conservator.[123] Most wool, woolfells and cloth were still exported to the Netherlands; but large quantities of wool and cloth were also shipped to Normandy, as were most hides and salmon, and almost all cod and herring. Trade with England was small and trade with Denmark and the Baltic was also limited. No other destinations are recorded.

Since no duty was collected by the crown on any but English imports – the petty customs levied on all goods passing through the ports were retained by the burghs – there is no national record of imports to compare with the customs accounts on exports. For much of the period under review the only evidence to be had is from foreign commentaries or archaeological finds. To these can be added in the fourteenth century occasional references in the *Exchequer Rolls* to purchases made on credit for the royal household; and in the fifteenth century occasional Aberdeen and continental court cases. From later in the century there are records of royal purchases in the *Accounts of the Lord High Treasurer*, customs accounts and notarial records from France and, most valuable of all, the *Ledger of Andrew Halyburton*. This records Halyburton's dealings in the Netherlands between 1493 and 1505 on behalf of mainly Scottish clients: the commodities they exported, their financial dealings with Italian bankers in Antwerp, Bergen-op-Zoom, Bruges and Middelburg, and the merchandise he sent back to Scotland on their instructions. Halyburton's ledger records the dispatch of: fine cloths; spices; beer; Rhenish, Malmsey, Anjou and Gascon wine; large consignments of iron, salt and soap; paints, dyes and mordants; books; feather beds; furs and clothing; monumental brasses; altarpieces and pictures; gold and silver ware.[124] The variety is remarkable. Though they formed only a very small part of Halyburton's trade, earlier Staple agreements and contemporary French records show that wheat, barley, nuts, fruit and vegetables were also shipped in bulk to Scotland.[125] But most of these imports would have been classed as luxury goods.

It is notable that the base metal wares and leather goods, which in earlier years had been a major feature of the Scottish import trade, are not recorded in the ledger. The Scottish crafts had developed greatly in the lean years after James I's reign, in fair measure because there were insufficient resources to finance imports on the same scale as before. Legislation to stem bullion exports and to try to force merchants to import gold and silver was frequent: a sure indication that it was ineffectual. Mint output was very low and the coinage was heavily debased in the course of the fifteenth century. Under James III (1460–1488) the monetary shortage became critical and a copper coinage was temporarily introduced.[126] To stem this haemorrhaging, it was James III who first took formal steps to ensure incorporation of crafts and to redefine standards of craftsmanship (derived in the case of the silversmiths from the craft standard of Bruges);[127] introduced sumptuary laws to limit the importation of costly materials;[128] pressed for the re-development of fisheries; and introduced a free trade policy. It is a remarkably enlightened, indeed revolutionary, catalogue that was to transform economic life. By the early sixteenth century foreign trade was less important in burgh affairs than it had ever been.

NOTES

1. I am indebted to my father Dr R. B. K. Stevenson, formerly Keeper of the National Museum of Antiquities of Scotland, for this and other archaeological information.

2. Anderson, *Early Sources*, 68.

3. *Libellus de Vita et Miraculis Sancti Godrici* (Surtees Society, 1847), 28–30.

4. *PSAS*, xxiv (1889–90), 66 n. 1.

5. *APS*, i, 11.

6. *ESC, passim.*

7. *APS*, i, 303–8.

8. *ESC*, nos. cliii, clxiii, ccix; *RRS*, i, nos. 223, 260.

9. *RRS*, i, no. 243.

10. *APS*, i, 308.

11. *ESC*, nos. lxxii, cxxii, ccxix, cxci, ccxlviii; *RRS*, i, no. 239.

12. M. M. Postan, 'The Trade of Medieval Europe: the North', in *Cambridge Economic History* (Cambridge, 1952), ii, 160.

13. *ESC*, nos. clxix and notes, ccxlviii, cclxviii; *RRS*, i, nos. 121, 171, 175; *RRS*, ii, nos. 97, 98, 388; Duncan, *Scotland*, 476–8.

14. T. H. Lloyd, *The English Wool Trade in the Middle Ages* (Cambridge, 1977), 1–24.

15. See MacQueen and Windram, Ch. 12, below.

16. *Leges Burgorum*, cc. 8, 9, 16, 25; *Assise Willelmi Regis*, c. 41; *RRS*, ii, no. 475.

17. *RRS*, ii, no. 467; *Aberdeen Burgh Chrs.*, no. 5.

18. Duncan, *Scotland*, 513.

19. *Cambridge Economic History*, ii, 182–4, 367–88; G. Sivery, *L'économie du royaume de France au siècle de Saint Louis*, (Lille, 1984), 151–95; N. J. G. Pounds, *An Economic History of Medieval Europe* (London, 1974), 306–10.

20. *APS*, i, 382.

21. *APS*, i, 387–8.

22. *RRS*, ii, nos. 433, 462.

23. Duncan, *Scotland*, 504–5; *RRS*, ii, no. 462.

24. B. Landström, *The Ship* (London, 1962), 62–73.

25. *The Black Book of the Admiralty*, ed. T. Twiss (London, 1873), ii, 226.

26. Duncan, *Scotland*, 514.

27. J. Craeybeckx, *Les vins de France aux anciens Pays Bas* (Paris, 1918), 21–2, 24, 93.

28. *Coinage in Medieval Scotland*, British Archaeological Report 45, (Oxford, 1977), 4, 8–10, 67–71.

29. *Ibid.*, 67–71, 85–98.

30. W. W. Scott, 'The use of money in Scotland, 1124–1230', *SHR*, lviii (1979).

31. *Dunf. Reg.*, 203–12; *Liber Sancti Thome de Aberbrothoc* (Bannatyne Club, 1848), 231–47; *The Priory of Coldingham* (Surtees Society, 1841), pp. cviii–cxvii; *Register of John de Halton* (Canterbury and York Society, 1913), 152–3.

32. W. Stubbs, *Constitutional History of England* (Oxford, 1878), ii, 579–81.

33. *Recueil de documents relatifs à l'industrie drapière en Flandre*, ed. G. Espinas and H. Pirenne (3 vols., Brussels, 1906–20), *passim*; G. Espinas, *La draperie dans la Flandre française au moyen âge* (2 vols., Paris, 1923), ii, 43–5.

34. *CDS*, i–ii, *passim*.

35. Duncan, *Scotland*, 507.

36. *ER*, i, 4, 159, 266, 293, 305, 331 etc.

37. *Assisa de Tolloneis*, c. 6.

38. *ER*, i, 69, 89, 161, 162, 198, 268.

39. *Ibid.*, 19, 516.

40. H. Pirenne, *Histoire de Belgique* (5th ed., Brussels, 1929), i, 265, n. 2.

41. Hume Brown, *Early Travellers*, 44.

42. *ER*, i, 5–6, 28.

43. Duncan, *Scotland*, 283, 428–9, 516.

44. *Chron. Bower*, ii, 130.

45. Lloyd, *Wool Trade*, Ch. 2.

46. Duncan, *Scotland*, 592.

47. Stevenson, *Documents*, i, nos. 233, 248.

48. *Inventaire des archives de Bruges*, ed. L. Gilliodts van Severen, i, 439; ii, 123.

49. Duncan, *Scotland*, 504.

50. *Ibid.*, 603–4.

51. Stevenson, *Documents*, ii, no. 335.

52. PRO, SC1/35/12. I am indebted to the staff of the SRO for this reference.

53. *Chron. Bower*, ii, 130.

54. *Chron. Walteri de Hemingburgh*, (Eng. Hist. Soc., 1848–9), ii, 96–9.

55. *ER*, i, 365–74, 419–29.

56. *Ibid.*, 52–541.

57. W. Stanford Reid, 'Trade, traders and Scottish independence', *Speculum*, xxix (1954) 210–22; *idem*, 'Sea-power in the Anglo-Scottish war, 1296–1328', *Mariner's Mirror*, xlvi (1960), 7–32; *Cartulaire de l'ancienne Estaple de Bruges*, ed. L. Gilliodts van Severen, i, nos. 136, 153, 168, 178, 187, 212, 242, 248; Nicholson, *Scotland*, 105–06; *APS*, i, 479–81.

58. *APS*, i, 514–5.

59. Pirenne, *Histoire*, (1st edn. Brussels, 1903), ii, 121–3.

60. *Inventaire Bruges*, i, 502–3; M. P. Rooseboom, *The Scottish Staple in the Netherlands* (The Hague, 1910), Appendix 10.

61. Stevenson, 'Thesis', 216–18.

62. J. A. van Houtte, *Bruges: essai d'histoire urbaine*, (Brussels, 1967), 24–76; M. H. I. Letts, *Bruges and its Past* (London, 1926), 103–19, 139–42.

63. Hume Brown, *Early Travellers*, 11.

64. *The Libelle of Englyshe Polycye*, ed. G. Warner (Oxford, 1926), 14.

65. *Halyburton Ledger*, 184.

66. Grant, *Scotland*, 80, 240; *APS*, i, 134 (1357), 144 (1367), 150, 174 (1370), 190 (1385), 210 (1398).

67. *APS*, i, 497–501; and see n. 31 above.

68. *ER*, i–iii, *passim*.

69. R. Vaughan, *Philip the Good* (London, 1970), 243.

70. *ER*, i–iii *passim*; E. M. Carus-Wilson and O. Coleman, *England's Export Trade, 1275–1547* (Oxford, 1963), *passim*.

71. T. H. Lloyd, *The Movement of Wool Prices in Medieval England* (Economic History Review Supplement No. 6, 1973).

72. Espinas and Pirenne, *Recueil*, i, 49; ii, 307; iii, 637.

73. *Recueil de documents relatifs à l'industrie drapière en Flandre (2e partie)*, ed. H. E. de Sagher *et al* (3 vols., Brussels, 1951–66), ii, 4–5, 16–7, 31–3, 45, 66–7, 108, 253–6, 275–81; iii, 413–7 [in the 1490s Tourcoing was Halyburton's main customer], 434–50, 527–31; Warner, *Libelle*, 13.

74. Grant, *Scotland*, 43–4.

75. *Inventaire Bruges*, iii, 462–6; *Bronnen tot de geschiedenis van den handel met Engeland, Schotland en Ierland*, ed. H. J. Smit (4 vols., The Hague, 1928–51), i, nos. 748, 791, 811, 827; *Précis analytique des documents des archives de la Flandre occidentale*, ed. O. Delepierre (3 vols., Bruges, 1843–5), i, 73.

76. Smit, *Handel*, i, nos. 784, 791, 827, 831, 834, 845, 847; *Inventaire Bruges*, v, 302–3; *Cartulaire Bruges*, i, 452–5; Rooseboom, *Staple*, Appendices 14, 15.

77. *Inventaire Bruges*, v, 302–3.

78. *Ibid.*, iii, 429, 430; v, 301; vi, 12, 39.

79. Rooseboom, *Staple*, Appendices 21 (article 6), 26 (article 5).

80. *Inventaire Bruges*, vi, 17.

81. *ER*, i, 69, 70, 159, 161, 162; ii, 156, 228, 294, 449, 575; iii, 42, 108; iv, 438; v, 32; Grant, *Scotland*, 238–9.

82. *ER*, i, 134, 161, 162.

83. E. W. M. Balfour-Melville, *James I* (London, 1936), 29, 31.

84. M. Mollat, *Le commerce maritime normand à la fin du moyen age* (Paris, 1952), 9.

85. *APS*, i, 568.

86. *ER*, ii, *passim*.

87. Mollat, *Commerce*, 19–95.

88. Fischer, *Scots in Germany*, 13–14.

89. Delepierre, *Précis*, i, 167, 168, 186.

90. de Sagher, *Recueil, passim*.

91. *Cartulaire Bruges*, i, 517–23; Delepierre, *Précis*, i, 186; Rooseboom, *Staple*, Appendix 18; J. Yair, *An Account of the Scotch Trade in the The Netherlands* (London, 1776), 49–55.

92. *Cartulaire Bruges*, i, 554; *Chron. Bower*, ii, 487; J. H. Munro, 'Industrial

protectionism in Flanders', in *The Medieval City*, ed. H. A. Miskimin *et al* (London, 1977), 241.

93. Rooseboom, *Staple*, Appendix 19.

94. *Cartulaire Bruges*, i, 554; *APS*, ii, 6 c. 27, 7 c. 6; *Chron. Bower*, ii, 487; Rooseboom, *Staple*, Appendix 21.

95. *APS*, ii, 12 c. 22; Grant, *Scotland*, 236–7 (Table 1), fails to take account of this change in weight and his figures for wool exports from 1426 onwards are not directly comparable with those for earlier years.

96. *APS*, ii, 6 cc. 22–3, 8 c. 19; *ER*, iv, 506, 604.

97. *APS*, ii, 16 c. 7.

98. *Ibid.*, 8 c. 16.

99. *Ibid.*, 86 c. 3 (1467), 178 c. 12 (1487).

100. *ER*, v–vi, *passim*; J. H. A. Munro, *Wool, Cloth and Gold* (Toronto, 1972), 112–9, 134–53; Mollat, *Commerce*, 90–91.

101. *ER*, v, 1–123.

102. *CDS*, iv.

103. *APS*, ii, 20 c. 2, 24 c. 10; *ER*, iv, 406, 408, 444, 478, 480, 536, 567, 569, 612, 616, 629.

104. *ER*, iv, 389, 413, 443, 444, 445, 472, 480, 483, 507, 531, 542, 570, 616, 621, 628.

105. *ER*, vi, 125, 202, 303, 494, 594.

106. A. I. Dunlop, *The Life and Times of Bishop Kennedy* (Edinburgh, 1950), 66–7; 89–101; Stevenson, 'Thesis', 75–82.

107. *ER*, iv–vi.

108. *APS*, ii, 87 c. 6.

109. *Ibid.*, c. 7.

110. Stevenson, 'Thesis', 87–102.

111. *Ibid.*, 202–06.

112. Smit, *Handel*, ii, 1187.

113. Mollat, *Commerce*, 59; *idem*, *Comptabilité du port de Dieppe au XVe siècle* (Paris, 1951), 38–111, 129.

114. Mollat, *Commerce*, 71, 85–7.

115. *Ibid.*, 95, 103–4, 159; H. Touchard, *Le commerce maritime breton à la fin du moyen age* (Paris, 1967), 194–200, 239; *Halyburton's Ledger, passim*.

116. Touchard, *Commerce*, 262, 269.

117. Mollat, *Commerce*, 157–9, 171.

118. *APS*, ii, 100 c. 10.

119. *ER*, vii *et seq.*

120. *ER*, xiii, 382.

121. *Halyburton's Ledger*, pp. xxi–ii, 71, 206, 270.

122. SRO, E71/29/2–3.

123. *James IV Letters*, nos. 160, 165; *RSS*, i, no. 2016.

124. *Halyburton's Ledger*, pp. lxxii–iii.

125. Rooseboom, *Staple*, Appendix 21; Mollat, *Commerce*, 159.

126. E. Burns, *The Coinage of Scotland* (3 vols., Edinburgh, 1887), i, 284–7; ii, 1–227; I. Stewart, 'Scottish mints' in *Mints, Dies and Currency* (ed) Carson, R. A. G., 228–42; C. E. Challis, 'Debasement: the Scottish experience in the fifteenth and sixteenth centuries', in BAR 45, *Coinage*, 171–96; J. E. L. Murray, 'The black money of James III', in BAR 45, *Coinage*, 115–28; *idem*, 'Unicorns and heavy groats of James III and James IV', in *Brit. Numis. Jour.*, xl (1971), 62–96; N. McQ. Holmes, 'A fifteenth century coin hoard from Leith', in *Brit. Numis. Jour.*, liii (1983), 78–107; *APS*, ii, 5 c. 16 (1425), 9 c. 5 (1426), 14 c. 2

(1427), 15 c. 1 (1428), 20 c. 2 (1431), 23 c. 7 (1431), 24 c. 13 (1436), 86 cc. 10–11 (1466), 88 c. 1 (1467), 90 c. 1 (1468), 105 cc. 11, 15 (1473), 106 c. 4 (1474), 118 c. 3 (1478), 144 c. 8 (1482), 166 cc. 10–11 (1484), 172 c. 16 (1485), 183 c. 13 (1487), 221 c. 14 (1489), 238 c. 4 (1493), 242 c. 11 (1503), 246 c. 48 (1503).

127. *Edin. Recs.*, i, 26–34, 47–9; *APS*, ii, 95 c. 5, 105–06 c. 17; Nicholson, *Scotland*, 450–51.

128. *APS*, ii, 100 c. 7.

Part Four

Urban Society and Administration

12

Laws and Courts in the Burghs

Hector L. MacQueen and William J. Windram

Early in the twelfth century certain Scottish towns and urban settlements began to acquire the status of 'burghs'. This meant that these places gained a trading monopoly over the surrounding areas of the countryside so that none might buy and sell there except in the market-place of the burgh where a toll would have to be paid by all those who were not the privileged inhabitants termed 'burgesses'. It was David I (1124–1153) who led the way in establishing burghs, erecting Berwick and Roxburgh as such even before he became king of Scots, and it seems clear that his main purpose was to modernise the Scottish economy along lines already established elsewhere in western Europe and England. Certainly he brought to and settled in his burghs men from furth of Scotland whom we may reasonably infer to have been merchants and tradesmen capable of employing new skills and techniques previously unknown in the kingdom. They were the first burgesses and they were drawn to Scotland by the assurance of individual rights and privileges within their burghs and in the kingdom at large.[1]

It has been rightly pointed out that in Scotland 'burgh' and 'burgess' were from the beginning essentially legal concepts[2] with the privileges implied by each no doubt enforceable by process of law; and there is evidence to show that David I did engage in law-making activity in setting up his burghs. A charter of his grandson, William I (1165–1214), in favour of Inverness, refers to three assizes (i.e. statutes) of David, which must relate to particular trading monopolies of burghs.[3] No-one is to make dyed or shorn cloth within the bailiary (*balliam*) of the burgh; buying and selling of certain unspecified items outwith the burgh is prohibited; and there are to be no taverns outwith the burgh except in villages whose lord is both resident and a knight. The charter also indicates that William has affirmed or re-enacted all these assizes. The prohibition embodied by each assize presumably applied to all except the burgesses within their burghs, and the effect would have been to confer upon them and their market place a monopoly in the activities mentioned. The assizes relate to obviously important matters. A monopoly of buying and selling within the area around the burgh was the fundamental burghal privilege, while the most significant industry in the twelfth-century burghs was the manufacture of cloth. The value of the privilege attached to the keeping of a tavern is not so immediately apparent but it has been persuasively suggested that it was connected with the trade in wine, a 'quality' item which had to be imported from overseas.[4]

There are also less specific references in twelfth-century documents to 'all the liberties and customs which burgesses have in common throughout the whole land at whatever port (*quibuscunque portubus*) they put in'[5] and, in William's charter to Inverness, to 'all laws and right customs which other burgesses living in the other burghs of Scotland have',[6] while there is also mention of an assize of the king's burghs concerning those who come to their fairs.[7] All this clearly shows the existence of a body of law, both legislative and customary in origin, applicable in all burghs and so not arising particularly out of individual or *ad hoc* grants, from early on in their histories. Probably its content was closely comparable with the urban laws and customs of contemporary western Europe and England. This is certainly true of the tenure by which the Scottish burgess held his lands in the burgh. References to holdings *in burgagio* can be found in the reign of David I associated with the characteristic duty of the burgess to perform his service of 'watch and ward' within the burgh.[8] By the reign of William I the tenure was so well established that it only needed to be indicated by the phrase *in libero burgagio* or *in liberum burgagium* without further elaboration.[9]

Despite this evidence of royal law-making in connection with burghs in the twelfth century, it is not necessarily the case that the best-known compilation of burgh laws, the *Leges Burgorum*, also dates from this period. The first manuscript containing the *Laws* is the so-called Berne MS dating from c. 1270 at earliest[10] and this provides a *terminus ante quem* for dating the *Laws*. How far back the collection or its constituent parts may be dated is uncertain. Traditionally but perhaps mistakenly a link with David I has been assumed from two facts: firstly, the text commences with a statement that it was 'constituted' by the king; and secondly, some twenty of its opening chapters are virtually identical with what is generally regarded as a mid-twelfth-century statement of the customs of Newcastle-upon-Tyne as they stood in the reign of Henry, king of England.[11] The connection between Newcastle and Scotland arises from the Scottish control of Northumberland between 1139 and 1157.[12] Indeed, it has recently been argued that the Newcastle custumal was produced at the command of David and then taken to Scotland for use there, the point being that the *Burgh Laws* chapters show a closer verbal resemblance to that document than do subsequent versions of the Newcastle customs.[13] But this argument assumes that the *Burgh Laws* is to be attributed to David's reign and then dates the custumal on the basis that, as it precedes the *Burgh Laws*, its composition must have been before 1153. Thus it appears that Scottish historians use the Newcastle customs to date the *Burgh Laws*, while Newcastle historians reverse the procedure. A fresh start seems to be needed on both sides.

The first point must be that the attribution to David in the text of the *Burgh Laws* is of no significance in itself. By the end of the thirteenth century it was commonplace in Scotland to ascribe laws to David; indeed *Regiam Majestatem* itself was to reflect this by declaring that it had been written at his command.[14] We may compare the attribution of English laws to Edward the Confessor, of Welsh law to Hywel Dda and of the Irish *Senchas Mar* to St Patrick; these statements meant no more than that the law so ascribed was the good old law of the land.[15] Indeed, the ascription to David might almost be regarded as evidence for a later date of compilation than during his reign just because the strong discernible tendency amongst the compilers of medieval legal treatises was to attempt to give authority to their works by attribution to earlier well regarded figures.

Moreover, even if the precise date of the Newcastle custumal could be established,[16] it would help little with the dating of the *Burgh Laws*. While it might be accepted that the compiler of the *Burgh Laws* had the former before him as he worked, it could not be said when he did so merely by dating the custumal. The customs of Newcastle were widely copied in the north of England during the twelfth century, presumably because the custumal provided a model and convenient statement of typical burghal law in articulate written form.[17] It is highly probable that it was also known in the neighbouring towns of southern Scotland and would therefore have been available to the compiler of the *Burgh Laws*. Professor Duncan has concluded that the *Burgh Laws* was 'probably drawn up under the influence or even precisely for Berwick',[18] which would make considerable sense.

Finally, it is important to recall that there is a great deal more to the *Burgh Laws* than the chapters duplicated from the Newcastle customs. Some of this additional material looks to be of thirteenth- rather than twelfth-century origins and there are hints of further connections with Newcastle.[19] This gives rise to two possibilities for the composition of the work: one is the suggestion of Professor Duncan that the text was built up gradually over a long period of time, starting perhaps in the late twelfth century;[20] the other is that it represents a gathering together of the laws and customs of the burghs made at some single point of time in the thirteenth century but including material from earlier periods. Until more work is done on the elements of the text and their origins, however, it will probably be impossible to say which of these possibilities is more likely.

Royal burghal charters such as those mentioned above provide a more securely dateable source for examining the laws and customs followed in the early Scottish burghs. There is little evidence for the formation of collections of the particular rights and privileges of individual burghs. However, a possible exception may be the so-called *Constitutiones Regis Willelmi*, the manuscript tradition of which is well evidenced by its occurrence in at least nine of the forty or so manuscripts of medieval Scots law.[21] It is a much smaller collection of material than the *Burgh Laws* but has its own considerable interest. The collection is headed by the well-known charter granted to Perth in 1209 by William I.[22] Then follow around twenty-four separate chapters.[23] The majority of these are concerned with burgh regulations, although some of the chapters have a wider ambit and include comment on matters such as the choosing of a judge, and giving way to animals being driven in narrow places or across bridges. The burghal material in the *Constitutiones* frequently echoes the provisions of the 1209 charter, much of which is taken up with the position and privileges of the merchant guildry and the relationship of the guild members with external merchants. For instance, the *Constitutiones* contain remarks on the penalties for non-payment of toll, the liability of pedlars under the law of 'dustyfootmen' (*piespoudres*) and a variety of matters affecting the good administration of the burgh, including a rising scale of penalties for thieves captured in the burgh and the measurement of burgh land.

Provisions like those of the Perth charter are found in other burgh charters of William I, while Alexander II specifically granted the customs of Perth to Aberdeen.[24] They also resemble the contents of a short collection of legal material which was copied into the *registrum vetus* of the diocese of Glasgow in what seems to be a thirteenth-century hand.[25] This collection is entitled *Constitutiones Nove*. The charter provisions are not reproduced exactly but there are strong similarities, apart from the first chapter which declares that no one outwith a burgh is to have a tavern unless he also has pit and gallows and even then is to have one only. There are also some resemblances to the assizes of David I and William mentioned in the latter's charter to Inverness and already discussed above. So the *Constitutiones* of William, taken with the evidence of the surviving charters, appear to point to his reign as a period when burgh law was being reduced to written form. The reign has been characterised by Professor Barrow as one of consolidation rather than dramatic incident.[26] It may be that at least part of his achievement was the recognition that uniformity of practice amongst the burghs would be assisted by clearly stated enactments in written form, which may have encouraged the collection of already existing rules of law and practice and the creation thereby of legal treatises.

It is common to present this law of the burghs as distinct from the law of the realm and to state that the difference arose because burgesses as traders needed to escape from the 'feudal' restrictions on landownership and freedom of movement in order to carry on their trading activities properly.[27] So, for example, the burgess held his land free of any services to the superior other than his rent, while on his death his heir would not be liable to pay the feudal casualty of relief to the superior in order to gain entry to his inheritance. Such a presentation is derived from an outmoded approach to medieval burghs which emphasised the development of urban liberties and privileges as the result of a struggle to escape from magnatial power in the countryside. But this cannot be convincingly applied to Scotland, where military feudalism and burghs arrived together and spread together under the patronage and encouragement of successive kings from the twelfth century on.[28] Indeed, far from engaging in a struggle with the burgesses, magnates of the twelfth and thirteenth centuries seem to have been eager to establish their own burghs at places such as Kirkintilloch, Prestwick and Dunbar.[29] The better view of burghal privileges is surely that they were introduced to Scotland by royal legislation, by the continuation of the settled customs and usages amongst burgesses outwith Scotland and perhaps by specific grants to individuals, rather than hewn out against a background of already-established feudal laws.

What the burgesses do seem to have had to establish was freedom from the burden of toll – that is, from the right of the owner of a market to claim payment from those desiring to buy and sell there.[30] We know that the Scottish king exacted toll from the numerous exemptions of ecclesiastical foundations from the burden found in the twelfth century; frequently this privilege is associated with a grant of freedom to buy and sell.[31] Probably, even certainly, other lords had similar rights, while the burgesses themselves claimed toll from those using their market. 'But those who took toll were anxious to be quit of toll'.[32] It is likely that from the beginning the Scottish burgesses sought relief from toll although it is only towards the end of the twelfth century that there is evidence showing the king making grants to them of this type.[33] The result was the freedom of the burgess to carry his goods around the country in pursuit of trade and profit: this probably had far greater practical significance for him on a day-to-day basis than the relative freedom of his landholding from the incidents of feudal tenure.[34]

It has been said, however, that there was a contemporary perception of a sharp distinction between the laws and customs of the Scottish burghs and the laws and assizes of the Scottish realm.[35] So, for instance, the 1292 inventory of the records of Scotland mentions two rolls, *de legibus et assisis regni Scocie et de legibus et consuetudinibus burgorum Scocie*.[36] But the entry continues, *et de quibusdam statutis editis per reges Scocie*; altogether, therefore, this is merely a description of the contents of the two rolls rather than a statement that the burghs existed under a regime of law cut off from the landward areas. Professor Dickinson suggested that a document preserved in the register of Glasgow Cathedral is also evidence for a contemporary distinction between the laws of the realm and the laws of the burghs.[37] The document, a charter of William I which Professor Barrow dates 1195 x 1211 and probably c. 1202 x 1210, refers to the protection of those coming to the Glasgow fair *secundum assisam burgorum meorum et terre mee*; but it seems that this should be taken to mean that the assize in question applies both in the king's burghs and in his land, since to get to a fair in a burgh the traveller must go through landward parts and without the assize would be liable to toll.

Nevertheless, the impression of a separate legal order within the burghs seems to gain support from the existence in the thirteenth century of a distinct structure of courts paralleling that of sheriff, justiciar and *colloquium* or parliament in the landward areas. This structure consisted of the courts of each of the burghs themselves, the chamberlain's court and the 'court of the four burghs'.[38] However, it cannot be assumed that this structure was established at the same time as the early burghs themselves, although it is highly probable that from the beginning each had its own court to settle the disputes arising amongst the members of its community and between them and outsiders. However, early documents suggest that while there were royal officers in the burghs – the *prepositi* and *ballivi* – they were under the control of the sheriff who may therefore have presided in the town courts.[39] We should also note the case of Baldwin, granted a toft in Perth by a royal charter c.1153 along with the right to be sued only before the king himself or his justice;[40] but it would be unwise to see this as evidence of the norm in the twelfth century since other parts of the king's charter exempt Baldwin from restrictions and obligations normally incumbent upon the burgess, suggesting that this right too was a special privilege.

A specifically burghal court presided over by the *prepositus* and the *ballivi*, the *curia burgensium*, first appears in documents early in the thirteenth century. The *prepositus* and the *ballivi* are royal officers still but chosen to act as such by the community of the burgesses. The removal of the sheriff from burgh affairs probably took place in the late twelfth century, and this may mean that the final emergence of a fully independent burgh court with its own officers only occurred at this period. Even less than this can be said about the origins of the chamberlain ayre and the court of the four burghs. But it may be speculated that since the chamberlain already headed the king's financial department in the twelfth century, his ayre of the burghs was introduced to maintain a grip on the royal income from burghs which were slipping the more immediate leash of the sheriff. The Court of the Four Burghs, on the other hand, seems much more likely to be the outcome of the burghs' own recognition after 1200 of their collective interest, in particular in response to the financial demands of the king.[41]

If the structure of burghal courts was a relatively late development connected with the growing independence of the burghs, it should still not be thought of as an indication that in some way the burgesses were subject to a regime of law quite separate and different from that under which all the rest of the king's subjects lived and worked. Both burgh and chamberlain courts were described as *curiae domini regis* in the thirteenth century,[42] that is, as courts held in the king's name by the king's officers and dispensing royal justice, even though the king himself was not present at all or any of their proceedings. In consequence the burgess owed suit at the burgh court just as landward tenants in chief owed suit at the sheriff court; in both cases this obligation would normally be discharged by attendance at the three *curiae capitales* held each year. Similarly, burgess and tenant-in-chief had an obligation of suit at the courts of the chamberlain and the justiciar respectively when their ayres came into the burgh and the sheriffdom; as suitors they and not the presiding officers would render judgement on disputes coming before the courts.[43] The basic conception of the burghal courts was thus identical to that of other courts found in medieval Scotland.

It is the argument of this essay that the distinction between the law of the burghs and the law of the realm has been drawn more sharply by modern historians than it would have been by those living and working in the middle ages. The distinction has some validity in that there were undoubtedly special burgh laws, defining the rights and privileges of burghs and burgesses and gathered together in texts like the *Burgh Laws*. But an examination of these materials coupled with a look at what actually happened in the burgh courts suggests that there was also a complex interaction between the jurisdiction and procedures of the burgh court on the one hand and the ordinary processes of the common law on the other.

This is most obvious in relation to crime. It is clear that the burgh court presided over by the *prepositus* and the *ballivi* had only a limited criminal jurisdiction in the medieval period;[44] this picture began to change only in the fourteenth and fifteenth centuries as burghs received charters giving their officers the powers and jurisdiction of the sheriff within the precincts of the burgh.[45] In this way the burgh court would have acquired jurisdiction to deal, for example, with cases of slaughter where the killer was taken 'red hand', of homicide that was not premeditated, and of theft where the thief was caught 'infangthief'.[46] The *Burgh Laws* provided that the pleas of the crown – that is, the most significant crimes such as murder, robbery and rape – were not to be determined within the burgh but were to await the coming of the justiciar on his ayre. However, on his arrival the burgess was to be tried *in curia burgi coram justiciario*, meaning that the suitors of the burgh court would be convened to hear the case under the presidency of the justiciar rather than of the burgh's own officers.[47] This seems to have been still the normal procedure in the fifteenth century to judge from an act of parliament in 1432 concerning slaughter within burgh, which provided for the imprisonment of the accused until the arrival of the judge 'having power to do the law'; it is clear from the context that this would not usually be the officers of the burgh. Presumably the appropriate judge would be the justiciar in the case of murder, and the sheriff (or the baron, where one had jurisdiction) where the killer was taken 'red hand' or where the homicide had been committed *chaudmelle*.[48] But the importance of the principle of trial by one's own peers[49] – that is, one's fellow burgesses – probably explains why it was sometimes possible for a burgess accused of crime to be repledged from the justice ayre where the assize would be made up of the suitors of the sheriffdom. Thus, for example, the burgh of Irvine can be found repledging its burgesses from justice ayres at Ayr in the 1460s and 1470s.[50] But clearly this could delay the execution of justice, and in 1488 parliament enacted that where it was sought to repledge a burgess to his own court the justiciar might instead call before him an assize (i.e. jury) of neighbouring burgesses – that is, burgesses from towns other than that of the accused – to dispose of the case.[51]

We might explain this restricted jurisdiction to deal with crime by the theory that the *raison d'être* of the burgh court was to deal with mercantile matters, the principal cause of litigation there. However, a better suggestion may be a connection with the relatively late appearance of the burgh court. The king and his officers were generally not much concerned with disputes between burgess and burgess, but crime and its punishment involved financial returns – from fines, escheats and pardons – which were too important to be left to an institution no longer under the control of directly appointed royal officers.[52] This view gains support from the early records and other evidence of the burgh courts' activities which show that they were primarily concerned, not with disputes of a trading character, but with those of a type which arose in all medieval communities, urban

H

and rural. And the evidence shows the burgh court dealing with these disputes as any other contemporary court would have done – that is, in accordance with the general law.

For example, in the earliest surviving burgh court record, that of Aberdeen in 1317, there are three cases of *wrang et unlaw*. These were actions in which the pursuer alleged breach of the king's protection, in the first two cases by defamation, in the third through disturbance of possession of land.[53] There was nothing distinctively burghal about the subject matter of the cases or in the legal concept of *wrang et unlaw*.[54] One year later parliament passed an act about the pleading of defences in actions of *wrang et unlaw*, laying down that a defender was not to be regarded as having failed to enter a defence if he simply denied the *wrang et unlaw* or if he sought to be repledged to the court of his lord. It was further provided, however, that this was not to effect the law and custom of the burghs to the effect that one could only deny the *wrang et unlaw* and could not claim another court.[55] This should be connected with the statements in the *Burgh Laws* that disputes arising in the burgh should be dealt with in its court and that in burgh pleas of *wrang et unlaw* the defence of 'twertnay' is used,[56] although we lack any other direct evidence that this phrase was actually used in the burgh courts. 'Twertnay' or 'thwertnay' means 'to deny completely': in northern and midland England in the thirteenth century there were grants of twertnay indicating a special privilege whereby use of the word by the defender meant that he did not have to contradict the claim against him in full, word by word, as would normally have been the case. In the borough of Leicester before 1277 it was essential to utter the thwertnay at the outset since otherwise the defender lost his action.[57] Finally, a passage found in two other medieval Scottish texts, the *Leges Portuum* and the *Liber de Judicibus*, states that if a man charged in the king's court carelessly replies with a twertnay he is to be regarded as having stated a defence and cannot be repledged to his lord's court.[58] Reading the *Burgh Laws* in this light and assuming that it reflects actual early practice, it would seem that originally the only defence to a claim of *wrang et unlaw* in the burgh court was to say 'Twertnay' and that one could not claim another court. The aim of the 1318 legislation seems to have been to make pleading in such cases in the landward areas similarly simple, while allowing the claim of another court to be entered as an alternative. It is this latter point on which burgh custom appears to differ and to be saved by the statute. But further, as the 1317 cases and others show, in the burgh and outwith the defender was no longer confined to his formal denial as the whole of his defence by the beginning of the fourteenth century; he could, if he wished, go on with new allegations of fact so that the denial was merely the start of more specific pleading on the pursuer's claim.[59] The 1318 act is therefore not evidence of a major difference between the law of the land and the law of the burghs; it is rather an indication of a major shift in all courts from rigidly formulaic pleading to a more flexible system designed to ensure that in general judgments were based on all the facts of a dispute.

Even in cases which might be thought most characteristically mercantile and therefore burghal – those involving the performance of personal obligations – we can see in use in the burgh court procedures identical to those known to have been used in the sheriff court. The enforcement of contracts and debts might be by one of the brieves *de compulsione*: the brieve *de convencione* to compel the performance of non-pecuniary contractual obligations and the brieve of distress for the recovery of debts. These brieves were used in the sheriff court and there are also a number of examples of the procedure in burgh court records.[60] So, for instance, in Aberdeen in 1406 Paul Crab sued his brother William by a brieve *de convencione*,[61] while in 1399 William de Strade claimed 22 shillings from William Chalmers by a royal brieve of distress.[62] In 1449 another defender was brought before the Aberdeen burgh court by a brieve of distress,[63] and it was probably around the same time that there was a similar action in the burgh court of Linlithgow where the judgement in the pursuer's favour was executed by giving him possession of the defender's tenement.[64] Again there was an action begun by brieve of distress in Ayr burgh court in 1458.[65] In all these cases the brieves gave rise to a procedure identical to that which would have operated in the sheriff court: the summoning of the defender by officers of the court, the proof of the debt or contract and of the defender's failure to pay or perform, and ultimately execution against the debtor's lands.[66]

Actions of debt and breach of contract did not need to be begun by brieve, however, and the procedure may have been relatively unusual. But in another important class of case brieves were apparently the essential first step. Chapter 43 of the *Burgh Laws* is the earliest known statement in Scotland of the rule that no man could be ejected from his lands except through court action begun by brieve.[67] It reads:

> If anyone is challenged for his lands or tenement in a burgh, he need not answer his adversary without the lord king's letters unless he freely wishes it. And he who is so challenged can resort to delays and to reasonable essonzies, once, twice and three times. And at the fourth day he shall come to warrant his essonzies and to answer before the bailies whoever they may be from time to time.

We know from other evidence that this rule was established as part of the general law before the end of the thirteenth century so that its enactment by parliament in 1318 was only an affirmation of the existing position which must be related to the contemporary political situation.[68] The rule continued in force throughout the fourteenth and probably the fifteenth centuries.[69] Its application to actions over lands in burghs before 1318 is confirmed by a case of the previous year in Aberdeen where William Duncan sued Philip Gaydon, alleging *wrang et unlaw* and claiming damages.[70] The complaint was of Philip's retention of the possession of a house against those to whom it had been leased by William. In the pleading it emerged that the house had been held by Philip's parents *in maritagium* – that is to say, jointly and heritably but inalienably until the third generation after the original couple[71] – yet nevertheless Philip's father had sold the house to William. Philip argued that his possession was based on a heritable title derived from the tenure of his parents and that accordingly he did not have to answer William's complaint unless it was made by a letter of the king's chapel. The court held for Philip.

In the landward areas the brieves rule compelled pursuers seeking to recover lands from intruders to use one of the brieves of novel dissasine, mortancestor or right, the choice depending upon which was appropriate to the circumstances of the case.[72] Someone seeking to regain sasine from the person who had ejected him had novel dissasine: someone who claimed that the defender was withholding lands pertaining to him by right of inheritance from certain relatives had mortancestor; and in any other situation the brieve of right would have to be used.[73]

The position of the burgess was different. Novel dissasine and mortancestor were ordinarily competent only in the court of the justiciar, and none of the surviving evidence about these forms of action suggests that they could be raised in the burgh court or that burgesses sought to use them before the justiciar. Only the brieve of right is found in a burghal context. Thus about 1290 Master Roger Bartholomew recovered his sasine of certain lands in Berwick by brieve of right in the burgh court.[74] In 1317 the Aberdeen burgh court dealt with a brieve of right raised by John, son of Laurence, and Marjory, his wife, against Marjory's sister, Emma de Cragy. The brieve still survives, sewn to the court rolls.[75] Actions by brieve of right are also recorded in the Aberdeen burgh court in 1405[76] and in the Haddington burgh court in 1425 and again in 1426.[77] Several actions begun by brieve of right are found in the Aberdeen burgh records of the 1430s and 1440s,[78] suggesting that there would be more evidence for the use of brieves of right in burgh courts if their records had survived in greater quantity. That the action was common seems to be borne out by the existence in the so-called registers of brieves of a style for the *breve de recto in burgo* separate from the equivalent brieve for use in the landward areas, even though the only actual difference in the form of the two brieves was that the former was addressed to the provost and bailies of the burgh, the latter to the sheriff and his bailies. Otherwise both brieves were commands to cause the pursuer to have full right of lands of which the defender was alleged to be deforcing him.[79]

In considering the significance of this, a comparison with the customs of some of the major boroughs in England and those parts of the British isles under English control is suggestive, for in their courts the writ of right seems to have been available but, as a general rule, not the petty assizes of novel disseisin and mort d'ancestor[80] which were the equivalents of the Scottish actions of novel dissasine and mortancestor. The twelfth-century text known as *Glanvill* states that 'for reasons of convenience' it had been enacted that burgage tenures could not be recovered by mort d'ancestor and the king had provided another remedy.[81] The nature of this other remedy is not stated. *Bracton*, a text compiled by an unknown author in the thirteenth century, explains that mort d'ancestor was excluded where local custom permitted the purchase of borough lands, because sometimes land which had been bought could be bequeathed by the purchaser in his will so that his heir under the normal rules of primogeniture might lawfully be excluded from them. However, the writer went on to comment that 'as to lands that descend hereditarily the assize could well lie, because they cannot be bequeathed any more than lands lying outside as to which the assize lies, and the reason why it does not is not clear'.[82] It would also seem that the English burgess almost never used novel disseisin but rather an action called the assize of fresh force,[83] and that the writs of entry (to which there was no Scottish equivalent) were not used at all in the borough courts. Thus the only one of the English real actions which was always competent to the burgess was that on the writ of right; and there is evidence to show that it could be applied there when in the ordinary courts of the common law mort d'ancestor would have been the appropriate writ.[84]

This is a much simplified picture of the position in the English boroughs, and it must be stressed that custom probably varied from borough to borough and from time to time. The purpose of these generalisations is merely to give a background against which the lack of evidence for novel dissasine and mortancestor in the Scottish burgh courts may be considered. It is important to recall also that Scottish burgh laws and customs appear far more uniform than was the case in England and to note that the burghs seem to have regarded mutual consistency of application and interpretation of the law as important.[85] With regard to novel dissasine, there does seem to have been an action of fresh force available in the burgh court. A chapter in the *Burgh Laws* declares that he who has been ejected from possession of lands without proper authority or judgement should be restored before any other claim to the lands is heard,[86] while a fragment found in many of the later legal manuscripts, said *in gremio* to be a statute of Robert I (1306–1329), lays down a procedure *super deforciatione recenti in burgo*.[87] This seems to modify what is said in the *Burgh Laws* in that the person complaining of recent ejection is to have his case heard immediately upon the debatable ground by an assize, to determine not just the possessory question of expulsion and restoration but that of ownership, 'so that he against whom it is decided shall never be heard thereupon afterwards'. Whether or not this was truly legislation of Robert I or any other king, two cases of *recens deforciamentum* were heard before assizes in Aberdeen burgh court in 1399, both proceeding upon the pursuer's complaint and giving of a pledge rather than upon a royal brieve.[88] In 1448 'fresch force' by a wrongful distress was alleged in Ayr burgh court; the court determined which party had right and declared that the losing party should 'nocht be herd . . . in tyme to cum'.[89] Here, then, we seem to have a case of the type provided for in the supposed statute of Robert I, and again there is no sign of a brieve initiating the action. It is apparent that the general requirement of a brieve to commence litigations over land was inapplicable to cases of this kind. This may mean that the action had indeed been grafted into the law by some legislative act which took fresh force out of the scope of the usual rule.

Regarding mortancestor, these is in *Regiam Majestatem* the passage from *Glanvill* that it had been enacted for reasons of utility that burgage would not be recovered by this action.[90] There is, however, no evidence of such a piece of legislation in Scotland. As to *Bracton's* remarks, the Scottish burgage could not be bequeathed by testament,[91] and its alienability was restricted to protect the interest of the heir. The burgess could alienate only his conquest – that is, the lands which he himself had acquired or purchased rather than inherited. However, alienation of conquest was prohibited when the burgess was on his deathbed, unless it was necessary through poverty.[92] Heritage could never be sold except in cases of necessity.[93] Necessity had to be determined by the procedures of the *retrait lignager*, which conferred a right of pre-emption upon the heir.[94] Only the heir who had knowingly failed to make use of this right could be prevented from subsequently challenging the validity of a sale to some other person. Where the lands were seized by a creditor in satisfaction of a debt (perhaps the most typical example of a transfer by reason of necessity), then they had to be offered to the debtor's heirs within a year and a day – that is, at one of the next three head courts.[95] All this shows that there would have been relatively few occasions when the heir of a deceased burgess could not claim to be entitled to the lands of his ancestor by right of inheritance. So it would seem that the Bractonian puzzlement at the general exclusion of burgage from the ambit of mortancestor might have been echoed in Scotland.

Whatever may be the reasons for the position in England, the most probable explanation for the structure of actions relating to land found in the Scottish burgh courts is surely to be found in the context of the overall development of the forms of action in Scotland. The history of the brieve of right probably goes back to the twelfth century.[96] An important factor leading to the introduction of the brieves of novel dissasine and mortancestor in the first half of the thirteenth century may have been the ability of the defender in brieve of right cases to claim trial by combat;[97] the new actions had always to be determined by an assize,[98] and their appearance could have meant that in what were perhaps the commonest type of complaints about the possession and ownership of land a rational mode of trial could be insisted upon. However, already in the twelfth century, the burgess seems to have been considered as normally immune from combat, if we may generalise from William I's grant of the privilege to the burgesses of Inverness in 1196 or 1197;[99] certainly he was regarded as exempt from combat under the *Burgh Laws*.[100] Therefore there would have been no need to narrow the scope of the brieve of right in the burgh court with special actions in which only the assize could be used.[101] Accordingly the brieve of right could be left as the sole remedy for the recovery of land in the burgh. After all its terms, alleging that the pursuer was being deforced by an intruder of lands which he claimed by a heritable title, were perfectly capable of application to the situation covered by the brieve of mortancestor, which simply restricted the class of ancestors from whose possession a title might be derived. Similarly the brieve of right could be used to deal with complaints of ejection such as would otherwise have been the subject of a novel dissasine.

In one respect, as the law developed, the *breve de recto in burgo* may have proved inadequate, and that would be in the provision of a remedy for ejection for those whose title was not heritable and who were accordingly not within the terms of the brieve. The fragment attributed to Robert I mentions two interests in land which were not heritable – holding in security of a debt or holding for one's lifetime only – presumably indicating that these might be recovered by the action of *recens deforciamentum* or fresh force. It may not be too far-fetched therefore to see this action as a later introduction, almost certainly borrowed from England and intended to cure a defect in the operation of the brieve of right in burgh. The chapter in the *Burgh Laws* that concerns the immediate restoration of a dispossessed person before any inquiry as to his right, refers to the rule in some versions as an assize of Newcastle-upon-Tyne[102] and may represent a first attempt at a solution by borrowing, with the Robert I fragment on fresh force being a further development of the law. Unfortunately of course this speculative reconstruction is not susceptible of proof and it would be rash indeed to try and provide it with a chronology: but it would explain what seem to be our only certain facts, that the dispossessed burgess had two remedies for his restoration, the brieve of right and the action of fresh force, and did not use the other brieves available in the landward areas, novel dissasine and mortancestor.

This essay has sought to make two main points. The first is that, although specific burghal laws can be traced back to the time of David I and must have been of the greatest importance in establishing the trading and other privileges of the first burghs, it by no means follows that all such laws are attributable to that period. Present knowledge does not allow us to date many of the laws, whether from the point of view of establishing their introduction or their obsolescence. Accordingly it is impossible to use the burgh laws as evidence for the workings of burgh society at any time in the middle ages unless other material can be given in support. Secondly, the existence of the burgh laws should not be taken as meaning that in legal matters the burgess was treated altogether apart from his landward neighbours. Trading rights and privileges apart, the evidence of the activities of the burgh courts suggests that the only significant distinctions were procedural rather than substantive ones and that sometimes, as the law in general moved on, they became of less practical importance, ultimately leaving the right of the burgess to claim his own court as the central point of independent treatment. Finally, the material considered here surely suggests that the immediate source for much burghal law was the laws of the English boroughs. In this, as in much else, there was little difference between the law of the burghs and the general law of the land.

NOTES

1. On the early development of burghs see especially Duncan, *Scotland*, Ch. 18, and Barrow, *Kingship*, Ch. 5.

2. Most recently by Dickinson and Duncan, *Scotland*, 104; B. Dicks, 'The Scottish medieval town: a search for origins', 27; and by Barrow, *Kingship*, 91.

3. *RRS*, ii, no. 475.

4. See generally Duncan, *Scotland*, 490–92.

5. *RRS*, i, no. 166. The use of the term 'port' here may simply be to mean 'market town' or 'town gate' rather than 'town with a harbour'. See Barrow, *Kingship*, 87; also P. H. Sawyer, 'Kings and merchants', in *Early Medieval Kingship*, edd. P. H. Sawyer and I. N. Wood (Leeds, 1977), 139–58 at 153–4, and Reynolds, *English Towns*, references in index *s.v.* '*portus*'.

6. *RRS*, ii, no. 475.

7. *RRS*, ii, no. 442.

8. *ESC*, nos. 241 and 248; see also *RRS*, i, no. 121. See n. 40 below for uncertainty as to the dating of the two latter documents.

9. See *RRS*, ii, nos. 131, 351, 518.

10. See *APS*, i, 178. The MS is SRO, PA 5/1. The *Leges Burgorum* commence at fo. 62r.

11. See Barrow, *Kingship*, 97–8 for a recent linking of David I and the *Leges Burgorum*. The Newcastle custumal is now PRO, C 47/34/1, no. 15. A text was printed in *APS*, i, 39–41 and from there in *Stubbs' Select Charters*, ed. H. W. C. Davis (9th ed., Oxford, 1913), 132–4, but the document appears to have been lost subsequently: see *Borough Customs*, i, introduction, p. xl, and A. Ballard, *British Borough Charters 1066–1216* (Cambridge, 1913), p. xxxvii. We are grateful to Dr T. M. Chalmers of the PRO who located the document for us. Subsequently we found that the text had in fact been previously recovered, in the early 1920s by Charles Johnson, who printed a new edition with translation and notes in *Archaeologia Aeliana*, 4th series, i (1925), 169–78. Another translation (from *Stubbs*) will be found in *English Historical Documents 1042–1189*, edd. D. C. Douglas and G. W. Greenaway (London, 1953), 970–71. *Pace Stubbs*, 133, and, following that source, C. Stephenson, *Borough and Town* (Cambridge, Mass., 1933), 125–6, and Mackenzie, *Scottish Burghs*, 27–8, the document does not bear to be the work of an inquest.

12. See Duncan, *Scotland*, 218–224, and Barrow, *Kingship*, 37–9, 47.

13. R. F. Walker, *The Origins of Newcastle upon Tyne* (Newcastle, 1976), 8–9.

14. See A. A. M. Duncan, 'Regiam Majestatem: a reconsideration', *Juridical Review*, vi (1961), 199–217 at 207–08; A. Harding, 'Regiam Majestatem amongst medieval law books', *ibid.*, xxix (1984) 97–111 at 109ff; *Regiam Majestatem*, prologue (*APS*, i, 597; Stair Society, vol. xi, 57).

15. See F. Pollock and F. W. Maitland, *The History of English Law before the time of Edward I* (2nd ed. Cambridge, 1898, reissued 1968), i, 95–104; J. G. Edwards, 'Hywel Dda and the Welsh law-books', in *Celtic Law Papers*, ed. D. Jenkins (Aberystwyth, 1971), 137–60; D. A. Binchy, 'The pseudo-historical prologue to the *Senchas Mar*', *Studia Celtica*, x–xi (1975–6), 15–28. See also D. Jenkins, 'The medieval Welsh idea of law', *Tijdschrift voor Rechtsgeschiedenis*, xlix (1981), 323–348, and A. Harding, 'Legislators, lawyers and law-books', in *Lawyers and Laymen*, edd. T. M. Charles-Edwards *et al* (Cardiff, 1986), 237–57.

16. On the palaeographical evidence, with which we have been assisted by Professor Barrow, the document appears to be of mid-twelfth century date. The reference to King Henry must be to Henry I. Even though the document does not so number him, it finds its most probable historical context in the reign of Henry II, when men looked back to the law of Henry I and explicitly sought its restoration (see especially W. L. Warren, *Henry II* (London, 1973), 262). Perhaps it is a product of the English recovery of Northumberland in 1157.

17. E.g. they were granted to Hartlepool by Adam de Brus (see confirmation in *Calendar of the Charter Rolls 1341–1417* (London, 1916), 370) and to Gateshead and Wearmouth by Hugh de Puiset, bishop of Durham 1153–1194 (see *The Boldon Buke*, ed. W. Greenwell (Surtees Society, xxv, 1852), appendix, xl–xlii). See Stephenson, *Borough and Town*, 126–7.

18. Duncan, *Scotland*, 482.

19. E.g. c. 99, which in the printed version is said to be an assize held at Newcastle (*APS*, i, 352; *Ancient Burgh Laws*, 48). But this part of the chapter is not given in the earliest MSS. The earliest version mentioning Newcastle is in a fifteenth-century MS and there it is not part of the *Leges Burgorum* but of a small collection entitled the 'statutis of the burowys' (NLS, Adv. MSS. 25/4/15, fos. 163–4, printed *APS*, i, 722–3, *Ancient Burgh Laws*, 168–70).

20. Duncan, *Scotland*, 481.

21. The earliest MS is BL, Add. MS. 18111.

22. *RRS*, ii, no. 467; but see Duncan, *Scotland*, 467–9, and *idem*, 'Perth', 30–50.

23. Versions of many of these are printed in the *Fragmenta Collecta* in *APS*, vol. i. See further P. G. Stein, 'Roman law in Scotland', *Ius Romanum Medii Aevi*, pars 5, 13b (1968), 1–51 at 10–12.

24. These may be studied together in *APS*, i, 86–9, and in *RRS*, ii, nos. 213, 244, 475.

25. *Glas. Reg.*, ii, no. 536 (with facsimile); also in *APS*, i, 666, and *Ancient Burgh Laws*, 97–8. For the date see G. G. Simpson and B. Webster, 'The archives of the medieval church of Glasgow: an introductory survey', *The Bibliothek*, iii (1962), 195–201 at 198.

26. G. W. S. Barrow, 'The reign of William the Lion, king of Scotland', *Historical Studies*, vii (Dublin, 1969), 21–44.

27. See e.g. W. C. Dickinson's introduction to *Abdn. Recs.*, pp. xxxv–vi; Duncan, *Scotland*, 479; Dickinson & Duncan, *Scotland*, 104–05, 107–08; Barrow, *Kingship*, 98–9.

28. For the outmoded nature of the old approach see Reynolds, *English Towns*, 99. For the spread of military feudalism see two works of G. W. S. Barrow, *The Kingdom of the Scots* (London, 1973), Ch. 10 and *The Anglo-Norman Era in Scottish History* (Oxford, 1980).

29. See the comment of Murray, *Early Burgh Organisation*, i, 312, quoted by W. Stevenson, 'The monastic presence in Scottish burghs in the twelfth and thirteenth centuries', 100, and the lists of magnatial and ecclesiastical burghs in Pryde, *Burghs* at 37ff.

30. See *RRS*, ii, 73, and Duncan, *Scotland*, 474–5 for toll. Note also Sawyer, 'Kings and merchants', at 152–3.

31. See *ESC*, nos. 153, 167, 168, 209, 210 and 242; *RRS*, i, nos. 200, 201, 222; and references in *RRS*, ii, 73 and n. 11.

32. Pollock and Maitland, *History of English Law*, i, 650.

33. These may be studied most conveniently in Ballard, *British Borough Charters 1066–1216*, 190–91 and A. Ballard and J. Tait, *British Borough Charters 1216–1307* (Cambridge, 1923), 254.

34. Cf. Pollock and Maitland, *History of English Law*, i, 650: 'perhaps the burgesses regarded freedom from toll as the most vital of all their rights'.

35. *Abdn. Recs.*, p. xxxvi, n. 1

36. *APS*, i, 114.

37. *Glas. Reg.*, i, no. 43 (now also printed in *RRS*, ii, no. 442).

38. See generally Dickinson's introduction to *Abdn. Recs.*, pp. cxvii–cxlv, and his article 'A chamberlain's ayre in Aberdeen 1399 x 1400', *SHR*, xxxiii (1954), 27–36; also G. S. Pryde, 'The burgh courts and allied jurisdictions', in *An Introduction to Scottish Legal History*, ed. G. C. H. Paton (Stair Society, 1958), 384–95. For the Court of the Four Burghs in the thirteenth century see Stevenson, *Documents*, i, 380–81, and *APS*, i, 724 c. 20.

39. See *Abdn. Recs.*, p. xxii; Duncan, *Scotland*, 481–4.

40. *ESC*, no. 248; *RRS*, i, no. 121. The grant was made to Baldwin by either David I or Malcolm IV.

41. The first appearance of a burgh court is in a quitclaim issued by the burgh of Berwick under its common seal in 1212 and said to have been made *in plena curia placitorum nostrorum* (*Melrose Liber*, i, no. 27). For early references to the *curia burgensium* see *St A Lib*, 284–5 and *Scone Liber*, no. 95. For the *prepositi* and *ballivi*, see *Abdn. Recs.*, p. lxxx; Duncan, *Scotland*, 483–4.

42. See *Arbroath Liber*, i, no. 229 and *Kelso Liber*, i, no. 34.

43. For all this see *Abdn. Recs.*, pp. cxvii, cxxviii–iv, and the *Iter Camerarii*, c. 3 (printed in *APS*, i, 694–5 and *Ancient Burgh Laws*, 135) along with Dickinson's introduction to the *Fife Court Bk.*, pp. lxxii–lxxxvi, and the *Ordo Justiciarie*, c. 12 (*APS*, i, 707).

44. *Abdn. Recs.*, pp. cxxvi–viii.

45. *Ibid.*, p. cxl.

46. *Fife Court Bk.*, appendix B, 335–8.

47. *Leges Burgorum*, cc. 6 and 7 (*APS*, i, 334; *Ancient Burgh Laws*, 5–6).

48. *APS*, ii, 21 c. 4. See further *Leges Burgorum*, c. 74, which in the Ayr MS provides for the jurisdiction in such cases of those who hold in barony in burgh (*APS*, i, 348; *Ancient Burgh Laws*, 36–7); also a fragment printed *APS*, i, 739 c. 14 and *Ancient Burgh Laws*, 185. There is discussion of baronial jurisdiction within burghs in *Abdn. Recs.*, pp. lxi–lxix, and in Stevenson, 'Monastic presence', 105–08.

49. For the expression of this principle in c. 7 of the *Leges Burgorum*, see *APS*, i, 334, and *Ancient Burgh Laws*, 6.

50. *Irvine Muniments*, i, no. 13. For the right of burghs to repledge, see *Leges Burgorum*, cc. 51 and 56 (*APS*, i, 342–3; *Ancient Burgh Laws*, 24–7).

51. *APS*, ii, 208 c. 10.

52. Compare the restricted criminal jurisdiction of borough courts in England: see Reynolds, *English Towns*, 101, and references there given.

53. *Abdn. Recs.*, 8, 10, 11. The defamation case at p. 10 is of particular interest since in it the pursuer claims damages of 20 shillings, showing that it is erroneous to say that 'defamation in the church and local courts ... only involved apology and sometimes penalty but not damages' (H. McKechnie, in *Introduction to Scottish Legal History*, at 268). See also on this S. D. Ollivant, *The Court of the Official in Pre-Reformation Scotland* (Stair Society, 1983), 75–7, and, for England, *Select Cases on Defamation to 1600*, ed. R. H. Helmholz (Selden Society, 1985), pp. xlviii–lxv.

54. On *wrang et unlaw* and the link with the king's peace, see A. Harding, 'The medieval brieves of protection and the development of the common law', *Juridical Review*, xi (1966), 115–49. For another mid-fifteenth century case of 'breking of the kingis pece' see Ayr Burgh Court Book 1428–1478, fo. 97. Formerly in the SRO as B6/12, the original went into the custody of Kyle and Carrick District Council at the Carnegie Library, Ayr in October 1984; also available in microfilm in EUL, Mic. M. 690.

55. *APS*, i, 471 c. 17.

56. *Leges Burgorum*, cc. 6 and 117, for the exclusive jurisdiction; c. 31 for twertnay (*APS*, i, 334, 338 and 356; *Ancient Burgh Laws*, 5–6, 16 and 57). Note also the rules about admissions in actions of *wrang et unlaw* in c. 96 (*APS*, i, 352; *Ancient Burgh Laws*, 46–7) apparently applied in Aberdeen in 1401: *Abdn. Recs.*, 205.

57. R. Stewart Brown, 'Thwert-ut-nay and the custom of "thwertnic" in Cheshire', *EHR*, xl (1925), 13–21, especially at 15–18; *Borough Customs*, i, 162–5.

58. *APS*, i, 735 c. 5. On the texts see Stein, 'Roman law in Scotland', 11–14, and W. J. Windram, 'What is the *Liber de Judicibus?*', *Journal of Legal History*, v (1984), 176–7.

59. See generally H. L. MacQueen, 'Pleadable brieves, pleading and the development of Scots law', *Law and History Review*, iv (1986), 402–21, and, in addition to references there given, *Abdn. Recs.*, 120.

60. For styles and discussion see *Reg. Brieves*, 37–9, and *Quoniam Attachiamenta*, Chs. 34 and 49–51 (*APS*, i, 653 and 657; Stair Society vol. xi, 342–6).

61. *Abdn. Recs.*, 232, 237.

62. *Ibid.*, 133.

63. Noted *ibid.*, p. cxxv n. 5.

64. SRO, Crown Office Writs, AD 1/52, first published by Lord Kames in his *Historical Law Tracts* (1st ed., 2 vols., Edinburgh, 1758), ii, appendix no. I (see also 4th ed., 1792, 459–60) and reprinted from there in *Borough Customs*, ii, 72. We are grateful to Mr Alan Borthwick who supplied the SRO reference for this document, a notarial instrument of

1451 which refers to an earlier litigation begun by brieve of distress. See further below, text accompanying n. 94.

65. Ayr Burgh Court Book 1428–1478, fo. 77v.

66. For examples of brieves *de compulsione* in the sheriff court between c. 1300 and c. 1460, see *Kelso Liber*, ii, no. 397; Fraser, *Wemyss*, ii, no. 49; Fraser, *Melville*, ii, no. 41, and *RMS*, ii, no. 375.

67. *APS*, i, 341; *Ancient Burgh Laws*, 21.

68. For the other thirteenth-century reference to the rule see PRO, Ancient Correspondence, SC 1/18/147, printed in A. A. M. Duncan and J. G. Dunbar, 'Tarbert Castle', *SHR*, 1 (1972), 1–16 at 15–16; for the 1318 statute, *APS*, i, 473 c. 25. See generally H. L. MacQueen, 'Pleadable brieves and jurisdiction in heritage in later medieval Scotland' (Edin. Univ. PhD, 1985), 125–8.

69. See *Abdn. Reg.*, i, 155; *Moray Reg.*, 209, 379; *APS*, i, 557–8; HMC, *Various Collections*, v, 77.

70. *Abdn. Recs.*, 10–14.

71. For *maritagium* see c. 41 of the *Leges Burgorum* (*APS*, i, 340; *Ancient Burgh Laws*, 20) and *Regiam Majestatem* II, 51–2 (in *APS*, i, 619; Stair Society vol. xi, 167).

72. See MacQueen, 'Thesis', Chs. 3 and 4.

73. See ibid; also MacQueen, 'The brieve of right in Scots law', *Journal of Legal History*, iii (1982), 52–70; the same author's 'Dissasine and mortancestor in Scots law', *ibid.*, iv (1983), 21–49; W. D. H. Sellar, 'Courtesy, battle and the brieve of right 1368 – a story continued', *Miscellany II* (Stair Society, 1984, 1–12), and A. Borthwick and H. L. MacQueen, 'Three fifteenth century cases', *Juridical Review* xxxi (1986), 123–51.

74. Stevenson, *Documents*, i, 384–6.

75. *Abdn. Recs.*, 8. For further proceedings see 9, 10, 12, 14–15.

76. *Ibid.*, 214.

77. SRO, B30/9/1, Haddington Court Book 1423–1514, fo. 1. The 1425 case is printed in *Proc. Soc. Antiq. Scot.*, ii (1855), 386.

78. ACA, CR, iv, 49, 213, 293, 295, 344, 363, 369; v(1) 61. We are grateful to Mr Alan Borthwick for drawing these references to our attention. Other entries bearing upon the cases cited will be found in close proximity to the pages given here. The original record is in the ACA, available also in microfilm in EUL, Mic. M. 839.

79. For the styles see *Reg. Brieves*, 39–40 and the register in the Cambridge MS entitled *Liber quem vulgus Regiam Majestatem vocat* (CUL, Ee/4/21) at fo. 273 (also available in microfilm in EUL, Mic. M. 11).

80. See for a summary A. Harding, *The Law Courts of Medieval England* (London, 1973), 42.

81. *Glanvill*, ed. G. D. G. Hall (London, 1965), XIII, 11. See also the editor's note on this passage.

82. *Bracton*, edd. G. E. Woodbine and S. E. Thorne (4 vols., Harvard, 1968–77), fo. 271 (iii, 295). Cf. *Borough Customs*, i, 243–5.

83. *Borough Customs*, i, 231–42.

84. *Ibid.*, i, 255.

85. See e.g the concurring letters sent to Aberdeen between 1467 and 1469 by Perth, Edinburgh and Dundee concerning inheritance from a burgess who had had two wives and issue by both (*Abdn. Counc.*, i, 26–9). Edinburgh and Dundee both cite a relevant section of the *Leges Burgorum*, c. 24 (*APS*, i, 337; *Ancient Burgh Laws*, 12). Cf. the letters of Perth, Lanark, Aberdeen and Newcastle on the burgess' right of alienation, printed *APS*, i, 723, and in *Ancient Burgh Laws*, 169–70. The date of these letters is uncertain: they come from

the 'statutis of the burowys' discussed above, n. 19. The court of the four burghs seems also to have been an agent of uniformity: see *Abdn. Recs.*, pp. cxliii–cxlv. On the whole question of the uniformity of burgh law see also *ibid.*, p. xxxvi, n. 1 and lxxix, n. 3.

86. *Leges Burgorum*, c. 99 (*APS*, i, 352; *Ancient Burgh Laws*, 48); see n. 19 above.

87. *APS*, i, 721–2 cc.12 and 13 (also in *Ancient Burgh Laws*, 165–7).

88. *Abdn. Recs.*, 65, 117.

89. Ayr Burgh Court Book 1428–78, fo. 52r.

90. *Regiam Majestatem*, III, 25 (in *APS*, i, 629; Stair Society vol. xi, 227).

91. There seems to be no evidence for testamentary freedom in relation to burgage in Scotland.

92. *Leges Burgorum*, cc. 21, 42, 101 (*APS*, i, 336, 340, 353; *Ancient Burgh Laws*, 11, 20–21 and 49). With regard to death bed see also the concurring statements of the customs of Perth, Lanark, Aberdeen, Newcastle and Edinburgh in *APS*, i, 723 and *Ancient Burgh Laws*, 169–70, discussed above at n. 85.

93. *Leges Burgorum*, c. 42 (*APS*, i, 340; *Ancient Burgh Laws*, 20–21).

94. See D. Baird Smith, 'The *retrait lignager* in Scotland', *SHR*, xxi (1924), 193–206, for the relevant provisions of the *Leges Burgorum* and some thirteenth-century examples; Stevenson, 'Monastic presence', 103; *Abdn. Recs.*, 3–7 and p. xxxix n. 1; Ewan, 'Thesis', 121, 151–2, for instances in the fourteenth-century *secundum leges burgorum*; and yet further fifteenth-century examples in the Ayr Burgh Court Book 1428–78 at fos. 76v.–77r, 88v.; *Stirling Chrs.*, 206; SRO, Crown Office Writs, AD 1/52 (for which see *Borough Customs*, ii, 72, and above, n. 64). For an earlier comparative account of the law by P. Chalmers, see *Spalding Misc.*, v, appendix to preface, 49–55.

95. *Leges Burgorum*, cc. 89–91 (*APS*, i, 351; *Ancient Burgh Laws*, 43–5).

96. See Harding, 'The medieval brieves of protection' at 124–31, and MacQueen, 'The brieve of right revisited', in *The Political Context of Law*, ed. R. Eales and D. Sullivan (Ronceverte, 1987), 17–25.

97. See G. Neilson, *Trial by Combat* (Glasgow, 1890), 86–90; Sellar, 'Courtesy, battle and the brieve of right', 6–8.

98. *APS*, i, 325 c.35

99. *RRS*, ii, no. 388. Immunity from combat was a typical burgess privilege in England and Europe: see Professor Barrow's editorial note; Reynolds, *English Towns*, 101; and R. Bartlett, *Trial by Fire and Water: the Medieval Judicial Ordeal* (Oxford, 1986), 54–62, 119–20.

100. *Leges Burgorum* cc. 12 and 13 (*APS*, i, 335; *Ancient Burgh Laws*, 8). See also the interesting 1475 case in *Abdn. Counc.*, i, 406–07, discussed in Neilson, *Trial by Combat*, 281–2.

101. We owe this suggestion to Mr David Sellar.

102. See n. 19 above.

13

The Community of the Burgh in the Fourteenth Century

Elizabeth L. Ewan

The sense of community in the medieval Scottish burghs can be traced back to the very beginnings of their history. From the eleventh and twelfth centuries the burghs were being founded as centres of trade by being granted privileges which would facilitate the development of commerce. Some burghs were formed by the grant of a charter to an already existing settlement; others were created from new by attracting settlers from the surrounding countryside, other parts of Scotland and even from other countries such as England and Flanders. If the burghs were to flourish, the best conditions for trade had to be encouraged and this involved the establishment of a peaceful and cooperative environment which would attract the country-dwellers to bring their produce to sell, craftsmen to settle and ply their trade, and merchants to build warehouses and set up centres from which they could extend networks of trading connections both throughout Scotland and overseas. Without a sense of community which would make such conditions possible, it was unlikely that a burgh would survive the early stages of development.

Several factors helped to promote this sense of community. Privileges were granted to the burgesses in common, helping to establish feelings of equality and joint responsibility for their upkeep. Many early charters such as those to Aberdeen and Perth[1] granted the burgesses a monopoly of trade in certain items over a large area of the burgh's hinterland and may have roused the resentment of those living in this area. The defence of these privileges by the burgesses would contribute to their sense of unity. By the early fourteenth century, charters were usually granted to 'the community of the burgh',[2] implying official recognition of this concept by the burgh overlord. The burgesses had been describing themselves as a community for some time before this: as early as 1275 a charter in Arbroath was dated 'in the presence of the community of the burgh of Arbroath'.[3]

The system of landholding within the Scottish burgh also helped to promote a sense of community. Unlike in English boroughs, where tenurial heterogeneity could lead to a jumble of overlords and jurisdictions, the burgage plots of most Scottish burghs were held of the burgh superior only, either directly or through a tenant-in-chief who was himself usually a burgess. A few burgh properties were held by lords outwith the burgh, but the *Burgh Laws*, a compilation of burgh customs dating from the twelfth to fourteenth centuries, stated that in such a case the tenant was subject first to the jurisdiction of the burgh.[4] An exception may have been made in the case of the abbey of Arbroath which was granted properties in several burghs in regality.[5] How far such jurisdiction was effective in practice is not clear – possibly it was merely used to control the alienation of these lands by the abbey's tenants. After about 1300 grants of burgh lands to ecclesiastical institutions outwith the burghs decreased,[6] and thus the problem of conflicting jurisdictions, which does not seem to have been very significant in earlier days, became even less important in the fourteenth century. It was not, it seems, until the late fifteenth or early sixteenth century, when burgh courts in Perth, Aberdeen and elsewhere acted to prevent their own burgesses resorting to other courts, ecclesiastical and secular, that the tangle of legal jurisdictions forced burghs to reassert their authority.[7]

For the burgh overlord one of the most important, if not *the* most important, functions of the burgh was to produce revenue through rents and tolls on trade. As well as helping the burgesses defend their trading rights, the overlord therefore had an interest in promoting the most efficient form of local administration. There was thus no inherent objection to the burgesses gradually taking over the administration of the burgh from the officials of the overlord as long as the efficient collection of revenues continued. Indeed the *Burgh Laws* imply that some measure of self-government was encouraged from an early date.[8] By the early fourteenth century there are signs that even the burgesses of small ecclesiastical burghs expected to have some say in the government of their community. In the burgh of Westerkelso in 1323 a dispute arose over the burgesses' practice of granting new men burgess status, a privilege which the abbot of Kelso claimed belonged to him. The outcome was that the abbot's right was confirmed, but it is significant that the right to approve those appointed by him was reserved to the burgesses.[9] A *modus vivendi* between overlord and burgh community resulted, which allowed the burgesses to prevent the introduction of any undesirable elements.

If such was the situation in a small burgh where the superior was often in attendance, it is likely that even more autonomy had been gained in burghs belonging to the king or great men of the church or state who were often absent and delegated the supervision of burgh affairs to their officers. During the upheavals and uncertainties of the first half of the fourteenth century, when royal administration was weakened by war and the absence of the king, the burgesses were probably able to increase their control over the government of the burgh. The chamberlain, the royal official in charge of finances, was supposed to conduct an annual inquiry into the affairs of each royal burgh, but in fact seems to have graced the burgesses more with his absence than his presence. However, exchequer audits, at which the collectors of burgh revenues accounted for the financial situation of the burgh, were held for most years from 1327[10] (except for a gap, 1333–56, during Edward Balliol's rule and David II's captivity in England) and thus ensured that the burgesses met their fiscal responsibilities to the crown or gave some reason for their default.

In the fourteenth century, the capacity of many burghs for self-government was recognised by the crown in the form of feu-ferme charters which granted all burgh revenues except customs on exports to the community of the burgh in return for a fixed annual payment. A charter to Aberdeen in 1319 led the way.[11] In fact, the significance of these charters may have been more symbolic than real. They probably had little effect either on the relationship between the crown and the royal burghs or on the administration of finance as many burghs were already in the habit of farming their burgh revenues by virtue of fixed-term leases from the chamberlain. Some burghs such as Peebles continued this practice for the rest of the century. The feu-ferme charter simply placed the arrangement on a more permanent footing. But the added security it gave probably aided the development of a sense of pride in the burgh, as the knowledge that there would usually be a steady source of surplus revenue for the 'common good' fund of the burgh would enable the burgesses to plan long-term projects which would enhance the community.

The Berwick *Statutes of the Guild*, a set of bye-laws enacted during the second half of the thirteenth century, shows a well-developed system of local burgh administration. During the fourteenth century there are glimpses of similar systems of government in other burghs, although the first detailed burgh records, those of Aberdeen, do not begin until 1398. From the evidence which does exist, however, it appears that certain offices were common to most burghs. In burghs with a fairly sophisticated form of government, the variety of offices could be quite great. Evidence from the Aberdeen records and other documents as well as from the *Burgh Laws* shows activity by the alderman or provost (also sometimes known as the mayor in some burghs), bailies, sergeands, liners, tasters of wine and ale, apprisers of flesh, treasurers, masters of the kirk work, the clerk of the community and even a 'custodian of the seal of the community'. As the names of these last two offices suggest, the duties of government were seen as being carried out for the benefit of the community.[12]

Of these offices, that with the most prestige was the post of alderman, who was the head of the community – charters to the burgh were often addressed to the alderman and community. He presided over certain burgh courts and witnessed important transactions involving burgh lands. However, it appears that in many cases this was more a ceremonial position than one conferring any great degree of power, although, when held by an enterprising individual, its authority could be used to lead the burgesses in community projects such as extending the burgh church. This was done in Aberdeen under the guidance of the alderman William de Leith in the 1350s.[13]

The real power in the burgh government lay with the bailies. It was they who were responsible for the day-to-day running of municipal affairs. Indeed, some burghs did not have an alderman at all during this period, the leadership being shared among the bailies. The office of bailie had developed in the first half of the fourteenth century. Earlier, the administration of most burghs had been entrusted to the *prepositi*, officers of the king or lord who collected the rents and other dues owed to the burgh superior and who, in the case of the royal burghs, presented their accounts yearly at the Exchequer. Originally appointed by the lord, these men came to be chosen from among the burgesses themselves. By the 1350s they had been replaced by bailies, burgesses elected by their fellows, who had a responsibility to both lord and burgh. At a local level, they were responsible for the financial administration of the burgh, setting mills, fishings and other burgh properties at ferm, and ensuring that the laws concerning trade, the basis of the burgh's prosperity, were observed. They also supervised the land transactions of the burgesses, giving sasine to the new tenant when a burgh property was alienated. The other officers of the burgh were answerable for their conduct to the courts presided over by the bailies.

The Aberdeen records show that the burgesses of that burgh conformed to the rule laid down in the *Burgh Laws* and chose their officials at the first head court after Michaelmas.[14] As well as holders of specific offices, a common council was chosen, varying in number of members from year to year. As representatives of the burgess community, the council members can probably be seen as the fourteenth-century equivalent of the 'good men of the burgh' mentioned in the *Burgh Laws*, in accordance with whose counsel the bailies were to swear to govern.[15] In small burghs, the 'good men' might mean all the burgesses (perhaps about one-third of the adult male population,[16] although women were sometimes burgesses as well), but in larger burghs it seems likely that the council came to represent the whole community of burgesses, except possibly at the head courts which every burgess had a duty to attend. Even then, the majority of the burgesses might confine themselves to giving assent to measures proposed by the burgh officials, rather than actively proffering advice. Unfortunately, there are no detailed proceedings which deal with the promulgation of burgh statutes in this period, although this is not surprising as the purpose of the written record was to record new laws, not to describe how they came to be passed. Certain actions taken collectively by the burgesses of Inverness and Irvine are stated to have been done 'with the assent of the community'.[17] There may have been some discussion, or even some opposition on at least one occasion in Inverness, as in 1359 a decision was made 'with the assent of *the major part* of the community'.[18]

The government of the burgh centred around the burgh court, usually presided over by the bailies, and in some burghs such as Elgin by other burgh magistrates as well.[19] Here disputes between burgesses were heard, alienations of burgage lands witnessed, infringements on burghal privileges by outsiders punished, and transgressions of burgh regulations by inhabitants fined.[20] The most important occasions were the head courts, usually held after Michaelmas, Yule and Easter,[21] as it was here that statutes were promulgated. A burgess wishing to alienate heritage land had to offer it for sale to relatives at three head courts before so doing.[22] An old burgh law which had parallels throughout Europe stated that an unfree man could become a burgess if he held undisputed possession of a burgage for a year and a day, which may have represented the period covered by four head courts.[23]

The head courts also dealt with ordinary judicial business, ruling on matters such as disturbance of the peace or failure to prosecute a case, but they were supplemented by two other sessions, the *curiae legales* which were usually held fortnightly, and the *curiae tentae per ballivos* which were held any day of the week and sometimes on several consecutive days. The existence of these extra courts suggests an increase in court business which might imply some growth of the population of many burghs in the fourteenth century. Of the two, the *curiae legales* were the more formal; it was at these sessions that the assize of bread and ale was announced periodically, and cases begun by the king's brieve or letters could be heard here as well as at the head court.[24]

The judgement of the court was apparently made by the burgesses who formed the body of the court as suitors. The bailies were merely the presiding officers. Thus the burgesses played an active role in the administration of the burgh laws. Or at least they did in theory – in practice, court cases were frequently postponed until the next sitting due to the lack of attendance of a sufficient number of burgesses.[25] Punishment for crimes could take the form of fines, loss of burghal privileges or the right to practise a trade for a certain period, or, at worst, banishment from the burgh. In 1405 an Aberdeen ordinance stated that anyone found guilty of abusing a burgh officer on a second occasion was to be 'placed on the cuckstool and befouled with egges, dung, mud and suchlike'.[26] Humiliation before the community was considered to be a powerful deterrent. Pledges were often taken for future good conduct from those accused of assault. Penalties for breaking such pledges could be severe, reflecting the importance attached to preserving the peace of the burgh.

As well as the burgh court, there was another institution in many burghs which concerned itself with the affairs of the community. This was the guild. The crown had granted the burgesses of certain burghs such as Perth and Stirling the right to have a guild in the thirteenth century. By 1400 at least nineteen burghs either had a guild or the right to possess one.[27] The function and composition of the guild have been the subjects of much controversy, with the guild being seen by some historians as an exclusive association of merchants determined to defend its members against any encroachments on their privileges by the burgh craftsmen. Recently this view of merchant-craftsman conflict has been called into question,[28] implying that the exclusive nature of the guild might also have been exaggerated. Any exclusion was probably aimed at those burgh inhabitants who did not possess burgess status – servants, journeymen, and the like – or at specific trades rather than at burgess craftsmen as a whole. Moreover, many burgesses combined the two roles of craftsman and merchant. The interpretation of an exclusive guild seems mainly to rest on the example of the Berwick guild, an organisation which should not be taken as typical of the guilds of most Scottish burghs, as at the time of the *Statutes of the Guild* in the late thirteenth century, the size and importance of Berwick far outstripped that of other Scottish towns, rendering it highly probable that its guild would be a much more complex organisation than that of most burghs.

From the little evidence which exists for guild activity before 1450,[29] it seems that the organisation acted largely as a department of the burgh government, concerning itself mainly with the trade in the staple goods of wool, woolfells and hides which made up the bulk of Scotland's exports until the fifteenth century. Privileges granted to the guilds in the thirteenth century suggest that at that time the main concern of the guild brethren was the cloth industry,[30] whose artisans – the weavers and waulkers – were often excluded from membership; but by the fourteenth century the export of staple goods had become a more important source of income for the burgess entrepreneurs. Thus the guilds of Forfar and Montrose in 1372 made an agreement to allow each other reciprocal trading rights in merchandise pertaining to the guild, while the guild of Cupar tried unsuccessfully to defend its claimed monopoly over staple goods against the men of St. Andrews.[31] But of equal importance to the daily life of its members were both the convivial fellowship and religious dimension it provided; through the guild the members were able to join together in an activity close to many burgesses' spiritual concerns – the upkeep of the burgh church.[32]

Guild rules and regulations were mirrored by the ordinances with which the burgh government sought to control the conduct of most occupations in the best interests of the community. The trades of most concern were those which had a direct bearing on the daily welfare of the burgh inhabitants. Hence, baking and brewing are mentioned again and again among both the *Burgh Laws* and the Aberdeen records. Bread and ale were the essential components of the medieval Scottish diet, and, as such, their production had to be closely supervised and controlled to ensure adequate supplies for the burgh population. The principle of equal opportunity for all burgesses can be seen at work here. Malt and grain were not to be sold secretly from individual houses but in the market or at least openly displayed in windows so that all might have the chance to buy. Brewsters were to sell all year round and were limited in the amount of malt they were allowed to purchase. Their ale was also subject to checks of quality by the official ale-tasters of the burgh (perhaps one of the more popular administrative offices). Bread was similarly subject to checks for size and quality. In Aberdeen the price of grain and malt was set by the burgh government and announced every few weeks.[33] Control by the community can be seen in operation here as the prices and checks were made by the burgh officials, not by the representatives of the crafts themselves.

Other crafts for which less documentary evidence survives were also essential to the wellbeing of the community. Archaeological evidence suggests the presence of fairly large quantities of meat in at least some towns.[34] Probably the ports had more access to meat than many areas of Scotland as the export trade in hides meant that a large number of cattle were brought to the burghs. The various regulations governing the butchery of animals and the sale and quality of meat suggest that the product formed a not unimportant part of many a burgess diet. Unexported hides were used by burgh craftsmen to make shoes, belts, sheaths and even cooking vessels, while other parts of the animal were used for making bone implements and ornaments, producing neat's-foot oil, and many other purposes.[35] Thus the export trade of the merchants had beneficial side-effects for the community as a whole. In return, local industries such as shipbuilding, of which there is evidence at Ayr and Inverness in the thirteenth century, supplied an essential tool for the expansion of the merchants' overseas trade.[36]

Although the evidence is too scarce to allow of more than speculation, it is possible that the disruption caused in the early part of the fourteenth century by the Wars of Independence may have encouraged the development of local burgh industries as the supply of imports decreased.[37] This appears to have been the case with the pottery industry where a major change can be seen in levels probably dating to the early fourteenth century; local wares begin to become predominant at many sites.[38] Possibly a re-expansion of the cloth industry also took place – dyes were being imported later in the century and an import tax was placed on English cloth in 1398.[39] The quality of woodworking at Perth suggests a high level of expertise, while the extensions to burgh churches such as St. Giles' in Edinburgh seem to have been entrusted to the skills of local craftsmen.[40]

In the early days of the burghs probably most trading was done by craftsmen who bought their raw materials and sold their finished products. With the expansion of overseas trade in the thirteenth century, however, a new group began to establish itself in burgh society – the overseas merchants. These were people who made a livelihood from buying and selling other people's products, both raw materials from the burgh hinterland and partially finished goods from the burgh, as well as goods and materials from abroad. As a national group, their significance to the crown increased markedly after 1357 when David II was released from his English captivity and a large ransom was agreed for his return. A large proportion of this was to be raised from customs revenues. As the custumars levied these customs in the burghs on the exports of wool, woolfells and hides shipped by the merchants, it was in the crown's interests to encourage the merchants' business.

The merchants' increasing importance in national affairs was acknowledged by the king in a 1364 charter which confirmed their privileges.[41] Any non-burgesses living in an area over which the burgh had a trading monopoly was to sell and buy staple goods only from the merchants of that burgh. Similarly, foreign merchants could trade only with the burgh merchants. The merchants' national role thus led to the safeguarding of the burghs' economic role, and the opportunity for prosperity for the whole community. Their growing participation in parliaments and general councils also meant that burgh interests were represented in some of the major decision-making bodies of the realm.

The increasing status of the merchants on a national level was reflected in their position in burgh society. Many of those involved in trade with England or the Continent were elected to burgh office and were prominent holders of burgh property. The predominance of such men, however, does not necessarily imply a diminishing sense of community amongst the different social groups of the burgh. It was expected in medieval society that the most prominent figures of the community would provide its leadership[42] and this is apparently what happened, although this did not mean that craftsmen burgesses were therefore excluded, as is sometimes alleged. There is not enough evidence to draw such a conclusion, while the presence of weavers and dyers in the fifteenth-century guilds of Perth and Dunfermline suggests that occupation was no bar to participation in burgh government.[43]

Social divisions did exist within the burgh, but these tended to exist, in the fourteenth century as later, more between those who enjoyed burgess privileges and those who did not, than between merchants and craftsmen.[44] Even the division between burgess and non-burgess did not necessarily lead to feelings of resentment in an under-privileged class. By the fourteenth century, the older burghs would have attracted many migrants from the countryside who lacked the resources with which to attain burgess-ship, but who could offer their services to families already established in the burghs, as servants, labourers, apprentices and journeymen. Such people appear only infrequently in the surviving records, but the conditions governing urban excavation mean that more evidence has been uncovered about what were probably their homes than about the dwellings of their burgess masters.[45] In general it seems that the more substantial homes of the burgh were built on the frontages of the burgages. Stretching out along the long narrow plots behind them were gardens, stockyards and various structures which could be workshops and small houses, perhaps providing accommodation for the servants of the burgess household.[46] Thus there was probably a connection between the various families living on a burgage plot, at least until the growth of population led to the subdivision of burgage plots in some burghs, a feature which seems to have been more characteristic of the fifteenth than the fourteenth century.[47] Such connections would probably reinforce the non-burgess family's identification with the interests of its employer rather than with other members of its social group, thus minimising the development of a separate group identity.[48]

Within the burgh itself there were tangible signs of the sense of community. Burgh plans focused on the marketplace, usually indicated by the widening of the main street, a market cross, and the presence of the townhouse or burgh church. As the centre of local trade, the market was the meeting-place of all the burgh inhabitants and also of visitors to the burgh. It was thus appropriate that it should be the site of the institutions of government and the meeting-place for head courts, for this was a government which depended for its functioning on the visible participation and consensus of the community. The market place was the focus for the proper working of the nexus of laws which governed the community.

Thus, in 1399, Paul Crab, burgess of Aberdeen, declared publicly at the tron his intention to pursue a claim against a fellow-burgess.[49] The market cross was the symbol of the burgh's position within the realm. When David II suspended the trading privileges of the town of Brechin, he ordered that the market cross be removed.[50] It was also at the cross that public proclamations, both burghal and royal, were made.

The symbolic importance of the marketplace was enhanced in many burghs in the fourteenth century by the construction of townhouses there. It had earlier been the practice, and still continued to be so in some fourteenth-century burghs, to hold courts and town meetings out of doors or in the houses of individual burgesses. The churchyard often provided a convenient meeting-place for the communities of Elgin and Inverness.[51] During the 1300s, a number of burghs were granted charters conferring on them the right to erect a townhouse 'for the ornament of the burgh'.[52] The building of the new Aberdeen townhouse at the beginning of the fifteenth century was made a responsibility of the whole community, free and unfree, every inhabitant being required to contribute one day's work to the construction or pay 4d.[53] Generally, these buildings were erected in or beside the marketplace, land which belonged to the burgh superior and therefore required his permission to build on. In some cases at least, the structures were of two storeys and their size and prominent site would have made them immediately recognisable as one of the most significant buildings of the burgh. In function, they combined the activities of burgh administration, legislation and justice; here burgh courts could be held, the council met, market tolls were collected and criminals imprisoned.

Another focus of community feeling was the burgh church. The urban parish almost invariably continued to conform to the original bounds laid down in the twelfth or thirteenth century,[54] but by the fourteenth century the structure of the parish church in some burghs was being extended and its fabric made more ornate. In two burghs, Edinburgh and Aberdeen, both documentary and architectural evidence survives of building work carried out by the burgesses on their churches in the fourteenth century.[55] From 1342 to 1360 the church of St. Nicholas in Aberdeen was the recipient of gifts from both individual burgesses and from the community as a whole. One of the officers of the burgh administration was the conservator of the church work; in the last years of the century four masters of the kirk work were appointed annually. In Edinburgh, St. Giles' was the focus of concern in 1365 when it was agreed that a register of charters to the church should be kept to minimise the disruption caused by war damage and English occupation to church muniments. In 1387 an indenture was concluded between the community and three masons to extend the church by the building of five chapels in the south nave. This may have been the result of damage caused by the English attack of 1385. It seems that the effect of English raids, warfare and occupation was to draw together more closely the community of the fourteenth-century burgh.

Other ecclesiastical institutions were also the focus of burgess interest. The early grants of burgh lands directed to the church had largely been made to abbeys and bishoprics; by the fourteenth century they were made rather to local religious houses of friars.[56] The men of such houses often played an active role in the community, providing spiritual guidance, education, medical care, and aid for the poor and old, and they thus gained the respect of the burgh inhabitants. In Aberdeen, the Carmelites seem to have been especially popular, although this impression may be due to the pattern of survival of the documents.[57] The possession of burgh lands and rents helped integrate the friaries further into burgh life – although not always amicably – as a number of disputes over them in the burgh court are recorded.

Community feeling was also expressed in actions which were taken by the community as a whole. Here the burgh church figured prominently. The presentation of a new chaplain to an altar after the death of the founder was generally entrusted to the alderman and the community.[58] The administration of lands and rents granted to the altar was likewise handled by the community. Often the land would be set at ferme to an individual burgess who would then pay the rent to the altar.[59] In such transactions, the assent of the community of the burgh was often represented by the phrase *teste communitate* (by the witness of the community)[60] or by the use of the burgh seal which was a physical symbol of the unity of burgh action. By the fourteenth century, most burghs had seals; they were used to ratify decisions both within the burgh and on a national level – seventeen burgh seals were appended to the document appointing burgess representatives to take part in the negotiations for David II's ransom in 1357.[61]

Lands held by the burgh in common were another focus for community action. Usually these lands lay around the perimeter of the burgh, outside the area occupied by the burgages. Some of them were divided up into individual holdings, originally pertaining to specific burgages, but by the fourteenth century being bought and sold as separate properties.[62] Other lands, however, were for common use. At Aberdeen, Rubislaw, which came into the burgh's possession in the mid-fourteenth century, provided grazing for all the animals of the burgesses. The burgh government appointed a herd to look after the livestock.[63] Grants of such lands were made to the community as a whole and were probably intended to provide an extra source of revenue as well as make available lands for agricultural use. Sometimes such grants included fishings and mills, although often these remained in the hands of the burgh superior. If the burgh did gain control, it tended to lease such properties to individuals, although not in perpetuity – at Aberdeen, the leases rarely exceeded three years. The divisions of fishings into shares as small as 1/32 meant that a maximum number of burgesses were able to participate. The mills were shared out among fewer burgesses, with an entire mill often being leased to only one individual.[64]

The sense of community went beyond the individual burgh. In the early part of the century there can be discerned traces of the community feeling which was to find political expression in the 1350s in the recognition of the Third Estate. There seems already to have been a general sense of common identity among the various burghs. This was reinforced by a lack of differentiation between royal and non-royal burghs in all matters except taxation. In the 1320s, when Robert I wished to know what privileges had formerly been enjoyed by the burgesses of Dundee, an assize of burgesses from both royal and ecclesiastical burghs reported that Dundee, which had earlier been a baronial burgh, enjoyed the same privileges as the other burghs of the kingdom.[65] Laws of one burgh were often adopted by another, while charters sometimes referred to the privileges of a certain burgh as the model for privileges being granted to another.[66] The Court of the Four Burghs was recognised as competent to declare judgment on the burgh laws of many of the Scottish burghs, and it was also common for one burgh to seek another burgh's advice on a point of burgh law or custom.[67]

Generally, relations between the burghs seem to have fostered cooperation rather than bred disruption. Sometimes alliances were made in the face of a threat to burghal trading privileges, as in the case of the agreement made in 1372 between Forfar and Montrose which excluded the men of Brechin from the reciprocal trading rights established between the two burghs.[68] In the 1350s appeals had been made to David II by both Dundee and Montrose, apparently acting in concert, against intrusions on their trading privileges by the men of non-burghal settlements.[69] In the late thirteenth century a joint appeal was made to the crown for protection of their trading privileges by the burgesses of the burghs north of the Mounth.[70] Sometimes, cooperation was enforced from above. The burgesses of Dundee and St. Andrews were given the right to trade in Cupar by parliament, which also dismissed a counter-claim by the burgesses of Cupar against the men of St. Andrews.[71] The few inter-burghal disputes of which there are records were settled from above in a similar fashion, the distinction between royal and non-royal burghs having little bearing on their outcome. The only place which lost its privileges, albeit temporarily, was Brechin, and it had long been in the unique position of enjoying market privileges without having burghal status.

A sense of community between the burghs was also fostered by the trading activities of the individual burgesses. There are a few references in the fourteenth century and many more in the fifteenth and sixteenth centuries to cooperation between burgesses of different burghs in overseas trading ventures. In 1370 two ships were loaded with the goods of men of Edinburgh, Perth and Dundee; it seems likely that the men of Perth and Dundee shared space in one ship.[72] An agreement with Bruges in 1348 was made on behalf of 'the four great towns of Scotland' – Edinburgh, Perth, Aberdeen and Dundee.[73] Moreover, men occasionally acquired burgess-ship in more than one burgh.[74] As this usually involved men from inland or west-coast burghs who became burgesses of east-coast burghs, it was probably access to continental trade which was the main motive. Other burgesses might send their goods from the west to be shipped through the east-coast burghs; the burgesses of Ayr were especially prominent in this practice.[75]

Politically, the fourteenth century saw the development of burgess representation in parliament. This process has been traced by a number of historians[76] – burgesses were probably present as petitioners in the early parliaments of Robert I and in 1326 they received official summons. They were present again in 1328 and 1341 and they seem to have attended regularly from 1357. The development of their political representation stemmed largely from the financial needs of the crown and the continued need for money to pay the instalments of David II's ransom from 1357 to 1373. The effect of this on burghal unity may have been twofold: those burghs represented in parliament were able to give concrete expression to their feeling of unity, but there may also have begun to be a division between those burghs and the ones not so represented, that is, most of the non-royal burghs. As yet, the split was not wide, but as the parliamentary burghs in the following centuries pushed for extra privileges on the grounds that they bore the burden of burgh taxation, the division would become more significant.

The burghs were also part of the community of the realm and had their part to play in the functioning of the kingdom. As centres of trade, they provided meeting-places for producers and buyers, for foreign and native merchants. They were often the scene for meetings of parliaments and general councils or the temporary home of the royal court. Justice courts of sheriffdom, church and king could all be held in the burgh. Burgh fairs brought merchants and traders from far and wide, while the weekly markets provided the opportunity for the meeting of town and country. The burgh was also constantly interacting with the hinterland because of its dependence on the countryside for food, raw materials for industry and building materials.[77] Even in the major exporting burghs, it is unlikely that the community could have survived long in isolation from the countryside.

The links between the burgh and its hinterland were given new expression in the fourteenth century by the increasing investment of wealthy burgesses in rural lands, although, as far as can be determined from the surviving records, the converse pattern of investment in burgh lands by country landowners as yet remained minimal.

Finally, the burgesses showed their solidarity with the community of the realm through their actions on the kingdom's behalf. Although some burghs cooperated with the English occupation in the Wars of Independence – and they may have had little choice – many, especially Aberdeen,[78] acted as centres of resistance, while individual burgesses of Inverness, St. Andrews, Edinburgh and Aberdeen among others, played an active role in supporting the Scottish cause by recovering castles, supplying provisions from overseas and aiding the Scottish forces in battle. In diplomacy as well the burgesses played their part. John Mercer of Perth and Adam Forrester of Edinburgh were prominent ambassadors in the second half of the century.[79] The duties of royal offices were often carried out by burgesses, acting as deputies to men of greater social standing who did little of the real work. Burgesses were closely involved in the running of the royal mints.[80] The royal office most commonly filled by burgesses was that of the custumar or collector of royal revenues from export duties, which emerged in the late thirteenth or early fourteenth century. In this post the close connection of the burgesses with the welfare of the crown and the economy of the kingdom as a whole can be seen. In the same way as they formed a community within their burghs, so they were part of the community of the realm.

NOTES

1. *Abdn. Chrs.*, no. iii; *RRS*, ii, no. 467.

2. *Abdn. Chrs.*, nos. vi–viii (1313–19).

3. BL, Add. MSS. 33245, fo. 80r.

4. *Fragmenta Collecta*, in *Ancient Burgh Laws*, c. 6.

5. *Arbroath Liber*, i, no. 344; ii, nos. 6, 8, 14, 40.

6. See Stevenson, Ch. 6, above.

7. M. Lynch, 'The crown and the burghs, 1500–1625', in *The Early Modern Town in Scotland* (London, 1986), 66–7.

8. See MacQueen and Windram, Ch. 12, above.

9. *Kelso Liber*, ii, no. 459.

10. See *ER*, vols. i–iii for details of these audits.

11. *Abdn. Chrs.*, no. viii. Berwick was granted a feu-ferme charter in the late thirteenth century and again in 1320 after it was recovered from the English (Nicholson, *Scotland,*

108) but the payments lapsed after it came under English rule again in the 1330s. For other burghs, see map in *Historical Atlas of Scotland* (2nd ed., forthcoming), which corrects the list given in *Abdn. Recs.*, p. lxxv.

12. See Ewan, 'Thesis', Ch. 2, for a more detailed discussion of these offices.

13. *St Nich. Cart.*, 16–17.

14. *Leges Burgorum*, c. 70; *Abdn. Recs.*, 23.

15. *Abdn. Recs.*, 100, 196; *Leges Burgorum*, c. 70.

16. Lynch, *Edinburgh*, 10.

17. *Moray Reg.*, no. 235; *Irvine Muniments*, no. 1.

18. My italics. *RRS*, vi, no. 225.

19. In 1392 the provost and bailies presided over a burgh court in Elgin (NLS, Adv. MSS. 9A.1.10, fo. 38). See MacQueen and Windram, Ch. 12, above, for further discussion of the burgh court.

20. See *Abdn. Recs.*, esp. pp. cxxv–xl, for the proceedings of the Aberdeen burgh court and its procedure.

21. This rule was not always strictly adhered to. No Yule head court was held in Aberdeen in 1399, while a Perth head court was held on 9 Feb. in 1369 (SRO, GD79/5/1).

22. *Leges Burgorum*, c. 42. The process can be seen in Perth (SRO, GD79/5/1), Dundee (Dundee Archives, TC/CC10, no. 5), and Aberdeen (SRO, GD52/393).

23. *Leges Burgorum*, c. 15; *Abdn. Recs.*, p. xxv, n. 2.

24. *Abdn. Recs.*, pp. cxxiii, 27, 34, 39, 41.

25. *Ibid.*, 35, 139.

26. *Ibid.*, p. cxxvii.

27. *RRS*, ii, no. 467; *Stirling Chrs.*, no. 7. A map of guilds merchant in *Historical Atlas of Scotland* (2nd ed., forthcoming) corrects the list in Gross, *Gild Merchant*, 203–07.

28. The view put forward by Gross, *Gild Merchant*, 213, Nicholson, *Scotland*, 263, and E. M. Barron, *Inverness in the Fifteenth Century* (Inverness, 1906), 32, has been questioned by M. Lynch, 'Whatever happened to the medieval burgh?', 12–13. See also Lynch, Ch. 15, below.

29. See Torrie, Ch. 14, below, for fuller details.

30. *RRS*, ii, no. 467; *Abdn. Chrs.*, no. iii.

31. MA, M/WC/1; *RRS*, vi, no. 462.

32. See Torrie, Ch. 14, below, as an example.

33. See *Leges Burgorum* and above, n. 24.

34. Details are given in G. W. I. Hodgson, 'The animal remains from medieval sites within three burghs on the eastern Scottish seaboard', in *Site, Environment and Economy*, ed. B. Proudfoot (BAR, International series, no. 173, 1983). See Spearman, Ch. 8, above, for the importance of cattle.

35. Duncan, 'Perth', 36–7; PHSE bone, 23.

36. *ER*, i, pp. lxxiv, 6. By the fourteenth century this industry may have declined due to the unsettled wartime conditions and a shortage of timber which had begun to affect Scotland.

37. See Spearman, Ch. 8, above, for further details of local industries, and Lynch, Ch. 15, below, for the impact of the development of craft industries in the fifteenth century.

38. N. MacAskill *et al*, *Pottery* in Holdsworth (ed), *Perth Excavns*.

39. *CDS*, iv, no. 462; *APS*, i, 571.

40. PHSE wood; *Edin. Chrs.*, no. 14.

41. *RRS*, vi, no. 316.

42. Reynolds, *English Towns*, 138.

43. My thanks to Marion Stavert, who is preparing an edition of the Perth guild book for the information on Perth. See Torrie, Ch. 14, below.

44. Cf. Lynch, Ch. 15, below.

45. Because burgess houses were generally on the street frontages which have been subject to intensive occupation right to the present day, it is rare to have the opportunity to excavate them. The backlands, in contrast, are often open land today and can be excavated more easily.

46. This picture is based on reports of excavations in Perth, Aberdeen and Inverness. Some of the Perth excavation reports are published in Holdsworth (ed), *Perth Excavns*. Aberdeen and Inverness excavations are published in *Abdn. Excavns*. and 'Inverness excavn'.

47. Or later, as in Perth. See Spearman, Ch. 3, above.

48. Such was apparently the case in England; Reynolds, *English Towns*, 88.

49. *Abdn. Recs.*, 37.

50. *RRS*, vi, no. 334.

51. *Abdn. Recs.*, 10; *An Account of the Familie of Innes* (Spalding Club, 1864), 54–6; *Moray Registrum*, no. 235.

52. Montrose Archives, M/WC/2; *Irvine Muniments*, no. 6.

53. *Abdn. Recs.*, 238.

54. See Cowan, Ch. 5, above.

55. See *St Nich. Cart.*, 12–20; *Abdn. Recs.*, 101; *St Giles Reg.*, nos. 1, 18; see also Stell, Ch. 4, above.

56. Stevenson, Ch. 6, above.

57. See AUL, Marischal College Charters, catalogued in *Aberdeen Friars: Red, Black, White, Grey*, ed. P. J. Anderson (Aberdeen, 1909).

58. *Aberdeen-Banff Illustrations*, iii, 43–4.

59. *St Giles Reg.*, nos. 8, 14.

60. SRO, RH6/199.

61. *Edin. Chrs.*, no. 6.

62. E.g. the croft territories of Aberdeen were part of an active land market in the 1300s; see *Abdn. Reg.* and Marischal Coll. Chrs. Remnants of the older system remained at Elgin: *Moray Reg.*, no. 232.

63. *Abdn. Recs.*, 91–2, 167.

64. *Ibid.*, 84, 169, 170, 171.

65. Dundee Archives, TC/CC, 14A.

66. *Abdn. Chrs.*, no. 3; *Dundee Chrs.*, 9–11.

67. Stevenson, *Documents*, i, 380–81.

68. See above, n. 31.

69. *RRS*, vi, nos. 120, 121.

70. *Abdn. Chrs.*, 290–91.

71. *Dundee Chrs.*, 12; *RRS*, vi, 136, 462.

72. *Rot. Scot.*, i, 948.

73. *HUB*, iii, no. 131. These towns are wrongly identified in Nicholson, *Scotland*, 154.

74. SRO, GD215/1862/2, fos. 17–19.

75. *ER*, ii, 374, 378, 471, 515.

76. Some of the conclusions in R. S. Rait, *The Parliaments of Scotland* (Glasgow, 1924) have been revised by A. A. M. Duncan, 'The early parliaments of Scotland', *SHR*, xlv (1966), 36–58.

77. See Ewan, 'Thesis', 251–8.

78. Ewan, 'The Age of Bon-Accord', 32-3.
79. Ewan, 'Thesis', 272-3, 331-2; Grant, *Scotland*, 71.
80. *ER*, i, 567, 584, 615-17; ii, 65, 159.

14

The Guild in Fifteenth-Century Dunfermline

Elizabeth P. D. Torrie

Guilds were a familiar and integral part of medieval life, with origins wherever groups of men came together with a common purpose.[1] They were known throughout much of Europe from the eighth century as friendly societies[2] and many adopted religious overtones, reinforced by pageantry and material support of the church. Within towns a further increasingly important aspect manifested itself: that of the guild as an economic organisation, devoting much of its corporate life to mercantile pursuits. The earliest authentic references would suggest that this was true of Scotland by the twelfth century. A body called the 'gild merchant' is referred to in the *Laws of the Four Burghs*, reputedly of the reign of David I,[3] and during the time of William the Lion royal recognition was confirmed.[4] The *Statutes of the Guild*, the statutes of the guild of Berwick, the earlier part attributed to 1249 and the later specifically dated 1281 and 1294, became the model for most Scottish guilds. The Dunfermline guild felt the *Statutes* still of sufficient relevance to the fraternity in the fifteenth century to copy many clauses *verbatim* into the Dunfermline Guild Court Book which was commenced in 1433. These early rulings, moreover, illustrate precisely that the guild merchant was a fraternity whose functions were social, religious and mercantile.

The Berwick guild appears to be of an earlier than thirteenth-century origin, and Perth and Roxburgh are known to have had guilds before 1189 x 1202.[5] These, along with Edinburgh (1209?), Dundee (1165? x 1214), Inverness (1165? x 1214), Inverkeithing (1165? x 1214), Aberdeen (1222), Ayr (1222?), Dumbarton (1222) and Stirling (1226), were the first recorded in Scotland. The thirteenth, fourteenth and fifteenth centuries saw the formation of many more such guilds; even so, the majority of guilds merchant were established in the century after 1560.[6] The early burghal laws and the *Statutes of the Guild* might indicate the theoretical purposes of the institution, but no guild records are extant until the fifteenth century to demonstrate how in practice the brethren conducted their lives. Consequently, the Dunfermline guild is of interest. Founded perhaps between 1365 and 1399, or earlier, its guild court book while dating from only 1433 is the earliest surviving in Scotland.[7] The volume gives a clear picture of the functioning of a guild merchant in Dunfermline in the fifteenth century, and perhaps also a relatively accurate reflection of the practices of earlier medieval guilds in Scotland as a whole. Information from the Guild Court Book may be supplemented by the later fifteenth-century burgh court records of Dunfermline and by the guild records of Aberdeen, Perth, Stirling and Ayr.[8]

A consideration of the Dunfermline guild has a merit beyond this: Dunfermline was a small town. Medieval population figures are elusive and the earliest firm numbers are as late as 1624, when the *Register of the Privy Council* specifies that,

> the wholl bodie of the towns, quhilk consisted of ellevin scoir of tenementis and fouretene scoir and sevin famileis, wer brynt and consumed, with the wholl plennessing of the houssis, besydis the barnis about the toun, quhairin thair was fyve hundreth bollis of victuall; quhairby this poore towne, sometyme a floorisheing member of the body of this commounweele, and haveing within it sevin hundreth communicantis, with saxteene scoir of bairnis, of whom the eldest is not past sax yeiris of aige, is totalie ruyned and undone.

Using a multiplier of 4.5 members per family suggests a total population of almost 1,300 which is not inconsistent with the total of 1,020 (700 adult communicants and 320 children under six). Such a population figure is based on the presumed veracity of the records; and Dunfermline, in appealing to other burghs for help, may well have exaggerated its plight. It seems, however, reasonable to surmise that there were no more than 1000 to 1100 inhabitants by 1500, and, according to an early sixteenth-century burgess roll, about 140 to 150 burgesses.[9] Small urban settlements were the norm in Scotland. There were between sixty and seventy burghs in 1450 but no more than four of them could make any claim to be large population centres.[10] Aberdeen, Dundee, Perth and Edinburgh were not typical of the Scottish urban scene. Their wealth and size set them apart from the mass of burghs.[11] An assessment of the Dunfermline guild in the fifteenth century offers an insight into the guilds of the many lesser burghs that have left few or no records.

In any one year throughout the fifteenth century there were, on average, fifty members of the Dunfermline guild. This indicates a high percentage of participation in guild business given a burgess population of approximately 140. An analysis of membership reveals two essential qualifications for entrance: a candidate must normally have been a burgess of Dunfermline and male. Otherwise, the fraternity was not a closed one. Entry was, however, most easy for a son, usually the eldest, of a guild member; or, on the failure of a male heir, for the husband of a daughter of a

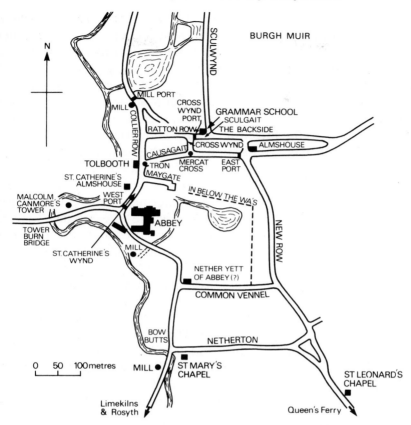

Dunfermline in 15th century

guild member. All of these entered the fraternity free, apart from a donation of spice and wine. A proportion might also be admitted free or at a reduced entry fee, through the intercession of the burgh superior, the crown, or a local notable family, or in recompense for good deeds. Otherwise a newcomer paid the full entry fee, usually forty shillings, plus the spice and wine. Edinburgh's entrance fee in 1463 was £3, Stirling's forty shillings in 1460, and Perth's usual payment in the 1460s was five merks. Both Edinburgh and Perth imposed the additional fee of wine and spices on certain members, whereas in Stirling wine and wax were demanded.[12] The Dunfermline guild entrance fee of 40s, compared with the normal 6s. 8d. burgess entry fee, suggests a measure of exclusiveness.

A group consisting of approximately one third of all male burgesses could, however, scarcely be called exclusive. The membership of the fraternity would appear to confirm this. Men of different social standing were represented: gentry, churchmen, graduates, merchants, town clerks, tavern keepers, cordiners, plumbers, weavers, masons and skinners. Clearly the guild was not a stronghold of merchants. Indeed, there are only three specific references to 'merchants' as such in the Dunfermline guild records in the fifteenth century. The rare use of the word does not imply that merchant representation within the guild was virtually non-existent, but rather that, as with other occupations, such designations were not of prime importance to the fifteenth-century Dunfermline guild. It may be advisable, in the case of Dunfermline and other smaller burghs, to treat with some scepticism the notion that in the fifteenth century merchants and craftsmen were engaged in a permanent struggle for power.[13] The charter of Abbot John confirming that Dunfermline should have its guild speaks of a 'gild merchant'. But throughout the fifteenth and sixteenth centuries the term 'gild merchant' was not used once by the scribe minuting the business of the Dunfermline guild. In the eyes of contemporaries the fraternity was simply the guild – open to both merchant and non-merchant alike. Nor was Dunfermline alone in this. The fifteenth-century records of other burghs indicate that craftsmen gained entry to guild fraternities, even though the *Burgh Laws* prohibited dyers, fleshers and soutars who practised their craft with their hands. The burgh charters of Perth, Stirling and Aberdeen specifically excluded weavers from guild membership, but the 'Perth Guildrie Book' shows weavers and a high proportion of other crafts, such as baxters, dyers, furriers and skinners, within its guild. Misconceptions about merchant domination and supposed disputes between merchants and craftsmen may have arisen through a misunderstanding of the term 'merchant'.[14] In Scotland a merchant was anyone who bought and sold, and consequently a man with no greater pretensions than to make his livelihood in his booth in the town, probably never moving out of Scotland and rarely far from home, merited the qualification 'merchant'. He might be a *grand entrepreneur*, often travelling overseas, but was not necessarily so. If this latter definition of a merchant is used exclusively, the Dunfermline guild was not a 'merchant' guild at all.

It is unwise when considering the medieval Scottish town to assume that what was true for the larger centres was inevitably so for the smaller. Increasing size and material wealth brought about both economic diversification and stratification within urban society. As bodies formalised, internal dissensions came to the fore, and in the late fifteenth and early sixteenth centuries there was in larger towns a hardening of rôles and the emergence of a certain élitism, in both craft and merchant organisations.[15] Yet Dunfermline – and probably most of the smaller burghs – were largely immune to such developments throughout the medieval period.

Throughout the fifteenth century the Dunfermline guild conducted its business under the leadership of a dean[16] supported by a sergeand, in regular meetings of the guild court in the tolbooth. By the fifteenth century Dunfermline was an ecclesiastical burgh and all indications are that a fair measure of freedom was accorded by the burgh superior, the abbot of Dunfermline. There is no evidence of unwanted interference in guild affairs on his part. Indeed, on two occasions, in 1441 and 1462, brethren were summoned before the guild court and censured for attempting to appeal to the abbot against its decisions.[17] The burgh as a whole appears to have been granted a significant measure of independence by the superior,[18] and there is little trace in Dunfermline or other early ecclesiastical burghs in Scotland, in sharp contrast with England, of the church being 'the most restrictive lord of all'.[19] Dunfermline's alderman and two bailies were usually representatives of well-known Dunfermline families; and there is no indication, as for example in the abbot's burgh of Arbroath, of one bailie being chosen by the superior.[20] The abbots of Dunfermline did, however, retain to themselves the right of correction of the bailies, although there is no evidence that it was ever enforced.[21] On the contrary, on the one occasion recorded that a bailie and an alderman were subjected to reprimand, it was by an assize of twenty-three of their peers.[22] The guild court and burgh court records suggest that Dunfermline's relations with its superior were harmonious and that town and abbot co-existed with mutual tolerance.

The Dunfermline regality court records have not survived for the fifteenth century[23] and it is possible that they might have revealed a stricter control of the burgh and guild by the abbots, but it is reasonable to surmise from what sources are available that the regality court encroached little upon the privileges of Dunfermline burgesses. This was a burgh with a fair degree of self-government and a wide participation in town affairs by many burgesses. This was of course one of the virtues of a small burgh, whatever its status: it was still possible for all burgesses to meet together to ratify, or at times initiate, decisions.[24]

An assessment of the officeholders in the burgh and guild reveals not only a relatively high identification between personnel but also a certain monopoly enjoyed by a few families of the positions of the alderman, two bailies and the dean of guild. There was moreover active participation at regular assizes by a large proportion of the burgesses, who inevitably included guild members. In consequence the guild as an institution acted in town affairs in matters quite specifically within its remit, but it also at times functioned as a municipal department in areas that might arguably be considered purely burghal. This was perhaps inevitable. Where a particular item of burgh business was transacted was not a matter of supreme importance as long as it received attention. Consequently the guild court might act much as a burgh court. Throughout most of the fifteenth century the guild and the burgh used the services of the same scribe; there are occasions when guild minutes appear in the burgh court book and possibly *vice-versa*. While formal divisions of authority can be extrapolated from the *Burgh Laws* and other documents, in practice the medieval burgh constitution did not work that way.

There were, however, matters that were specifically the prerogative of the guild. Probably most noticeable was the control which the guild had over the commercial activities of the town. Saturday was market day,[25] and the length of the Causagait or High Street of Dunfermline became an extended trading area. The market precinct had of necessity to be linear, because of the narrowness of the main street, and by the fifteenth century pressure for space had resulted in booths being sited outside the town ports. The topography of the town did not permit the conventional siting of market cross and tron beside each other. The tron was in all probability outside the tolbooth, in which the town weights were kept, at the west end of the town, and the market cross was sited further east in the centre of the main street. It was to this market and to the two annual fairs that the inhabitants of the surrounding countryside came.

A town's livelihood was dependent on successful interaction with its hinterland; and the Dunfermline guild kept a close surveillance that there was no encroachment into its trading area. The four regality burghs of Dunfermline, Kirkcaldy, Queensferry and Musselburgh had been granted the right to trade freely throughout the regality of Dunfermline lands in 1363 by David II.[26] This was an important concession, but contained within it potential difficulties if any one burgh became over-ambitious at the expense of its neighbours. North of the Forth the regality lands were divided between Kirkcaldy and Dunfermline. South-west Fife was, consequently, apportioned into three major trading zones, Inverkeithing also having its commercial hinterland.[27] Fife was perhaps unusual, as most of Scotland's urban trading areas were characterised by overlapping jurisdictions and continually changing boundaries throughout the fifteenth and sixteenth centuries.[28] The Dunfermline regality lands, by contrast, were clearly defined.[29] The practical enforcement of the trading boundaries between Inverkeithing, Kirkcaldy and Dunfermline could, however, never be totally effective, and rivalry persisted, especially between Kirkcaldy and Dunfermline. Both burghs claimed the sole right of trading in Goatmilk, and in 1448 an appeal was made to the abbot to settle the dispute, the decision being made in Dunfermline's favour.[30] It is significant, however, that by 1583 the Kirkcaldy burgh records make it clear that not only was Goatmilk considered to be within its trading area,

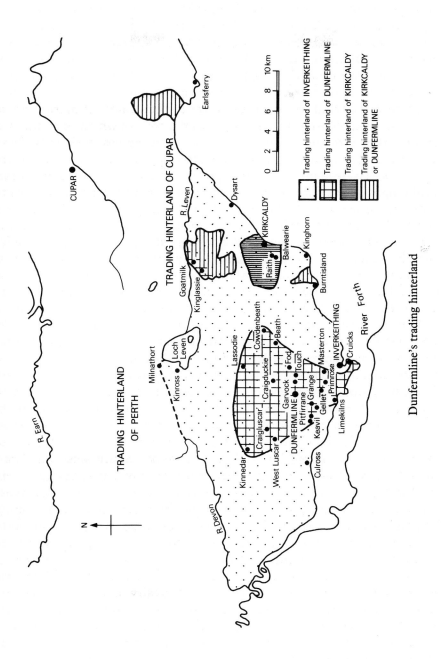

Dunfermline's trading hinterland

but so also was Kinglassie.[31] In general, protection of one's own hinterland was such that not even royal intervention could successfully intrude on this patchwork of jurisdictions. In 1585 two merchants arrived in Dunfermline with a licence granted by the crown to trade in all burghs throughout the realm. The Dunfermline guild's response was that Dunfermline has been 'erectit ane frie brucht of regaltie quharvpoun the kingis ma may [sic] nocht justlie intrude uny persoun vpoun thame for hurting of thair liberties'.[32] The guild kept a close watch for any malpractice throughout this hinterland. Forestalling, the purchase of goods before they reached market, thus avoiding the payment of toll, and regrating, the purchase in bulk and possible hoarding of goods in order to sell at an advantageous time when prices were high, were heavily punished. All trading was to take place in the open market, where not only could fair dealing be seen, but also allowing the town to benefit financially from the payment of tolls and fees by vendors at its market. Such measures were of benefit to the entire town; but the guild was not acting in a deliberately altruistic manner. Monopoly played a major role in guild business, and it was monopoly designed to favour the guild. Dealing in the staple goods – hides, furs, skins, wools and woolfells – throughout the hinterland was the sole prerogative of the fraternity. This right was sometimes shared by the brethren by rote; but so that all would benefit equally, surplus was to be offered initially to the other members of the guild at cost. Any non-guild member who attempted to trespass in such trafficking was fined by the guild court.

The guild also claimed exclusive rights to control the burgh's overseas trade. The Dunfermline merchant traded to the continent as freely as his neighbours from royal burghs.[33] Flanders was the usual destination in the fifteenth century, although there was some trade further north. In 1445, for example, the *Bargia* was seized at sea by an armed Bremen ship. Among those whose goods were confiscated were two Dunfermline merchants.[34] Trading with Danzig and other Baltic ports was well established by the sixteenth century, and was, in all probability, practised in the fifteenth. International trade, while playing a minor role, was not insignificant in Dunfermline's economic life. Where evidence does exist, it is clear that the commodities exported were the same as in royal burghs – wool, woolfells, hides, rough cloth and salmon. Dunfermline merchants used the ports of Dysart and Leith for overseas trade. Their own port of Limekilns was about three miles from the burgh, but there is no medieval evidence of international trade from there. It may have served more specifically as the port for local or coastal trade – the mainstay of the Dunfermline guild.

The guild also had within its remit the responsibility for the lucrative cloth and leather industries. In a town that was not to witness its first two craft incorporations, those of the hammermen and the weavers, until the second half of the sixteenth century,[35] a simpler mode of craft supervision continued, which was regulation by the men who were the economic backbone of the town, the guild. This virtually total dominance of the commercial life of the town may well have been resented. It was most certainly envied if the frequent attempts to break the guild privilege are taken into account. Recourse was sought not by attempts to set up rival craft organisations but by joining the controlling guild. It is, perhaps, not over-speculative to suggest that this is not a measure of the compliance of the crafts nor indeed of the aggression of the guild, but rather a comment upon the small size of the town.

While altruism may not have been the primary motivation of the guild, it is undeniable that guild activities brought considerable economic benefit to the town as a whole. The fraternity can often be seen working alongside the burgh officials in the control of price and quality of commodities such as wheat, ale, malt and bread, as well as in imposing restrictions on the sale of food supplies outwith the town during the time of plague. But the town gained also from less obvious gestures on the part of the guild: the waiving of the payment of the customary guild entrance fee in exchange for the new members purchasing and maintaining the town weights; assisting in the repair of the tolbooth; repairing the aisle of the parish church; upgrading a section of the road to Limekilns; and other good works.

The *Guild Court Book* of Dunfermline, for a number of years, offers relatively full accounts of income and expenditure. An analysis of these serves to highlight the guild's financial role in the town.[36] The guild was dealing with far larger sums of money than was the burgh as a whole. It is evident that many of the major town projects, such as road paving and repair, port building, tolbooth mending and roofing were largely or wholly financed by the guild. In 1448 and 1449 for example, £26 3s. 4d. was spent on making improvements to the tolbooth; £21 18s. 6d. of this came directly from the guild. Although never explicity stated, both the guild and burgh records imply some particular guild responsibility for the material fabric of the town, also pinpointed by the guild's interest in lining decisions. Loans from guild to town were commonplace – for payment of taxes or the fee of the common clerk – and there is no evidence of these loans ever being repaid. The guild purse and the common purse were quite distinct; but it is abundantly clear that the latter, often slim or even empty, was fed largely by the former.

The origins of fifteenth-century urban families are not easy to ascertain. For Dunfermline, the little evidence there is would suggest both a highly localised catchment area, incomers being in the main from Fife and areas to the north-east, and that the guild relied for survival on this new blood.[37] A nucleus of fifteenth-century Dunfermline families did, however, survive, at least seven of them entering their fourth generation by the early sixteenth century. The average guild brother of Dunfermline had probably more in common with his rural neighbours than with the great merchants of the capital.

The town – here and elsewhere in Scotland – was still very much of the country, and a fair measure of self-sufficiency from an inhabitant's own toft and common pasturage outside the burgh was the norm for even the wealthiest guild brother. The guild itself possessed extensive lands to the south of the Netherton during the earliest part of the fifteenth century.[38] These it maintained and hedged, and probably used for grazing. Guild life was also at the time sufficiently unpretentious that amongst its possessions was a quarrying mallet that was hired out to members. Life was precarious and tempered by harsh realities. Fear of plague, the need to provide an adequate supply of food for the family, squabbles with neighbours over lining marks and maintenance of property were their routine concerns. There are indications, however, that some guild brethren achieved, for a small town, a relatively high standard of living. Homes with well-designed, interconnecting chimneys and roofs, drainage and possibly sewers, with separate sleeping rooms and living quarters were available for the wealthier members of the guild. It may, however, be significant that in 1522 the only surviving inventory of goods of a deceased guild brother, dean of guild John Wilson, a literate, wealthy man, suggests that he did not possess a book or a clock, and that his lifestyle still demanded the possession of humble tools and spinning and weaving equipment in the home, although the itemisation of a mirror, nightshirt, spurs, feather bed and hangings, holy water vat and 'best sark' set him well above the bulk of Dunfermline society.[39] The level of luxury or sophistication of the Dunfermline guild brethren must not, however, be exaggerated. Their lifestyle displayed a traditional pattern: a concern for the material and moral support of their town and church; a certain mistrust of strangers; a subservient role for women who, although permitted to become burgesses, were not allowed to hold office or become guild members; and an apparent lack of interest in national affairs. The guild followed an introspective, conservative and even simple way of life.

The majority of the guild brothers must, however, have been numerate in order to run their businesses adequately. Dunfermline was possibly endowed with two schools: a song school was in existence by the time of the Reformation, and probably much earlier; and a grammar school attached to the abbey may have benefited from the teaching of Robert Henryson.[40] The sons of guild brothers, as the wealthiest and worthiest of the town, were the most likely to gain benefit from these schools. A number of less fortunate, however, received some formal education, in due course attended St. Andrews University as 'paupers', returned to their home town as graduates, and eventually entered the ranks of the guild. But graduates were not the only literates amongst the guild brethren. A few deans of guild were capable of not merely signing their names, but also of writing the minutes in the *Guild Court Book* rather than leaving this task to the clerk. There is also evidence of one woman, both a sister and wife of guild brothers, signing her name in 1493 – a very early example of a woman not of the rank of nobility or gentry with this capability.[41] Literacy was still, however, a limited skill, here and in other towns.[42] In 1559, for example, of seven guild brothers only three could sign their names unaided; and in 1594 of twenty-two members of the fraternity, ten still required the hand of the notary to guide theirs.

For these relatively simple men membership of the fraternity demanded two things: support for the church and active fellowship. It was perhaps inevitable in a burgh under the superiority of an abbot that the ties between church and burgh should be strong. The abbey buildings physically dominated the town; and church influence was pervasive in virtually every aspect of burgh life, not least in the routine of the guild fraternity. A significant proportion of guild funds went directly to the support of the church, mainly for the regular supply of wax and candles and for maintenance of altars in the parish church, which was situated to the west of the conventual church in the nave of the original 1150 abbey church.[43] Together with the burgh authorities, the guild played a dominant part in the organisation of the 'licht sylvir', a fund for the lighting of the church by candles, and in the appointment of gatherers who collected throughout the town. The guild took three altars more closely under its patronage. These were The Holy Blood Altar, first recorded in the *Guild Court Book* in 1491, St. Salvator's Altar and, to a lesser extent, St Ninian's Altar. Not only do the guild records reveal a careful apportionment of income for the maintenance of these altars and their chaplains, but also that rentals destined for the guild purse were diverted to this cause.

Inadequate documentation precludes a precise assessment of the material trappings of parish and conventual churches. However, it is perhaps not over-speculative to suggest that the interior of one of the most renowned of the Scottish abbeys would have been decorated in a costly, if not sumptuous, manner. The abbey itself was furnished with books, ornaments and other ecclesiastical jewels,[44] but was not the financial responsibility of the town, although there is some evidence of guild support.[45] The interior of the parish church, however, was maintained by the town; it would have been adorned with stone and wood carvings, as well as paintings and rich vestments,[46] all of which were paid for by the burgesses, and in particular by the guild. Religious fervour manifested itself, however, in other, less materialistic ways. Church festivals were the stimulus for processions and communal enjoyment; and in these the guild played its part. The 'guild cross' was probably carried ahead of the brethren whilst processing, and consequently a cover was bought in 1446 for its protection against the elements. Masses for the dead and attendance of all members at the burial of a guild brother were obligatory, and there is evidence that the guild and burgh officials demanded diligent service from the chaplains they maintained.[47]

Within the confines of the guild the small but significant proportion of clerical members, including in 1440 Richard Wallod, sacristan and future abbot of Dunfermline, must have had some influence on the group. More generally, for the town as a whole, churchmen were invaluable members of the community not only for their legal expertise and education, whether they functioned officially as notaries public, schoolmasters or clerics, but also for their assistance on a more informal basis in the counsels of the burgh and the guild. The proliferation of altars and chaplains within the parish church accentuated this. Most of the chaplains lived in the town, conducting their lives in a similar fashion to their lay uncles, nephews, brothers and fathers. Sir James Allansone, for example, who conducted the morning service in the parish church, was a guild member and held property on the west side of Collier Row.[48] Sir James Gudeswane by 1502 was vicar of Carnbee and chaplain of the Holy Blood Altar in the parish church. He was, however, sufficiently active as a member of the guild to serve as dean in 1485, 1486 and 1487.[49] Church and society were intertwined. The very timing of town life was determined by the routine of the church. Burgh head courts coincided with church festivals, as did the settlement dates for rentals and fines; and church bells announced the start of the working day, and the curfew at night.[50] A number of Dunfermline townspeople must have found work within the abbey precincts. While quantification is impossible, an abbey that looked to the town for kitchen staff and plumber might well require much casual labour, be it that of washerwoman or gardener.[51]

Ultimately, however, there was one facet of guild life that dominated all others. It was a fraternity whose essential qualities were those both of freedom and obligation. A member might not enjoy the one without being bound to the other. It was not sufficient merely to pay money, perform good deeds, or claim the right by inheritance to enter the guild. A man had also to be accepted by the brethren and he, in his turn, was bound to promise to obey rules and keep fraternity secrets before being permitted into this community. The guild court was equally concerned to preserve good neighbourhood amongst members as it was to punish those who trespassed on guild privileges from outside or abused them from inside.

Charity was not reserved solely for town improvement and church maintenance: within the guild, support of those who fell upon hard times, participation at burials by a display of solidarity and the saying of masses, as well as the care of widows and orphans were of paramount importance. Membership of the guild meant a commitment to a life of mutual self-help. Four notable guild brothers fled Dunfermline when plague struck in 1475. They were brought before the guild court and censured for acting against the common good. It was not deemed worthy that they should have abandoned those less fortunate in the town, 'and left it desolate in the tym of the pestilence'.[52] On the other hand, on joining the brotherhood a man entered a privileged state. He might benefit financially from the guild mercantile prerogatives: he would gain in social standing; his opinion would bear more weight in burgh affairs; and in case hard times fell upon him, he gained some form of built-in insurance against total destitution. But far more was offered: camaraderie that often expressed itself in merrymaking. Processions, plays and the appointment of Robin Hood until well into the sixteenth century could involve all the town,[53] but the *Guild Court Book* reveals a further aspect of guild life: the routine business of the guild was sustained by alcoholic refreshments and eating on a large scale. The accounts for 1443 show that nearly three-quarters of guild expenses went on alcoholic drink. By the end of the century there was an annual guild feast. In 1503 a breakdown of the expenses for this feast reveals its priorities: coal was purchased for 6d and bread for 18d; wine was 14d, ale 3s and a barrel of beer 30s. This was essentially a brotherhood, a group of men who joined together for many reasons, and not least for a bond of friendship. This close association had, ultimately, one supreme merit: mutual support was guaranteed not only through the harsh realities of their worldly existence, but also along the path to the next.

The sixteenth and seventeenth centuries were to see the gradual evolution of the Dunfermline guild into an élitist trade organisation, which became the preserve of merchants often to the detriment of craft interests, maintaining little in common with the early notion of the guild merchant as portrayed in the *Statutes of the Guild*. Such a hardening of role was perhaps inevitable as burgh society increased in size, wealth and sophistication, and as incorporations of crafts emerged there did develop an exclusiveness, both in burgh politics and in merchant and craft organisations. That the Dunfermline guild could retain so much of its original character until well into the sixteenth century was determined by a number of factors, not least the relative smallness of the town, the conservatism of its people and perhaps also its seeming desire to maintain the traditional, apparently harmonious, interdependence of abbot and burgh. The guild merchant had a significant role to play in the municipal and economic aspects of life in the burgh, but to overstress these functions would be to miss one aspect of its nature – it was a society for mutal self-help, conviviality and support of the church, retaining much in common with the early socio-religious guilds. The fifteenth-century records suggest that Dunfermline remained an essentially medieval town, not yet subjected to the social stratifications and economic tensions faced by larger and later burghs. It is probable that the practices and values of the guild in Dunfermline bore a strong resemblance to those of other small burghs, and serve to give a relatively clear reflection of the medieval guild merchant.

NOTES

1. If specific references are not cited, information has been gained from SRO, B20/10/1, MS Burgh Court Book of Dunfermline [BCBD], edited by E. Beveridge as *Dunf. Recs.*, or MS Guild Court Book of Dunfermline, 1433-1597 [*GCBD*] edited by E. P. D. Torrie.

2. E. Coornaert, 'Les ghildes médiévales', *Revue Historique*, xcix (1948), 22-55, 206-43.

3. *Leges Burgorum*, cxciv.

4. *Assise Regis Willelmi*, ccxxxix.

5. They are referred to in a charter of Roger, bishop of St Andrews when the guild merchant was established there in 1189 x 1202; copied onto fo. 35r of 'Registrum evidentiarum civitatis Sancti Andree', St A. UL, B65/1/1.

6. E. P. D. Torrie, 'Guilds merchant established by 1550', in *Historical Atlas II*. See anon. review of Gross, *Gild Merchant* in *The Scottish Review*, xxxii (1898), 61-81, which includes a date list of commencement of guilds given by Gross at i, 203-07, suggesting that 31 of 56 guilds merchant in Scotland were founded after 1560. See also Mackenzie, *Scottish Burghs*, 101.

7. A grant during the abbacy of John, possibly of Strathmiglo, to the burgesses of Dunfermline that they might have a guild merchant may have been merely confirmatory, since reference is made to the property held by the guild 'of old'.

8. BCBD; ACA, CR, vol. ii (1441-1465); Perth Museum and Art Gallery, Archive 1|1, 'The Guildrie Book'; CRA, PD6|1|1, MS Stirling Guild Recs., 1460-75; SRO, PA5/2, 'The Ayr Manuscript', fos. 8v-10, 85v.

9. *RPC*, xiii, 510-11; 'The Burrow Roll of Dunfermline', in BCBD, 364-7. See also Torrie, 'Thesis', app. vii, p. 357.

10. Precise figures of numbers of burghs at a given date are not possible; early burghs might lapse and some may never have had any real existence; see Pryde, *Burghs*.

11. See Lynch, Ch. 15, below.

12. *Edin. Recs.*, i, 20; MS Stirling Guild Recs., *anno* 1460; MS Perth Guildry Book, 38.

13. See e.g. *Abdn. Recs.*, pp. c-ci; Gross, *Gild Merchant*, i, 214; I. F. Grant, *The Social and Economic Development of Scotland before 1603* (Edinburgh, 1930), 135-6; Wormald, *Scotland*, 48; Lythe, 'Economic life', 71.

14. Patten, 'Urban occupations in pre-industrial England', 302.

15. See Lynch, Ch. 15, below.

16. The burgh had an 'alderman' or *prepositus*, both terms being used synonymously in

the Dunfermline records. He was the primary official within the burghal organisation; and as such held a dominant position within the guild. It is clear, however, that the dean as head of the guild court could dictate to the alderman; and there is no suggestion, as, for example, in Aberdeen (*Abdn. Recs.*, p. cii) that the alderman was the head of the guild, not even that the term 'alderman' was 'a title taken over from the gild' (Mackenzie, *Scottish Burghs*, 103).

17. *GCBD*, fos. 5, 9.

18. The royal charter issued on 19 August 1488 granting the right to the abbot of Paisley to erect a burgh of barony at Paisley, citing as examples Dunfermline, Newburgh and Arbroath, specifically entitled the superior to retain to himself far-reaching burghal domination (*Pais. Reg.*, 263). In the event the abbot's charter of 1490 (*Pais. Chrs.*, 35, 38) transferred the appointment of lesser officials (but not bailies and aldermen) to the burgesses, as presumably had happened in Dunfermline, Newburgh and Arbroath.

19. Reynolds, *English Towns*, 115. See also W. G. Hoskins, and H. P. R. Finberg, *Devonshire Studies* (London, 1952), 189, and W. R. G. Robinson, 'Swansea', in *Boroughs of Medieval Wales*, ed. R. A. Griffiths (Cardiff, 1978), 279, for some detail of the struggles of Tavistock, Abingdon, Bury St. Edmunds and Swansea to gain any true measure of municipal independence.

20. G. Hay, *The History of Arbroath to the Present Time, with notices of the Civil and Ecclesiastical affairs of the neighbouring district* (Arbroath, 1876), 115.

21. *Dunf. Reg.*, no. 396.

22. *Dunf. Recs.*, 118.

23. The earliest surviving records of the regality court dealings commence in 1531 with the 'Court Book of the Regality of Dunfermline' (SRO, RH11/27/6), transcribed by J. M. Webster and A. A. M. Duncan (*Dunf. Ct. Bk.*).

24. See Ewan, Ch. 13, above; Grant, *Development*, 378. In large burghs, despite the forum of the headcourt, all burgesses met together only rarely – as in Perth in 1560; see Lynch, Ch. 15, below.

25. *GCBD*, fo. 9v. Markets and fairs were not the preserve of royal burghs; cf. Grant, *Development*, 367.

26. *Dunf. Reg.*, no. 390.

27. Disagreements over trading zones were a common feature of the fourteenth and fifteenth centuries: e.g. Cupar's litigation against St Andrews in 1369 and 1498, Glasgow's resentment of Rutherglen and Dumbarton, and Dundee's rivalry with Perth (T. Keith, 'The trading privileges of the royal burghs of Scotland', *EHR*, xxviii, 463). Ayr forbade dealing with Irvine in hides in 1432 ('Ayr MS', fo. 85v), and the arguments between Brechin, Forfar, Dundee and Montrose brought a free trade agreement between Montrose and Forfar in 1372, to the exclusion of Brechin (Montrose Burgh Archives, M/W1/1/1) as well as long-term disputes, mainly between Montrose and Dundee (*HMC*, 2nd Report (1871), 206).

28. See Map III in *Dunf. Ct. Bk.*

29. *GCBD*, fos. 5, 26, offer documentary evidence of the scope of Dunfermline's jurisdiction.

30. *Dunf. Reg.*, no. 424; GBCD, fo. 100.

31. *Kirkcaldy Burgh Recs.*, ed. L. Macbean (Kirkcaldy, 1908), 82.

32. *GCBD*, fo. 82.

33. Arguments that overseas trade was confined to royal burghs are incorrect; cf. Wormald, *Scotland*, 42, and Lythe, 'Economic life', 81.

34. Staatsarchiv Bremen, 1/Bc/1445, Juli 15.

35. D. Thomson, *The Dunfermline Hammermen. A History of the Incorporation of*

Hammermen in Dunfermline (Paisley, 1909), 26–8; D. Thomson, *The Weavers Craft, being a History of the Weavers Incorporation of Dunfermline* (Paisley, 1903), 72.

36. Torrie, 'Thesis', 209–21, 262–85.

37. Of the 152 documented entries to the guild in the fifteenth century, forty claimed through 'inheritance', or through their wives; eighty-three committed themselves to the payment of the full entry fee; nine entered as a result of good service to the guild; and sixteen through influence (of the crown, abbot, or Stewarts of Rosyth).

38. For a discussion of the guild lands, their site and extent, and their removal from guild possession, see Torrie, 'Thesis', 200–04, and app. vii.

39. BCBD, 209.

40. There is no conclusive evidence that Robert Henryson, the poet, was the Dunfermline schoolmaster. The witnessing of three deeds by Robert Henryson, notary, in Dunfermline in 1478 ('Registrum de Dunfermelyn', NLS. Adv. Ms. 34–1–3A, fo. lxii (or 98), lxiiv (or 98v) and lxiv (or 99)) does not indicate that he was the schoolmaster and poet, although the combined post of notary and schoolmaster as held by John Moffat in Dunfermline was not uncommon (J. Durkan, 'The early Scottish notary', 27). William Dunbar's lament on the death of the poet would confirm some connection with Dunfermline (*The Poems of William Dunbar*, ed. J. Kinsley (Oxford, 1979), 180). The title page of William Dunbar's version of *Aesop's Fables* in 1570 (published by Henry Charteris and printed by R. Lekprevik) speaks of 'Maister Robert Henrisone, Scholemaster of Dunfermeling'; and this is repeated in *The Testament of Cresseid*, published by Charteris in 1593. See R. Dickson and J. P. Edmond, *Annals of Scottish Printing* (Camb., 1890), 240, 396. The indications are that the notary, poet and schoolmaster were one man.

41. BCBD, 45. Cf. R. K. Marshall, *Virgins and Viragos* (London, 1983), 58, which gives the earliest known signature of a 'middle-class' Scotswoman as 1530.

42. Nine of nineteen Stirling guild brethren could sign their names in 1559 (Central Region Archives, PD6/1/1, fo. 11). Thirty-one of 259 Perth burgesses required to sign their names in 1561 could do so; but this disproportionate number of illiterates is explicable since the signatories included all categories of burgesses, not merely guild brothers (Perth Museum, MS 2/1, no. 23a).

43. *Dunf. Recs.*, 45, 293; NLS, 'Huttons Collections', Adv. MS. 28.4.2, vi, fo. 258.

44. *CPL*, xii, 297.

45. Torrie, 'Thesis', 205–06.

46. *Dunf. Recs.*, 264, 266; I. B. Cowan, 'Church and society', in Brown (ed.), *Scottish Society*, 121.

47. *Dunf. Recs.*, 30, 203; GBCD, fo. 22v.

48. *GCBD*, fo. 28; *Dunf. Recs.*, 160, 275.

49. *Ibid.*, 125.

50. *Ibid.*, 138.

51. *Ibid.*, 126, 168; R. B. Dobson, 'Cathedral chapters and cathedral cities: York, Durham and Carlisle in the fifteenth century', *Northern Studies*, xxix (1983), 28.

52. *GCBD*, fo. 11v.

53. *The Booke of the Universall Kirk of Scotland* (Bann. Club, 1839), i, 375.

15

The Social and Economic Structure of the Larger Towns, 1450–1600

Michael Lynch

In the three quarters of a century after 1450 the larger Scottish towns seemingly underwent the greatest changes since their legal foundation two or three centuries before. From an early stage the government and community of the burgh had been focused on the head court and guild merchant. Yet by the reign of James III parliament had intervened to rearrange burgh elections so as to bypass the forum of the head court in which all burgesses had formerly been expected to meet. Various crafts were coming to be accorded formal and separate status as incorporated guilds by burgh courts. In Edinburgh, where these developments came earliest, the skinners, who had had their own altar in the burgh church since 1451, were incorporated in 1474; a further five crafts followed in the course of the next fifteen years and by 1523 fourteen craft guilds had been formed. Other burghs followed, if at a more modest rate; by 1540 Dundee and Perth each had nine incorporated crafts and Aberdeen and Stirling seven apiece.[1] Yet these developments, even if they ran in tandem,[2] were not intended to be innovative. Few enactments of medieval parliaments or urban establishments were. They were designed to deflect or counteract change, not to herald it.

The characteristic institutions of medieval burgh society – the single-parish burgh church, the merchant guild and the head court – remained, but they absorbed and camouflaged a complex process of change which would by 1600 transform the structure of urban society as well as the basis on which it was run. As burgh churches in many of the larger towns were granted collegiate status – St Giles' (Edinburgh) in 1466, St Mary's (Haddington) and St Nicholas (Aberdeen) in 1540[3] – and individual craft altars for each of the newly incorporated guilds were erected in them, the notion of the burgh as a single *corpus christianum* gave way to a *mélange* of civic and occupational piety. The burgh still worshipped as a community but also as a series of distinct units, a fact which would greatly complicate the spread of Protestantism, both before and after the Reformation of

261

1560.[4] The merchant guild remained as an association of merchants and employers, but the emergence of craft guilds allowed 'the best and worthiest'[5] of the craft masters closer control over quality and colleagues alike as well as reflecting the increasing – but probably still sluggish – diversification of the town economy. The head court still assembled three times a year, and in smaller burghs like the Canongate the ritual recording of absentees still had real point, even in the closing years of the sixteenth century; in larger burghs its role was fast receding as an increasing divide opened up between burgh councils and the community of burgesses they represented.

The evidence for the study of the Scottish town, although it burgeons considerably in the sixteenth century,[6] is usually too incomplete to give a detailed or all-embracing picture of urban society before the later seventeenth century. A number of technical difficulties block the construction of an occupational study of the Scottish town. The term 'merchant' embraced both overseas trader and market-based retailer, accounting, for example, for about 45% of known occupations in sixteenth-century Edinburgh, and making distinctions between distribution and merchandising difficult as well as between wholesaling and retailing.[7] Exporters and importers rarely specialised in any one commodity.[8] The crafts pose their own difficulties. Norwich had seventy-nine different trades in 1525, whereas Edinburgh, which was of comparable size, had less than twenty for most were conglomerate organisations; the hammermen, who comprised the largest of the crafts in the capital, were more than a guild of smiths and had from their date of incorporation in 1483 comprised seven different trades which included workers in leather, pewter, gold and tin, and the record does not always distinguish one from the other.[9] Burgess or freemen's rolls, which exist for some burghs from the early sixteenth century, only slowly come to give an occupation with any consistency and are seldom specific where merchants are involved. Voluminous testamentary evidence exists for the last thirty years of the sixteenth century for Edinburgh but little for the other large towns, making impossible a comparative survey of merchant probate material.[10] The merchants and members of the incorporated craft guilds together made up only about 30% of adult males in most towns of any size, and much the most intractable task confronting the historian is to analyse the remainder. Tax (or stent) rolls exist for a number of royal burghs in the sixteenth century and a batch of fourteen even exists for fifteenth-century Aberdeen, but they have severe limitations; the early Aberdeen rolls only occasionally give an occupation and those for Edinburgh list craftsmen individually only from 1583.[11] The basis for inclusion in the rolls came to be defined, at the end of the sixteenth century, as inhabitants paying £100 rent or owning 2,000 merks of moveable property. But it is unlikely that this was taken literally for it would have missed all but a small fraction of society; two-thirds of all households in Edinburgh paid less than £40 a year in rent in 1635 and nearly a third less than £10. Tax was not meant to fall on the urban poor; the crown in 1533 ordered assessors to leave untaxed 'cardsters, spinners and such other miserable persons'; and an attempt by the Aberdeen council in 1558 to force assessors to lower the tax threshold to include every inhabitant worth '£40 Scots in goods and land' provoked resignations *en bloc*.[12] The real difficulty for the historian is trying to estimate what proportion of the middling sort was taxed, as the criteria for assessment seem to have fluctuated before 1600 and indeed also appear to have varied from one burgh to another. In practice sixteenth- and seventeenth-century tax rolls probably reveal, at best, only 40% of the male working population.

There are large sections of urban society which the records rarely reach and usually underestimate when they do. Single women or widows comprised 22% of households in Edinburgh according to a unique, comprehensive survey made in 1635 but they usually accounted for no more than 7% to 10% of taxpayers.[13] The poor scarcely appear in numbers in Scottish urban records at all; the Aberdeen kirk session accounts for 1626–7, which are fuller than most, list just thirty-seven 'pensioners of the burgh' to whom regular relief was given.[14] It may be that Scotland's towns did not in the sixteenth century experience the widespread migration of rural poor as happened in some English towns, but it would be surprising if Scottish urban society did not match the figures of 30% to 40% which are conventionally taken to mark the proportions of the population at or below the poverty line in English towns, even in normal economic circumstances. The census of 1,175 poor made by the kirk session in Perth in November 1584 probably falls in line with such figures, for Perth's population is not likely to have been much above 4,500. This is, however, the only specific indicator of the severity of the problem of urban poverty in sixteenth-century Scotland. Perth was a town with a discernible pattern of plague epidemics and short-term mortality and subsistence crises, but it is unlikely to have been unique.[15] Lawyers, like the poor, conventionally evaded paying tax[16] and they, along with other elements like visiting nobles and lairds with peripatetic households, who frequented towns but were not part of the burgh community as such, leave little trace in record.

It is therefore difficult, in the absence of comprehensive data, even to be sure of the simple percentages of people in various occupations in Scottish towns before the late seventeenth century. It would be difficult to *prove* that more than 50% of the occupational population were engaged in manufacturing in any Scottish town before 1600, although it is virtually certain that this was the case in the 'craft town' of Perth, as it was in the 1690s.[17] It is, nonetheless, possible to construct a reasonable facsimile of urban society if a variety of evidence – relating to trade, tax, urban wealth and occupations – is used. The resulting picture does not always conform to the conventional view of the Scottish town, which uses the institutions of urban society – merchant guild, crafts and burgess-ship – as the sole arbiters of its structure. Various forces, both internal and external, were at work on urban society in the late medieval period and these institutions were not immune from them. Although the picture is often necessarily incomplete, it is possible to detect in most towns whether the status or wealth of certain groups, like manufacturing or service trades, was rising or falling and it is possible, albeit with caution, to highlight the position of similar groups in different burghs. The overall impression which suggests itself is that by the sixteenth century, if not before, the larger towns were coming to distance themselves from other towns in their social make-up as well as in the amount of diversification their economies had undergone since 1300. But, equally strikingly, the largest towns of all – the 'four great towns of Scotland'[18] which had emerged by the middle of the fourteenth century – also differed significantly, one from the other.

The dynamics of the changes ushered in during the reign of James III are both complex and obscure, and their effects imperfectly understood. The stream of legislation from the parliaments of the reign on burghs, beginning in 1469, had the effect of concentrating power in the hands of merchant-dominated councils now able to re-elect themselves to office with impunity. This new – or newly consolidated – monopoly of political power in the hands of the merchants, it is often argued, came into collision with the gradual emergence of the craftsmen as a distinct and increasingly disruptive voice in burgh affairs.[19] Much urban history of the late medieval period has come to concentrate on the friction between merchants and craftsmen, at the expense of noting shifts in status of one craft against another, or fluctuations in the struggle against unfree craftsmen in suburbs and satellite towns, or the unincorporated craftsmen who operated within the burgh boundaries. Tensions did exist between merchants and craftsmen: the boundaries between the activities of manufacturers and retailers of manufactures were often contentious and were reiterated in favour of merchants by an act of 1467. In Edinburgh the trade in hides and skins, which had come to take on a new importance with the fall in the wool trade, seems to have been the particular focus of attention by the burgh council.[20] There was political tension too. The legislation of 1469 had referred to 'great trouble and contention' at burgh elections, and fear of craft agitation seems to have gripped various parliaments of the 1490s. In Edinburgh 'six or eight' seats on the council were demanded in 1508 by 'a part of the craftsmen', presumably from a similar number of guilds. The 1530s and 1540s were marked in Perth by sustained agitation by the craft guilds for representation on the town council; by 1534 they had two craftsmen on the council and by 1544 a bailie as well but much of the next twenty years was taken up by efforts to consolidate their gains. By 1538 Edinburgh, too, had a pair of craftsmen sitting on its council. Yet there craft agitation for further political representation was much more subdued. It was not until the early 1580s that the capital's craftsmen pressed the question with any force and gained, through the revised burgh constitution drawn up by a royal commission in 1583, further seats for six of the craft deacons. In Aberdeen serious disputes between merchants and craftsmen belonged to the 1580s and early 1590s; in Dundee they were concentrated in the period between 1600 and 1610 and in Stirling to the decade after that.[21]

Did this amount to a deep fissure in late medieval Scottish urban society? The troubles in Perth took place in a town which had, as will be seen, a highly distinctive economy. These campaigns were not usually marked by riots but by a calculated withdrawal from the necessary business of burgh government or by an appeal to outside authority. Craftsmen took to the courts rather than the streets to seek redress. There were occasional riots in sixteenth-century Scottish burghs but these usually took the form of a protest by a single craft, usually baxters or fleshers, on a specific issue like price-fixing by burgh councils of basic foodstuffs, rather than a revolt of the artisans.[22] It is striking that, if a deep-seated rivalry between merchants and craftsmen did exist, it was not exploited in the unsettled periods provoked by the Reformation crisis of 1559–60 or the civil war which followed the deposition of Queen Mary in 1567. The one example of a concerted campaign by craftsmen in different burghs, in the mid-1550s, is deceptive. It was triggered by the act of parliament of 1555 which, like that of 1427, abolished the office of craft deacon in all burghs. The act provoked a wave of resentment which threw the government into a flurry of activity and resulted in the withdrawal of the legislation by the end of 1556. It was a characteristic of such legislation to find its justification in the alleged general nature of the dangers it sought to counteract; but in fact the act of 1555 was the work of the Edinburgh merchant lobby 'great in court at the time', just as the act of 1469 had been. The irony of the act of 1555 was that it provoked for a short time the very danger it professed to suppress.[23]

Disputes between merchants and craftsmen were localised rather than general, and sporadic rather than continuous. Half a century or more separated the craftsmen's campaign in Perth from those elsewhere. It may be the case that craft agitation – or the alarm which greeted it in parliament and the privileged circles of burgh power – seemed to peak in the last quarters of both the fifteenth and sixteenth centuries but it would be difficult to use these as the pegs on which to hang a thesis of some kind of general crisis hanging over Scottish urban society for the better part of a century and a quarter. The economic circumstances of the two periods were very different. The late fifteenth century saw a decline in overseas exports, a squeeze on merchants' profits and a concomitant shift in the economic climate in favour of urban craftsmen.[24] This was a predictable scenario for the flowering of commercial jealousies; they in turn probably helped to give extra stimulus to the demands of craftsmen in some burghs for representation on the council as those councils attempted to redress the balance of fortunes by various means. In Edinburgh the council between 1492 and 1500 extended the term of apprenticeship in the cloth trade to seven years, imposed new taxes on the drink trades, renewed its attempts to hold down both prices and wages, pursued bakers for selling imported flour and fashioned general legislation to restrict the retailing activities of skinners.[25] Yet the late sixteenth century saw a drastic change in the economic climate: the export trade was expanding, quite sharply by the 1590s; overseas merchants' activities and wealth were decidedly on the upswing. The combination of sharply rising food prices, occasional outbreaks of plague, especially in the late 1580s, and sluggish demand for manufactures had resulted in falling wage rates for many ordinary urban craftsmen and journeymen and, at best, stagnating returns for their masters.[26] The craftsmen from the metal, leather and food trades, who had in Perth been the foremost beneficiaries of the political gains of the 1530s, had to fend off the claims of rival crafts half a century later when their own economic position was slipping.[27] The craft aristocracy which had been moulded in the circumstances of the late fifteenth century was itself being refashioned and that was as much at issue in late sixteenth-century controversies as political rivalry between craftsmen and merchants.

The configuration of the craft aristocracy and the changes in it varied from town to town, and appearances can be deceptive. In Dundee the food trades, the baxters and fleshers, continued to play a prominent role in craft politics into the seventeenth century.[28] Yet both there and probably in Perth, too, prosperity was increasingly shifting to trades like the maltsters and dyers, unincorporated, without political representation and anxious to shrug off the control exercised over them by incorporated crafts. The dyers in Perth, whose entry into the merchant guild had been bitterly contested by the old-established crafts in the 1550s, were by the end of the seventeenth century the most prosperous and well-housed of all the town's commercial groups, including the merchants.[29] In Edinburgh the extra seats on the council gained in 1583 went to just six of the fourteen incorporated crafts; they were either in the service or luxury sectors, like tailors and goldsmiths, or in old-established crafts, like the skinners, whose overall position was deteriorating but where a small coterie of masters was more than holding its own as boundaries between manufacturing and retail were being redrawn to give more scope to its activities.[30] Craftsmen admitted to the merchant guild were acting more like retailers. The old rules governing servants and apprentices were tacitly being bent to suit the new breed of craftsman-employer. This was all part of the quiet and often disguised transformation of the society of the late medieval burgh which accompanied the slow diversification of its economy during the sixteenth century.

Much of the history of the medieval town can properly be explained in terms of its institutions, such as the merchant guild. It is increasingly necessary, however, from the fifteenth century onwards to take account of the differences in composition of the guild from one town to another as well as variations in its rules. It is difficult to believe that the institution of the guild operated in the same way in Aberdeen, where there were sixty-three members in 1445, and in Perth, a somewhat smaller town, where there were over a hundred in the guild in the 1450s.[31] The new craft guilds also appear much the same from one burgh to another; they had the same occupational saints, similar seals of cause and much the same general status, if judged by their position in civic ritual like the Corpus Christi procession. This impression is reinforced by the volume of apparently general legislation passed by parliament on issues affecting crafts. Yet this kind of analysis almost certainly gives too rigid a picture of the urban economy, for part of the motive for putting the guild structure on a more formal basis was to reinforce both trading monopolies and occupational specialisation in manufacturing processes which were lengthy and involved.[32] The task for the historian is to judge how successfully urban establishments managed to fashion these economic straitjackets during a period when many circumstances pointed in the opposite direction. The historian needs to exercise caution in using legislation as evidence, whether of parliament, privy council or Convention of Royal Burghs; it is easy to construct a general problem – which in fact did not exist – out of legislation which was usually passed to solve a specific or local difficulty.

Such was the 'problem' of merchant and craft conflict. Yet, viewed as a whole, Scottish urban history did not usually revolve around persistent trench warfare between the merchant and craft guilds. The problem, such as it was, was mostly confined to the larger towns, where the ruling oligarchy was widened, even if reluctantly, to accommodate the leading masters from the more prestigious crafts in the course of the period 1450–1600; but the timing and constituents of the process varied from town to town. A degree of conflict resulted, but it again varied in its seriousness from town to town. There were a series of more subtle and equally important processes going on as well: the absorption of the craft aristocracy into the urban oligarchy had the effect of widening still further the gap between rulers and ruled, masters and servants. The divide between the overseas merchants and the middling sort, the humble retailers, who usually did not belong to the merchant guild and who were probably coming to specialise in one commodity, was widening. A gap was also opening amongst the craftsmen between the service and manufacturing sectors of the economy and, to a lesser extent, between different parts of the food and drink trades. The line between wholesaler and retailer was being redrawn, as was the ranking of the hierarchy of crafts.[33]

It is common for medieval historians to talk of 'the Scottish burgh', for both royal founding charters and the two sets of regulations laid down in the twelfth and thirteenth centuries, the *Burgh Laws* and the *Statutes of the Guild,* had presumed and regulated a common pattern of activity in the king's newly created burghs. Yet it is likely that minor specialisations existed, even at this early stage, beyond the three basic groups of trades – food and drink, clothing and building.[34] This process must have been accelerated by the end of the thirteenth century with the virtual collapse of the wool trade on which the bulk of burghs, situated on the North Sea trading route to Flanders, depended. So it is increasingly important, from 1300 onwards, to try to accommodate the likelihood, despite the paucity of evidence, that various circumstances combined to encourage different towns to diversify their economies to some extent. By 1450 it is possible to identify these economic circumstances more clearly, although quantitative data as to the numbers in each sector of the urban economy seldom materialises until at least a century later.

The 'four great towns of Scotland' recognised by the Bruges staple after the fall of Berwick – Edinburgh, Aberdeen, Perth and Dundee – remained the leading towns for more than three centuries. In the 1370s their combined share of customs revenue, the vast bulk of which still came from wool, was 58%; by the 1590s, when customs were derived from a much wider range of commodities exported, it was 80%. Almost half of the remaining 42% of customs revenue in the 1370s was paid by four other towns – Linlithgow, Haddington, Lanark and Montrose. By the 1590s the composition of the exporting towns ranking 5th to 8th had changed – they were now Haddington, Montrose, Dumbarton and the group of Fife ports around Pittenweem – and their overall share had shrunk to rather less than 10%.[35] Yet if the four largest towns had consolidated their position over the course of this period, they had done so in rather different ways. This is clearly revealed by the sixteenth century, when data for the percentage of national taxation paid by each burgh, which was calculated on a broader base than income derived from the export trade, becomes available to set against the statistics derived from customs revenue. Set against each other, the two sources reveal quite tellingly the difference between the four largest towns.

Table 1. Customs revenue and burgh taxation, 1460–1599[36]

	Edinburgh	*Dundee*	*Aberdeen*	*Perth*
Average customs revenue, 1460–1599	59.39%	6.45%	11.73%	2.86%
Average of total burgh taxation, 1535–1594	26.81%	11.54%	9.02%	6.9%

Much the most obvious of the patterns which had set in from the fourteenth century onwards were the slightness of the impact of Perth on the export trade and the growing stranglehold exercised by Edinburgh over most sectors of it. Edinburgh had 32% of the wool trade in the 1370s and 71% by the 1490s and, a century later, monopolised it. But this was an increasing grip over a trade which was in steepening decline after 1400. The absolute volume of the trade in both woolfells and hides also contracted in the course of the fifteenth century, but in the course of recovery in the first half of the sixteenth century they too came to be concentrated in Edinburgh, especially from the 1520s onwards. In the 1460s Edinburgh's share of the trade in hides was 28% but by the 1590s it was 83%, and Dundee was the only other town to have a significant stake in it. By the late 1590s Edinburgh also had 80% of the trade in fells, with the bulk of the remainder being shared, in a ratio of about three to two, between Aberdeen and Dundee. By contrast, Dundee exported almost four times the value of woollen cloth of Aberdeen, although both were badly affected by the collapse in the Baltic market after 1570; Edinburgh, nonetheless, had 76% of what was generally an expanding trade by the end of the sixteenth century.[37] The details of the customs returns are complex, indicating different patterns for different commodities, but their overall picture is unmistakable. Edinburgh's ability to exercise a near-monopoly in most staple commodities indicates an appreciable broadening of its base as a reception centre – and perhaps also as a finishing centre. In 1478–9 nearly 90% of its customs returns were made up of wool, hides and woolfells; by the end of the sixteenth century it had considerably extended the range of exports, capturing a share, somewhere between 25% and 30%, of the rising trade in fish and salt, and more than 65% of that in coal.[38]

Dundee had the most volatile history of the four: it had to weather the loss of its share in the wool trade in the fourteenth and early fifteenth centuries by developing interests in the trade in coarse woollen cloth, fish, hides and skins, but the sixteenth century would see, largely as a result of a reduction in parts of the Baltic trade, a drop in Dundee's share of the trade in hides and skins as well as inroads being made, especially by Edinburgh, into its other spheres of interest.[39] The shifting sands of sixteenth-century overseas trade seem to have affected Dundee more than the other large towns; it alone of the four saw its tax payments both rise and fall appreciably in the course of the century, lifting quite sharply after 1535 but dropping in the 1570s, although they ended the century above what they had been in 1535. Aberdeen, by contrast, had a more even passage through the century: its tax returns remained stable until a slight drop in the 1590s, reflecting its unrivalled position as a provincial centre which allowed it to retain or increase its share of inland trade and remain in contact with the rural craftsmen in its hinterland as well as its ability to maintain its 40% share of the lucrative export trade in salmon.[40]

The customs returns tell one story and in some respects the tax returns tell another. What is striking is the point at which they differ. The sixteenth century saw a series of changes in the destinations of the overseas trade, rises and falls in the volume of exports and shifts in the commodities traded. Yet, for the four largest towns at least, the tax returns reflect little of this – in distinct contrast to middling towns, many of which, from the evidence of the tax rolls, seem to have followed a recurrent course of short-term crisis and recovery. It was small to middling ports, too, which, like Dysart or Pittenweem, showed the most striking rise in activity.[41] This would seem to indicate two points about the larger burghs which are to some degree paradoxical. Their natural position – as administrative centres and regional as well as local market places – gave them a broad economic structure with a base in the food, drink and clothing trades which was not easily affected by temporary shifts in trade patterns or even, as the case of Perth indicates, by short-term demographic or natural setbacks, like plague or local bad harvests. But the fact that the other three large towns managed to survive the successive inroads made by Edinburgh into different sectors of overseas trade may point to some growth in inland trade as well as to a degree of specialisation, either in inland trade or in urban handicrafts, which gave each of them a rather different character.[42]

There are few precise indicators of the occupational structure of the burghs of Perth and Dundee although it is clear that they were very different towns. Perth was self-confessedly a 'craft town', where the craftsmen claimed to pay as much taxation as the merchants, whereas in Dundee, it may be deduced from a half-complete assessment of 1588, the incorporated crafts paid 27% of all tax, and the unincorporated dyers and maltmen a further 14.7% between them, leaving the mariners with 20% and the merchants with a little under 40%.[43] Perth had probably begun to lose much of its share of the wool trade to Dundee before 1320, and by the sixteenth century, as the Tay silted up, it was in a real sense a good deal further from the sea than it had been in the fourteenth. By 1560 Perth's craftsmen were able to claim that it, as a 'dry town' which was 'far from the sea', was not like other 'merchant towns' in Scotland. The picture of its merchant community drawn by the craftsmen during their political campaign in the 1550s as 'dry' or inland merchants, largely made up of chapmen, hucksters, carters, fish buyers and stablers, is overdrawn but not too misleading. The limited evidence of testamentary wealth which survives suggests a much narrower differential between merchants and craftsmen than in other large towns. There was a correspondingly higher proportion of craft masters in the merchant guildry: 44% of entrants in the late 1560s were craftsmen, whereas in Edinburgh in the 1560s the proportion was 14%. The result was a distinct blurring in Perth of the traditional boundaries between craftsmen manufacturers and merchant retailers; the craft documents even talk of 'merchant craftsmen', especially amongst the leading trades, metal workers, goldsmiths, baxters and skinners.[44]

Perth falls into a pattern which was common enough in England but rare in Scotland where most of the leading towns depended on direct access to the North Sea trade routes: it was pre-eminently an inland town dominated by its manufacturing trades.[45] These served both its own population, which was probably growing at a modest rate in the sixteenth century, and a rural hinterland which extended beyond the sheriffdom. The hammermen, who were the largest craft in the burgh, made domestic utensils largely for the home market and agricultural implements for customers as far away as Inverness and Kincardine, as well as for the local market which naturally lay within fifteen miles' range. Few of its handicrafts were destined for an international market for, in distinct contrast to its neighbour at the mouth of the Tay, the documentary and physical evidence of the presence of a textile industry, as distinct from finishing trades, is slight. Its leather craft also seems to have had wide marketing: there were complaints from Edinburgh's skinners in 1558 that Perth craftsmen were selling 'made work' in the capital. Some of its bakers were probably really wholesalers in grain and flour supplying noble households as well as ordinary rural demand; one Perth baxter was owed £200 by the widow of Lord Ruthven. In Edinburgh the regulations governing bakers were much stricter; they could import flour for baking but were forbidden to sell surpluses.[46] So Perth was a manufacturing centre which had a social make-up unlike other large Scottish towns, except perhaps Glasgow, where the specialisms were in some respects different and the population still rather smaller, but it too should in the sixteenth century still be considered as an inland town.[47] Both were to some extent immune to the shifts in foreign trade and accordingly prospered modestly.

Perth had as yet little of a textile industry, in contrast to both its neighbours, Stirling and Dundee, where output was geared to an international market, mostly in the Baltic, as well as a local or regional one.[48] There was probably a greater concentration in Dundee of both cloth manufacturing and the finishing processes than in any other town, although it is impossible to say, here or elsewhere, how much of the lengthy, preliminary processes of carding and spinning, which usually involved as much labour as actual manufacture, was carried out within the town.[49] This was the kind of workforce, often female and invariably poor, that never surfaces either in burgess rolls or tax assessments. Dundee's main rival as a cloth centre was Edinburgh, although weavers and waulkers made up a modest proportion of the capital's overall workforce. It is difficult to know how effective was the attempt made by the Edinburgh council in 1530 to restrict carding to a domestic industry within the town limits but by the second half of the century much of the capital's textile workforce had, to judge from the declining numbers on its tax rolls, migrated to the suburbs (see Table 2). Yet the dyers seem to have remained, increasing in wealth rather than numbers, so that by 1635 the finishing process was controlled by a handful of entrepreneurs. It is impossible to say how many dyers there were in Dundee but their tax assessment – 6.67% of all taxation – was proportionately higher than that on any single craft in the capital, including even its boom industry of tailoring.[50] Dundee was thus a port where one-fifth of its taxation stemmed from those directly connected with the sea but the remainder was split fairly evenly between merchandising and manufacturing. This may help to explain why its overall tax assessment (see Table 1) was so much higher than its percentage of customs revenue derived from exports. It had two specialisms beyond its natural status as a centre of large consumption: it was a manufacturing centre of coarse woollen cloth and an overseas exporter, particularly to the Baltic, of cloth, together with hides, skins and fish.[51] This gave it a narrower manufacturing base than Perth and a more restricted interest in overseas trade than Edinburgh; both elements probably combined to cause its chequered economic performance in the sixteenth century.

More detailed material, derived from burgess and tax rolls, exists for an analysis of Edinburgh and Aberdeen. The economy of both was undoubtedly dominated by retailing and distribution rather than manufacturing, but they were in many respects very different towns. Their respective merchant communities were superficially similar in outline; Aberdeen had some 350 in its merchant guildry in the early seventeenth century and Edinburgh had about 400 merchants in the 1580s. But only seventy-five in the Aberdeen guildry were overseas traders whereas in Edinburgh it has been estimated, on the basis of a sample of testaments, that some 43% of merchants had an interest in overseas trade.[52] There were no less than 175 exporters of skins and 192 in hides out of the port of Leith in 1561–3. Many of the Aberdeen exporters specialised in cloth but as yet few Edinburgh merchants, big or small, specialised in the export of a single staple commodity; the largest exporter of hides held just 4% of the market.[53] The merchant princes of the capital together controlled only 40% of the overseas trade in staple commodities in the early seventeenth century; they were turning to new avenues of trade, and especially to grain, to make their real profits.[54] There were three basic differences between the two merchant communities: Aberdeen had rather more merchants than the capital, relative to its population size (see Table 2);[55] there was, not surprisingly, a far greater concentration of wealth at the top of the mercantile elite in Edinburgh;[56] and there was also a marked difference in both the wealth and the activities of the middling sort. In Aberdeen this group, constituting the bulk of the burgesses of guild, were local traders; but in the capital the middling sort, who included many small retailers or cramers who were *not* in the guildry, made a useful sideline out of the concentration of the export trade through Leith. In Aberdeen the boundary between inland and overseas trade was much more clearly drawn despite the fact that more of its merchants were in the guildry. Appearances belie reality: there were more merchants in the guildry in Aberdeen but fewer actually operating in trade overseas; there were fewer in the Edinburgh guildry but more, both inside and outside it, involved in the export trade.

The bulk of Aberdeen merchants consisted of small men who swamped the merchant guild and drew on inland trade with the network of market centres and smaller towns in the shire for their livelihood. Its ruling patriciate was largely made up, not of overseas merchants, but merchant lairds whose families had over the course of centuries laid down roots in the rural hinterland, both by intermarriage with the gentry and by direct investment in landed estates.[57] The major issue in burgh politics was not a conflict between merchants and craftsmen but the relationship between town and country, which could raise itself in a number of forms. By the 1590s there were complaints that too many small merchants had been allowed into the guildry, which threatened to ruin the town's prosperity.

The overseas merchants had reacted by transferring their activities for part of the year to other ports, especially Leith and Dundee, leaving the burgh 'a dry pond'. It was a coalition of the disaffected – overseas merchants, and unenfranchised lawyers as well as craftsmen – which combined to form the nucleus of the opposition to the entrenched ruling oligarchy in the early 1590s.[58]

The differences between the manufacturing sectors of the two towns is more simply illustrated.

Table 2. Numbers of craftsmen and merchants in Glasgow, Aberdeen and Edinburgh[59]

Craft	Glasgow 1605	Aberdeen 1637	Edinburgh 1558 Masters	Edinburgh 1558 Servants	Edinburgh 1583	Edinburgh 1634
Tailors	65	14	81	72	116	134
Maltsters	55	3	(13)	(8)	(37)	(18)
Cordiners	50	13	41	8	29	31
Weavers	30	24	13	13	20	9
Hammermen	27	10	66	85	52	42
Baxters	27	11	45	55	55	38
Coopers	23	6	—	—	9	—
Skinners	21	3	42	21	60	46
Wrights	21	14	—	—	19	29
Fleshers	17	8	—	—	40	24
Masons	11	3	—	—	13	12
Bonnetmakers	7	—	14	39	8	7
Dyers	5	6	(8)	(11)	(11)	(11)
Surgeons	2	—	15	10	15	12
Goldsmiths	—	1	14	6	19	14
Candlemakers	—	1	—	—	(18)	(11)
Waulkers	—	—	38	5	6	4
Furriers	—	—	9	—	3	—
Others	—	10	—	—		
Craftsmen	361	127	399 masters	333 servants	530	602
Merchants	213	c370	285 masters (def.)	411 servants (def.)	414 (including 44 widows)	613

Just as Aberdeen had proportionately more merchants than Edinburgh, so it had distinctly fewer craftsmen. Both the documentary record and physical remains indicate that Aberdeen had few developed manufacturing industries; although few traces of large-scale smithies have been found in any Scottish medieval town, the small number from the metal trades listed in tax rolls distinguishes Aberdeen from both Perth and Edinburgh. Surprisingly few are found in the various branches of the leather trade in Aberdeen too, although it is possible that those involved in tanning were either located in the suburbs or too poor to pay taxation.[60] There was, from this evidence at least, no particular concentration of craftsmen in any one quarter of the burgh, except for a colony of fourteen weavers in the Green; but the dyers lived elsewhere. It is clear that by the middle of the seventeenth century much of the plaiding which was exported out of Aberdeen was made in the network of small towns around it rather than in the burgh itself;[61] but, in the absence of specific evidence, it is not possible to say whether the numbers of weavers based in Aberdeen itself were declining, as they were in Edinburgh, or whether most textile work had long been put out to rural industry. The overall picture of Aberdeen's manufacturing sector shows a markedly restricted economy, which must have depended to a far greater extent than the other large burghs on its hinterland for a range of products. It was also clearly not the same kind of market centre as Perth, which supplied a wide range of manufactured products to its hinterland.

Perth and Aberdeen were two towns which, on the face of it, were similar – provincial centres, the seats of sheriffdoms and of roughly comparable size; but town and country interacted rather differently. Also in both, much the same hierarchy of crafts existed; the hammermen were the most prestigious guild in Perth and they had pride of place in Aberdeen in civic ritual. Yet this resulted from the fact that both towns copied 'the example of Edinburgh', which had in its turn imported much of its civic religious ritual from the Bruges staple at the time of craft incorporation.[62] There is real danger in assuming that crafts had the same importance in different urban economies merely because they had similar constitutions or saints.

It was in Edinburgh that the process of incorporation of crafts was first begun and the capital had rather more craft guilds – and consequently a more elaborate web of controls over its economy – than any other town. It also had more markets; there were six in sixteenth-century Stirling but no less than fifteen in different parts of Edinburgh as early as 1477, some held on two or three different days of the week. These brought attendant social problems; the meal market was moved away from the High Street in 1541 because of the 'multitude of ... miserable creatures' who thronged the street daily to make their living.[63] The authorities were equally worried by the encroachment of suburban craftsmen threatening the monopoly of the burgh's guilds but uncertain how to deal with them. They oscillated from a policy of outright prohibition, banning them from the market place, to one of licensed control, admitting them to burgess-ship.[64] The suburbs seem to have particularly attracted workers in the textile and clothing trades and the capital turned both to parliament and the Convention of Royal Burghs to seek a remedy. It seems, from the outright drop of both weavers and waulkers in the closing years of the sixteenth century, that there was an unchecked flight to the suburbs of certain crafts.[65]

The reasons for the drop in numbers of other crafts, such as the skinners and fleshers, may be more complicated. These were trades where a closer job description is necessary. The range of activity of a craftsman was potentially wide: he could be no more than a workman, perhaps with a single apprentice or servant; he could, in a slightly larger workshop, act more like a foreman or, if he was admitted to the merchant guildry, he would act as an employer who did not himself work with his hands; the precise amount of retail business permitted varied from craft to craft and also, it seems, to some extent from town to town; and lastly, the doors of the guildry might open up new avenues in trade, either in the commodity with which he was associated, or in others. Fleshers could be more concerned with the hide than the carcass, skinners more interested in the profits to be made from dealing in skins and hides rather than in supplying them to other parts of the leather trade.[66] Amongst the 278 exporters of hides and skins out of Leith in 1561–3 there were sixteen skinners, fully a third of the masters in that craft, as well as five furriers and nine fleshers; oddly enough, there was also a baxter and a tailor.[67] So the drop in numbers of both skinners and fleshers after 1583 is likely to have been caused by a fall in their share of overseas trade.

This impression is confirmed by the evidence of the proportionate income of each craft, based on a number of sixteenth-century tax rolls. The income of skinners and fleshers fell by nearly a half in the twenty years after 1565, which coincides with the drop in the Baltic trade in skins and hides.[68]

Table 3. Percentage tax payments of Edinburgh incorporated crafts, 1565–83[69]

Craft	1565	pre-1574	1574	1583
Skinners & Furriers	22.8	18	20.07	12.12 (11.89 & 0.23)
Baxters	15.59	17.62	13.02	11.09
Fleshers	14.1	13.12	9	7.03
Tailors	12.62	14.27	18.07	25.77
Hammermen	11.13	13.27	13.27	11.62
Wrights & Masons	7.05	7.14	8.17	5.84 (4.45 & 1.39)
Cordiners	5.94	6.67	6.67	4.85
Goldsmiths	4.47	4.56	6	13.69
Barbers & Surgeons	3.33	3.06	3.06	3.65
Websters, Waulkers & Bonnetmakers	2.97	2.67	2.67	4.34 (1.49, 1.39 & 1.46)

These figures also reveal the declining fortunes of another of the town's oldest incorporations, the baxters. The regular setting of bread prices had been a feature of burgh council controls since the early fifteenth century but was more damaging a century later, in a period of accelerating price inflation.[70]

In 1583, as part of the re-ordering of the burgh constitution, Edinburgh's craftsmen were assessed individually for tax rather than each craft paying a fixed quota. These individual returns reveal the composition of the craft aristocracy, which claimed the new seats on the town council awarded to the craftsmen in 1583 and paid more appropriate sums for their newly-won privileges. A half of this aristocracy, as measured by their tax returns, consisted of tailors. They were accompanied by goldsmiths and surgeons, whose status was in process of being transformed in the later sixteenth century, as well as by a few skinners, cordiners and wrights, together with masters from the more skilled sections of metal working, such as the cutlers, saddlers and pewterers. The craft hierarchy established in the late fifteenth century had been transformed in the rather different circumstances of the late sixteenth century. Wealth accrued to three kinds of occupations, in Edinburgh and elsewhere: where the master craftsman was able to take greater control of the lengthy process of manufacture or processing; where craftsmen could most easily turn into retailer or even exporter; and in those trades, like tailoring and goldsmithing, which were most likely to benefit from a growing, more sophisticated market. Correspondingly, other craft occupations which did not meet these criteria saw declining profits, real falls in wages and, in some cases, a flight from the urban environment to effect lower costs of production.[71]

Yet there are clearly substantial parts of the urban economy which tax rolls never reach; their most serious deficiencies lie in the domestic-based industries largely staffed by female labour such as brewing and, where it existed, in the preliminary processes of the textile industry. The fifteenth-century Aberdeen rolls, which variously list between 290 and 445 taxpayers, have always a certain percentage of women but it rarely exceeds 10%; equally, the 1637 roll, which has 569 entries, has only 51 women on it.[72] Yet occasional censuses do exist for the brewing industry, which was subjected to close council control: 157 brewers, evenly spread around the town and 80% of them wives of burgesses, were listed in Aberdeen in 1509; 288 were made to find sureties in Edinburgh in 1530, the vast bulk of them again burgess wives or widows, but here 45% of them were concentrated in the south-eastern quarter.[73] Such information simply does not exist for other domestic industries but it was the usual policy of burgh councils to try to restrict the ancillary parts of the town economy to the households of freemen; the Edinburgh council ordered that carding and spinning should be done only by widows and 'failed householders' and it deplored the habit of female domestic servants setting up in separate households and supporting themselves through brewing or selling foodstuffs.[74] Burgh councils feared masterless women as well as masterless men.

Neither a study of tax rolls nor of guild material readily reveals another vagary of the occupational structure of Scottish towns – the likelihood that the lower down urban society, the more frequent was the resort of both men and women to more than one means of earning a living. There are a number of examples in the Edinburgh tax roll of 1583 of tailors and cordiners from the lowest end of the crafts earning part of their income from brewing. There is in the Stirling records a case of a baxter illicitly weaving coloured cloth as well as numerous entries, which could be duplicated elsewhere, of all sorts of craftsmen and merchants and their wives infringing the *Burgh Laws* by buying and selling, particularly in foodstuffs and drink.[75] Both the proximity of the rural hinterland and the diversity of most manufacturing processes made inevitable widespread evasion of market regulations which were largely unchanged since their introduction in the twelfth century.

The other serious breach in the *Burgh Laws* came with the development of larger-scale workshops. Bakers were restricted to three servants but an Edinburgh muster roll of 1558 gives details of ten bakehouses; six of them had between six and nine workers.[76] There were other means of evasion of the letter of the *Laws*. Edinburgh tailors were in the 1580s criticised for employing workmen in the guise of fee'd servants.[77] Middlemen could employ unlimited rural labour on a contractual basis. Almost certainly the links between town and country were closer than has usually been supposed yet this was, by its very nature, a two-way process. The ways by which the town reached out into the countryside have yet to be fully explored. The development of manufactories properly belongs to the seventeenth century,[78] but much of it was likely to have been an extension or rationalisation of a system of putting-out which had gone on for some time before. Most of the early manufactories were located near Edinburgh or financed by Edinburgh merchant capital. Edinburgh merchants had greater investments in salting and coal mining – the raw materials of a number of manufacturing processes – than has hitherto been suspected.[79]

The other major deficiency of sixteenth-century tax rolls, which is particularly serious for Edinburgh, is that they usually give no indication of the size or wealth of the professional classes. Lawyers were exempt from taxation throughout this period; they appear on some tax rolls after 1630 but only in so far as they were engaged in other activities, such as moneylending or trading.[80] The evidence available for seventeenth-century Edinburgh indicates that the professions were the fastest-growing sector of society; in 1635 they made up 8% of all households and by the 1690s this figure had almost doubled. The evidence before 1600 is scarce but revealing. A voluntary contribution list was drawn up in 1565, which included thirty-one lawyers as well as the fourteen crafts and 357 merchants. The lawyers' assessment amounted to 85% of the tax paid by all the town's 400 craftsmen and 27.5% of the total levied on the merchants.[81] The lawyers already belonged amongst the upper reaches of the burgh establishment; Edinburgh was already rather more than a merchants' town.

The conclusions to be drawn from detailed study of the 'four great towns' of late medieval Scotland underline how far each by 1600 had progressed from the norm of towns which until 1300 must largely have been dedicated to the wool trade. And each had since then gone its separate way. The most important factor in determining the markedly different shapes of the major Scottish towns was the distinctive pattern of Scottish overseas trade after the slump in the wool trade and the increasingly central role taken by Edinburgh in it. Yet it was probably only in the sixteenth century that Edinburgh underwent significant population increase to match its economic role. By 1560 it had about 12,500 within its walls and by 1635 this had increased to somewhere over 20,000. This was, of course, nothing like the phenomenal rate of growth of London in the same period or the differential which marked it out from provincial towns like York or Norwich, which were by 1600 less than a tenth of the size of the capital. Edinburgh was certainly no more than three times the size of any of the three other towns discussed here.[82] Yet, because of the marked tendency of the export trade to funnel itself through its port of Leith, the Scottish capital exercised something like the same kind of influence over the other east coast burghs, both large and small, at least until the growth of Glasgow's overseas trade after 1650s. It is possible to demonstrate, from late seventeenth-century evidence, how the economy of the capital affected the structure of the smaller towns, like Dalkeith or Musselburgh, which lay within a twenty-mile radius of it.[83] It is likely that that had already begun to happen much earlier. However, there is some evidence from before 1600 to demonstrate the capital's effects on larger towns.[84] Overseas merchants from Aberdeen were beginning to base themselves in Leith for part of the year in the 1590s. It is likely that Dundee was another port which felt the same kind of squeeze. Leith was fast becoming the entrepôt for the bulk of Scottish shipping and Edinburgh the mecca for both the export and import trade in most commodities. The beneficiaries were not only the capital's merchant princes but also a significant proportion of its middling sort. This marked them out from the middling sort of traders in other ports who were often in difficulties, as well as from those who were solely dependent

K

on handicrafts, where profits had been stagnant and real wages falling since the 1570s.[85]

The changing winds of Scottish overseas trade provide one explanation of the changes in the structure of the large towns. Another is provided by the shifting boundaries between town and country which were becoming increasingly obvious by the 1590s. Until now historians have tended to emphasise the threat to the royal burghs posed by burghs of barony.[86] The threat certainly existed in a real form by the late sixteenth century. Yet towns were already trying to respond to it in a variety of ways: by greater investment in farming of livestock for the urban market;[87] by a certain amount of investment, which may have been confined to Edinburgh merchants, in coal and salt works; by putting out parts of some manufacturing processes; and by taking firmer control of their suburbs. These were complex patterns and they affected no two towns in the same way.

A third reason for the underlying differences in the structure of many towns stemmed from the fluctuating boundaries between wholesale and retail, and in the varying access to the export trade. All these considerations point to the limitations involved in trying to analyse urban societies in the process of change with the traditional blunt instruments. The study of burgh institutions and the terminology of merchants and craftsmen lend a misleading uniformity to Scottish urban society. There was no general struggle between merchants and craftsmen. The most that can be said is that at various times different groupings of craftsmen vied with different kinds of merchants in rather different towns. At other times these craftsmen tried to hold off the demands of other craftsmen who did not enjoy the same privileges as themselves; in Perth the hammermen, baxters and skinners, who had gained power in the 1540s, tried to resist the claims of the other crafts in the 1580s.[88] The certainties, enshrined in late medieval parliamentary and burgh legislation, of who in burgh society constituted 'the best and worthiest' amongst the craft masters, were under review. The merchant guild was itself a rather different institution in these four towns in terms of membership. It was rarely, as is often thought, an exclusive merchants' club. It was increasingly an organisation of employers and wholesalers.

The changes in the status of various groups in burgh society and in the minutiae which regulated their working lives are signs of a more fundamental reshaping of the larger Scottish towns in the closing decades of the sixteenth century. With the increase in populations of towns many of the traditional ways by which the burgh community had been organised and governed since their foundations were being abandoned. The mechanism of the head court, which had been sidestepped by the act of

1469 allowing burgh councils to conduct elections, was progressively abandoned. The old principle which had associated burgess-ship with the ownership of a toft or tenement was virtually irrelevant by the sixteenth century; taxation could be based on income as well as ownership of property. Much of the conduct of burgh government was carried on in secret, conducted by increasingly oligarchical bodies which met behind closed doors, either in the council chamber or the kirk session.[89] Yet there was a real reappraisal of the community of the burgh in the late sixteenth century and much of it was performed by the reformed church. The 1580s and 1590s saw censuses of both adult communicants and the poor undertaken in Edinburgh, Perth and Aberdeen. Real attempts were made to re-establish a *corpus christianum* in the form of model urban parishes. That meant ending the historic link between the burgh community and the single burgh church. The reformers aimed at eight parishes in Edinburgh, each with a thousand adult communicants; they settled in 1598 for four. Both Glasgow and Aberdeen were split – at first into two parishes. And in Aberdeen the ministers drew lots to decide their parishes.[90] If there was a single moment which marked the end of the medieval burgh community, it was this.

NOTES

1. J. D. Marwick, *Edinburgh Guilds and Crafts* (Edinburgh, 1909), 47–73; E. Bain, *Merchant and Craft Guilds: a History of the Aberdeen Incorporated Trades* (Aberdeen, 1887), 308; Murray, *Early Burgh Organisation*, i, 359; Verschuur, 'Thesis', 152, 260; *Stirling Recs., 1519–1666*, 274–7.

2. See Dickinson & Duncan, *Scotland*, 285; Lythe, 'Economic life', 72.

3. Cowan & Easson, *Medieval Religious Houses*, 213–28.

4. Lynch, *Edinburgh*, 28–9, 216.

5. The same phrase was used in the act of 1487 and Edinburgh's revised consistution of 1583 (*APS*, ii, 178; *Edin. Recs.*, iv, 267); see Lynch, 'Whatever happened to the medieval burgh?', 14, 19n.

6. See Flett and Cripps, Ch.2, above.

7. Lynch, *Edinburgh*, 10, 51–2; cf. Patten, 'Urban occupations in pre-industrial England', 302.

8. Lynch, *Edinburgh*, 52; Brown, 'Thesis', 33–4, 113–24. Some Aberdeen merchants specialised in cloth export (Macniven, 'Thesis' 114, 145).

9. J. F. Pound, 'The social and trade structure of Norwich, 1525–1575, *Past & Present*, xxxiv (1966), 55; *Edin. Recs.*, i, 47–9. A sixteenth-century English observer also pointed to the comparatively small number of handicraft occupations in Scotland (*CSP Scot.*, xii, no. 906).

10. See Sanderson, 'The Edinburgh merchants in society, 1570–1603', 183–99. A limited amount of testamentary evidence exists for Perth; see Verschuur, 'Thesis', 142–4.

11. Lynch, *Edinburgh*, 10; the Edinburgh 1583 tax roll is printed in *ibid.*, 378–92. Fourteen tax rolls are recorded in ACA, CR, vols. iv, v(i), vi, for the period 1448–72; an earlier roll, of 1408, is printed in *Abdn. Chrs.*, 312–17.

12. *APS*, iv, 141–2; the Edinburgh census of c.4,000 households, made in an annuity tax roll of 1635, is analysed by W. H. Makey, 'Edinburgh in mid-seventeenth century', in Lynch, *Early Modern Town*, 206–15; Edinburgh had 1,245 taxpayers in 1583 but an estimated 8,000 adult communicants (Lynch, 'Whatever happened', 7). *Acts of Council*, 399; *Abdn. Counc.*, i, 309; ACA, CR, xxii, 704.

13. ECA, MS Annuity Tax Roll (1635); I am grateful to Dr. Makey for this point. Women accounted for 6.67% of the Edinburgh taxpayers in 1583, 10.5% of Aberdeen's in 1623 and 8.96% in 1637 (Macniven, 'Thesis', 101; ACA, MS Stent Rolls, 1596–). A survey, probably of householders, made in Stirling c.1550 had 18.7% (*Scottish Antiquary*, vi (1892) 175–8).

14. ACA, MS Kirk Session Accts (1602–1705), 'The collection book of the session of New Aberdeen for 1627'; they were paid £424 3s 4d *pa*.

15. P. Clark (ed.), *Country Towns in pre-industrial England* (Leicester, 1981), 10, 54–64; Patten, 'Urban occupations', 297; cf. Wormald, *Scotland*, 46. NLS, Advocates MSS 31.1.1, Perth Kirk Session Recs., 23 Nov., 14 Dec. 1584; 1660 loaves per week was the extent of the relief. See below, n. 82, for Perth's population and Spearman, Ch. 3, above; see also M. Flinn (ed.), *Scottish Population History* (Cambridge, 1977), 109.

16. Lynch, *Edinburgh*, 35; Macniven, 'Thesis', 101.

17. In the 1690s, according to the poll tax, 63.5% of Perth's workforce was engaged in manufacturing, but only 36% of Edinburgh's and 28.7% of Aberdeen's (I. D. Whyte, 'The occupational structure of Scottish burghs in the late seventeenth century', in Lynch, *Early Modern Town*, 224). This description of Perth, made c.1560, is one of a series of documents drawn up for the burgh's craftsmen (Perth Museum and Art Gallery, MS Convener Court Book [CB], no. 34), and reproduced in Verschuur, 'Thesis'. Cf. N. Goose, 'English pre-industrial urban economies', *Urban History Yearbook* (1982), 25; J. Langton, 'Industry and towns, 1500–1730', in *An Historical Geography of England and Wales*, ed. R. A. Dodgshon & R. A. Butlin (London, 1978), 185.

18. *HUB*, iii, no. 131.

19. See Lythe, 'Economic life', 71; Dickinson & Duncan, *Scotland*, 284–9.

20. *APS*, ii, 86; *Edin. Recs.*, i, 86–7.

21. *APS*, ii, 95, 226–7, 234, 238; *Edin. Recs.*, i, 118; iv, 268–9, 275; Verschuur, 'Thesis', 264, 366–7. There are a number of early sixteenth-century lists reproduced in an appendix to *Edin. Recs.*, iii, which purport to be council lists and have craftsmen on them; these were, however, craft deacons attending meetings where the common good was at issue and are not lists of councillors as such. The list for 1538–9 (*ibid.*, ii, 93; iii, 295) is, however, a council and includes a skinner, Wm. Loch, and tailor, Andrew Edgar. The claim that craftsmen were on the council as early as 1508 mistakes the 'great council of the town' for the burgh council (Nicholson, *Scotland*, 564).

22. Lynch, 'Whatever happened', 15–16.

23. *APS*, ii, 14, 497–8; CB, no. 34; Verschuur, 'Thesis', 404–08, 426–8; Lynch, *Edinburgh*, 71–3; cf. Dickinson & Duncan, *Scotland*, 288.

24. Grant, *Scotland*, 85–6; Stevenson, 'Thesis', pp. iv, 262–3; Murray, *Early Burgh Organization*, i, 346.

25. *Edin. Recs.*, i, 65, 67, 82, 86–7. Cf. Reynolds, *English Towns*, 182.

26. S. G. E. Lythe, *The Economy of Scotland in its European Setting, 1550–1625* (Edinburgh, 1960), 30, 113–4, 248, 251–2; Guy, 'Thesis', 173.

27. Verschuur, 'Thesis,' 262–4, 276.

28. *RPC*, vii, 94–100, 551–2, 585, 735–7.

29. CB, no. 34; Flinn, *Population History*, 194.

30. Lynch, *Edinburgh*, 53.

31. ACA, CR, v(2), 651. I am grateful to Marion Stavert, who is preparing an edition of the Perth Guildry Book for the SRS, for this information. It is difficult to be sure of numbers in the Edinburgh guildry before 1520; 200 were admitted 1521–40, and 336 in 1551–70. See also Introduction, Ch.1, above.

32. L. A. Clarkson, *The Pre-industrial Economy in England, 1500– 1750* (London, 1971), 99–100, 103; Spearman, Ch. 8, above.

33. Lynch, *Edinburgh*, 64; Sanderson, 'Edinburgh merchants', 194–5; cf. Patten, 'Urban occupations', 302–04, 311; Langton, 'Industry and towns', 182–4; Clarkson, *Economy*, 104.

34. Goose, 'Urban economies', 34; Langton, 'Industry and towns', 185.

35. Stevenson, 'Thesis', 228n; Guy, 'Thesis', 20.

36. Guy, 'Thesis', Tables 1a–1d. The average of burgh taxation is calculated from ten taxes, 1535–1594, printed in *Burghs Convention Recs*, i. Customs returns 1500–99 and tax assessments 1535–1707 for individual burghs are tabulated in M. Lynch, 'Continuity and change in urban society', in R. A. Houston and I. D. Whyte (eds.), *Scottish Society, 1500–1800* (Cambridge, 1988), 98, 115–16.

37. Stevenson, 'Thesis', 258, 290; Nicholson, *Scotland*, 439; Guy, 'Thesis', 50, 77, 92–4, 96. The redistribution of the export trade in hides is analysed in M. Lynch, 'Towns and townspeople in fifteenth-century Scotland', in J. A. F. Thomson (ed.), *Towns and Townspeople in the Fifteenth Century* (Gloucester, 1988), 173–89, tables 1, 2.

38. Nicholson, *Scotland*, 439–40; Guy, 'Thesis', 116, 141–7, 158.

39. Stevenson, 'Thesis', 172, 210, 223, 254, 258; Guy, 'Thesis', 77, 90, 94, 96; cf. Lythe, *Economy*, 159–61.

40. Guy, 'Thesis', 116; Lythe, *Economy*, 182, 218; Lynch, 'Continuity', 115–16.

41. Lynch, *Early Modern Town*, 12; Lynch, 'Continuity', 115; Dysart's assessment rose sharply from 1574; Pittenweem, first taxed in 1579, paid 50% more by 1583. Their equally striking decline in the seventeenth century is charted in T. C. Smout, *Scottish Trade on the Eve of Union, 1660–1707* (Edinburgh, 1963), 136–7, 282–3.

42. See Table 2.

43. CB, nos. 22, 34; Verschuur, 'Thesis', 151, 578, 616; Maxwell, *Old Dundee*, 287–9.

44. Stevenson, 'Thesis', 249; Pitcairn, *Trials*, i, 418; CB, nos. 29, 34; Verschuur, 'Thesis', 144, 155, 507. The Edinburgh figures are calculated from the printed burgess roll and accounts of the dean of guild. There were craftsmen in the Edinburgh merchant guild in numbers before the decreet of 1583; historians who have denied this may have been misled by the habit of the record not recording occupations in a promotion from burgess-ship to guildry – e.g. John Bawtie, a skinner, was only marked 'burgess of before' when entered in 1561 (*Edin. Burg.*, 50). Yet this may not necessarily mark a 'transition from craftsman to merchant' (Dickinson & Duncan, *Scotland*, 287) but to employer or middleman; both categories encompassed a range of activities and entry to the guildry probably usually entailed increased interest in the long process of manufacturing or the wholesale purchase of raw materials. By the seventeenth century 27% of guildry entrants were craftsmen (MacMillan, 'Thesis', 38).

45. Cf. Clark, *Country Towns*, 4–5, 12; Goose, 'Urban economies', 25, 27.

46. C. A. Hunt, *The Book of the Perth Hammermen, 1518–1568* (Perth, 1889), 1;

Verschuur, 'Thesis,' 158–9; cf. Langton, 'Industry and towns', 185, 188; Spearman, Ch. 8, above. *Edin. Recs.*, i, 65, 69; iii, 24.

47. See Table 2 for Glasgow. Leith was also a craft town as well as a port; its skills were often used by the crown.

48. R. C. Fox, 'Stirling, 1550–1700', 62; Stevenson, 'Thesis', 254; Guy, 'Thesis', 50, 72–3, 77; *Wedderburne Compt Bk.*, 84.

49. Langton, 'Industry and towns', 175.

50. See Table 2; *Edin. Recs.*, ii, 40; Marwick, *Edinburgh Guilds*, 137–41, 145. Maxwell, *Old Dundee*, 288; Edinburgh's tailors paid 25.77% of craft taxation, or 5% of total taxation (Table 3; Lynch, *Edinburgh*, 53).

51. Dundee exported 11.93% of woollen cloth, 11.74% of skins, 7.2% of hides and 13.21% of salmon over the period 1460–1599 (Guy, 'Thesis', pp. 116, 134, Tables 3.5a, 4.5a, 4.9a, 5.1a). See Ditchburn, Ch. 10, above.

52. Macniven, 'Thesis', 101, 134; Lynch, *Edinburgh*, 51–2 and Table 2, above; Sanderson, 'Edinburgh merchants', 194, but the 43% figure takes account only of testaments 'clearly indicative' of overseas trading. Small-scale exporting, which is a feature of the Edinburgh customs returns (see n.67, below), would not always show up in testament inventories.

53. SRO, Edinburgh Customs Accts, 1561–3 (E71/30/12); Macniven, 'Thesis', 279. Exporting was supposed to be the preserve of members of the merchant guild, but only 86 of 278 dealers in hides and skins in Edinburgh belonged to it.

54. Brown, 'Thesis', 114–6, 120, 124, 148.

55. This is strikingly illustrated in the poll-tax returns of the 1690s: 9% of Edinburgh's pollable population were merchants, 22% of Aberdeen's (Whyte, 'Occupational structure', 224).

56. The top 10% of taxpayers paid 56% of taxation in Edinburgh but only 30% in Aberdeen, although tax was assessed on property and income only within the burgh (Lynch, 'Whatever happened', 11).

57. Ewan, 'The age of Bon-Accord', 41; White, 'Thesis', 14–15; Macniven, 'Thesis', 104–06.

58. White, 'Thesis', 309, 319, 321–4, 329–32; ACA, CR, xxxii, 622, 631, 640.

59. These comparative tables need to be treated with some caution as they are not always based on the same yardsticks: although the Glasgow figures are based on meetings of merchants and craftsmen who were members of the merchant guild, they are liable to be fairly inclusive (Murray, *Early Burgh Organisation*, i, 484); the Edinburgh 1558 totals are derived from a muster roll (ECA, MS Co. Recs., ii, fos. 126v–137v) which is defective, missing out three crafts and the merchants in the N.E. quarter; the other tables are based on tax rolls (ACA, MS Stent Rolls, 1596 – ; ECA, MS Stent Rolls, vols. i & ii). The total numbers of taxpayers were Aberdeen 569 (1637); Edinburgh 1245 (1583), 1606 (1634); I am grateful to Dr Makey for all information regarding the 1634 roll. The crafts which were incorporated also varied from burgh to burgh; the bracketed totals for Edinburgh indicate unincorporated crafts; 19 of the 38 waulkers listed in 1558 lived in the suburb at the West Port.

60. Cf. Murray, *Abdn. Excavns.*, 248.

61. A. Skene, *Memorialls for the Government of Royall Burghs in Scotland* (Aberdeen, 1685), 102–05; Gordon, *Description*, 5.

62. Hunt, *Perth Hammermen Book*, pp. ii, 2; *Abdn. Counc.*, i, 18; *Edin. Recs.*, i, 32; D. McRoberts, *The Fetternear Banner* (Glasgow, n.d.), 16–17; Murray, *Early Burgh Organization*, i, 392–8; Bain, *Aberdeen Guilds*, 57–8.

63. Fox, 'Stirling', 54, 59–60; *Edin. Recs.*, i, 34–5; ii, 104–05.

64. Marwick, *Edinburgh Guilds*, 95, 137–8, 140–41, 155–6; *Burghs Convention Recs*, i, 436, 454.

65. *Edin. Recs.*, iv, 365–9, 404. The problem also affected Dundee. See *APS*, iii, 579; *Burghs Convention Recs.*, i, 155–6, 238, 436, 454.

66. See Langton, 'Industry and towns', 182–3; Clarkson, *Economy*, 104; Patten, 'Urban occupations', 305. Scottish urban historians have not as yet explored the range of activities of various trades; for fleshers, see Bain, *Craft Guilds*, 306; *Statuta Gilde*, c.30.

67. SRO, E71/30/12. There were 42 masters in the skinner craft and 9 in the furrier in 1558 (see Table 2); the 9 fleshers probably represented a quarter of their craft (*Edin. Recs.*, i, 114, 116).

68. Guy, 'Thesis', 90, 102–04, suggests a fall somewhat earlier than Lythe, *Economy*, 160, which dates it c.1600.

69. The assessment on Edinburgh crafts was fixed at 20%, and merchants at 80% until 1583, when all were assessed individually. Assessment on various crafts varied, however, from year to year, as shown. The pre-1574 figures add up to more than 100 but the difference is insignificant. The overall amount paid by craftsmen after 1583 remained virtually the same as before, at 20.5%. See Lynch, *Edinburgh*, 377–92, for the 1565 and 1583 amounts, Marwick, *Edin. Guilds*, 100, for the others.

70. Lynch, 'Whatever happened', 15–16; *Abdn. Recs.*, p. xlivn.

71. Lynch, *Edinburgh*, 53, 63–4; Lynch, 'Continuity', 109–10. Alternative distinctions as to the comparative wage levels of craftsmen are made in Lythe, *Economy*, 30, 113.

72. See n. 11, above for fifteenth-century rolls, and Table 2 for the 1637 roll.

73. ACA, CR, viii, 1205–09; *Edin. Recs.*, ii, 44, 46.

74. *Ibid.*, ii, 27, 40.

75. Lynch, *Edinburgh*, 388–92; *Stirling Recs.*, *1519–1666*, 24, 34, 80, 174–6.

76. ECA, MS Co. Recs., ii, fo. 137r; *Leges Burgorum*, c.lxi; see also Balfour, *Practicks*, 69.

77. *Edin. Recs.*, iv, 366–9.

78. A useful list, in which only three pre-date 1600, is given in G. Marshall, *Presbyteries and Profits* (Oxford, 1980), 284ff.

79. J. Brown, 'Merchant princes and mercantile investment in early seventeenth-century Scotland', in Lynch, *Early Modern Town*, 138–9.

80. A handful appear on the Aberdeen 1637 roll.

81. Makey, 'Edinburgh', 208; Whyte, 'Occupational structure', 224; Lynch, *Edinburgh*, 377.

82. P. Corfield, 'Urban development in England and Wales', in *Trade, Government and Economy in Pre-industrial England*, eds. D. C. Coleman and A. H. John (London, 1976), 217–20, 232. Estimates of Scottish urban populations before the later seventeenth century are notoriously unreliable. Lythe's suggestion of 7–8,000 for Dundee and Aberdeen in 1600 and c.5,500 for Perth is flawed because it uses a gross over-estimate of 30,000 for Edinburgh in 1560 as a bench-mark (*Economy*, 117). The more modest estimate of 4,000 for Aberdeen in Mackenzie, *Scottish Burghs*, 138, is more plausible. Edinburgh's population is, however, fairly certain; a kirk session census of 1592 counted 8,000 adult communicants, suggesting a total population of c.13,500. But this was only within its walls and did not count suburbs, its port of Leith or the adjacent burgh of the Canongate. The likelihood that the populations of most other Scottish towns were well under 4,000 even after a century of increase, is underlined by a 1639 table of valued rents, printed in Lynch, 'Continuity', 102–03.

83. Whyte, 'Occupational structure', 236, 238.

84. ACA, CR, xxxii, 622, 637, 640, are enactments of the guild court deploring the trend;

I am grateful to Dr. Allan White for these references.

85. Cf. Brown, 'Thesis', 114–20.

86. E.g. Mackenzie, *Scottish Burghs*, 80, 85; Lynch, 'Whatever happened', 17. A list of burghs of barony is given in Pryde, *Burghs*, 51ff.

87. W. Coutts, 'Provincial merchants and society: a study of Dumfries, 1600–1665', in Lynch, *Early Modern Town*, 148–50.

88. Verschuur, 'Thesis', 276, 486.

89. M. Lynch, 'From privy kirk to burgh church: an alternative explanation of the Protestantization of burgh society', in *Church, Politics and Society in Scotland, 1408–1929*, ed. N. Macdougall (Edinburgh, 1983), 88; *Edin. Recs.*, ii, 72; Lynch, *Edinburgh*, 15, 42. The problem of change is discussed in a longer-term context in Lynch, 'Continuity', esp. 87–90, 110–14.

90. ECA, MS Moses Bundles, no. 195, doc. 7029; Lynch, 'Whatever happened', 7; Scott, *Fasti*, iii, 451, 473; vi, 36; *Abdn. Counc.*, ii, 145–6; the Convention of Royal Burghs recommended in 1596 that every large burgh should subdivide its parish (*Burghs Convention Recs.*, i, 491). Perth had also stretched the jurisdiction of its kirk session to include three of its suburbs in the 1590s (MS Perth Kirk Session Reg., 1592 & 1597).

Bibliography

Archival sources are listed by Archive and then as far as is possible by registration number and title.

Printed sources and secondary works conform to the *List of Abbreviated Titles of the Printed Sources of Scottish History to 1560*, published as a supplement to the *Scottish Historical Review* of October 1963. Abbreviations not included in that list conform in general to the principles upon which the list was constructed. Secondary works which are not abbreviated appear in their alphabetical position by author(s) and date.

Archival Sources

ACA
  Aberdeen Council Archive

ACA, —
  Sasine Register, 1484–

ACA, —
  Stent Rolls, 1596–

ACA, —
  Kirk Session Accounts (1602–1705)

ACA, CR
  ACA, MS Council Register

ACA, CR
  Aberdeen Council, Baillie & Guild Court Books 1398–

Archiv der Hansestadt Lübeck,
  Anglicana (Correspondence)

AUL
  Aberdeen University Library Archive

AUL, MS.M.390, Mass 1–19
  Marischal College Charters

Ayr Arch. (see Kyle & Carrick D.)

BA
  Berwick Archive

BA, B1/1; B2/1
  Guild Minute Books

BL
  British Library

BL, MS. Add. 18111
  Constitutiones Regis Willelmi

BL, MS. Add. 33245
  Registrum de Aberbrothock

Bruges, Rijksarchief,
  Registre du Franc de Bruges

Bruges, Stadsarchief,
  Letterbook of Anselm Adornes

Brussels, Arch. Gen. du Royaume,
  Papiers d'Etat et de l'audience

CRA
  Central Region Archive, Stirling

CRA, PD6/1/1
  Stirling Guild Recs.

CUL
  Cambridge University Library Archive

CUL, Ee/4/21
  Liber quem vulgus Regiam Majestatem vocat

DA
  Dundee Archive

DA, —
  Book of the Church c. 1480–1524 In Burgh Court Book vol. 2

DA, —
  Dundee Town Charter Chest

DA, —
  Dundee Town Council Minutes

DA, —
  Dundee Burgh Treasurer's Accounts 1590

DA, —
  Dundee Burgh Laws drawn furth of the Act of this Burgh 1550–1646

DA, —
  Dundee Burgh Lockit Buik

DA, —
  Dundee Burgh Cartularies (c. 1820)

DA, —
  Dundee Protocol Book 1526–28

DA, TC/CC 10
Burgh Writs: fourteenth century

DA, TC/CC, 14A
Return to royal enquiry re privileges of Dundee, 1325

ECA
Edinburgh City Archive

ECA, —
Annuity Tax Roll (1635)

ECA, —
Council Recs.

ECA, —
Stent Rolls

ECA, —
Moses Bundles

Gemeentearchief, Obdrachten, R.

Gemeentearchief, Bergen-op-Zoom, Poorterboeken

Gemeentearchief, Veere, Poorterboeken

Historisches Archiv der Stadt Köln, Brb.34/35
Briefbucher (Correspondence)

Historisches Archiv der Stadt Köln, Schreinsurk. Schöff.
Schreinsurkunden Schöffenschrein (Judicial records)

Kyle & Carrick DC Archive, B6/12
Ayr Burgh Court Book 1428–78

Lille, Archives départmentales du Nord,
Chambre de Comptes, série B

MA
Montrose Archive

MA, M/WC
Royal charters

NLS
National Library of Scotland, Edinburgh

NLS, Adv. MS. 9a.1.10
Hutton transcripts (chartularium de Elgin)

NLS, Adv. MS. 25.4.15
Statutis of the burowys

NLS, Adv. MS. 29.4.2
Huttons Collection

NLS, Adv. MS. 31.1.1
Perth Kirk Session Records

PA
Perth Archive, Sandeman Library

PA, MS 1359/25/2/29

Perth Museum & Art Gallery Archive 1/1
The Perth Guildry Book

PRO
Public Record Office

PRO, C 47/34/1
Newcastle custumal

PRO, E 122/
Berwick Customs Accounts

PRO, SC1/
Ancient Correspondence

Rijksarchief, Middelburg, Water Bailiff Accts.

SCA
Scottish Catholic Archives, Edinburgh

SCA, Fort Augustus MS A1

SRO
Scottish Record Office, Edinburgh

SRO, AD 1/52
Crown Office Writs

SRO, B20/10/1
MS Burgh Court Book of Dunfermline [BCBD]

SRO, B30/9/1
Haddington Court Book 1423–1514

SRO, E71/1/1
Aberdeen Cocket Bk 1499–1500

SRO, E71/29
Leith Cocket Bk

SRO, E71/30
Edinburgh Customs Accounts

SRO, GD215/1862/2
Beveridge Papers

SRO, GD52/393
Lord Forbes Collection

SRO, GD79/5/1
King James VI Hospital, Perth

SRO, PA 5/1
Leges Burgorum

SRO, PA 5/2
The Ayr Manuscript

SRO, RH6/199
Register House Charters

St A. ULA
St Andrews University Library Archive

St A. ULA, B65/1/1
Registrum evidentiarum civitatis Sancti Andree

Staatarchiv Bremen, 1/Bc
Britannica (Correspondence)

Vatican Archives, MS. Reg. Supp.
Register Supplicationum

WAP
Wojewodzkie Archiwum Panstwowe

WAP Gdańsk, 300D
Dyplomy i korespondenga (diplomata and correspondence)

WAP Gdańsk, 300D/8
Correspondence with Lithuanian towns

WAP Gdańsk, 300D/36a
Correspondence with Bytów, Lebork and Leba

WAP Gdańsk, 300D/69
Correspondence with Toruń

WAP Gdańsk, 300/59
Ksiega Miejske i libri memorandorum kancelarii Gdanskiej (Town books)

WAP Gdańsk, 300/19
Kamora Palowa (Customs records)

WAP Toruń, Kat.I.686
Letter from Aberdeen to Gdańsk, 1st Dec. 1410

Printed Sources and Secondary Works

Abdn. Chrs.
Anderson, P J (ed) *Charters and other Writs illustrating the History of the Royal Burgh of Aberdeen*
Aberdeen 1890

Abdn. Counc.
Extracts from the Council Register of the Burgh of Aberdeen
[Spalding Club] 1844–48

Abdn. Friars
Anderson, P J (ed) *Aberdeen Friars: Red, Black, White and Grey*
Aberdeen 1909

Abdn. Recs.
Dickinson, W C (ed) *Early Records of the Burgh of Aberdeen 1317, 1398–1407*
[SHS] 1957

Abdn. Reg.
Registrum Episcopatus Aberdonensis
[Spalding & Maitland Clubs] 1845

Abdn.-Banff Illustrations
Illustrations of the Topography and Antiquities of the Shires of Aberdeen and Banff.
[Spalding Club] 1843

Abdn.-Banff Coll.
Collections for a History of the Shires of Aberdeen and Banff
[Spalding Club] 1843

Acts of Council
Thomson, T *et al* (eds) *The Acts of the Lords of Council in Civil Causes*
Edinburgh 1839, 1918–

Adams, I H *The Making of Urban Scotland*
London 1978

AHCAG
Archaeological & Historical Collections relating to Ayrshire and Galloway
1878–99

Aitken, W G 'Excavation of bloomeries in Rannoch, Perthshire and elsewhere' In *PSAS* 102 (1969–70) 188–204

Alcock, L & Driscoll, S T *Excavations at Dundurn, St Fillans, Perthshire, 1976–77 A Revised Interim Report*
[Glas. Univ. Archaeology Dep] 1985

Alcock, L *Arthur's Britain*
Penguin Bks 1971

Ancient Burgh Laws
Innes, C (ed) *Ancient Laws and Customs of The Burghs of Scotland 1124–1424*
[SBRS] 1868

Anderson, *Early Sources*
Anderson, A O (ed) *Early Sources of Scottish History, 500-1286*
Edinburgh 1922

Anderson, J *The Black Book of Kincardineshire*
Stonehaven 1843

Anderson, M O 'St Andrews before Alexander I' In Barrow, G W S (ed) *The Scottish Tradition*
Edinburgh 1974

Anderson, M O 'The Celtic church in Kinrimund' In *Innes Review* xxv
(1974) 67-76

Anon. 'List of the inhabitants of Stirling, 1544-1550'
In *Scottish Antiquary* vi (1892) 175-8

APS
Thomson, T & Innes, C (eds) *The Acts of the Parliaments of Scotland*
Edinburgh 1814-75

Arbroath Liber
Liber S. Thome de Aberbrothoc
[Bannatyne Club] 1848-56

Archiwum Miasta Gdańska
Warsaw 1970

Assisa de Tolloneis
Innes, C (ed) Assisa de Tolloneis In *Ancient Burgh Laws*
[SBRS] 1868

Assise Regis Willelmi
Innes, C (ed) Assise Regis Willelmi In *Ancient Burgh Laws*
[SBRS] 1868

Ayr Accts.
Pryde, G S (ed) *Ayr Burgh Accounts 1534-1624*
[SHS] 1937

Ayr Burgh Chrs.
Charters of the Royal Burgh of Ayr
[AHCAG] 1881

Ayr Friars
Charters of the Friars Preachers of Ayr
[AHCAG] 1881

Bain, *Aberdeen Guilds*
Bain, E *Merchant Craft Guilds: a History of the Aberdeen Incorporated Trades*
Aberdeen 1887

Baird Smith, D 'The retrait lingnager in Scotland' In *SHR* xxi (1924) 193-206

Balfour-Melville, E W M *James I*
London 1936

Ballard, A *British Borough Charters 1066–1216*
Cambridge 1913

Ballard, A & Tait, J *British Borough Charters 1216–1307*
Cambridge 1923

Balmerino Liber
Liber Sancte Marie de Balmorinach
[Abbotsford Club] 1841

Barron, E M *Inverness in the Fifteenth Century*
Inverness 1906

Barrow, G W S *Robert Bruce and the Community of the Realm of Scotland*
Edinburgh (1st ed.) 1965

Barrow, G W S 'The reign of William the Lion, king of Scotland' In *Historical Studies* vii
(Dublin 1969) 21–44

Barrow, G W S *The Kingdom of the Scots*
London 1973

Barrow, G W S *The Anglo-Norman Era in Scottish History*
Oxford 1980

Barrow, *Kingship*
Barrow, G W S *Kingship and Unity: Scotland 1000–1306*
London 1981

Bartlett, R *Trial by Fire and Water: The Medieval Judicial Ordeal*
Oxford 1986

Bateson, *Borough Customs*
Bateson, M (ed) *Borough Customs* (2 Vols)
[Selden Soc.] 1913

Beveridge, E *The Churchyard Memorials of Crail*
Edinburgh 1893

Biddle, M (ed) *Winchester in the Early Middle Ages*
Oxford 1976

Biegánska, A 'A note on the Scots in Poland, 1550–1800'
In Smout, T C (ed) *Scotland and Europe, 1200–1850*
Edinburgh 1986

Binchy, D A 'The pseudo-historical prologue to the Senchas Mar' In
Studia Celtica x-xi (1975–6) 15–28

Black, G F *The Surnames of Scotland*
New York 1945

Blanchard, *Perth, Canal St Exc.*
Blanchard, L M *et al* 'An excavation at 45 Canal Street, Perth, 1978–9'.
In *PSAS* cxiii (1983) 489–519

Blanchard, *Perth, King Edward St Exc.*
Blanchard, L M *et al Excavations at King Edward Street, Perth, 1982*
Forthcoming

Blanchard, *Perth, Kirk Close Exc.*
Blanchard, L M *et al* 'Excavations at Kirk Close, Perth' In Holdsworth, P (ed)
Excavations in The Medieval Burgh of Perth 1979–1981
Soc. of Ant. of Scotland, Monograph Ser. 1988

Blanchard, *Perth, Meal Vennel Exc.*
Blanchard, L M *et al Excavations at Meal Vennel, Perth; an Interim Report*
[Privately available: SUAT]

BOEC
Book of the Old Edinburgh Club
1908–

Boece, *Historiae*(1527)
Boece, Hector *Scotorum Historiae a prima gestis origine*
Paris 1527

Bogdan, N Q & Wordsworth, J W *The Medieval Excavations at the High Street, Perth*
Perth 1978

Booton, H 'Thesis'
'Burgesses and Landed Men in North-East Scotland in the Later Middle Ages: a Study in
Social Interaction'
[Abdn. Univ. Ph.D.] 1988

Bracton
Woodbine, G E & Thorne, S E (eds) *Henry de Bracton, de legibus et constietudinibus Angliae*
Harvard 1968–77

Brämer, C 'Die Entwicklung der Danziger Reederei im Mittelalter' In *Zeitschrift des
Westpreussisches Geschichtsverein* lxiii (1922)

Brechin Reg.
Registrum Episcopatus Brechinensis
[Bannatyne Club] 1856

Brill, E V K 'A sixteenth-century complaint against the Scots' In *SHR*
xxvii (1948) 187–91

Brooks, N P & Whittington, G 'Planning and growth in the medieval Scottish burgh: the
example of St Andrews' In *Trans. Inst. Brit. Geogs.* xxxiv (1977) 278–95

Brooks, N P "St John's House': its history and archaeology'
In *St Andrews Preservation Trust Annual Report* (1976) 11–16

Brooks, N P 'Urban archaeology in Scotland' In Barley, M W (ed)
European Towns, their archaeology and early history 19–33
London 1977

Brown, *Scottish Society*
Brown, J M (ed) *Scottish Society in the Fifteenth Century*
London 1977

Brown, 'Thesis'
Brown, J J 'The Social, Political and Economic Influences of the Edinburgh Merchant Elite, 1600–1638'
[Edin. Univ. Ph.D.] 1985

Brown, J A 'Provand's Lordship; the bishop's almshouse'
In *TSES* ix (1927–30) 13–22

Brown, J J 'Merchant princes and mercantile investment in early seventeenth-century Scotland' In Lynch *Early Modern Town*
London 1986

Brown, P H *Scotland in the Time of Queen Mary*
London 1904

Burghs Convention Recs.
Marwick, J D (ed) *Records of the Convention of the Royal Burghs of Scotland*
Edinburgh 1866–90

Burns, E *The Coinage of Scotland* (3 vols)
Edinburgh 1887

C. A. Chrs.
Easson, D E (ed) *Charters of the Abbey of Coupar Angus*
[SHS] 1947

Cal. Chtr. Rolls
Calendar of the Charter Rolls
London 1903–27

Cambuskenneth Reg.
Registrum Monasterii S. Marie de Cambuskenneth 1147–1535
[Grampian Club] 1872

Cameron, A I 'The Vatican Archives, 1073–1560' In McKechnie, H (ed) *Sources of Scots Law*
[Stair Soc.] 1936

Cameron, J K (ed) *Letters of John Johnston and Robert Howie*
St Andrews Univ. Pub. 1963

Cant, R G *The College of St Salvator*
Edinburgh 1950

Cant, R G *Old Elgin: a description of old buildings*
[Elgin Society] 1954

Cant, R G 'The church in Orkney and Shetland. . .in the middle ages' In *Northern Scotland* i (1972) 1–18

Cant, R G 'The building of St Andrews Cathedral' In *Innes Review* xxv (1974) 77–94

Cant, R G 'The medieval kirk of Crail' In O'Connor, A C & Clarke, D V (eds) *From the Stone Age to the Forty-five* 368–83
Edinburgh 1983

Cant, R G 'Historical notes: Western St Andrews, Argyle, Rathelpie, Kinburn'
In *St Andrews Preservation Trust Report and Year Book* 1984
1984

Carus-Wilson, E M & Coleman, O *England's Export Trade, 1275–1547*
Oxford 1963

Cast. & Dom. Arch.
MacGibbon, D & Ross, T *The Castellated and Domestic Architecture of Scotland* (5 vols).
Edinburgh 1887–92

CCR
Calendar of Close Rolls
London 1902–

CDS
Bain, J (ed) *Calendar of Documents Relating to Scotland*
Edinburgh 1881–8, 1987

Challis, C E 'Debasement: the Scottish experience in the 15th & 16th centuries'
In Metcalf, *Coinage*
Oxford [BAR xlv] 1977

Christensen, T L 'Scoto-Danish relations in the sixteenth century' In *SHR*
(1969) 64–79, 124–50.

Chron. Bower
Goodall, W (ed) *Joannis de Fordun Scotichronicon cum Supplementis et Continuatione Walteri Boweri*
Edinburgh 1759

Chron. Hemingburgh
Chronicle Walteri de Hemingburgh
[Eng. Hist. Soc.] 1848–9

Chron. Holyrood
Anderson, M O (ed) *A Scottish Chronicle known as the Chronicle of Holyrood*
[SHS] 1938

Chron. Melrose
Anderson, A O *et al* (eds) *The Chronicle of Melrose*
London 1936

Chron. Perth
The Chronicle of Perth
[Maitland Club] 1831

Chron. Pluscarden
Skene, F J H (ed) *Liber Pluscardensis*
Edinburgh 1877–80

Clark, *Country Towns*
Clark, P (ed)*Country Towns in Pre-Industrial England*
Leicester 1981

Clarkson, *Economy*
Clarkson, L A *The Pre-industrial Economy in England, 1500–1750*
London 1971

Cochran-Patrick, R W *Records of the Coinage of Scotland* (2 vols)
Edinburgh 1876

Cock, W B & Morris, D B (eds) *Extracts from the records of the Merchant Guild of Stirling 1592–1846*
Glasgow 1916

Coldingham Corresp.
The Correspondence, Inventories, Account Rolls and Law Proceedings of the Priory of Coldingham
[Surtees Soc.] 1841

Coldstream Chartulary
Chartulary of the Cistercian Priory of Coldstream
[Grampian Club] 1879

Colgrave, B (ed) *Eddius Stephanus, Life of Wilfred*
Cambridge 1927

Colvin, H M *History of the King's Works*
London 1963

Conzen, M R G 'Alnwick, Northumberland: a study in town-plan analysis' In
Inst. Brit. Geogs. xxvii (1960) 1–120

Cooper, J 'The church and convent of the Grey Friars, Elgin'
In *Trans. Aberdeen Ecclesiol. Soc.* ii (1890–3) part v 45–53

Coornaert, E 'Les ghildes medievales' In *Revue Historique* xcix (1948)
22–55, 206–43

Cornfield, P 'Urban development in England & Wales' In Coleman, D C & John, A H
Trade, Government & Economy in Pre-Industrial England
London 1976

Coutts, W 'Provincial merchants & society: a study of Dumfries
1600–1665' in Lynch, *Early Modern Town*
London 1986

Cowan, I B & Dunlop, A I *Calendar of Scottish Supplications to Rome 1428–32*
[SHS] 1970

Cowan & Easson, *Religious Houses*
Cowan, I B & Easson, D E *Medieval Religious Houses, Scotland*
London 1976

Cowan, I B & Shaw, D (eds) *The Renaissance and Reformation in Scotland*
Edinburgh 1983

Cowan, I B 'The development of the parochial system in medieval Scotland'
In *SHR* xl (1961) 43–55

Cowan, I B 'The religious and the cure of souls in medieval Scotland' In *RSCHS* xiv (1962) 215–30

Cowan, I B 'The Vatican Archives: a report on pre-Reformation Scottish material' In *SHR* xlviii (1969) 227–42

Cowan, I B 'The early ecclesiastical history of Edinburgh' In *Innes Review* xxiii (1972) 16–21

Cowan, I B 'Church and society' In Brown, *Scottish Society* London 1977

Cowan, *Parishes*
Cowan, I B *The Parishes of Medieval Scotland*
[SRS] 1967

CPL
Bliss, W H *et al* (eds) *Calendar of Entries in the Papal Registers relating to Great Britain and Ireland: Papal Letters*
London 1893–

CPR
Calendar of Patent Rolls
London 1901–

Craeybeckx, J *Les vines de France aux anciens Pays Bas*
Paris 1918

CSP Scot.
Bain, J *et al* (eds) *Calendar of the State Papers Relating to Scotland and Mary Queen of Scots 1547–1603*
Edinburgh 1898–

Davidson, J & Gray, A *The Scottish Staple at Veere*
London 1909

Davidson, J M 'St Kentigern's Church, Lanark' In *PSAS* xlvi (1911–12) 133–9

Defoe, D *A Tour through the Whole Island of Great Britain*
1724–6; 1968 reprint

Delepierre, O (ed) *Précis analytique des documents des archives de la Flandre occidentale* (3 vols)
Bruges 1843–5

Dickinson & Duncan, *Scotland*
Dickinson, W C & Duncan, A A M *Scotland from the Earliest Times to 1603*
Oxford (3rd ed) 1977

Dickinson, W C 'A chamberlain's ayre in Aberdeen 1399–1400' In *SHR* xxxiii (1954) 27–36

Dickinson, W C (ed) *The Sheriff Court Book of Fife*
[SHS] 1928

Dicks, B 'The Scottish medieval town' In Gordon, G & Dicks, B (eds) *Scottish Urban History*

Aberdeen 1981

Dickson, R & Edmond, J P *Annals of Scottish Printing*
Cambridge 1890

Dilley, J 'German merchants in Scotland 1297–1327' In *SHR* xxvii (1948) 142–55

Discovery & Excavation
Scottish Group of the Council for British Archaeology (eds) *Discovery and Excavation in Scotland*
[Scottish Group Council for Brit. Archaeology] 1955–

DN
Diplomatarium Norvegicum
Kristiania 1848–1919

Dobson, R B 'Cathedral chapters and cathedral cities: York, Durham and Carlisle in the fifteenth century' In *Northern Studies* xxix (1983)

Dodd, W 'Ayr: a study in urban growth' In *Ayrshire Arch. Nat. Hist Colls.* x (1972) 302–81

Dollinger, P *Die Hanse*
Stuttgart (3rd ed.) 1976

Donaldson, G *The Sources of Scottish History*
[Privately available in Univ. Libraries] 1978

Donaldson, R 'An early printed fragment of the "Buke of the Howlat" — Addendum' In *Edin. Bib. Trans.* (1983) 27–8

Dow, J 'A comparative note on the Sound Toll Registers, Stockholm Customs Accts and Dundee Shipping Lists' In *Scand. Ec. Hist Rev.* (1964) 79–85

Dow, J 'Scottish trade with Sweden 1512–1580' In *SHR* xlvii (1969) 64–79

Dryburgh Liber
Liber S. Marie de Dryburgh
[Bannatyne Club] 1847

Duke, W 'Notice of the fabric of St Vigean's Church, Forfarshire' In *PSAS* ix (1870–72) 481–91

Dunbar, J G *The Historical Architecture of Scotland*
London 1966 edn.

Duncan, A A M & Dunbar, J G 'Tarbert Castle' In *SHR* l (1971) 1–16

Duncan, 'Perth'
Duncan, A A M 'Perth: the first century of the burgh' In *Trans. Perth. Soc. Natural Sciences*, Special Issue (1974) 30–50.

Duncan, *James I*
Duncan, A A M *James I King of Scots 1424–37*
[Univ. of Glas.] 1984 (2nd ed.)

Duncan, *Scotland*
Duncan, A A M *Scotland: The Making of the Kingdom*

Edinburgh 1975

Duncan, A A M 'Regiam Majestatem: a reconsideration' In *Juridical Rev.*
vi (1961) 199–217

Duncan, A A M 'The early parliaments of Scotland' In *SHR* xlv (1966) 36– 58

Duncan, A A M 'Taxation of Burghs' In McNeill, P & Nicholson, R (eds)
Historical Atlas I 64, 175
St Andrews 1975

Duncan, J D *House, Nos 3–7 Castle Street*
[Regality Club] 1889

Dundee Chrs.
Hay, W (ed) *Charters, Writs and the Public Documents of the Royal Burgh
of Dundee*
Dundee 1880

Dunf. Ct. Bk.
Webster, J M & Duncan, A A M (eds) *Regality of Dunfermline Court Book*
Dunfermline 1953

Dunf. Recs.
Beveridge, E (ed) *The Dunfermline Burgh Records*
Edinburgh 1917

Dunf. Reg.
Registrum de Dunfermelyn
[Bannatyne Club] 1842

Dunlop, A I *The Life and Times of Bishop Kennedy*
Edinburgh 1950

Dunlop, A I (ed) *The Royal Burgh of Ayr*
Edinburgh 1953

Durkan, J 'Notes on Glasgow Cathedral' In *Innes Review* xxi (1970) 51– 69

Durkan, J 'The great fire at Glasgow Cathedral' In *Innes Review* xxvi
(1975)

Durkan, J 'The early Scottish notary' In Cowan, I B & Shaw, D (eds)
The Renaissance and Reformation in Scotland
Edinburgh 1983

Durkan, J 'The bishop's barony of Glasgow in pre-Reformation times'
In *RSCHS* xxii (1986) 277–308

EAA 1879
Edinburgh Architectural Association Sketch Book, ii
Edinburgh 1878–9

Eccles. Arch.
MacGibbon, D & Ross, T *The Ecclesiastical Architecture of Scotland* (3 Vols)
Edinburgh 1897

Edin. Accts.
Adam, R (ed) *Edinburgh Records: The Burgh Accounts*
Edinburgh 1899

Edin. Burg.
Watson, C B B (ed) *Roll of Edinburgh Burgesses and Guild-Brethern 1406– 1700*
[SRS] 1929

Edin. Chrs.
Charters and other Documents relating to the City of Edinburgh
[SBRS] 1871

Edin. Recs.
Extracts from the Records of the Burgh of Edinburgh
[SBRS] 1869–92

Edwards, J G 'Hywel Dda and the Welsh law books' In Jenkins, D (ed)
Celtic Law Papers
Aberystwyth 1971

EHD
Douglas, D C & Greenway, G W (eds) *English Historical Documents*
London 1953

EHR
English Historical Review
1886–

Ekwall, E *The Concise Oxford Dictionary of English Place Names*
Oxford 1960

Ellison, 'Archaeological survey'
Ellison, M 'An archaeological survey of Berwick-upon-Tweed' In
Clack, P A G & Gosling, P F (eds) *Archaeology in the North*
Durham [Northern Archaeological Survey] 1976

ER
Stuart, J *et al* (eds) *The Exchequer Rolls of Scotland*
Edinburgh 1878–1908

ESC
Lawrie, A C (ed) *Early Scottish Charters prior to 1153*
Glasgow 1905

Espinas, G & Pirenne, H (eds) *Recueil de documents relatifs à l'histoire de l'industrie drapière en Flandre* (4 vols)
Brussels 1906–24

Espinas, G *La draperie dans la Flandre française au moyen âge*
Paris 1923

Ewan, E 'The age of Bon-Accord: Aberdeen in the fourteenth century' In
Smith, J S (ed) *New Light on Medieval Aberdeen*
Aberdeen 1985

Ewan, 'Thesis'
Ewan, E L 'The Burgesses of Fourteenth Century Scotland — a Social History'
[Edin. Univ. Ph.D.] 1984

Familie of Innes
An Account of the Familie of Innes
[Spalding Club] 1864

Fawcett, R 'Late Gothic architecture in Scotland: considerations on the influence of the
  Low Countries' In *PSAS* cxii (1982) 477–96

Fawcett, R *Edinburgh Castle* (Official Guide)
HMSO 1986

Feachem, R 'The hillforts of northern Britain' In Revet, A L F (ed)
The Iron Age in Northern Britain 59–88
Edinburgh 1966

Fenton, A & Stell, G (eds) *Loads and Roads in Scotland and Beyond*
Edinburgh 1984

Ferguson, J *Ecclesia Antiqua, or a history of an ancient church,*
St Michael's, Linlithgow
Edinburgh & London 1905

Ferguson, J *Linlithgow Palace; its history and traditions*
Edinburgh 1910

Fife Court Bk.
Dickinson, W C (ed) *The Sheriff Court Book of Fife 1515–22*
[SHS] 1928

Finlayson, 'Thesis'
Finlayson, W H 'The Scottish Nation of Merchants in Bruges'
[Glas. Univ. Ph.D.] 1951

Fischer, T A *The Scots in Germany*
Edinburgh 1902

Fischer, *Prussia*
Fischer, T A *The Scots in Eastern and Western Prussia*
Edinburgh 1903

Flett, 'Thesis'
Flett, I 'The Conflict of Reformation and Democracy in the Geneva
of Scotland'
[St Andrews Univ. M. Phil] 1981

Flinn, *Population History*
Flinn, M (ed) *Scottish Population History*
Cambridge 1977

Forbes, *Lives*
Forbes, A P *Lives of St Ninian and St Kentigern*
Edinburgh 1874

Foster, J & Sheppard, J *British Archives*
London 1982

Fox, R C 'Stirling 1550–1700: the morphology & function of a pre-industrial Scottish burgh' In Gordon, G & Dicks, B (eds) *Scottish Urban History*
Aberdeen 1983

Fox, R C 'Urban development, 1100–1700' In Whittington, G & Whyte, I D (eds) *An Historical Geography of Scotland*
London 1983

Fragmenta Collecta
Innes, C (ed) Fragmenta Collecta In *Ancient Burgh Laws*
[SBRS] 1868

Fraser, C (ed) *Northern Petitions*
[Surtees Soc.] 1981

Fraser, *Douglas*
Fraser, W *The Douglas Book*
Edinburgh 1885

Fraser, *Eglinton*
Fraser, W *Memorials of the Montgomeries Earls of Eglinton*
Edinburgh 1859

Fraser, *Grandtully*
Fraser, W *The Red Book of Grandtully*
Edinburgh 1868

Fraser, *Grant*
Fraser, W *The Chiefs of Grant*
Edinburgh 1883

Fraser, *Melville*
Fraser, W *The Melvilles Earls of Melville and the Leslies Earls of Leven*
Edinburgh 1890

Fraser, *Southesk*
Fraser, W *History of the Carnegies, Earls of Southesk and their Kindred*
Edinburgh 1867

Fraser, *Sutherland*
Fraser, W *The Sutherland Book*
Edinburgh 1892

Fraser, *Wemyss*
Fraser, W *Memorial of the Family of Wemyss of Wemyss*
Edinburgh 1888

Friedland, K 'Hanseatic merchants and their trade with Shetland' In Withrington, D J (ed) *Shetland and the Outside World*
Aberdeen 1983

Fritze, K *Am Wendepunkt der Hanse*
Berlin 1967

GCBD
Torrie, E P D (ed) *Guild Court Book of Dunfermline*
[SRS] 1986

Gemmell, W *The Oldest House in Glasgow*
Glasgow 1910

Geog. Coll.
Macfarlane, W *Geographical Collections relating to Scotland made by Walter Macfarlane*
[SHS] 1906–8

Gibb, *Glasgow*
Gibb, A *Glasgow – The making of a City*
London 1983

Gifford, J et al *The Buildings of Scotland, Edinburgh*
(Penguin Bks.) 1984

Gilbert, J 'The usual money of Scotland and exchange rates against foreign coin' In Metcalf, *Coinage*
Oxford [BAR no. xlv] 1977

Gilliodts van Severen, L *Inventaire des archives de la ville de Bruges*
Bruges 1871–82

Gilliodts van Severen, L (ed) *Cartulaire de l'ancienne Estaple de Bruges* (9 Vols)
Bruges 1904–8

Glas. Chrs.
Charters and other Documents Relating to the City of Glasgow
[SBRS] 1895–1906

Glas. Friars Munimenta
Robertson, J (ed) *Liber Collegii Nostre Domine: Munimenta Fratum Predicatorum de Glasgu*
[Maitland Club] 1846

Glas. Reg.
Registrum Episcopatus Glasguensis
[Bannatyne & Maitland Clubs] 1843

Goose, N 'English pre-industrial urban economies' In *Urban History Yearbook* (1982) 24–30

Gordon, G & Dicks, B (eds) *Scottish Urban History*
Aberdeen 1981

Gordon, *Description*
Gordon, J *Aberdoniae utriusque descriptii: A description of both towns of Aberdeen*
[Spalding Club] 1842

Gouldesbrough, P *Formulary of Old Scots Legal Documents*
[Stair Soc.] 1985

Gourlay, R & Turner, A *Historic Dumfries: the archaeological implications of its development*
Glasgow [Scottish Burgh Survey] 1977

Graham, A 'Archaeological notes on some harbours in Eastern Scotland' in *PSAS* ci (1968–9) 200–85

Graham, A 'Old harbours and landing-places on the east coast of Scotland'
In *PSAS* cviii (1976–7) 332–65

Grant, *Scotland*
Grant, A *Independence and Nationhood: Scotland, 1306–1469*
London 1984

Grant, G G 'The use of documentary sources by the archaeologist: a viewpoint from Scotland' In *Archives* xiii No 60 (Autumn 1978) 206–210

Grant, I F *The Social and Economic Development of Scotland, before 1603*
Edinburgh, London 1930; Connecticut 1971

Grant, J *Old and New Edinburgh*
Edinburgh 1882

Greenwell, W (ed) *The Boldon Buke*
[Surtees Soc.] 1852

Greig, *Abdn., Queen St Midden Exc.*
Greig, J C 'Queen Street Midden Area' In Murray, J C (ed), *Abdn. Excavns.*
Soc. Ants. Monograph no 2 1982

Grose, *Antiquities*
Grose, F *The Antiquities of Scotland* vol i
London 1789

Gross, *Gild Merchant*
Gross, C *The Gild Merchant*
Oxford 1890

Guy, 'Thesis'
Guy, I 'The Scottish Export Trade, 1460–1599'
[St Andrews Univ. M.Phil.] 1982

Hall, G D G (ed) *Glanville*
London 1965

Hall, *Perth Blackfriars*
Hall, D *Excavation and the Blackfriars, Perth: an Interim report*
[Privately available: SUAT]

Halton Reg.
Register of John de Halton
[Canterbury & York Soc.] 1913

Halyburton's Ledger
Innes, C (ed) *Ledger of Andrew Halyburton, Conservator of the Privileges of*

the Scottish Nation in the Netherlands, 1492–1503
Edinburgh 1867

Harding, A 'The medieval brieves of protection and the development of
the common law' In *Juridical Review* xi (1966) 115–49

Harding, A *The Law Courts of Medieval England*
London 1973

Harding, A 'Regiam Majestatem among medieval law books' In *Juridical
Review* xxix (1984) 97–111

Harding, A 'Legislators, lawyers and law-books' In Charles-Edward, T M
et al (eds) *Lawyers and Laymen* 237–57
Cardiff 1986

Hay, G *The History of Arbroath to the Present Time, with notices
of the Civil & Ecclesiastical affairs of the neighbouring district.*
Arbroath 1876

Hay, G 'A Scottish altarpiece in Copenhagen' In *Innes Review* vii
(1956) 5–11

Hay, G 'The late medieval development of the High Kirk of
St Giles, Edinburgh' In *PSAS* cvii (1975–6) 242–60

Heinemann, O *et al* (eds) *Pommerisches Urkundenbuch*
Stettin 1868–

Helmholz
Helmholz, R H *Selected Cases on Defamation to 1600*
[Selden Soc. 1985]

HHUB
Lappenberg, J M *et al* (eds) *Hamburgisches Urkundenbuch*
Hamburg 1842–1933

Hilton, R 'Towns and societies in medieval England' In *Urban
History Year Book* (1982) 7–13

Historical Atlas I
McNeil, P & Nicholson, R (eds) *An Historical Atlas of Scotland*
St Andrews 1975

Historical Atlas II
—— *Historical Atlas of Scotland* (2nd ed.)
forthcoming

HMC
Royal Commission on Historical Manuscripts *Reports of the Royal Commission on Historical
Manuscripts*
London 1870

Hodgson, G W I 'The animal remains from medieval sites within three burghs on the
eastern Scottish seaboard' In Proudfoot, B (ed) *Sites Environment & Economy*
[BAR International Ser. No 173] 1983

Holdsworth, *Perth Excavns.*
Holdsworth, P (ed) *Excavations in the Medieval Burgh of Perth 1979–1981*
Society of Antiquaries of Scotland, Monograph Series No. 5, 1988

Holm Cultram Reg.
Grainger, F & Collingwood, W G (eds) *The Register and Records of Holm Cultram*
[Cumberland & Westmorland Ant. & Arch. Soc.] 1929

Holmes, N 'A fifteenth century coin hoard from Leith'
In *Brit. Numis. Jour.* liii (1983) 78–107

Holyrood Liber
Liber Cartarum Sancte Crucis
[Bannatyne Club] 1840

Hoskins, W G & Finberg, H P R *Devonshire Studies*
London 1952

Hoskins, W G *Local History in England*
London 1972

Houston, J M 'The Scottish burgh' In *Town Planning Review* xxv (1954) 114–27

HR
Koppmann, K *et al* (eds) *Die Recesse und Andere Akten der Hansetage* (three series)
Leipzig 1870–1913

HUB
Hohlbaum, K *et al* (eds) *Hansisches Urkundenbuch*
Halle, Leipzig and Weimar 1879–1939

Hume Brown, *Early Travellers*
Brown, P Hume (ed) *Early Travellers in Scotland*
Edinburgh 1891

Hunt, *Perth Hammermen Bk.*
Hunt, C A *The Book of the Perth Hammermen, 1518–1568*
Perth 1889

Hunter, J 'The Church of St Nicholas, Aberdeen' In *PSAS*, cv (1972–4) 236–47

Hurd, R *Gladstone's Land*
[Nat. Trust for Scot., Saltire Soc.] 1966

Inchaff. Chrs.
Charters, Bulls and other Documents relating to the Abbey of Inchaffray
[SHS] 1908

Inglis, H R G 'Roads and bridges in the early history of Scotland'
In *PSAS* xlvii (1912–13) 303–33

Inglis, H R G 'The most ancient bridges in Britain' In *PSAS* xlix (1914–15) 256–74

Inglis, J A 'Financial and administrative records 1264–1724' In McKechnie, H (ed)
An Introductory Survey of the Sources and Literature of Scots Law

[Stair Soc.] 1936

Irvine Muniments
Muniments of the Royal Burgh of Irvine
[AHCAG] 1890–91

Iter Camerarii
Innes, C (ed) Iter Camerarii In *Ancient Burgh Laws*
[SBRS] 1868

James IV Letters
Hannay, R K & Mackie, R (eds) *The Letters of James IV 1505–1513*
[SHS] 1953

James V Letters
Hannay, R K & Hay, D (eds) *The Letters of James V*
Edinburgh 1954

Jenkins, D 'The medieval Welsh idea of law' In *Tijdschrift voor Rechtseschiedenis* xlix (1981) 323–348

Jexlev, T 'Scottish history in the light of records in the Danish National Archives' In *SHR* xlviii (1969) 98–106

Kames, Lord *Historical Law Tracts*
Edinburgh 1758

Keith, T 'The trading privilages of the royal burghs of Scotland'
In *EHR* xxviii (1913) 678–690

Kelham, 'Thesis'
Kelham, C A 'Bases of magnatial power in later fifteenth-century Scotland'
[Edin Univ. Ph.D] 1986

Kelso Liber
Liber S. Marie de Calchou
[Bannatyne Club] 1846

Keussen, H *Köln im Mittelalter. Topographie und Verfassung*
Bonn 1918

Kinsley, J (ed) *The Poems of William Dunbar*
Oxford 1979

Kirk, J (ed) *The Second Book of Discipline*
Edinburgh 1980

Kunze, K (ed) *Hanseakten aus England 1275–1412*
Halle 1891

Laing, L *The Archaeology of Late Celtic Britain and Ireland*
London 1975

Lamb, A C *Dundee: Its Quaint and Historic Buildings*
Dundee 1895

Lanark Recs.
Renwick, R (ed) *Extracts from the Royal Burgh of Lanark*
Glasgow 1893

Landstrom, B *The Ship*
London 1962

Langton, J 'Industry and towns, 1500–1730' In Dodgshon, R A &
Butlin, R A (eds) *An Historical Geography of England & Wales*
London 1978

Lawrie, *Annals*
Lawrie, A C (ed) *Annals of the Reigns of Malcolm and William, Kings of Scotland*
Glasgow 1910

Leges Burgorum
Innes, C (ed) Leges Burgorum In *Ancient Burgh Laws*
[SBRS] 1868

Lennox Cartularium
Cartularium Comitatus de Levenax
[Maitland Club] 1833

Letts, M H I *Bruges and its Past*
London 1926

Lewis, J H 'Excavations at Lanark Castle' In *TDGAS* 3rd ser liii (1977– 8) 129–32

Lind. Cart.
Chartulary of the Abbey of Lindores
[SHS] 1903

Lind. Lib.
Liber Sancte Marie de Lundoris
[Abbotsford Club] 1841

Lindsay, *Elgin Excavns.*
Lindsay, W J (ed) *Excavations in Elgin*
forthcoming

Lindsay, I G 'The Scottish burgh' In Scott-Moncrieff, G (ed)
The Stones of Scotland 77–102
London 1938

Lindsay, W J 'Digging up Auld Ayr, an excavation at 102–104
High Street' In *Ayrshire Coll.* xiv no. v (1985) 194–224

Livingstone, M *Guide to the Public Records of Scotland*
[SRO] 1905

Lloyd, T H *The Movement of Wool Prices in Medieval England*
[Econ. Hist. Rev. Supp. no 6] 1973

Lloyd, T H *The English Wool Trade in the Middle Ages*

Cambridge 1977

LUB
Urkundenbuch der Stadt Lubeck
Lubeck 1843-1905

Lyall, R 'Scottish students and masters at the universities of Louvain
and Cologne in the fifteenth century' In *Innes Review* xxxvi (1985), 55-73

Lynch, M 'From privy kirk to burgh church: an alternative explanation of the
Protestantization of burgh society' In Macdougall *Church, Politics & Society*
Edinburgh 1983

Lynch, M 'Whatever happened to the medieval burgh?' In *Scot. Econ. & Soc.
Hist.* iv (1984) 5-20

Lynch, M 'Continuity and change in urban society', In Houston, R A and Whyte, I D (eds),
Scottish Society, 1500-1800
Cambridge 1988

Lynch, M 'The crown and the burghs, 1500-1625' In Lynch, *Early
Modern Town*
London 1986

Lynch, *Early Modern Town*
Lynch, M (ed) *The Early Modern Town in Scotland*
London 1986

Lynch, *Edinburgh*
Lynch, M *Edinburgh and the Reformation*
Edinburgh 1981

Lynch, Towns
Lynch, M 'Towns and townspeople in fifteenth-century Scotland',
In Thomson, J A F (ed), *Towns and Townspeople in the Fifteenth Century*
Gloucester 1988

Lythe & Butt, *Economic History*
Lythe, S G E & Butt, J *An Economic History of Scotland, 1100-1939*
Glasgow 1975

Lythe, S G E 'Scottish trade with the Baltic 1550-1650' In Eastham, J K (ed)
Essays in Commemoration of the Dundee School of Economics 1932-55
Coupar Angus 1955

Lythe, S G E *The Economy of Scotland in its European setting 1550-1625.*
Edinburgh 1960

Lythe, 'Economic life'
Lythe, S G E 'Economic life' In Brown, *Scottish Society*
London 1977

MacAskill, N M 'The Pottery' In Holdsworth (ed) *Perth Excavns.*
Society of Antiquaries of Scotland, Monograph Series 1988

Macbean, L *Kirkcaldy Burgh Records*
Kirkcaldy 1908

McBrien, H & Kerr, B 'Recent work in Glasgow by the Scottish Urban Archaeological Trust'
In *Glas. Arch. Soc. Bull.* xx (Oct. 1985).

Macdougall, N *James III: A political study*
Edinburgh 1982

Macdougall, *Church, Politics and Society*
Macdougall, N (ed) *Church, Politics & Society in Scotland 1408–1929*
Edinburgh 1983

MacGavin, *Perth, Mill St Exc.*
McGavin, N *et al Excavations at Mill Street, Perth 1979–80*
Society of Antiquaries of Scotland, Monograph Series. Forthcoming

MacGregor, G *The History of Glasgow*
Glasgow & London 1881

Mckechnie, *Sources of Scots Law*
McKechnie H (ed) *An Introductory Survey of the Sources and Literature of Scots Law*
[Stair Soc.] 1936

Mackenzie, *Scottish Burgh*
Mackenzie, W M *The Scottish Burgh*
Edinburgh 1949

M'Kerlie, P H *History of the Lands and their Owners in Galloway* (5 vols.)
Edinburgh 1870

Mackie, J D & Pryde, G S *The Estate of the Burgesses in the Scots Parliament*
St Andrews [Univ. Pub.] 1923

Mackie, R L *et al Arbroath Abbey* (Official Guide)
HMSO 1982

Mackie, J D *Provand's Lordship*
n.d.

Mackintosh, H B *Elgin Past and Present*
Elgin 1914

McLaren, T 'Early plans of Perth' In *Trans. Perthshire Soc. of Nat. Science*
x pt. 1 (1943) 1–22

MacMillan, 'Thesis'
MacMillan, J 'A Study of the Edinburgh Community and its Economic Activity, 1600–1680'
[Edinburgh Univ. Ph.D.] 1984

Macniven, 'Thesis'
Macniven, D 'Merchant and Trader in Aberdeen in the Early Seventeenth Century'
[Abdn. Univ. M.Litt.] 1977

MacQueen, J *St Nynia*
Edinburgh & London 1961

MacQueen, 'Thesis'
MacQueen, H L 'Pleadable brieves and jurisdiction in heritage in
later medieval Scotland'
[Edin. Univ. Ph.D.] 1985

MacQueen, H L 'Pleadable brieves, pleading and the development of
Scots law' In *Law and History Review* iv (1986) 399–418

MacQueen, H L 'The brieve of right revisited' In Eales, R and Sullivan, D (eds)
The Political Context of Law
Ronceverte 1987

McRoberts, D (ed) *The Medieval Church of St Andrews*
Glasgow 1976

McRoberts, D *The Fetternear Banner*
Glasgow n.d.

McUre, J *A View of the City of Glasgow*
Glasgow 1736

McWilliam, C *The Buildings of Scotland, Lothian except Edinburgh*
Penguin Bks. 1978

Makey, W H 'Edinburgh in the mid-seventeenth century'
In Lynch, *Early Modern Town*
London 1986

Malcolm, C A 'Sheriff and other local court records' In McKechnie, H (ed)
Sources of Scots Law
[Stair Soc.] 1936

Marshall, G *Presbyteries and Profits*
Oxford 1980

Marshall, R K *Virgins and Viragos*
London 1983

Marwick, J D (ed) *Extracts from the Records of the Burgh of Glasgow 1573–1642*
Glasgow 1876

Marwick, *Edinburgh Guilds*
Marwick, J D *Edinburgh Guilds and Crafts*
Edinburgh 1909

Mary of Lorraine Corresp.
The Scottish Correspondence of Mary of Lorraine
[SHS] 1927

Matheson, C *A Catalogue of the Publications of Scottish Historical
and Kindred Clubs, 1908–27*
Aberdeen 1928

Maxwell, *Old Dundee*
Maxwell, A *The History of Old Dundee*
Dundee 1884

May Recs.
Stuart, J *Records of the Priory of the Isle of May*
Edinburgh 1868

Mears, F C 'Notes on a medieval burgess's house at Inverkeithing'
In *PSAS* xlvii (1912–13) 343–8

Melrose Liber
Liber Sancti Marie de Melros
[Bannatyne Club] 1837

Merriman, M H 'The "Rough Wooing" of 1544–50' in McNeill, P & Nicholson, R (eds)
Historical Atlas I 83, 194–5
St Andrews 1975

Metcalf, *Coinage*
Metcalf, D M (ed) *Coinage in Medieval Scotland*
Oxford [Brit. Arch. Reports no 45] 1977

Millar, A H (ed) *Roll of Eminent Burgesses of Dundee 1513–1886*
Dundee 1887

Milne, R (ed) *Rental Books of King James VI Hospital*
Perth 1891

Miner, J N 'Church and community in later medieval Glasgow: an introductory
essay' In *Histoire Sociale* xv (1982).

Moeller, B *Imperial Cities and the Reformation*
Philadelphia 1972

Mollat, M *Comptabilité du port de Dieppe au XVe siècle*
Paris 1951

Mollat, M *Le commerce maritime normand à la fin du moyen age*
Paris 1952

Moncrieff, G I Scott (ed) *The Stones of Scotland*
London 1938

Moray Reg.
Registrum Episcopatus Moraviensis
[Bannatyne Club] 1837

Morris, J A *The Brig of Ayr*
Ayr 1912

Munro, J H *Wool, Cloth and Gold*
Toronto 1972

Munro, J H 'Industrial protectionism in Flanders' In Miskimin, H A *et al* (eds)
The Medieval City
London 1977

Munro, R W *Scottish Lighthouses*
Stornoway 1979

Murray, *Abdn. Gallowgate Exc.*
Murray, H 'Excavation of 45–47 Gallowgate, Aberdeen' In *PSAS* cxiv (1984) 303–13

Murray, *Abdn. Excavns.*
Murray, J C (ed) *Excavations in the Medieval Burgh of Aberdeen 1973–81*
Society of Antiquaries of Scotland Mon. No.2 1982

Murray, *Early Burgh Organisation*
Murray, D *Early Burgh Organisation in Scotland*
Glasgow 1924

Murray, A L 'Foreign trade and Scottish ports 1471–1542' In McNeil, P &
Nicholson, R (eds) *Historical Atlas I*
St Andrews 1975

Murray, H 'Medieval wooden and wattle buildings excavated in Perth and
Aberdeen' In Simpson, A & Stevenson, S *Town Houses and Structures*
Glasgow [Scottish Burgh Survey] 1980

Murray, J C 'The Scottish Burgh Survey — a review'
In *PSAS* cxiii (1983) 1–10

Murray, J E L 'Unicorns and heavy groats of James III and James IV'
In *Brit. Numis. Jour.* xxxx (1971) 62–96

Murray, J E L 'The Black money of James III' In Metcalf, *Coinage*
Oxford [BAR xlv] 1977

Nat. MSS. Scot.
Facsimiles of the National Manuscripts of Scotland
London 1867–71

Neilson, G *Trial by Combat*
Glasgow 1890

Neish, R *Old Peterhead*
Peterhead 1950

Newbattle Reg.
Regestrum S. Marie de Newbotle
[Bannatyne Club] 1849

Nicholson, *Scotland*
Nicholson, R Scotland: the Later Middle Ages
Edinburgh 1974

NLS
National Library of Scotland

NLS Cat. MSS since 1925
NLS Catalogues of Manuscripts, Charters and other Formal
Documents acquired since 1925
[HMSO] 1966

L

NLS Summary Cat. of Advoc. MSS
NLS *Summary Catalogue of the Advocates' Manuscripts*
[HMSO] 1971

NMRS
National Monuments Record of Scotland, RCAHMS

NRA
National Register of Archives

O'Connor, A & Clarke, D V (eds) *From the Stone Age to the Forty-Five: studies presented to R B K Stevenson*
Edinburgh 1983

Ollivant, S D *The Court of the Official in Pre-Reformation Scotland*
[Stair Soc.] 1983

OPS
Origines Parochiales Scotia
[Bannatyne Club] 1851–5

Pais. Chrs.
Metcalfe, W M *Charters and Documents relating to the Burgh of Paisley*
Paisley 1902

Paisley Reg.
Registrum Monasterii de Passelet
[Maitland Club] 1832

Patten, J 'Urban occupations in pre-industrial England' In *Trans. Inst. Brit. Geogs.* new ser. ii (1977) 296–313

Peddie, J M D 'Description of an old timber building in the Lawnmarket, Edinburgh' In PSAS xviii (1883–4) 465–76

Perth Blackfriars
Milne, R (ed) *The Blackfriars of Perth*
Edinburgh 1893

PHSE
Perth High Street Excavation (Archive Material c/o
Scottish Development Department, Historic Buildings & Monuments)

PHSE bone
Hodgson, G W I, Jones, A & Smith, C The Animal Remains from the Medieval Levels at Perth High Street
1975–77. Perth High Street Excavation — Fascicule IX: Environmental.
(un-pub 1983)

PHSE botanical
Fraser, M Perth High Street Plant Remains in -Perth High Street Excavation
Reports — Fascicule X: Environmental 2
(un-pub 1983)

PHSE buildings
Murray, H Wooden and Clay Buildings from Perth High Street Excavation —
Fascicule II: The Archaeology.
(un-pub 1983)

PHSE glass
Hunter, J R 'The Medieval Glass' In Perth High Street Excavation — Fascicule VIII:
The Miscellaneous Finds
(un-pub 1983)

PHSE leatherwork
Thomas, M C Perth High Street Excavation — Fascicule VI: The Leatherwork
(un-pub 1983)

PHSE metalwork
Perth High Street Excavation Committee Archival list of metalwork. Perth High Street
Excavation — Fascicule IV: The Metalwork.
(un-pub 1983)

PHSE stone
Perth High Street Excavation Committee Archival list of worked stone. Perth High Street
Excavation
(un-pub 1983)

PHSE textile
Bennett, H, Muthesius, A & Ryder, M L Perth High Street Excavation — Fascicule VII:
The Textile
(un-pub 1983)

PHSE wood
Curteis A, Martin, C & Wright, D The Worked Wood : Perth High Street Excavation —
Fascicule V: The Wood
(un-pub 1983)

PHSE worked bone
MacGregor, A Worked Bone, Antler, and Ivory from the Perth High Street — in
Perth High Street Excavation — Fascicule VIII: Miscellaneous Finds
(un-pub 1983)

Pirenne, *Histoire*
Pirenne, H *Histoire de Belgique*
Brussels (5th ed.) 1929

Pitcairn, *Trials*
Pitcairn, R (ed) *Criminal Trials in Scotland from 1488 to 1624*
[Bannatyne & Maitland Clubs] 1833

Plummer, C (ed) *Bede's Ecclesiastical History*
Oxford 1896

Pococke, *Tours*
Kemp, D W (ed) *Tours in Scotland. . .by Richard Pococke, Bishop of Meath*
[SHS 1st series] 1887

Pollock & Maitland, *History of English Law*
Pollock, F & Maitland, F W *The History of English Law before the time of Edward I*
Cambridge 1898 & 1968

Pollock, D C 'Saracen Head excavation 1980/81' In *Glas. Arch. Soc. Bull.* xii
(Autumn 1981)

Pollock, D C 'Recent excavations under Glasgow' In *Glas. Arch. Soc. Bull.*
xiv (Autumn 1982)

Postan, M M *et al* (eds) *The Cambridge Economic History of Europe* (3 Vols)
Cambridge Vol. i (2nd edn. 1966), ii (1952), iii (1963)

Pound, J F 'The social and trade structure of Norwich, 1525–75'
In *Past & Present* xxxiv (1966)

Pounds, N J G *An Economic History of Medieval Europe*
London 1974

Prot. Bk. Carruthers
Reid, R C (ed) *Protocol Book of Mark Carruthers 1531–61*
[SRS] 1956

Prot. Bk. Young
Donaldson, G (ed) *Protocol Book of James Young 1485–1515*
[SRS] 1952

Pryde, G S 'The burgh courts and allied jurisdictions' In Paton, G C H (ed)
An Introduction to Scottish Legal History
[Stair Soc.] 1958

Pryde, G S 'The city and burgh of Glasgow' In Miller, R & Tivey, J (eds)
The Glasgow Region
Glasgow 1958

Pryde, *Burghs*
Pryde, G S *The Burghs of Scotland, a critical list*
Oxford 1965

Pryde, *Kirkintilloch Court Bk.*
Pryde, G S (ed) *Court Book of the Burgh of Kirkintilloch*
[SHS] 1963

PSAS
Proceedings of the Society of Antiquaries of Scotland
1851–

Quoniam Attachiamenta
Cooper, Lord T M (ed) *Regiam Majestatem et Quoniam Attachiamenta*
[Stair Soc. xi]

Radford, C A R *Glasgow Cathedral*
[HMSO] 1970

Raine, J *The History and Antiquities of North Durham*
London 1852

Rait, R S *The Parliaments of Scotland*
Glasgow 1924

Rankin, W E K 'Scottish burgh churches in the fifteenth century'
In *RSCHS* vii (1941) 63–75

Rankin, W E K *The Parish Church of the Holy Trinity St Andrews*
Edinburgh 1955

RCAHMS, Dumfries
Royal Commission on the Ancient & Historical Monuments of Scotland *Inventory of the monuments in the county of Dumfries*
HMSO 1920

RCAHMS, East Lothian
Royal Commission on the Ancient & Historical Monuments of Scotland *Inventory of monuments in East Lothian*
HMSO 1924

RCAHMS, Edinburgh
Royal Commission on the Ancient & Historical Monuments of Scotland *Inventory of monuments in the City of Edinburgh*
HMSO 1951

RCAHMS, Fife
Royal Commission on the Ancient & Historical Monuments of Scotland *Inventory of monuments in the county of Fife, Kinross & Clackmannan*
HMSO 1933

RCAHMS, Kirkcudbright
Royal Commission on the Ancient & Historical Monuments of Scotland *Inventory of monuments in the county of Kirkcudbright*
HMSO 1914

RCAHMS, Midlothian
Royal Commission on the Ancient & Historical Monuments of Scotland *Inventory of monuments in Midlothian and West Lothian*
HMSO 1929

RCAHMS, Orkney
Royal Commission on the Ancient & Historical Monuments of Scotland *Inventory of monuments in the counties of Orkney & Shetland*
HMSO 1946

RCAHMS, Peeblesshire
Royal Commission on the Ancient & Historical Monuments of Scotland *Inventory of monuments in Peeblesshire*
HMSO 1967

RCAHMS, Roxburghshire
Royal Commission on the Ancient & Historical Monuments of Scotland *Inventory of monuments in Roxburghshire*

HMSO 1956

RCAHMS, Stirlingshire
Royal Commission on the Ancient & Historical Monuments of Scotland *Inventory of monuments in Stirlingshire*
HMSO 1963

RCAHMS, West Lothian
Royal Commission on the Ancient & Historical Monuments of Scotland *Inventory of monuments in Midlothian and West Lothian*
HMSO 1929

RCAHMS, Wigtownshire
Royal Commission on the Ancient & Historical Monuments of Scotland *Inventory of monuments in Wigtownshire*
HMSO 1912

RCHME, York
Royal Commission on Historical Monuments (England) *Inventory of monuments in the City of York*
HMSO 1972

Reg. Brieves
Register of Brieves In *APS* i 653–657
Edinburgh 1814

Regesta Norvegica
Oslo 1978

Regiam Majestatem
Cooper, Lord T M (ed) *Regiam Majestatem et Quoniam Attachiamenta*
[Stair Soc. 1947]

Regiam Majestatem [APS]
Regiam Majestatem In *APS* i 619–29
Edinburgh 1814

Reid, R C 'Mauchline Castle' In *TDGAS* 3rd ser. xvi (1929–30) 166–71

Reid, R C 'The caput of Annandale or the curse of St Malachy'
In *TDGAS* 3rd ser. xxxii (1953–54) 155–66

Reid, W Stanford 'Sea-power in the Anglo-Scottish war, 1296–1328'
In *Mariner's Mirror* xlvi (1960) 7–32

Reid, W Stanford 'Trade, traders and Scottish Independence' In *Speculum* xxix (1954) 210–22

Renwick, R & Lindsay, J *History of Glasgow*
Glasgow 1921

Renwick, R *Abstracts of Protocols of Town Clerks of Glasgow*
Glasgow 1894–1900

Renwick, R *Glasgow Memorials*
Glasgow 1908

Reynolds, *English Towns*
Reynolds, S *An Introduction to the History of English Medieval Towns*
Oxford 1977

Richardson, J S *The Medieval Stone Carver in Scotland*
Edinburgh 1964

Riden, P *The Medieval Town in Britain*
Cardiff 1980

Rigby, S H 'Urban decline in the later middle ages: the reliability
of the non-statistical evidence' In *Urban History Year Book* (1984) 45- 60

Riis, T 'Scottish-Danish relations in the sixteenth century'
In Smout, T C (ed) *Scotland and Europe 1200–1850*
Edinburgh 1986

Riis, T *Should Auld Acquaintance be Forgot: Scottish/Danish
Connections 1406–1717*
Odeuse Univ. Press 1986

RMS
Thomas J M *et al* (eds) *Registrum Magni Sigilli Regum Scotorum*
Edinburgh & London 1882–1914

Robertson, J *The Book of Bon-Accord*
Aberdeen 1839

Robinson, P 'Tenements: a pre-industrial urban tradition'
In *ROSC* i (1984) 52–64

Robinson W R G 'Swansea' In Griffiths, R A (ed) *Boroughs of Medieval Wales*
Cardiff 1978

Rooseboom, *Staple*
Rooseboom, M P *The Scottish Staple in the Netherlands*
The Hague 1910

ROSC
Review of Scottish Culture
1984–

Ross, T *et al* 'The Tailors' Hall, Cowgate' In *BOEC* xi (1922) 125–72

Rot. Scot.
Macpherson, D *et al* (eds) *Rotuli Scotiae in Turri Londinensi et in Domo Capitulari
Westmonasteriensi Asservati*
London 1814–19

RPC
Burton, J H *et al* (eds) *The Register of the Privy Council of Scotland*
Edinburgh 1877–

RRS i
Barrow, G W S (ed) *Regesta Regum Scotorum, Vol 1, Acts of Malcolm IV
1153–1165.*
Edinburgh 1960

RRS ii
Barrow, G W S (ed) *Regesta Regum Scotorum Vol II, Acts of William I 1165-1214*
Edinburgh 1971

RRS vi
Webster, B (ed) *Regesta Regum Scotorum Vol vi, The Acts of David II 1329-71*
Edinburgh 1982

RSCHS
Records of the Scottish Church History Society
1923-

Ruddock, E C 'Bridges and roads in Scotland: 1400-1750' In Fenton & Stell (eds) *Loads and Roads in Scotland and Beyond* 1984 67-91
Edinburgh

Ruffmann, K H 'Engländer and Schotten in den Seestadten Ost- und Westpreussens' In *Zeitschrift für Ostforschung* vii (1958)

St Andrews Copiale
Baxter, J H (ed) *Copiale Prioratus Sanctiandree*
Oxford 1930

St Andrews Liber
Liber Cartarum Prioratus Sancti Andree in Scotia
[Bannatyne Club] 1841

St Giles Reg.
Registrum Cartarum Ecclesiae Sancti Egidii de Edinburgh
[Bannatyne Club] 1859

St Mary Lib.
Liber Collegii Nostre Domine: Registrum Ecclesie B. V. Marie et S Anne infra Muros Civitatis Glasguensis 1549
[Maitland Club] 1846

St Nich. Cart.
Cartularium Ecclesiae Sancti Nicholai Aberdonensis
[New Spalding Club] 1888-92

Sagher, H E *et al* (eds) *Recueil de documents relatifs à l'industrie drapière en Flandre*
Brussels 1951-66

Samsonowicz, H 'Engländer und Schotten in Danzig in Spätmittelalter' In Friedland, K & Irsigler, F (eds) *Seehandel & Wirtschaftswege Nordeuropas*
Ostfildern 1981

Samsonowicz, H 'Handel zagraniczny Gdańska w drugiej polowie xv wieku', In *Przeglad Historyczny* xvii (1956)

Sanderson, M H B 'The Edinburgh merchants in society 1507-1603' In Cowan & Shaw (eds) *The Renaissance and Reformation in Scotland*
Edinburgh 1983

Sattler, C (ed) *Handelsrechnungen des Deutschen Ordes*
Leipzig 1887

Sawyer, P H & Wood, I N (eds) *Early Medieval Kingship*
Leeds 1977

Sawyer, P H 'Kings and merchants' In Sawyer & Wood (eds) *Early Medieval Kingship*
Leeds 1977

SBRS
Scottish Burgh Records Society
Edinburgh 1868–

Schofield, J *et al* 'Excavations south of Edinburgh High Street 1973–4'
In *PSAS* cvii (1975–6) 155–241

Scone Liber
Liber Ecclesie de Scon
[Bannatyne and Maitland Clubs] 1843

Scott, W W 'The use of money in Scotland, 1124–1230' In *SHR* lviii (1979) 105–31

Scott, W W 'Sterling and the usual money of Scotland' In *Scot. Ec. & Soc. Hist.* v (1985) 4–22

Scott, *Fasti*
Scott, H (ed) *Fasti Ecclesiae Scoticanae*
Edinburgh [revised edition] 1915–

Scoular, J (ed) *Handlist of the Acts of Alexander II*
[Privately produced] 1959

Sellar, D 'Courtesy, battle and the brieve of right' In *Stair Soc. Misc.* xxxv
[Stair Society] 1984

Sharrat, P & F *Ecosse romane*
St Leger-Vauban 1985

Shead, N 'Glasgow in the 12th and 13th centuries' In *Glas. Arch. Soc. Bull.* New ser. xiii (Spring 1982)

SHR
The Scottish Historical Review
1903–28, 1947–

SHS
Scottish History Society Publications
1893–

Simpson, G G & Webster, B 'The archives of the medieval church of Glasgow: an introductory survey' In *The Bibliotheck* iii (1962) 195–201

Simpson, G G (ed) *Handlist of the Acts of Alexander III, the Guardians & John*
1960

Simpson, G G (ed) *Scotland's Medieval Burghs, an archaeological heritage in danger*
Edinburgh [Soc. of Ant. of Scot.] 1972

Simpson, W D 'The architectural history of Rothesay Castle'
In *TGAS* n.s. ix (1939) 152–83

Simpson, W D 'The architectural history of Rothesay Castle, a further note'
In *TGAS* n.s. x (1941) 78–9

Simpson, W D *A History of Saint John's Kirk of Perth*
Perth 1958

Sivery, G *L'économie de royaume de France au siècle de Saint Louis*
Lille 1984

Skene, A *Memorialls for the Government of Royall Burghs in Scotland*
Aberdeen 1685

Slezer, *Theatrum Scotiae*
Slezer, J *Theatrum Scotiae*
1693 (and later edns)

Small, J W *Scottish Market Crosses*
Stirling 1900

Smit, H J (ed) *Bronnen tot de geschiedenis van den handel met Engeland, Schotland en Ierland* (4 Vols)
The Hague 1928–51

Smith, D M *English Episcopal Acta, i, Lincoln 1067–1185*
London 1980

Smith, J S 'The physical site of historical Aberdeen' In Smith, J S (ed)
New Light on Medieval Aberdeen
Aberdeen 1985

Smout, T C *Scottish Trade on the Eve of the Union, 1660–1707*
Edinburgh 1963

Smout, T C 'Coping with plague in sixteenth and seventeenth century
Scotland' In *Scotia* ii (1978) 19–33

Spalding Misc.
Miscellany of the Spalding Club
[Spalding Club] 1841–52

Spearman, *Perth, Canal St Exc.*
Spearman, R M 'Excavations at 45–63 Canal Street, Perth' In Holdsworth, P (ed)
Excavations in the Medieval Burgh of Perth 1979–81
Society of Antiquaries of Scotland, Monograph Series 1988

Spearman, *Perth, Methven St Exc.*
Spearman, R M 'Excavations at the Clydesdale Bank, 29–30 South Methven St.,
Perth, 1979' In Holdsworth, P (ed) *Excavations in the Medieval Burgh of Perth 1979–81*
Society of Antiquaries of Scotland, Monograph Series. 1988

Spottiswoode, *History*
Spottiswoode, J *History of the Church of Scotland by J Spottiswoode* (3 Vols)
[Bannatyne Club] 1850

SRA
Scottish Record Association (newsletter)
1977–

SRS
Scottish Record Society (newsletter)
1980–

St A Lib
Liber Cartarum Prioratus Sancti Andree in Scotia
[Bannatyne Club] 1841

Statuta Gilde
Innes, C (ed) Statuta Gilde In *Ancient Burgh Laws*
Edinburgh [SBRS] 1868

Stein, P G 'Roman law in Scotland' In *Ius Romanum Medii Aevi*
pars 5, 13b (1968) 1–51

Stein, W (ed) *Akten zur Geschichte der Verfassung und Verwaltung der
Stadt Köln im 14. und 15. Jahrhundert*
Bonn 1895

Stell, G 'Architecture: the changing needs of society' In Brown, *Scottish Society*
London 1977

Stell, G 'Scottish burgh houses 1560–1707' In Simpson, A T & Stevenson, S
(eds) *Town Houses and Structures in Medieval Scotland: a seminar*
Glasgow (Burgh Survey) 1980

Stell, G 'The earliest tolbooths: a preliminary account'
In *PSAS* cxi (1981) 445–53

Stell, G 'Castles and towers in south-western Scotland, some
recent surveys' In *TDGAS* 3rd ser. lvii (1982) 65–77

Stell, forthcoming
Stell, G 'By land and sea in medieval and early modern Scotland'
In *ROSC* iv
forthcoming

Stephenson, *Borough & Town*
Stephenson, C *Borough and Town*
Cambridge, Mass 1933

Stevenson, J H & Wood, M *Scottish Heraldic Seals* (3 Vols)
Glasgow 1940

Stevenson, W 'The monastic presence in Scottish burghs in the twelfth and
thirteenth centuries' In *SHR* lx (1981) 97–118

Stevenson, 'Thesis'
Stevenson, A W K 'Trade Between Scotland and the Low Countries in the Later Middle

Ages'
[Abdn. Univ. Ph.D.] 1982

Stevenson, *Documents*
Stevenson, J *Documents Illustrative of the History of Scotland 1286– 1306*
Edinburgh 1870

Stewart, I 'Scottish Mints' In Carson, R G A (ed) *Mints Dies and Currency: essays in Memory of Albert Baldwin*
London 1971

Stewart Brown, R 'Thwert-ut-nay and the custom of "thwertnic" in Cheshire' In *EHR* xl (1925) 13–21

Stirling Chrs.
Renwick, R (ed) *Charters and other Documents relating to the Royal Burgh of Stirling*
Glasgow 1884

Stirling Recs.
Renwick, R (ed) *Extracts from the Records of the Royal Burgh of Stirling*
Glasgow 1887–9

Stoppelaar, J H (ed) *Inventaris van het oud archief der stad Middelburg 1217–1581*
Middelburg 1873

STR
Bang, N (ed) *Tabeller over Skibsfart og Varetransport gennem Øresund 1467–1660*
Copenhagen 1906–33

Stubbs, W *Constitutional History of England*
Oxford 1878

SUAT
Scottish Urban Archaeological Trust Ltd.,
Methven St., Perth

TA
Dickson, T & Paul, Sir J Balfour (eds) *Accounts of the Lord High Treasurer of Scotland*
Edinburgh 1877–1916

Talbot, E J 'Scottish Medieval Burghs' In Riden, P (ed) *The Medieval Town in Britain* 1980 15–21
Cardiff

Taylor, L B *Aberdeen Shore Work Accounts 1596–1670*
Aberdeen 1972

Taylor, *Journey*
Taylor, J *A Journey to Edenborough in Scotland*
1903

TDGAS
Transactions Dumfries & Galloway Natural History and

Antiquarian Society
1862–

Terry, C S *Catalogue of the Publications of Scottish Historical and Kindred Clubs and Societies 1780–1908*
Glasgow 1909

TGAS
Transactions of the Glasgow Archaeological Society
1857–

The Book of the Universal Kirk of Scotland
[Bannatyne Club] 1839

The First Book of Discipline
Cameron, J K (ed) *The First Book of Discipline*
Edinburgh 1972

Thoms, *Perth, St Ann's Lane Exc.*
Thoms, L M 'Trial excavations at St Ann's Lane, Perth' in *PSAS* cxii (1982) 437–456

Thomson, D *The Dunfermline Hammermen. A History of the Incorporation of Hammermen in Dunfermline*
Paisley 1909

Thomson, D *The Weavers Craft, being a History of the Weavers Incorporation of Dunfermline*
Paisley 1903

Torrie, E P D *The Gild Court Book of Dunfermline 1433–1597*
[SRS] 1986

Torrie, *forthcoming*
Torrie, E P D 'Guilds merchant established by 1550' In *Historical Atlas II* forthcoming

Torrie, 'Thesis'
Torrie, E P D 'The Gild of Dunfermline in the Fifteenth Century'
[Edin. Univ. Ph.D.] 1984

Touchard, H *Le commerce maritime breton à la fin du moyen age*
Paris 1967

TSES
Transactions of the Scottish Ecclesiological Society
1903–

Twiss, T (ed) *The Black Book of the Admiralty*
London 1873

Ure, D *The History of Rutherglen and East-Kilbride*
Glasgow 1793

van Houte, J A *Bruges: essai d'histoire urbaine*
Brussels 1967

Vaughan, P *Philip the Good*
London 1970

Verschuur, 'Thesis'
Verschuur, M 'Perth and the Reformation: Society and Reform, 1540–60'
[Glasgow Univ. Ph.D.] 1985

Vet. Mon.
Theiner, A (ed) *Vetera Monumenta Hibernorum et Scotorum Historiam Illustrantia*
Rome 1864

von Bunge, F G *et al* (eds) *Liv-Esth-und Curlandisches Urkundenbuch*
Reval 1853–1910

von Klocke, F *Alt Soester Burgermeister aus sechs Jahrhunderten, ihre Familien und ihre Standesverhaltnisse*
Soest 1927

von Wechmar, I & Biederstedt, R 'Die schottische Einwanderung in Vorpommern im 16. und 17. Jahrhundert' In *Greifswald-Stralsunder Jahrbuch* v (1965) 1–27

Walker, R F *The Origins of Newcastle upon Tyne*
Newcastle 1976

Walker, V M 'Medieval Nottingham: a topographic survey' In *Trans. Thoroton Soc.* lxvii (1963) 44–5

Warden, *Burgh Laws*
Warden, A J *The Burgh Laws of Dundee*
Dundee 1872

Warner, G (ed) *The Libelle of English Polycye*
Oxford 1926

Warren, W L *Henry II*
London 1973

Warrender Papers
Cameron, A I *The Warrender Papers*
[SHS] 1931–2

Watson, C B B 'List of owners of property in Edinburgh, 1635'
In *BOEC* xiii (1924) 93–146

Watt, D E R *A Biographical Dictionary of Scottish Graduates to A.D. 1410*
Oxford 1977

Watt, *Fasti*
Watt, D E R *Fasti Ecclesiae Scoticanae Medii Aevi*
[SRS] 1969

Webster, *Scotland*
Webster, B *Scotland from the Eleventh Century to 1603*
Cambridge 1975

Wedderburne Compt Bk.
Miller, A H (ed) *The Compt Buik of David Wedderburne, Merchant of Dundee*
[SHS] 1898

White, 'Thesis'
White, A 'Religion, Politics and Society in Aberdeen, 1543–1593'
[Edinburgh Univ. Ph.D.] 1985

Whitehand, J W R & Alauddin, K 'The town plans of Scotland: some preliminary considerations' In *Scot. Geog. Mag.* lxxxv (1969) 109–21

Whittington, G & Whyte, I D *An Historical Geography of Scotland*
London 1983

Whyte, I D 'The occupational structure of Scottish burghs in the seventeenth century' In Lynch, *Early Modern Town*
London 1986

Windram, W J 'What is the Liber de Judicibus?' In *Journal of Legal History* v (1984) 176–7

Wood, M & Hannay, R K *Records of the Burgh of Edinburgh 1589–1603*
Edinburgh 1927

Wordsworth, *Inverkeithing Exc.*
Wordsworth, J 'Excavations in Inverkeithing, 1981' In *PSAS* 113 (1983) 520–50.

Wordsworth, *Inverness Exc.*
Wordsworth, J 'Excavation of the settlement at 13–21 Castle Street, Inverness 1979' In *PSAS* (1982) 322–382.

Wordsworth, *St Andrews, Kirkhill Exc.*
Wordsworth, J *Excavations at St Mary's Kirk Hill, St Andrews*
forthcoming

Wordsworth, J 'Friarscroft and the Trinitarians in Dunbar'
In *PSAS* cxiii (1983) 478–88

Works Accts.
Paton, H M *et al* (eds) *Accounts of the Masters of Works*
Edinburgh 1957–

Wormald, *Scotland*
Wormald, J *Court, Kirk and Community: Scotland 1470–1625*
London 1981

Yair, J *An Account of the Scotch Trade in the Netherlands*
London 1776

Index

This is primarily an index of persons and places. As an index of subjects it is selective rather than exhaustive since most themes and concepts will be readily found within the appropriate sections dealing with sources, the Church, trade and industry, and social structure and administration.